DATE DUE			
FEB 1 5 '95			
NOV 1 8 '96			
MAY 2 7 '97			
MAY 2 1 1998			
MAY 2 9 1998			
NOV 1 1 2003			
NOV 2 5 2003			
DEC 0 9 2003			

DEADLY
BLESSINGS

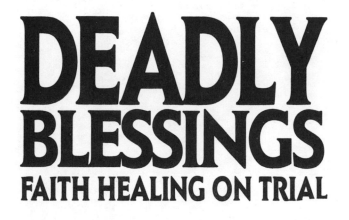

DEADLY BLESSINGS
FAITH HEALING ON TRIAL

RICHARD J.
BRENNEMAN

PROMETHEUS BOOKS
Buffalo, New York

Library of Congress Catalog Card Number 90-60906

ISBN 0-87975-580-6

To Dad, for more than I can say.
And to all those friends along the way
who still believe as I once did.

CONTENTS

ACKNOWLEDGMENTS

Every writer is deeply indebted to others. A writer is a professional student, always learning. And when I am learning, I look to those who have mastered their craft while remaining dedicated to honesty and thoroughness. My life has been touched by many colleagues. This list does not begin to encompass them all.

First on my list is Denny Walsh, an insightful, honest, and incorruptible reporter with an unparalleled understanding of the hidden channels of power in American society.

Others include: Ron Funk, an editor who trusted; Dan Moldea, advisor and inspiration; Jim Drinkhall, an exemplar; Bill Beebe, a wise gentleman; Tom Wilson, first city editor; Judith Watkins, impeccable researcher and writer; Elisabeth Sherwin, thoughtful and clear; John Peer Nugent, ever intrepid; Tom Franks, teacher; and to Russell Chandler, Bill Missett, Russell Carrollo, Ira Rifkin, Bob Bayer, and Bob Ballenger.

The pages you are about to read were streamlined and finetuned by Bob Basil, senior editor for Prometheus Books. Most of his suggestions I followed, and this book owes much to his efforts.

The next group is "the skeptical crew." This is a remarkable collection of folks who are putting remarkable claims to the test. The first here is James "The Amazing" Randi, an autodidact and conjurer extraordinaire, beneath whose mysterious outer identity works a great journalist.

Also to be thanked are: Robert Steiner, Terence L. Sandbek, Wayne R. Bartz, Saul Silverman, B. Premanand, David Alexander, Mark Plummer, Bela Scheiber, Barry Karr, Ken Frazier, Paul Kurtz, Joe Morrow, Morgan Sherwood, Jack Foran, and all the others.

My deepest thanks are owed to those who were willing to open up sensitive areas of life to me, the people whose stories are told in the following pages.

To those who gave of their time and experience, named and pseudonymed: David F. Wells, David P. Druliner, Jerry Smith, Gerald Uelmen, Nathan A. Talbot, the late David W. Rennie, Oscar Janiger, Mark Levin, Deborah Monheit, Robert Schibel, Lynard Hinojosa, Sunny Tucker, the late Sidney Cohen, Leo Breiman, Hank Walker, Bill Sturgeon, Marty Goldstein, Beatrice and Keith Lowenstein, Mara Huston, Randy Jones, and the others.

Thanks, too, to friends who helped along the way, including Michael Biber, the Douglases (Don, Alexa, Jim), Jim Kelly, Pat and David Geffner, Tanya Charter, Bob Lee, and Alice Adee.

Special thanks to three judges: Charles Woodmansee, Richard Neidorf, and Steve Trott, who helped a reporter learn about the law.

To two remarkable Westerners, now gone: Bill Willoughby and Louis L'Amour, for never-discouraging words.

To Laurie Butler, for help in keeping my life and household together.

Finally, to my family, whose presence comforts, delights, inspires: Derald, who knows how to question; Jacqueline, a scholar in the making; Samantha, a force of nature; and Laura, helper, editor, nurse, friend, lover, spouse.

Sacramento, California
February 1990

INTRODUCTION
HEALING AND THE NEW AGE

The great shuddering irrevocable shift overtaking us now is not a new political, religious, or philosophical system. It is a new mind—the ascendance of a startling worldview that gathers into its framework break-through science and insights from the earliest recorded thought.

—Marilyn Ferguson,
The Aquarian Conspiracy, 1980

America loves a mystery, a miracle; it has from the beginning. The evidence is right there on the back of the dollar bill, on the Great Seal of the nation. There's a pyramid, 1776 carved in Roman numerals at its base, capped with a levitating, all-seeing, ray-streaming mystical eye. Above is the legend ANNUIT COEPTIS, "He has smiled on our undertakings." Below, an unfurled streamer announces the NOVUS ORDO SECLORUM—"New Order of the Ages."

The birth of the nation heralded the dawn of a new age—the country's first, but by no means last.

American belief in a here-and-now fulfillment of human destiny owed much to a movement that revealed itself in public for the first time in London in 1717. Whatever its origins—and here theories abound—the emergence of Freemasonry revealed the existence of a brotherhood committed to the liberal ideas of fraternity, religious tolerance, human perfectibility, and compassion.

George Washington was a Mason, and took his first inaugural oath on a Masonic lodge's Bible—the same one George Bush used for his first inaugural oath two centuries later. Fellow brethren included John Hancock, Paul Revere, Robert Livingston, and Edmund Randolph. The young nation's most famous ally, the Marquis de Lafayette, was a brother. Many military leaders and officers on both sides of the Revolutionary War were Masons, as were a goodly number of line troopers. Lodges met in camps on both sides of the battle lines, and an officer might have been in a lodge presided over by an enlisted man. Masonic regalia captured with an enemy camp found its way back across the lines.

Some authors attribute the British loss of the colonies to a reluctance of self-perceived brothers to wage unlimited war on fellow Masons fighting for the ideals they shared.[1,2]

With its emphasis on hidden meanings and symbols (the pyramid side of the Great Seal is a Masonic design), secret traditions, mystical initiation, human perfectibility, and, above all, brotherhood, Freemasonry's spread in the New Land at the start of its own New Age paved the way for future, less rational, beliefs.[3]

*   *   *

Along with the Masonic concept of social unity came the notion of magnetic unity. Thanks to Masonic brother/writer/postmaster/fire chief/inventor of stoves and bifocals/wet weather kite-flyer/premier political intriguer/humorist/bald-headed, pot-bellied, primitive-dressing sexual swordsman Benjamin Franklin, electricity had become the rage of the age— a media sensation akin to the euphoria that would greet the promise of nuclear power in the days before Three Mile Island. Franklin was supremely positioned in his day to spread the Gospel of Progress.

Electromagnetism was about *invisible, inexhaustible energy* uniting all creation. Newton's gravity had confined us to earth; electricity promised the stars. Destiny could be changed.

Mesmerism seized on the public fascination with its promise of boundless power and unity, becoming a popular fad attracting thousands in the Old and New Worlds. Named after Franz Anton Mesmer, mesmerism was a "scientific" technique that could supposedly alter the magnetic flux of the body, curing disorders of body and mind.

A Viennese physician, Mesmer began treating patients with what he called "animal magnetism" in 1774, moving to Paris four years later (where Masonry flourished and where exactly ten years later Benjamin Franklin would pass negative judgment on mesmerism as a member of a royal commission called to investigate the matter).[4]

Rooted in astrology, Mesmer had come to believe that a healer could act as a conductor for universal energy fields that could restore the sick to health.[5] To evoke this wonder of the age, patients sat around large tubs filled with dilute sulphuric acid—battery acid—either holding hands or gripping iron bars extending from the liquid.

Still evolving, the craze reached London soon after the Revolutionary War and arrived in the United States by the 1820s, becoming a popular cult within a decade. Gone by then were the acid-filled vats. Self-proclaimed "mesmerists" toured the country, making "magnetic passes" over the bodies of their patients, claiming miracles. The techniques developed by scientists and charlatans alike were to evolve into what is today called "hypnosis."

*   *   *

If planetary, magnetic energies could be transmitted through the person of a healer, why not spiritual energy, soul energy? Indeed, since we all possessed an immortal essence, why couldn't those who have Gone Beyond transmit their presence back to us here on the Material Plane?

In 1848, spiritualism swept the nation. Upstate New York sisters Katherine and Margaret Fox played a typical children's prank: They started making things go bump in the night (apples on strings and cracking toe-joints), attributing the rapping to spirits who had Gone Beyond. But this ghost story was believed, and the children were captured by their own creation.

From simple nocturnal knocks, a "science" soon evolved, centering around the person of a gifted soul who could step out of consciousness and allow Discarnate Entities to take possession of the vacated material body to convey reassuring words to living loved ones. Donations were gladly accepted. The Fox sisters were the first "mediums," and their success bred instant imitation. Thousands swore to the authenticity of the voices that soon replaced the much more laborious rapping. One enthusiastic believer was the nation's First Lady some years later, Mary Todd Lincoln, who held seances in the White House (just as a later First Lady would try to steer the life of her spouse with the help of an astrologer).

But mere voices and thumps weren't enough. Folks always wanted more, what the Bible called "signs and wonders."[6] And what the people wanted, the mediums provided. Marvels followed: Words materialized on sealed slates; trumpets floated on air, uttering prophecies; glowing or unseen hands touched the believer's knees (under the seance table, usually); ghostly forms of dead souls appeared. To allay skeptical claims of trickery, some mediums even allowed themselves to be tied and placed in locked "cabinets": Spirits—and donations—still appeared.

These bizarre happenings were endorsed by a small but influential number of well-known and highly regarded scientists, doctors, lawyers, professors, and publishers. Sir Arthur Conan Doyle, creator of the cerebral detective Sherlock Holmes, was a passionate believer and wrote a glowing history of the movement. Sir Oliver Lodge, one of the premier physicists of the age, endorsed mediumship (though lust, rather than reason, seems to have been the overriding reason). Spiritualism fit into the scheme of the age, of this great nineteenth century. Science had plumbed the forces of the physical; now it would illuminate the metaphysical. As within, so without; as above, so below.

Spiritualism has remained a cultural force in one form or another ever since. The close of the nineteenth century saw a resurgence of spiritualism. It became especially strong in England with the onset of the First World War with its bloody toll. At one point the movement was strong enough there to support a daily newspaper and numerous other periodicals, many featuring in-depth interviews with departed celebrities.

There was another powerful strain at work in American society, the transcendentalist movement.

The United States was first a colonial outpost of the British Empire. Another colony was India. While the English (and French and Portuguese) sought to impose their own values on the Asian land, Indian thought filtered back throughout the realm.

Hinduism is a religion of master and student, of revelation and sur-render. The essence of Hindu mysticism is denial, rejection, and retreat: denial of the evidence of the material senses, rejection of material values, and retreat into a realm of subjective feeling.

Hinduism offers an incredible diversity of paths to liberation. At the same time, Hinduism embraces a strong caste tradition and fatalism. Birth was everything. Caste determines options; horoscopes set further con-straints. Custom and religion are inseparable; thousands of *shastras*, Sanskrit religious texts, prescribes techniques for eating, sleeping, breathing, love-making, walking, talking, sneezing, and singing. Throughout the religion's history, astrologers would pick marital partners, determine vocations, and tell kings when and where to start wars.

The material world is *maya*, illusion. The ego projects kama, desire, on the objects of the senses, creating attachment, which leads inevitably to suffering. The goal is *moksha*, liberation from the great wheel of death and rebirth, from attachment. This spiritual realization was achieved by *karma*, action—either through *bhoga*, disciplined indulgence, or *yoga*, disci-plined denial.

*   *   *

What California is to contemporary society, Boston was to the United States of the years before the Civil War. A seaport and the seat of the nation's leading university, Boston was a bohemian community, fertile ground for Indian beliefs. There, in 1836, the "Transcendental Club" was founded.[7] Its most famous members were Ralph Waldo Emerson, Henry David Thoreau, Bronson Alcott (author and father of Louisa May Alcott), and Margaret Fuller (great-aunt of R. Buckminster Fuller, who was to become a luminary of another New Age to come).

Boston Transcendentalism was Yankee mysticism, more pragmatic idealism than fatalistic acceptance; it was Hindu detachment wed to American Manifest Destiny—prosperity with the Oversoul.

The nineteenth century also witnessed the rise of evolutionary theory. Despite Darwin's inherently physical orientation, mystics and metaphysicians saw in material evolution a parallel of spiritual evolution. Humanity was on the march toward a goal of immortal perfection realized in the here-and-now. What remained was to transcend the warm fuzziness of the Transcendentalists and tie faith firmly to science, making reason and revelation coincide. Two remarkable Victorian women accomplished that task.

The Theosophical Society was the invention of a massive, gruff medium named Helena Petrova Blavatsky. Theosophy was her marriage of spiritualism to the Indo-Tibetan worldview, with its *gurus, avatars, chakras* (a seven-leveled series of "esoteric energy centers"), and *siddhis,* supernatural powers. Though the goal was freedom from physicality, some enlightened beings, *mahatmas* and *boddhisattvas*, remained on earth to guide others on the path to enlightenment. Meditating in caves high in the Himalayas, they beamed their thoughts into Blavatsky's mind. With the aid of followers, she created a movement that still endures.[8]

As Western physical scientists had delved into the realm of matter, conducting experiments and discovering the rules of natural law, so metaphysical scientists of the East had explored the domain of Spirit, comprehended its laws, Theosophists declared. What these Asian masters had discovered was a science of being as complete and well-tested as Newton's optics or Boyle's chemistry.

Blavatsky's revelation of these hidden truths promised the dawn of a millennium, heralded in 1897 when Theosophist Katherine A. Tingley launched *The New Century*, a magazine to help "construct practically a new 'order of the ages.' "[9]

But the bottom line was still miracles, and Blavatsky produced them. She and virtually all her fellow mediums were exposed as frauds and charlatans at some point in their careers.[10] But exposure didn't necessarily spell the end of their lucrative careers. Mediums were childlike beings, eager to please and not in full control of their powers. Like children, they could be naughty. Sometimes they resorted to trickery, but that didn't mean they always did, reasoned those whose desire to believe mattered more than anything else. Only when their energies were low did they resort to parlor tricks, went the rationale, one still heard today among the ranks of "psi" supporters.[11]

The other woman was Mary Baker Eddy, Discoverer, Founder, and

Leader of Christian Science. She began her career as a disciple of Phineas Parkhurst Quimby, a mesmerist turned mental healer. Though Mrs. Eddy and her church minimize her debt to Quimby, critics say Mrs. Eddy borrowed many, if not most, of her concepts and language from him.[12] But Mrs. Eddy made no compromises with matter, which she declared unreal. Pills and prayers were incompatible, she declared. The Truth she discovered would meet "every human need."

Mrs. Eddy's insistence on "radical reliance" on her revelation alone for healing proved too austere for some to whom the idea of mind-is-all remained attractive. A series of alternative churches arose that still held to the basic idea that matter was an illusion, but accepted that medicine offered some real, tangible benefits. Science of Mind, Religious Science, Unity, and a number of other, smaller sects hence arose.

*   *   *

If there's a single dominant factor coloring this century's resurgence of New Age beliefs, it's a chemical—lysergic acid diethylamide-25: LSD, or "acid."

A few molecules derived from a deadly fungus tickled some cells that squirted some chemicals inside the skull, setting off a literal brainstorm. While the drug experience often shattered old perceptions of the world, what acid didn't do was provide any lasting answers. The tripper always came down, always to the same world.

Not all acidheads became otherworldly mystics. The Weather Underground's materialist revolutionaries lived an acid-washed life, as did the Hells Angels and Cary Grant. There was a time when the drug had been the in-house high at the CIA, when exuberant spooks tried to dose the 1954 Company Christmas party punch.[13]

Millions tried acid, peyote, magic mushrooms, and the other psychedelic alkaloids. Save for a relative few pushed over already tenuous boundaries into full-blown psychosis, acidheads eventually found themselves drawn back from counterculture to mainstream culture, where today they run companies, practice law and medicine, build houses, tend children. What they kept was a sense of Something Beyond, a world where normal rules didn't apply and where, as the Bard said, "there is nothing either good or bad, but thinking makes it so."[14]

When the cosmic hallucinations of the acid revolution hit at the dawn of the current New Age, the spiritualists, theosophists, and mind-is-all folks were ready to step in with their own explanations, their own institutions. They were joined by a host of gurus from the East, most visibly the Maharishi Mahesh Yogi and his Transcendental Meditation cult.[15] Acid-eroded old Western categories were replaced by others, just as old but different.

Mediumship has survived, but in a new incarnation. They are *channellers*. For the most part, they have relinquished the old repertoire of magic tricks. Channellers rely on stage presence instead, performing in the full glare of TV cameras, uttering hybrid accents—purportedly those of beings from Atlantis, Lemuria, outer space (the Pleiades are popular), and the oceans (dolphins send to a few dry-landers). They make millions.

The prototype of the modern medium was Jane Roberts, who began to channel a "multi-dimensional" being called Seth.[16] By stripping mediumship of its easily debunked parlor tricks, Roberts and those who followed her succeeded in winning new respectability for the trade. By robbing mediumship of its one consciously learned talent, Roberts also enabled the suggestible to set out to become mediums themselves. It had become possible to become an utterly sincere "channeller."[17]

*   *   *

Many writers date the birth of the current incarnation of the New Age to 1971, when the eclectic *East-West Journal* first appeared.[18] But the movement erupted into public consciousness in 1980 with the publication of writer Marilyn Ferguson's *The Aquarian Conspiracy: Personal and Social Transformation in the 1980's.*

The idea of the "dawning of the Age of Aquarius" was injected into mass culture by the 1967 acidified rock musical *Hair*. For Ferguson, it was a banner under which a whole range of beliefs could be united.[19] To be part of the Aquarian Conspiracy, the opening words of the book's first chapter proclaimed, was to be part of "a leaderless but powerful network . . . working to bring about radical change in the United States. Its members have broken with certain key elements of Western thought, and they may have broken continuity with history."[20]

The idea of a break with history means the breakdown of categories. Old rules no longer apply. Mutually contradictory doesn't mean mutually false. To be part of the New Age is to be part of a movement that embraces meditation, chakra balancing, aura reading, crystal healing, acupuncture, homeopathy, channelling, astrology, UFOs (especially in the new form of mysterious, semi-divine extraterrestrial abductors), vegetarianism, hypnotism, psychics and faith-healers of all persuasions, martial arts, fire-walking, yoga, palmistry, alchemy, *Kabbalah*—the list literally goes on for pages.[24]

A final element in today's New Age is physics, and the revolutionary discoveries of relativity, quantum mechanics, and chaos theory. Matter and energy are one and mysterious, each capable of an alchemical transformation into the other by forces operating over vast distances. Apparently solid forms are illusions, masking a constant, ever-shifting interplay of cosmic forces, governed by immutable laws. All of which seems to meld nicely with the ever-shifting visions of the psychedelic experience.

As a culture, Americans identify themselves by decades. "She's a woman of the '80s." "He's a child of the '60s." The approach of a year ending with double zeros seems to inspire a certain nuttiness. Mesmerism and Masonry seized public attention at the dawn of the nineteenth century. Spiritualism, Theosophy, and Christian Science flourished near the dawn of the twentieth century. The approach of a year ending with triple zeros promises an unprecedented array of inventive and imitative weirdness.

*   *   *

Today's New Age movement is deeply involved with healing. If the forces governing the universe are spiritual, and if we are spiritual beings, then what is disease? After all, the spiritual is infinitely more powerful, more real, than the material.

Medical science had long since been forced to acknowledge that mental states sometimes play a significant role in preventing and recovering from illness. The "placebo effect" is real and powerful: Significant numbers of patients suffering from a significant number of real diseases report significant degrees of relief when a doctor gives them a sugar pill.

Clearly, *something* is at work.

For several decades, physicians shrugged off the placebo effect, focusing their energies on conditions they could treat with material remedies, with drugs, surgery, radiation, diet, and exercise. But recent studies have begun to define a complex relationship between thought and health. Scientists have discovered natural opiates manufactured by the brain. Other studies seem to show that simply thinking good thoughts helps the body prevent and fight a wide range of disorders. Anger, for example, can provoke heart attacks.

The relationship between thought and health is still ill-defined. The fact remains, however, that thinking is a human behavior which can and does influence health. The evidence also seems to show that it's not so much *what* you believe as *that* you believe. The fact of belief itself confers real benefits, whatever its object.

*   *   *

Deadly Blessings examines three forms of "alternative healing," one from the pre-twentieth century New Age (Christian Science) and two from the stirrings of the pre-twenty-first century New Age (psychic surgery and psychedelic psychotherapy).

It does so through the lens of the law. It examines the relationship of society to the individual, both social and legal. It charts the boundaries of the legal and illegal, of civil and criminal rights and wrongs, of state-imposed limitations on spiritual action.

NOTES

1. Michael Baigent and Richard Leigh, *The Temple and the Lodge* (New York: Arcade Publishing; Little, Brown, 1989).

2. See also John J. Robinson's *Born in Blood, The Lost Secrets of Freemasonry* (New York: M. Evans, 1989).

3. Mary Baker Eddy approved of Freemasonry, in part because it buried her first husband and rescued her from abandonment, in part because it accorded her religion equal status with all others.

4. The commission concluded that the phenomenon was the product of suggestibility.

5. See, for example, Ronald C. Clark's *Benjamin Franklin* (New York: Free Press, 1983), pp. 389-391, for a discussion of the Royal Academy's review of Mesmer's claims. As for hypnosis and its fruits, see E. M. Thornton's *Freud and Cocaine: The Freudian Fallacy* (London: Blond & Briggs, 1983).

6. Acts 14:3.

7. Dagobert B. Runes, ed., *Dictionary of Philosophy* (Totowa, N.J.: Littlefield, Adams, 1962), p. 320.

8. Blavatsky launched her career in England, and traveled the world making converts. Her movement later split, as movements do. Her disciples declared a young Hindu child, Jiddu Krishnamurti, the Avatar of the Age, Godhead incarnate—a mantle he later renounced.

9. Quoted in Hillel Schwarz's *Century's End: A Cultural History of the Fin de Siecle from the 990's through the 1990's* (New York: Doubleday, 1990), p. 158.

10. The one notable exception was Daniel Home, a Scotsman who never performed except when in total control of his environment. See Trevor H. Hall's *The Enigma of Daniel Home* (Buffalo, N.Y.: Prometheus Books, 1984).

11. Mediums received a major setback early in the twentieth century when they encountered Harry Houdini. A great friend of Arthur Conan Doyle, Houdini wanted very much to believe in life after death. His mother was the most cherished figure in his life, and when she died, he sought out mediums in the hope of reestablishing contact with her. But his professional magician's eye revealed fraud and deceit everywhere. Houdini became a great debunker, challenging and exposing mediums and other miracle-mongers at every opportunity.

12. Indeed, he seems to have coined the very name "Christian Science" in an essay written in 1863, long before the appearance of the first edition of *Science and Health*. See *The Quimby Manuscripts*, Horatio W. Dresser, ed. (Secaucus, N.J.: Citadel Press, 1976, reprint of 1921 edition), p. 388.

13. M. A. Lee and B. Schlain, *Acid Dreams*, p. 29.

14. A quotation cited by Mary Baker Eddy on the opening page of *Science and Health*.

15. The Maharishi claims meditators can catalyze world peace and even levitate (although his "yogic flying" turns out to be mere cross-legged mattress bouncing).

16. Jane Roberts, *Seth Speaks*, et al.

17. When Dr. Betty Grover Eisner's group began experimenting with mediumship, the New Age term hadn't come into the popular tongue. So to describe their art, they named it after Roberts's entity. They *sethed.*

18. See J. Gordon Melton, "A History of the New Age Movement," in *Not Necessarily the New Age*, Robert Basil, ed. (Buffalo, N.Y.: Prometheus Books, 1988), p. 35.

19. *New Age* itself is not a New Age term, but is borrowed from the Theosophists.

20. Los Angeles: J. P. Tarcher, p. 23.

21. See, for example, *The New Age Catalog*, a 244-page compendium by the editors of *Body, Mind & Spirit Magazine* and published by Dolphin Doubleday (New York) in 1988.

PART I

NESTLING'S FALTERING FLIGHT

THE SHORT LIFE AND DEATH OF SETH IAN GLASER

THE MOTHER'S EVENING PRAYER

Oh gentle presence, peace and joy and power;
   O Life divine, that owns each waiting hour,
Thou Love that guides the nestling's faltering flight!
   Keep Thou my child on upward wing to-night.

Love is our refuge; only with mine eye
   Can I behold the snare, the pit, the fall:
His habitation high is here, and nigh,
   His arm encircles me, and mine, and all.

Oh make me glad for every scalding tear,
   For hope deferred, ingratitude, disdain!
Wait and love more for every hate, and fear
   No ill,—since God is good, and loss is gain.

Beneath the shadow of His mighty wing;
   In that sweet secret of the narrow way,
Seeking and finding, with the angels sing:
   'Lo I am with you alway,'—watch and pray.

No snare, no fowler, pestilence or pain;
   No night drops down upon the troubled breast,
When heaven's aftersmile earth's tear-drops gain,
   And mother finds her home and heavenly rest.

—Mary Baker Eddy

This is a hymn sung in
every Christian Science church
and a frequent source of inspiration
to Mary Baker Eddy's followers.

THE CALL

For Mary Reynolds, a veteran Santa Monica police officer, it began with a radio call ten minutes before midnight, 28 March 1984. She and her partner were sent to look into the death of a child. A report she neatly hand-printed at the finish of the incident tells the following story:

Pulling up outside the home, Reynolds was met by a man identifying himself as Lawrence Hall, of the House of Hall Mortuary in Los Angeles. He told her he had been called more than eight hours earlier by the home's owner, for "advice and help regarding procedures about what to do about a death that had just occurred."

When Hall arrived at the house ninety minutes after the call, he was met by the parents of a seventeen-month-old boy. They asked him "if they could have more time to pray." Hall told them to call back whenever they were ready. That call finally came at 9:30 P.M. Hall returned to Santa Monica and called the Los Angeles County Coroner's office for permission to move the body. The coroner refused, instructing Hall to wait until police could investigate.

The uniformed officer talked to the infant's parents and the owner of the house, a Christian Science practitioner. The parents were Christian Scientists, and told Reynolds the child had not been seen by a doctor since a checkup six weeks after birth. He had never been vaccinated, never suffered any unusual illnesses prior to the short, fierce fever that had ended in his death. Just how high the fever was, they didn't know: They never took his temperature. The parents told the officer they had sent the undertaker away because they wanted to get help from another Christian Science practitioner, one "who had revived people who had been dead." Only when that practitioner's efforts failed did they again call the mortuary.

Admitted to the house, the police officer found the corpse face-up on a sofa, clad in a disposable diaper, a blue Donald Duck T-shirt, and white socks. That the child had been dead for some time was evident by signs of post-mortem lividity, a pooling of blood on the back where it had settled after his heart stopped.

The officer asked the parents what medical steps they had taken before the child succumbed—or "passed," as the parents referred to the death. "I asked if they gave him aspirin, any medication, a sponge bath, or anything physical to help him. They all said no. I asked if they ever took him to a doctor or consulted with a doctor and they said no. I asked why." The mother answered that "the Christian Science religion doesn't work that way, that they believe in healing through prayer."

Reynolds called her supervisor, Sergeant Legurski, who also came to the house. His supervisor, Lieutenant Mapes, ordered Reynolds to complete a detailed report, which would "be forwarded to the district attorney's office for possible prosecution."

*   *   *

Seth Ian Glaser was dead. The cause? According to the coroner's office, a bacterial infection of the brain normally responsive to antibiotic treatment. His parents, Lise Erwin and Eliot Dixon Glaser, and the practitioner, Mrs. Virginia Scott, were charged with murder. The Glaser case, one of three similar California cases and seven nationwide, illustrates the conflict between the rights of a child and its parents, and between a rich, sophisticated, and politically powerful church and the state.

DISCOVERER, FOUNDER, LEADER

Why pray for the recovery of the sick, if you are without faith in God's willingness and ability to heal them? If you do believe in God, why do you substitute drugs for the Almighty's power, and employ means which lead only to material ways of obtaining help, instead of turning in time of need to God, divine Love, who is an ever-present help?

Treat a belief in sickness as you would sin, with sudden dismissal. Resist the temptation to believe in matter as intelligent, as having sensation or power.

—Mary Baker Eddy

Christian Science is at once an extremely worldly and a radically unworldly religion: worldly in its demands for material success and in its political savvy; unworldly in its denial of life's tragedies. The religion cannot be understood outside the context of the era which gave it birth and the woman whose idea it was: the Discover, Founder, and Leader.

Just who was this Mary Morse Baker Glover Patterson Eddy?

The only comprehensive historical source is closed, the Archives of the Mother Church. Robert Peel, a writer and dedicated Christian Scientist, is the only biographer thus far allowed access to these files. His massive, three-volume biography is scholarly but partisan, and there is no way to judge its thoroughness. "Outsiders" Georgine Milmine and Edwin Franden Dakin have portrayed Mary Barker Eddy in a far less flattering way in their biographies.

While a comprehensive, objective biography remains to be written, much can be said.

Christian Science was shaped by an era in which women had no political power beyond moral persuasion. They couldn't vote, often couldn't own property in their own names. One medium of communication and influence open to them was sex, an act Christianity labeled the Original Sin. Biological urges were just as strong in the Victorian era, of course, as they are today. (The resulting conflict was wonderfully described by Mark Twain in the second of his *Letters from the Earth:*[1] "From youth to middle age all men and all women prize copulation above all other pleasures combined, yet it is actually as I have said: it is not in their heaven; prayer takes its place.")[2]

In Mrs. Eddy's formative years, the options women faced were narrowly circumscribed. Women born or married into wealth had the greatest freedom. But, for the most part, the professions and the political world were closed even to them. For those born into poverty, there were two options: marriage, or menial labor at home, in a sweatshop, or a factory. To be a mother was to be tied to home and children in a day before microwaves, disposable diapers and bottles, vacuum cleaners, clothes- and dish-washers, electric irons, gas- or electric-fired stoves and furnaces, not to mention indoor toilets. Many made their own thread, wove their own cloth, dressed their families in homespun. Universal free education didn't exist. Epidemics ravaged the land; children often got sick and died. A mother was part-time teacher, part-time doctor. Pasteur hadn't discovered bacteria, Darwin hadn't published, Einstein hadn't been born. There were no anesthetics, and most "medicines" did more harm than good. Life was governed by terrible, mysterious forces.

At the same time, there was an expansive spirit about the land. The nation was young, growing, constantly pushing at its borders. It was a land of immense resources and industry. Steam was king, and every day brought some new technological wonder.

*   *   *

Mrs. Eddy was a product of New Hampshire, where hard livings were won by stubborn folk who fiercely valued their independence. Born in July 1821, as a child she knew veterans of the American Revolution. Her family was politically active; one brother's meteoric political rise was ended only by untimely death.

She was a troubled child, often missing school. Just what she suffered from isn't clear. Critics have call her a hypochondriac, a lonely, insecure child who staged illness to win sympathy. Believers portray the same events as stages in spiritual evolution, a process of learning the futility of seeking happiness in the material world.

She was bright, and largely self-educated. She married three times. Her first husband, George Washington Glover, was a young entrepreneur who soon died, leaving her penniless, pregnant, and far from home. Her second mate, Daniel Patterson, was an amiable dentist whose affections were as itinerant as his practice; their divorce came simultaneously with her "discovery" of Christian Science. Her final marriage was to a disciple, Asa Gilbert Eddy, whose main legacy was his name.

Her course in life was always lonely. Ultimately, she was estranged from her family and her son, and saw many of her students fall away in anger and bitterness. Her first anointed healer, Richard Kennedy, was cast out, declared a malicious mesmerist, and (unsuccessfully) sued. When her third and last husband died, she declared that he had been the victim of "mesmeric poison," apparently administered by "one of my students, a malpractitioner."[3] Both her birth son and a second "son," a disciple adopted as an adult, challenged her mental competence in court during her final years, and her last, most successful disciple, Augusta Stetson, was cast out of the fold on her orders.

But she learned from her lessons. By the time of her death she had founded a church which would perpetuate her leadership, launched what was to become one of the world's most respected newspapers, and established a way of life centering on the adoration of her personality. Within her religion, she had found a higher purpose in her sorrow: "The loss of material objects of affection sunders the dominant ties of earth and points to heaven."[4] Experience taught her that "whatever is loved materially as mere corporeal personality, is eventually lost."[5] Human personalities were not to be trusted. The only way to preserve her true child, her church, was by casting out all personalities save one.

*   *   *

There was another powerful strain at work in American society, with its roots in the same New England soil that gave rise to Mrs. Eddy. ("Mrs. Eddy" is her own preferred reference, the term normally used by her followers and critics alike.) This was the transcendentalist movement.

In 1836, when Mrs. Eddy was fifteen years old, the "Transcendental Club" was founded in Boston.[6] Its most influential member was Ralph Waldo Emerson, whose poems were an obvious influence on Mrs. Eddy. Another of the Boston transcendentalist "Brahmins" was Bronson Alcott, whose endorsement Mrs. Eddy was to proudly cite.[7]

Phineas Parkhurst Quimby, a mesmerist dubbed "the Portland Healer," was Mrs. Eddy's guru during the troubled years of her second marriage. Seeking relief for a vague, unending series of complaints, she turned to the Maine healer—who by all accounts was a sincere believer in his craft.

Though Mrs. Eddy later denied Quimby any role in the genesis of her religion, she studied with him, and it was he who coined the very term "Christian Science." Quimby was a self-professed healer, and taught others. What he could not do was build a movement.

Another, parallel, phenomenon was spiritualism, the religion of trance mediums, seances, and materialization.

Mesmerism and spiritualism both portrayed a world of complex, subtle influences. What might appear a disease to the "material senses" might in fact be merely the representation of disturbed thinking or demonic influence. A gifted adept could discover the metaphysical causes of physical events, and offer the promise of healing either through a miracle or through a material prescription or practice. Though she was to give each a chapter in her sacred text, Mrs. Eddy was to deny both beliefs any positive role in the evolution of her own "science."

Indeed, not only did Mrs. Eddy deny that any of these philosophical and religious currents had any influence in her thinking, she also insisted that the brilliant structure she created glorify her person for all time. Her church decreed in 1906, four years before her death, "that no one on earth to-day, aside from Mrs. Eddy, knows anything about Christian Science except as he has learned it from her and from her writings; and Christian Scientists are honest only as they give her full credit for her extraordinary work. . . . Strive it ever so hard, The Church of Christ, Scientist, can never do for its Leader what its Leader has done for this church; but its members can so protect their own thoughts that they are not unwittingly made to deprive their Leader of her rightful place as the revelator to this age of the immortal truths testified to by Jesus and the prophets."[8] The church she created also contained a militant, ever-vigilant structure for ensuring that the media offered only acceptable images of her and her religion.

There are many areas of doubt in the official version of Mrs. Eddy's life. For instance, she certainly could not have become a Church-endorsed healer with her name listed in the *Christian Science Journal*. The application form for *Journal* listings asks: "Are you completely free from the use of drugs, sedatives, or material remedies?" For several periods during her years as leader of her church, Mrs. Eddy could not have answered yes. She relied on opiates to kill the pain of kidney stones. The Christian Science Board of Directors was forced to acknowledge this when, after her death, memoirs of household members surfaced in the press. To what extent she used the drug is uncertain. In his diaries, her devoted aide Calvin Frye describes multiple instances of morphine use by the prophetess. He tells of another household member, Adam H. Dickey, refusing her the drug and declaring "it was the old morphine habit reasserting itself."[9]

Unauthorized biographies depict a woman of violent mood swings attributed to the evil workings of M.A.M., malicious animal magnetism, the conscious effort to turn her science against her and work harm.[10] In one of her most lurid public moments, she claimed that the death of her third and final husband, Asa Gilbert Eddy, came by "arsenical poisoning," "not material poison but mesmeric poison." The physician who examined the body found clear evidence of a less mysterious malady, heart disease.[11]

To a Christian Scientist, Mary Baker Eddy is nothing less than the vehicle chosen for the second coming of the Christ, the healing power of God's presence demonstrated by Jesus of Nazareth. Believers hold that the Christian Science textbook, *Science and Health with Key to the Scriptures* by Mary Baker Eddy, is the "little book" described in St. John's vision of heaven.[12]

For at least eight years, "Mrs. Eddy" was "Mother Eddy." In "Class, Pulpit, Students' Students," an article in *Miscellaneous Writings 1883-1896*, she wrote "to the students whom I have not seen that ask, 'May I call you mother?' my heart replies *yes*, if you are with me in God's work. When born of Truth and Love, we are all of one kindred."[14]

But by 1903, she was to write that "in the year eighteen hundred and ninety-five, loyal Christian Scientists had given to the author of their textbook, the Founder of Christian Science, the individual, endearing term of Mother. At first Mrs. Eddy objected to being called thus, but afterward consented on the ground that this appelative in the Church meant nothing more that a tender term such as sister or brother. In the year nineteen hundred and three and after, owing to the public misunderstanding of this name, it is the duty of Christian Scientists to drop the word *mother* and to substitute Leader, already used in our periodicals."[15] What happened in 1903 was a Mark Twain satire on Christian Science, skewering the faithful for their endless reverential references to "Mother." The name "Mother Church" was retained, however, and Mrs. Eddy is for all time to come Pastor Emeritus, Discoverer, Founder, and Leader.[16]

But if Mary Baker Eddy was the mother, who was the father? There is no question that she was a plagiarist; only the degree of unattributed borrowing is in question. One major issue still not convincingly resolved is whether or not she stole large sections from two manuscripts to which she apparently had access during the time she was writing the first edition of *Science and Health*.[17]

The Metaphysical Religion of Hegel by Francis Leiber was allegedly mailed to Hiram Crafts in Boston by Leiber, for presentation to the local "Kantian Society." Crafts was Mrs. Eddy's first student; she lived in his home. The late Walter Martin, a conservative Christian whose special focus was cults, declares, "It is demonstrably true that Mrs. Eddy copied thirty-three pages verbatim and one hundred pages in substance" into *Science and Health*. He then gives parallel columns of identical or virtually identical text.[18]

The other manuscript was by none other than Phineas P. Quimby, and bears strong resemblance to the textbook's central chapter—the one used as the basis of formal instruction of authorized healers. (A computerized comparison of Mrs. Eddy's work with Lieber's and Quimby's could be quite interesting.)

There is yet another point to be made about Mrs. Eddy, and that is her peculiar use of the word "science." Hers clearly derives from her old mentor, Quimby, and is akin to the mystical connotation of "knowing." "Science" to Mrs. Eddy is a process of perceiving that heals all sense of limitation and mortality. The very act of perceiving changes the "material" sense of being, and brings about a "demonstration" of our true, spiritual being. While material science has certainly changed reality through its technological fallout, Mrs. Eddy's was the true science, of which the human material tinkering was the merest shadow.

The most significant tool of human knowledge, the scientific method, she rejected in its entirety. The scientific method declares that for a phenomenon to be studied, it must first be quantified, defined, limited. For conclusions to be considered valid, they must be independently repeatable by others.

Mrs. Eddy distrusted numbers, except when she could use them in her favor (as when she claimed "millions" of followers at a time when her church numbered fewer than 90,000 members). The power that healed was unlimited, infinite, innumerably potent and loving, and attempting to circumscribe it would be admitting doubt, something fatal to a healing. So no numbers were permitted, a rule incorporated into the By-laws of her Church.[19] Mrs. Eddy defined seven synonyms for God: Soul, Life, Truth, Love, Spirit, Mind, and Principle. Hers was not a corporeal God, not a God to be perceived through the five senses. God was a living, vital, eternal, creative power. God was good, incapable of creating conflict, crisis, or tragedy. The process of recognizing, of realizing, the identity of the individual as an eternal idea in divine Mind, Love, all-harmonious good, conveyed a power to vanquish any illusion of human tragedy. This was the "science" of Christ.

"Understanding" as defined by Christian Science is not the recognition of relationships between events in the world of the five senses. It is the result of an active, demanding, disciplined immersion. The believer must "*spiritually* understand," must "see through" the "false claims" of sin, death, sickness; must "know" in "Absolute Science" that these supposed sources of human misery are "errors," "lies," illusions of "mortal mind," the "false sense" of God and His "perfect reflection," man. Adherents believe a "Christianly scientific" understanding of the divine will insure a demonstration of healing.

"Demonstration" is another big word: It defines an active process, the circumstances and mental working-out that leads to a "healing," which, by definition, must bless all involved. It is frequently invoked in testimonials and religious articles.

While Christian Scientists are taught that the "mortal senses" are the fruits of a deceptive "false belief" about the nature of human existence, the religion provides a wealth of sensory experience. But the overwhelming medium is the eye, which beholds the flood of writing that the faithful consume, sometimes for hours a day. Christian Scientists are people of The Books: the Bible and *Science and Health*, the ordained "pastors" of the faith. To the Christian Scientist, the Bible is largely unknowable without *Science and Health.*

Science and Health describes three basic ways of knowing: belief, faith, and spiritual understanding. *Belief* is a thing of the head, *faith* brings in the heart's expectancy of good, and *spiritual understanding* results in demonstration. Science is divine Truth perceived so clearly that the physical illusion falls away and man arises as he always has been, a timeless, beautiful, glorious, immortal idea at play in divine Mind. Healings are miracles only to "mortal sense"; in Absolute Science there is nothing to heal.

A person possessed of such insight, such Absolute Divine Science, could survive unharmed standing at ground zero of a hydrogen bomb blast. "Divine Love always has met and always will meet every human need," writes Mrs. Eddy.[20]

*   *   *

Two of the most frequently used tools in Christian Science are *A Complete Concordance to the Writings of Mary Baker Eddy*, Authorized Edition, and a biblical concordance (*Cruden's Complete* and *Strong's Exhaustive* are popular, the latter because it includes a dictionary of the original Greek and Hebrew). Purists even specify the English language dictionary to use when delving into Mrs. Eddy's Victorian prose.

Most Christian Scientists own not only the basic writings, but subscribe to "the periodicals," the Mother Church's daily, weekly, monthly, and quarterly periodicals. Of these, the most important is the *Christian Science Quarterly*, which spells out the weekly "Lesson-Sermon," a collection of thirteen readings of passages from the Bible and *Science and Health* chosen in order from twenty-six topics mandated by Mrs. Eddy. While the topics are fixed, the readings themselves are varied, selected at church headquarters in Boston.

The lesson-sermon unites every Christian Scientist in every country in a common ritual, an infinitely varied psychological kaleidoscope on which all attention is focused. The lesson-sermon is a powerful, unifying discipline, directing the thought of every follower, reinforcing orthodoxy. It creates a context, a structure, through which the believer relates to self, fellow believers, and the outside world.

After a week of studying the lesson-sermon—often with extensive concordance use—the follower attends the Sunday "service." A First Reader recites all the lesson-sermon passages from *Science and Health*, and a Second Reader recites the biblical passages. The First Reader leads the service, selecting hymns from the *Christian Science Hymnal* (frequently including one of seven drawn from poems written by Mrs. Eddy). Churches also have an organist and a singer, who may be nonbelievers.[21]

There are Wednesday gatherings as well, called "meetings," which include readings from the Bible and *Science and Health*, which Mrs. Eddy officially ordained as the only "pastors" of the church after various schisms had split the movement.[22] The First Reader selects the topic and related scriptural selections and hymns, which take about half the hour-long meeting, leaving the remaining time for testimonials from the floor. One after another, Christian Scientists rise amid the silence to share a demonstration or an insight. The blind see, the deaf hear, the lame walk, at least in words. There is no doubting their sincerity.[23]

Lise Glaser describes these meetings:

I would go Wednesday nights to the testimony meetings and I'd hear all these people talk about testimonies, and I could see how loving they were and how wonderful they were, and I could see healings. People would come in and they'd look awful, and a couple of days later I'd see them and they'd be just fine—and I didn't quite understand it.

"WE ARE INVESTIGATING THE DEATH"

We have different methods of treatment, but sometimes just a word, when you look up the references to something like that in the Bible or in the Textbook, sometimes just the right reference is what is needed in a healing and that's the end of it, you know. I've seen instantaneous healing, I've seen something healed right in front of my eyes. So sometimes something like that is the key. It's not faith as we understand it. It's understanding. That's what we call it.

—Lise Glaser

The two detectives were clear. They told Mrs. Glaser, "We are investigating the death. The purpose of our investigation is to determine if there is any criminal negligence. Statements that you make may be indications of criminal negligence. As a result, then, you would be suspect. Because of that, we're going to be required to give you your Constitutional rights." For her statement to be allowed as evidence in a criminal proceeding, the officers must have first made certain she gave an *informed consent*.

DETECTIVE SHANE TALBOT: "You have the right to remain silent. Anything you say can and will be used against you in a court of law. You have the right to talk to a lawyer, before we talk to you and to have him present while we talk to you. If you cannot afford to hire a lawyer, one will be appointed to represent you before any questioning free of charge. Do you understand these are your rights as I just told you?"
MRS. SCOTT: "Yes sir, I do."
TALBOT: "Do you wish to discuss the case with me now?"
MRS. SCOTT: "Yes sir, I do."
TALBOT: "Do you wish to have an attorney present?"
MRS. SCOTT: "No, no I don't."

Mrs. Scott and the child's parents agreed to talk. At her own request, Mrs. Scott preceded her first interview with a call to Al Carnesciali, the Christian Science "Committee on Publication" (COP) for Southern California, the regional political, media, and local-church-affairs watchdog reporting directly to church headquarters in Boston.

In his interview with Mrs. Glaser, Detective Cooper explained why police had become involved. "You have to understand that we are representing Seth. We are legally empowered to do that. That's why we're here, and that's why you're here, because we are representing him because nobody else has the authority to represent him."

Seth Glaser's rights did not end with death, Cooper later told Mrs. Scott. "The state gives us a certain authority. And that authority says, 'Here you are to step into that child's shoes and be the protector of his rights.' So at this point, we are Seth's people."

Seth Glaser had a right to live, and the destruction of his life was a wrong. If his life had been destroyed by negligence, by abandoning the standard of what a "reasonable person" would do, then a crime had been committed, the ultimate violation of Seth's rights.

Here the law becomes very sticky. Just what is a *reasonable* person? There are many Christian Scientists in positions of great power and influence in our society. Two of the past three Directors of Central Intelligence have been Christian Scientists: incumbent William Webster and Stansfield Turner. John Ehrlichman and H. R. Haldeman, respectively domestic and foreign policy advisors to President Richard Nixon, were Christian Scientists. There are many in the media, in commerce, in all walks of life, making intelligent, well-informed professional decisions. Are they all unreasonable? If so, how can one account for their success?

A BORN SCIENTIST
AND A CONVERT

A miracle fulfills God's law, but does not violate that law. This fact at present seems more mysterious than the miracle itself. . . . The miracle introduces no disorder, but unfolds the primal order, establishing the Science of God's unchangeable law. Spiritual evolution alone is worthy of the exercise of divine power. The same power which heals sin heals also sickness.

—Mary Baker Eddy

For Virginia Scott, Christian Science came by birth. Her mother practiced the faith, though her father did not. "Gina," as she is known to clients and friends, has always been a believer, she told Detective Talbot.

Mrs. Scott took Christian Science class instruction in Portland, Oregon. Teachers, she explained, "are people who have advanced work in knowing how to do this." Class itself was inspirational, very intensive, "hard to equate with other kinds of study. I think different teachers do it differently. We'went to class for three hours every morning and then spent our afternoons and evenings studying various references."[24] All pupils become part of an "association," consisting entirely of the students of one teacher. Members are expected to attend an annual one-day association meeting, at which they are introduced to the new graduating class and hear an inspirational address by the teacher (or an invited speaker if the teacher has "passed on"). Class is a time of considerable reinforcement, when lifelong friendships are formed.

Like Mrs. Scott, Lise Glaser was class-taught. The daughter of an Episcopalian priest, she went to his services every Sunday until the age of eighteen, when she went to college. She attended a music conservatory in Cleveland, where she met her future husband in September 1977. They were married the following June. She went on to graduate from a conservatory in St. Louis with a Bachelor's of Music. "I didn't know there was such a thing as a Christian Science church until I met my husband."

As a child, Lise Glaser was frequently ill, "but it was just things that you wouldn't see a doctor for, like a cold or the flu." She was one of six children, and when they saw a doctor, it was one of her father's parishioners. "My father would get a large discount, so we made use of them when we needed them. There was a very loved doctor, he was a great guy. I still love my doctor. He came to my wedding and had some good things to say actually, because he knew I was marrying into a Christian Science family."

Since joining the church the only time she had seen a physician was during her pregnancy with Seth.

*   *   *

Virginia Scott works in a small office in her large, two-story hilltop home in one of Santa Monica's wealthiest neighborhoods. "We used to call Franklin Street 'Pill Hill,' " she says, "because almost everybody but us on the hill was a doctor or dentist. And when our children were little, we had a doctor next door and another doctor across the street . . . and we were all good buddies. One day one of the wives told me that she had heard the two of them out there talking, and one of them said, 'I don't get it. Your kid has the mumps, my kids have the mumps, the Scott kids play with her, they don't get the mumps. Dammit, I belong to the wrong church.'

"Where other children would be sick two weeks, ours would be back in school in five days. We have had this experience, and I'm not trying to sell you on it. I'm trying to point out that that's why we don't think to turn to medicine, because, A, we don't have faith in it, and, B, we've seen our system work frankly better in so many cases." But it didn't always work, even in Mrs. Scott's family. Her husband, though apparently recovered from epilepsy, suffers from other afflictions.

Eliot Glaser was born into a Christian Science family in Pasadena, California, a community known as a stronghold of the religion. As a young child, he was later told, he developed all the symptoms of polio and was healed through Christian Science. The disorder was never medically diagnosed. He had never sought a doctor's help in his life, although he did receive the inoculations necessary to enter school. He doesn't even go to a dentist, Lise Glaser said, though "he has in the past and his parents do."

Like his wife, Eliot Glaser has a degree in music. The couple moved to California in 1982, while Lise was pregnant with Seth, in part to have more financial security. Eliot went to work for his father and took part-time jobs as an organist at several churches, not all of them Christian Science.

*   *   *

Mrs. Scott became a *Journal*-listed practitioner of Christian Science in February 1977, after showing character references and "convincing evidence" of three healings to the Mother Church in Boston. She described the healings:

The first was of a friend, a "lady who had some kind of growth in her mouth. Now I never saw it; I can't describe it to you. But she said it was something that just didn't belong there. So I worked with her for maybe two weeks, ten days to two weeks, and it just totally disappeared."

The second was a young woman's three-day recovery from a sprained ankle. The third patient "had a problem of deafness in one ear that was healed very promptly also—I would say in two or three days." None of the three had been seen by a physician, she said. By church policy, she couldn't treat anyone undergoing medical care—unless the patient were a Christian Scientist under involuntary treatment, as in the case of a wounded soldier under treatment at a military hospital or an unconscious victim of an auto accident.

When Seth Glaser died, Mrs. Scott was handling about twenty-five to twenty-eight individual patients in the course of a day. Much of a practitioner's work is done over the phone. It's not even necessary to know the human identity of the caller or the affliction for a healing to be brought about. A single disembodied "Help!" is all that's needed for the healer to launch into the "prayerful work."

Mrs. Scott never charged the Glasers for her services, Mrs. Glaser said. "She's been very close to the family. She didn't feel that she could charge us."

*   *   *

Seth was an early walker and talker. "He could communicate very well. He was way ahead of other kids in vocabulary and understanding," his mother told police. He was last seen by a physician at the age of six weeks. "Up until he was about a year old, whenever he was sick I would call a practitioner and I did every time thereafter. But I know he was just really healthy. There was one time when he seemed to have a cold. I'd say he was about seven months old. He had a cold for about two days and that was healed."

There was an earlier sickness, she said. When Seth was three months old, "I seemed to have food poisoning. I didn't have it diagnosed, but I was suddenly violently ill and I was vomiting and had the runs and everything, just violently." She called Mrs. Scott and "felt much better." But the next day, when she picked up Seth to nurse, "he just didn't seem to want to do that, which was unusual for Seth," and she "immediately called . . . Mrs. Scott—you know I call her Gina, [we're] on a first name basis—I said, 'I'm afraid that maybe whatever I had has been transmitted through the milk.' So then she said, 'I'll get to work on it right away,' and within a half hour he was perfectly fine. He was a little pale but his color came back. He nursed, he was awake, he was smiling, a total change, which was very reassuring, comforting."

He had had three or four colds and one fever in the seven months prior to his death.

"One incident was serious for us. We were very scared and I, the practitioner had heard of such a thing before, and she said, 'Well, I think this is called croup.' He had a cough and his breathing was very labored and very loud and he had a fever and he didn't have very much energy and I called the practitioner repeatedly.

"When you work with a practitioner, you call whenever you're afraid or whenever you think the symptoms are getting better or worse. So I must have called her every two or three hours for like three days, and at that point the present situation wasn't getting any better. It wasn't getting worse, but it wasn't getting any better. She felt advised to call Mr. Carnesciali and let him know because there's a big stink right now about Christian Scientists' children and when something looks serious they want to make this man aware of it." Mr. Carnesciali is a practitioner and teacher of Christian Science, as well as the regional Committee on Publication.

Mrs. Scott "thought it would be wise to come and visit us," said Mrs. Glaser. "So she came and visited, then talked with us and talked with Seth. And he was still eating and drinking all this time—not much, but he was eating and drinking, and she felt very calm and peaceful about it and helped us to feel that way in the Christian Science work, and we continued Christian Science treatment, and he improved rapidly after that point. And I think he was healed, totally free—just about his normal business about a day and a half later. That was in early December."

*   *   *

Lise Glaser's attraction to Christian Science rose from her love of her husband. His music brought her inside the doors of a church; she first attended services to critique his organ playing. "I resisted Christian Science teaching when I first met my husband." But, she said, "I loved him and he lived it and I saw healings."

Right before they married, she went home to see her parents, *Science and Health* in hand, struggling with doubt: "I [thought], look, you know, [Eliot]'s really off his rocker." She went through the book with her pastor-father "and my dad pointed out some really good things about it. I mean he wanted to knock it down but he couldn't. He said it just looked like they're turning their back and ignoring things. Eliot was very careful not to push anything. He didn't care whether I ever became a Christian Scientist or not. That wasn't the point."

Still, she wrestled. Her biggest difficulties were the obvious physical afflictions of her new in-laws. "I said, 'Look, if Christian Science heals—and I'm being perfectly honest with you—why is your father blind and your mother hard [of] hearing? You know, if it heals, what's going on here?' I had a lot of doubts."

Then she found herself in the middle of one of the largest concentrations of young Christian Scientists on earth, Principia College in Elsah, Illinois, where Eliot had landed temporary work. Principia, she explained, is "the only Christian Science college there is in the world, and it's not part of the church. It's just a private college for Christian Scientists." A four-year liberal arts school, Principia accepts only students who are practicing Christian Scientists. Actor Robert Duvall is an alumnus.

While at Principia, she took a year off from music school and found herself immersed in the social life of the young Scientists. "I lived in that community where everybody, they did not smoke, they did not drink, and did not go to doctors. There was no pressure, and there are plenty of people involved in it whose spouses are not Christian Scientists, but I saw people healed. I saw some people who the doctors had given up on who were healed. . . . and there was so much love—and I, at that point, began to read the literature. I had never done it before. I didn't know anything about it. I didn't want to know anything about it. I read it and I didn't quite always understand what I read." She kept at her reading when she returned to school to finish her degree at a conservatory in nearby St. Louis.

Then she began to have healings, she said, though she still hadn't joined the church or read *Science and Health* from cover to cover. "I just read a few of these things that came out. Then I began—I would test things, you know. I would say, 'Okay, it hurts, I'm going to call a practitioner.' And I would be well either within an hour or the next day. Then I began to learn to understand it better and do it myself, so after a while I had healings without any practitioner. The ones that were tougher for me I would call a practitioner."

She had to make a decision. "Nobody told me that, but I thought, you know, 'Am I going to do this or am I not.'" She had reservations, especially regarding her feelings for her father, "but after a while it just seemed the right and natural thing to do and I wanted to be part of it. I wanted to be engaged in this work of healing and loving."

Lise Glaser joined the Mother Church.

"THE STRUCTURE OF
TRUTH AND LOVE"

The Rules and By-laws in the Manual of The First Church of Christ, Scientist, Boston, originated not in solemn conclave as in ancient Sanhedrim. They were not arbitrary opinions nor dictatorial demands, such as one person might impose on another. They were impelled by a power not one's own, were written at different dates, and as the occasion required. They sprang from necessity, the logic of events,—from the immediate demand for them as a help that must be supplied to maintain the dignity and defense of our Cause; hence their simple, scientific basis, and detail so requisite to demonstrate genuine Christian Science, and which will do for the race what absolute doctrines destined for future generations might not accomplish.

—Mary Baker Eddy

Mrs. Eddy continues to run her church from the grave, through her 89th and final edition of the *Church Manual of the First Church of Christ Scientist, in Boston, Mass.*, "the *Manual*." To become a member of The First Church of Christ, Scientist, of Boston, Massachusetts, the *Manual* decrees that an applicant must be at least twelve years old, have severed ties with any former religion, believe in the doctrines as taught by Mary Baker Eddy, and rely only on her writings for study, teaching, and practice.[25] Applications must be signed by another Mother Church member and countersigned by a teacher of Christian Science or one of the five directors of the Mother Church.[26] Members are formally united with the church during a vote prior to the annual general membership meeting in Boston.

What a Scientist receives in return for membership is a sense of belonging and the opportunity to become a church-recognized healer—a vital legal protection. The church has few hidden doctrines,[27] and the *Manual* defines clearly the relationship between the member and Mary

Baker Eddy, between the Mother Church in Boston and its satellite "branches," and between the church and society. The member has one primary obligation, spelled out in Article VIII, Section 6 of the *Manual*, "Alertness to Duty":

> It shall be the duty of every member of this Church to defend himself daily against aggressive mental suggestion, and not be made to forget or neglect his duty to God, to his Leader, and to mankind. By his works he shall be judged,—and justified or condemned.[28]

There is only one The First Church of Christ Scientist, the "Mother Church" in Boston, Mrs. Eddy's church. All others are branches, not entitled to use the imperial "The." Local churches stand in unique relationship to the Mother Church in Boston. Because Mrs. Eddy dictated the structure and content of services, branch church services differ only in matters of detail. The only power a First Reader does have is at the Wednesday services, where he acts as censor on testimonials that run on, describe symptoms too graphically, are obviously insane, or which challenge the founder or her revelation. The reader may occasionally offer an impersonal rebuttal to some particularly offensive "claim of error."

Branch churches and societies are incorporated under state laws and governed by boards of directors elected from the membership. Members are received by election. The readers are similarly elected by the members, and must be members of the Mother Church,[29] but they need not have received class instruction. Local churches have financial autonomy. A "church" requires at least sixteen members, one of whom must be a Boston-authorized practitioner. Anything smaller is a "society."

The Mother Church is undemocratic, governed by the self-appointing five-member Christian Science Board of Directors drawn from the ranks of authorized healers. Mrs. Eddy appointed its first members, and all subsequent candidates during her lifetime had to pass her scrutiny. It can dismiss one of its own members by a majority vote, and it elects a Church President to serve a one-year term, repeatable only once in three years. It was on the board that all Mrs. Eddy's powers devolved upon her "passing."

The board is responsible for discipline in the church. Its duties in this regard are spelled out in the longest single Section of the Church By-Laws in the *Manual*:

> Law constitutes government, and disobedience to the laws of the Mother Church must ultimate in annulling its Tenets and By-Laws. Without a proper system of government and form of action, nations, individuals, and religion are unprotected; hence the necessity of this By-Law and the warning of Holy Writ: "That servant, which knew his lord's will, and prepared not himself, neither did according to his will, shall be beaten

with many stripes."

It is the duty of the Christian Science Board of Directors to watch and make sure that the officers of this Church perform the functions of their several offices promptly and well. If an officer fails to fulfill all the obligations of his office, the Board of Directors shall immediately call a meeting and notify this officer either to resign his place or to perform his office faithfully; then failing to do either, said officer shall be dismissed from this Church, and his dismissal shall be written on the Church records.

It is the duty of any member of this Church, and especially one who has been or who is the First Reader of a church, to inform the Board of Directors of the failure of the Committee on Publication or of any other officer in this Church to perform his official duties. A Director shall not make known the name of the complainant.

If the Christian Science Board of Directors fails to fulfill the requirements of this By-Law, and a member of this Church or the Pastor Emeritus [Mrs. Eddy] shall complain thereof to the Clerk and the complaint be found valid, the Directors shall resign their office or perform their functions faithfully. Failing to do thus, the Pastor Emeritus shall appoint five suitable members of this Church to fill the vacancy. The salary of the members of the Board of Directors shall be at present two thousand five hundred dollars each annually.[30]

Mary Baker Eddy worked by design. She recognized that religious sects rise and fall on the charismatic personalities of their creators. So she carved out three titles, exclusively allotted to her alone: Discoverer of Christian Science, Founder of the Church of Christ, Scientist; and Leader. Then she sought to quite literally institutionalize her personality, while preaching that she sought not to.

Christian Scientists tend to be models of New England rectitude. They are formal, reserved, respectful, sincere. In this they are very much akin to the Mormons, followers of another religious leader whose roots are in the same region and era. Mrs. Eddy recognized the role of the Victorian man. Indeed, one attraction of her religion for women of the day was its promise of the ability to change external reality solely by power of divinely inspired *thought*. Women were considered more spiritual, more emotional, more sentimental; men were the world-dealing pragmatists.

Her chapter "Marriage" in *Science and Health* mirrors the age, and one passage may help explain her movement's lack of attraction for modern feminists: "Man should not be required to participate in all the annoyances of domestic economy, nor should woman be expected to understand political economy."[31] But marriage was a relative, human institution. "Suffer it to be so now" is the tone of her thought.

There are no infant baptisms, no wedding ceremonies, no funerals in Christian Science branch churches. To sanctify these by allowing them into the church would be to sanctify the very lie of man's birth, progress, and death in matter.[32]

Another attitude career-oriented women today would find hard to take is found in this declaration: "Marriage is the legal and moral provision for generation among human kind." Marriage [read sex] is not permissible except for procreation, itself a lie. She closes the passage with these lines: "Jesus said, 'The children of this world marry and are given in marriage: But they which shall be accounted worthy to obtain that world, and the resurrection from the dead, neither marry, nor are given in marriage.' "[33]

Asceticism is a vital part of Mrs. Eddy's religion. Spiritual man takes no pleasure in matter, knowing that each of matter's pleasures bears pain— and matter, mortal mind, always wars against Spirit, which dwells not in the limited and time-bound.

Mrs. Eddy rejected *all* drugs for *all* reasons, save one: to numb pain, the purpose for which she resorted to them. Alcohol, coffee, tobacco, tea— all were mortal mind's seductions claiming power over God's man.

*　　*　　*

While there is no formal clergy in Christian Science, and anyone who studies Mrs. Eddy's writings can become a healer, to become a church-endorsed practitioner requires the believer take an intense ten-day indoctrination into the faith taught by a church-recognized teacher.

Teachers are, in turn, instructed by the Massachusetts Metaphysical College, the church "Normal School," which holds sessions for seven days, once every three years. Thirty students, drawn from the ranks of church-recognized practitioners, are taught by an established teacher from a curriculum that must provide "Not less than two thorough lessons . . . on the subject of mental practice and *malpractice*" (emphasis in original). One student in each class must prepare a paper on the subject to be read, discussed, and understood in class—after which the original and any copies are handed to the teacher for destruction. It is the church's most vital doctrine, and the most sensational in Mrs. Eddy's day.

To her believers, the doctrine is not difficult to accept. Indeed, it is the most essential, because it offers a means of rationalizing failure. Why should a baby die, when an authorized practitioner and the Committee on Publication were on the case? And when they prayed on a scientific basis, with Mrs. Eddy's writings and the Bible close at hand?

Malpractice provided the out. The serpent-belief of mind in matter was exercising its most subtle, insidious lie—the claim of minds separate from Mind, capable of being seduced away from Truth by devious, serpentine chains of false reasoning. Malpractice was the lie that the evil will of another could take possession of one's body. Malpractice was oriental witchcraft, black magic. It was voodoo, hypnotism, occultism. Malpractice was error's counterfeit of genuine Science, stirred up by the "chemical-ization" of Truth on the lies of personal sense.

Mrs. Eddy believed herself and the movement to be ceaseless targets of malpractice, usually aimed by the mortal minds of "disloyal" students who had fallen away. In her later years, she surrounded herself with a phalanx of students whose sole duty was to serve as metaphysical bodyguards for her and the Church, maintaining constant prayer in two-hour shifts.[34]

The concept, rarely explicitly described in the available authorized editions of her writings, is as central to her Science as it was to her life. It forms a major element of the "primary class instruction" taken by all approved healers, and is the central theme of the teachers' class. The higher the Scientist rises, the greater the threat of malpractice. As error counterfeits Truth at every stage, its attacks become subtler, deadlier, as the student "grows in Science." It was malpractice that would hammer the faithful to the cross of matter with the nails of sin, disease, and death.

It was the malpractice of her first student which slew her last husband, by mimicking the symptoms of arsenic. "After a certain amount of mesmeric poison has been administered," she wrote after Asa Gilbert Eddy's death, "it cannot be averted. No power of mind can resist it."[35]

*　　*　　*

Active graduates of the Massachusetts Metaphysical College are those whose *Journal* listings contain the letters "C.S.B.," or Bachelor of Christian Science, the degree conferred by the school.

The college is governed by a three-member board: a president and a vice-president appointed annually by the Christian Science Board of Directors, and a teacher they select. Teachers are powerful figures in their churches, exerting considerable moral force over the "class-taught" students who form the majority of the movement. All teachers must be members of the Mother Church, answerable to the Board of Directors. Teachers who have been excommunicated cease to exist, as do their associations. Students are told they may apply to accredited teachers for proper in-struction and membership in a new association. One prominent teacher, a former lecturer and editor of the periodicals, was ousted for turning to dialysis in 1982 when his kidneys failed. Carl J. Welz, formerly of Santa Rosa, California, was for a decade, one of the most prominent names in the movement. After his expulsion, he continued to write and publish unauthorized but orthodox Christian Science propaganda.[36]

The Directors also appoint a Board of Lectureship, elected annually and staffed by practitioners and teachers who give lectures at branch churches—which are required to sponsor at least one a year. These talks, the closest Christian Science comes to conventional sermons, must address specific contemporary issues and bear tribute to Mrs. Eddy; they are pre-screened by the Mother Church in Boston.[37] Local churches advertise lectures in the media, and these are usually the best-attended events at a branch church (although the audience in urban areas is usually largely drawn from the congregations of other Christian Science churches). The lectures also serve as a means for teacher-lecturers to reach potential students.

Lectures are exciting to "the field," the branches. A popular speaker will produce a rarely seen packed church, because the lecturers are one of the few sources of genuine human charisma allowed in the movement. Some of the lecturers are remarkable. I remember a brilliant, old-fashioned English orator named Geith Plimmer, C.S. His voice was forceful, masculine, passionate, persuasive, and delightfully British. He had a florid, Dickensian complexion, and a profusion of veins on the temples that can indicate great medical problems. (I found my own teacher, a World War II Marine captain, on the lecture circuit. He was still a commander, the embodiment of earnest conviction, rectitude, discipline, and honor. *Semper fidelis.* I never asked him about what now seems a very real medical problem, a stiff arm and gait, which I somehow connected with a war wound.)

*   *   *

The greatest single presences in the believer's life after the daily lesson-sermon are "the periodicals." These are the publications of the Christian Science Publishing Society.

Also appointed by and answerable to the Christian Science Board of Directors, the Publishing Society prints and distributes authorized editions of Mrs. Eddy's writings, pamphlets, tape and disc recordings, Bibles and "approved" literature on Mrs. Eddy and the church. Day-to-day business is run by a manager and a staff of editors, appointed by the Christian Science Board of Directors for one-year, repeatable terms. The publishing board chooses its own members, subject to the approval of the Christian Science Board of Directors.[38]

Its major publications are:

- *The Christian Science Quarterly* (containing the lesson-sermons studied daily and read aloud each Sunday in all churches);
- *The Christian Science Journal,* the monthly magazine featuring editorials, articles (always by Mother Church members), statements from the Board of Directors, items of interest to branch churches, and the monthly listings of churches and societies, teachers and practitioners, nurses, and COPs;

- *The Christian Science Sentinel*, a weekly, with an emphasis on pragmatic articles and editorials, which lists upcoming authorized Christian Science lectures;
- *Der Herold Der Christian Science*, foreign language magazines similar to the *Sentinel*; and, perhaps most significantly,
- *The Christian Science Monitor*, the paper's only recognized missionary.[39]

Mrs. Eddy had done everything she could. By ordaining the Bible and *Science and Health* as the only pastors of her faith and creating the elected, lay readers, she had eliminated the schisms inevitable with a charismatic clergy. She had brought the branches totally under the control of her board in Boston.

She provided an ongoing, never-ending course of study in her writings—the Christ Science itself, full and complete—and the periodicals. She cut off the threat of secularization of the church by ordering that the buildings could be used for nothing except services, testimony meetings, lectures, church business meetings, and staff offices. She created Reading Rooms, controlled, approved environments for study and prayer. She allowed a modest expression of charisma in the teachers and the Board of Lectureship—all firmly controlled by Boston. And in the Committee on Publication she created a mechanism for enforcing orthodoxy, promptly and at all levels of the church, and for "handling" media, legislature, and the courts.

*   *   *

As a new Scientist, Lise Glaser didn't join a branch church immediately. Eliot's appointment at Principia was ending, and they would be moving soon. She felt she should attend services for several months before joining a particular branch. "So it just happened rather naturally, without any pressure."

She never told her parents she had made an out-and-out commitment to the religion "until a few months" before Seth's death, "because I wanted to be sure I was ready for the criticism. I wanted to be sure I was out-and-out committed on my own and that I believed in it in such a way that I didn't really care whether or not they cared."[40]

"I have come into it of my own choosing and have found that it's met my every need up to this point," she told the officers.

WHEN A CHILD IS SICK

If the case is that of a young child or an infant, it needs to be met mainly through the parent's thought, silently or audibly on the aforesaid basis of Christian Science. The Scientist knows that there can be no hereditary disease, since matter is not intelligent and cannot transmit good or evil intelligence to man, and God, the only Mind, does not produce pain in matter. The act of yielding one's thoughts to the undue contemplation of physical wants or conditions induces those very conditions. A single requirement, beyond what is necessary to meet the simplest needs of the babe is harmful. Mind regulates the condition of the stomach, bowels, and food, the temperature of children and men, and matter does not. The wise or unwise views of parents and other persons on these subjects produce good or bad effects on the health of children.

—Mary Baker Eddy

The detectives were making a record, gathering evidence. They had to establish both the motives and actions of those adults aware of Seth's condition before his death.

In criminal law, motive is everything, and death is a matter of degree. There was no dispute in this case that the parents had denied Seth medical attention. The question was *why?* What was it about Christian Science that caused believers to reject medical help, even for an infant in obvious peril? This is Lise Glaser's explanation: "Now about doctors. I was just asked by a friend who was concerned about Seth two weeks ago, because I was a Christian Scientist, 'What would you do if he ever got ill?' I get it from my family all the time. I don't get it all the time, but I get it. And I told her, you know, that 'we've always had [healings] and they've always been quick. I can't forsake it if I know it works.' . . . And I would tell her that [in] an extreme situation where something had gone on for a long time and I didn't think Christian Science was going to do it, I'd go to the doctor. Anyway, she said, 'But what about doctors? All the wonderful healing that they do and the relief they bring, and so on?' She said, 'How can you neglect that? God has given them the power.' And I said, 'I love doctors, I love good people and so on.' But I said, 'When you come right down to it, Christian Science has a better success rate than the doctors.' "

What about the time Seth had what she thought might be the flu, Detective Cooper asked. Instead of a Christian Science healing, could it have been just the normal passing of the disease? Her response: "Yes, that's entirely possible. I wouldn't discount that in the least."

"I have always gotten, ever since I was pregnant, questions, 'What would you do if Seth was really ill and Christian Science wasn't working? Would you go to a doctor?' And I said, 'If Christian Science wasn't working, I said—I've never been in that situation before and I would have to really search deeply, but if Christian Science wasn't working and I had more faith that a doctor could do better, I would take him to a doctor.'

"In this case, it was, at least for us, it, it was so quick. I didn't even have a chance to really do it. And I don't say this to excuse myself or anything else, but it was rather quick. I don't think anybody was aware of how serious it was until we actually started to take him over to Mrs. Scott's."

*   *   *

One week prior to his death, Seth had a cold.

On the twenty-first, before the family left for the Wednesday testimonial meeting, he was fine. Later that night he had a cough which "came up pretty quickly and a runny nose and sneezing" which would wake him. His mother called Mrs. Scott that night, "and on the next morning he still had it but he was feeling much, much better so that Eliot and I went off to a concert that night," leaving the child with Eliot's parents.

When they returned at 10 P.M., Seth woke up coughing. They stayed an hour, then took him home. "His cough was over by then," Mrs. Glaser said. The next day mother and child went to the Christian Science Reading Room, where Seth was left with a child-care attendant. "He still had a little bit of a runny nose."

Mrs. Scott said Mrs. Glaser called her on the morning of the twenty-seventh. "Seth seemed to have another cold such as we had worked [on]. He had had other colds several times during his life and they had called me and I had prayed for him as we do. And he had been healed. And she said he seemed to be ill again. In fact, she called me, oh I don't know, a week or two before. I forget exactly when, and he'd been fine as soon as we worked. It just worked right away. It was just like a little cold that he had had before, and we just took care of it."

The next day, Saturday, Lise and Eliot went to a square dance, leaving Seth with a member of their baby-sitting cooperative. "I remember a mother saying how she couldn't get him to stop eating. He was eating like a horse. . . . On Sunday he was fine. . . . There wasn't a stitch of a cold. In fact, that day he was so active he didn't take a nap. He did early in the morning but he was just running all over the place."

Here testimony conflicts. By the mother's statement, the healing was not instantaneous. It started seven days before his death, and he retained a runny nose and persistent cough for at least three days. It was probably here, according to the opinions of prosecution medical experts, that Seth contracted the slow-festering illness that was to kill him. Mrs. Scott's testimony that "he'd been fine as soon as we worked" is an honest statement in the context of Christian Science. She had *known* his absolute spiritual nature as the ever-cherished child of the all-loving "Father-Mother God, all-harmonious."[41] She had seen through the lie of sickness.

By a process of "scientific" reasoning, the practitioner's role was to detach any sense of illness from her mental image of Seth Ian Glaser. Simply to name a disease is to give it power. Disease must be unseen, revealed as mortal error, "self-seen and thus destroyed." Mrs. Eddy barred the use of formulae, specific readings to be used invariably with specific diseases, but there are certain standards of Christian Science, emphasized in class, readings, and articles, to which believers often turn when in crisis. One is the Scientific Statement of Being: "There is no life, truth, intelligence, or substance in matter. All is Infinite Mind and its infinite manifestation, for God is All-in-all. Spirit is immortal Truth; matter is mortal error. Spirit is the real and eternal; matter is the unreal and temporal. Spirit is God, and man is His image and likeness. Therefore, man is not material; he is spiritual."[42] Other favored platforms for prayer are the 91st and 23rd psalms, the Sermon on the Mount, and the Lord's Prayer.

*　　*　　*

On Monday, Lise Glaser went over to Mrs. Scott's. "I wanted to give her a loaf of bread that Eliot had made, kind of as a thank-you for her work on the cold." While at Scott's, Seth coughed once. "He may have had a cough on and off. I think so, cause he would say 'cough.' " It wasn't a raspy cough, and it came infrequently, "like maybe once an hour Monday night."

Eliot said he told her Tuesday morning that Seth had a little fever, but "I didn't pay any attention to that."

That morning Seth lay down. When it was clear he couldn't sleep, his mother said, she asked, "'Do you want to go to church?' " She said he answered "'church' and 'Danny'—this little boy he knows is named Danny, who goes pretty often too. And so we went." Because he was "acting a little grumpy," his mother told the attendant the boy might want to nap, though he had outgrown a regular nap schedule. She left him at 10 A.M., returning ninety minutes later. "He was asleep in [the attendant's] arms." They left the reading room in time for Mrs. Glaser to make a rehearsal at her home with four fellow musicians.

Seth didn't eat much, a little yogurt, but he drank a lot of water. "Even then I didn't think he was warm, you know. I felt his head. I wondered if he was ill, and he didn't seem highly unusual." She thought he was tired because he had fallen asleep in the reading room, so she put him down on his bed, closed the door, and went on with the rehearsal. He wasn't coughing, didn't seem to have a runny nose, didn't seem feverish.

Later in the day, she said, he "very obviously had a fever." The rehearsal ended at 2:30, and "I thought maybe these guys can meet him and maybe he's awake. So I opened up his door and he was lying on his bed and he turned up and looked at me. I said, 'Why don't you come out and meet the music people.' So he came walking out." The day was hot, and his room was warm, she noticed, even with the window open. "He was very flushed, and he came walking out and I said, 'Well, say hi.' But he acted so shy I picked him up and held him.

"As soon as they left, I saw he was hot all over. I called Mrs. Scott, and then I gave him something to eat. He didn't eat much," but he drank "a lot."

When Seth had come out at 2:30, Mrs. Glaser noticed his right eyelid was half closed. She had not seen the symptom before, and because she had "just been noticing some new spiders around the house. . . . I wondered if it was a spider bite." She suggested that to Mrs. Scott, "so we worked on that." When Eliot called her at 4:30 to say he was about to bicycle home from work, she told him, "I want you to know that Seth has a pretty high fever and I want you to pray about it on the way home.

"In Christian Science treatment we, we keep aware of what's going on physically because, you know, a lot of times you can feel a peace and healing before the evidence has changed and then after that then it starts to change, there is. . . . you know, I've had many healings at this point and right in the middle I've had fevers and stuff, right in the middle of a very, for me it's a very high fever. I didn't have it measured or anything. I really felt calm that I was being taken care of even though I was right in the middle of a very not comfortable experience. But when I really knew that I was being taken care [of] then, and only then did the evidence begin to change. If I slipped farther and farther into the evidence that is before me, the physical evidence, deeper into it, it makes it harder and harder to know that God is in control of the situation."

*   *   *

By Tuesday, the twenty-seventh, Monday's cough has been joined by inflammation and fever—which have to be understood in a Christianly scientific way. As Mrs. Eddy teaches, "Matter cannot be inflamed. Inflammation is fear, an excited state of mortals which is not normal."[43] What needs to be handled first and foremost in all child cases, Christian Scientists are repeatedly advised, is the fear of the parents. Fear is mortal sense; there is no fear in divine Love, Soul, Spirit. Fear is the serpent thought, the suggestion that divine Life can somehow be attached to matter and thus extinguished.

> MRS. GLASER: "What do I know about fevers? Okay. Raised in a normal family with normal medical things, and also we took a childbirth class and a child care class before we had Seth. They talked a lot about fevers. They said children get fevers pretty often because children haven't built up their immune system and resist infections and the way that children react to infections is a lot of times they have fevers."

She once subscribed to *Parents* magazine, she said, and recalled "reading an article about fever convulsions, not to be out-and-out worried, because it happens to children but it means they are reaching a crest. . . . I know with children dehydration is a very dangerous thing and with fevers sometimes children don't want to drink and the same with diarrhea. But when I was a kid and had fevers, we would have children's aspirin. My mother would make sure that we drank a lot. I remember not wanting to eat much, and they would be taking my temperature constantly to see how the fever was going."

And their childbirth class instructor told them that medical science "didn't even really know what to do about fevers."[44] The pediatricians and pediatric nurses at the hospital said "for fever the best we can do is to . . . sometimes sponge them down if they are very hot and if it's very dry sometimes there's going to be problems in addition, but we give them aspirin and we try to keep, sometimes they put them in a cool shower to bring the temperature down, a cool bath, but you have to be careful not to cause chills. I remember turning to Eliot and saying, 'Well, they might not have success, but I know Christian Science does.

"If a fever goes on for very long I know it can cause brain damage, which in turn I guess can cause other things in the body. A very high fever can kill someone, I know that. I'm aware of that. Eliot may not because he grew up in a Christian Science environment."

They never took Seth's temperature. "I was asked at one point if I had a thermometer by the coroner and the police and I think we have one in his drawer, but we never use it. It's not compatible when you're around Christian Science treatment to rely on medical practices. Now taking a temperature might not seem like medical practice to you but it is measuring a disease."

In Christian Science, she explained, "quality of thought determines your experiences. Anything that is manifested physically has its source in thought and as you get more . . . and more into the physical evidence, a lot of times that delays the healing."

As Mrs. Eddy affirms: "Error is not real, hence it is not more imperative as it hastens towards self-destruction. The so-called belief of mortal mind apparent as an abscess should not grow more painful before it suppurates, neither should a fever become more severe before it ends."[45]

*   *   *

DETECTIVE COOPER: "What I would like to ask you is how do you think Seth was feeling? He's not aware, he's not developed, his mind isn't developed, the same mind where he can make a determination."

MRS. GLASER: "Seth has had fevers before, this has healed fevers before and he knew, I'm sure he knew at one point that he wasn't feeling well and that he was again. . . . He's had plenty of bumps and when he was in pain, he's always let you know. Kids let you know one way or another. . . . I knew he was uncomfortable. I mean, I can look back now and I can just think all kinds of horrible things. I mean he died. . . . Seth, because he has responded to Christian Science before and has always trusted us before, I don't think he was feeling betrayed. I mean, it's the law that we can practice it. I have to live with the result one way or the other. But, you know, the law has changed and this, this may result in the law being changed."

COOPER: "When he was undergoing these convulsive reactions and he was unable to hold his head up and he . . . couldn't focus on anything and you felt he was delirious, then, did you ever consider that he was possibly in pain?"

MRS. GLASER: "No. No I did not. Because, you know, if I really sat down and thought about it, I would have figured, well, I guess this is painful."

Lise Glaser went on to recount that during the previous episode of the "croup," "his morale was low. He wasn't communicating at all, but he was communicating his distress. Whether he had the energy to cry or not, he was communicating it. I mean at no time at all, I didn't ever get a sense of that." She had also read testimonials in the Christian Science literature describing healings of broken bones in which the pain was healed before the bone was made whole. "I was not worried that he was in pain. I didn't get the message to think that was true."

Talbot and Cooper then asked what she would do in other, similar circumstances. "A compound fracture? I would call up a practitioner . . . and my teacher said, you know, you do, you always—the church doesn't tell you what to do."

Talbot and Cooper pressed again: What would *she* do?

> MRS. GLASER: "Yeah, but, you know, he said do what you do, but, you know, if something like—with the practitioner, if you decide to pray about something yourself, and if you're not getting relief, you call a practitioner. And he said with children you call a practitioner right away, which I always did. If ever anything came up, I called a practitioner right away. But, excuse me, you know if you asked me this before Seth passed on, I would probably say, 'Well, I'd call a practitioner about it and if I wasn't getting any relief, well then, maybe in a day or two.' "

But why, Talbot asked, "if God gives a person the ability to go through and endure, and medicine, and gives society the ability to develop all these things . . . then [isn't it] a gift to benefit them?"

> MRS. GLASER: "With Christian Science, the only reason it fails is the human application. We believe it is that law that Jesus had but didn't spell out. We believe it's spelled out as a law, like, you know, maybe—Eliot brought this up, but it's an easy thing. Two plus two equals four. If you make it two plus two equals five, then you've got the mathematics wrong."
>
> COOPER: "Do you feel [Seth's] rights were being neglected. Answer that: do you or don't you?"
>
> MRS. GLASER: "No, I do not."
>
> COOPER: "So you don't believe . . . that you could have done something to protect him better than you did?"
>
> MRS. GLASER: "No. If the symptoms, when they became alarming, had gone on much longer, I probably would have called the doctor, Dr. Hale probably.[46] I mean, I've never been in this position before. The croup was serious, but I can't even say really whether I would or I wouldn't. But I would have asked him what is, you know, what does this seem to be, because sometimes if you find out what the world thinks it is, it's easier to heal sometimes. And if . . . I thought a doctor could do better, I would take him. My dad underwent a colostomy and there is, you know, he doesn't have part of himself any more and my mother's lost her uterus. I mean, everybody in my family has less of their body with them. And I know that Christian Science has healed these things and people are still intact."
>
> TALBOT: "You don't have a lot of faith in doctors."
>
> MRS. GLASER: "No I don't, not any more."

Earlier, she had said it this way: "Some Christian Scientists when they break a bone, they go to a doctor immediately and have it fixed. Some have it healed through prayer. If it's not healed right away, they go and have it set. Christian Scientists do not oppose doctors and medicine for those who wish to use it. Christian Scientists have just found that Christian Science is more reliable. I know that doesn't sound, isn't a good thing to say right now in this case. They have found it more reliable and health insurance companies, many of them have also found it [so], otherwise they wouldn't insure them. And I love Dr. Hale."

At another point in the interview, Mrs. Glaser addressed the detectives directly: "I don't know whether you're Christians or not. It doesn't matter what you believe. But how far are you going to discount the fact that Jesus heals? I mean the fact that Christian Scientists—you can't discount some success, okay? There are some states. . . . now [in which] you can't practice Christian Science."

*   *   *

At 4:30, Eliot Glaser called Lise Glaser, who in turn called Mrs. Scott. Eliot arrived home about 5 P.M. Between the time Eliot got home and when they went to bed, Seth did not get up and walk around, his mother said. "He stayed hot, and he was in his bed, and he said 'drink,' and I said, 'okay.' See, he wasn't screaming in pain; he wasn't acting out-and-out weak or anything. He would talk and look at us and we would sit up and he would say 'drink' and I would give him a drink, come in and talk to him and rub his back, make him feel loved. At that point I had no idea that there was anything ultraserious going on because he didn't even seem as hot."

After dinner Seth's mother again called the practitioner, "because I wanted to keep in touch with her and I noticed he was breathing fast and his heart was beating fast, and when I noticed each of those things I called her up. I wondered if he was just having a hard time breathing, was that another thing that we needed to work on? And then I thought, maybe it's his heart that's making him do that."

"I don't really remember" the specifics of Tuesday's calls, Mrs. Scott told the detectives. "But we did talk two or three times, which is customary."

When the Glasers woke at five the next morning, Wednesday, Seth's eye was still half-closed, but he was conscious and could talk. "He didn't want to sit up, he just wanted to lie down. After he ate something and when I picked him up, he would clutch at me like he had lost his balance. I would pick him up and he would hold me a little bit stronger, and he acted like he was dizzy."

She sat him in her lap. "He reached down and picked up the peaches and put them in his mouth. He reached down and picked up the cup and drank. His head was just a little warm, but his body was fine." He had also begun to shake, and would cry if his mother stood him up. "He acted like, you know, he had no sense of balance and that he was worried of falling over." Lise Glaser called the practitioner and told her that it seemed like the fever was gone, but the eye was still swollen, that he was shaking a little bit, and wanted to sleep.

Mrs. Scott remembered the call. "She called early and said that it was very bad."

Seth went back to sleep till 7 or 8, then woke and asked for a drink. They "sat him up again. . . . He would hold on like he was shaking, and at that point I asked Eliot to stay home. I just said, 'Why don't you stay home from work and let's really work on this and see this thing through.'" Eliot called in and said he would be in later. "We had full expectancy that it would change. And then Seth threw up and I called Mrs. Scott right away."

This was about 9 A.M. She told Mrs. Scott that Seth had thrown up, that his temperature seemed to be going up, that "his breathing was still very fast. His heart was fast, and his face—when we would sit him up—would turn purplish, and then he would be fine when we . . . laid him down."

After the first call, Mrs. Scott said, she had worked and prayed for Seth. When the second call came, she had no reason to be alarmed— despite the mother's statement, "it's just really gone bad again." The practitioner "had had a very very strong feeling that the prayer was being effective. Sometimes you do and sometimes you don't. And I really was joyous because I felt that it really was."

When he spit up a second time, Lise Glaser again called Mrs. Scott. " 'Can we come visit you? Can we bring Seth, and can we come visit you?' and maybe that would help, because of the last instance of the croup when she came over, you know, things improved. His breathing was bothering me, and the fact that he was weak. . . . I was worried."

Lise Glaser asked Mrs. Scott if they could come over after lunch. Talbot asked, why *after* lunch? "Why not right then?" The response: "I didn't want to disturb her lunch." But, she added, had she known how serious it was, she would have asked to take him right then. "I was tired, I was plain tired, me waking up so early and working very hard the way we do in Christian Science . . . and I said, 'Eliot, you know, would you mind if I take a half-hour nap?'" She lay down, asked to be awakened at 12:30, in time for the 1 P.M. appointment with Mrs. Scott.

Awakening, Mrs. Glaser made herself a sandwich; then the anxious parents took Seth to the car. She sat beside him in the back seat. By now he couldn't hold his head up. They feared he might vomit and choke, and had brought a change of clothing in case he threw up over himself in the car. He did.

"When we got him in the car seat, he slumped down and he was conscious," she told the detectives. "But I couldn't get him to hold my gaze and he, he seemed delirious and his body would thrust every now and then. His body would tense, he'd kind of flail out and he would relax. He'd kind of thrash out with his arms and I would grab his hands and hold his hands and his head." She noticed Seth was convulsing when she put him into his car seat. The drive lasted about twelve minutes; Seth convulsed about every ninety seconds. It was while they were on the way to the practitioner's house that Mrs. Glaser felt Seth's condition was becoming serious. He was now completely nonresponsive.

When the parents called and asked Mrs. Scott to receive them at her home, the practitioner said she told them, "I'm glad to come there or you may come if you want to." Mrs Glaser told her, " 'Yes, we want to come,' and I didn't think a thing about it. His folks live right behind us, and I thought, 'Well, maybe they're coming to grandmother's, I don't know.' So I said, 'Fine, if you want to bring him.' "

When the Glasers arrived, they told Mrs. Scott Seth had become delirious on the drive over. Mrs. Scott recalled: "He didn't seem to be functioning, and he wasn't. He was sort of, his eyes were open. But they weren't seeing eyes. I mean that he wasn't really taking in the picture around him." But she didn't notice any convulsions. Detective Cooper said the father had told him that at some point Seth started to lose control. He couldn't keep his head up, and his arms and legs were cold. Eliot knew they were severe symptoms, "indicating the body is trying to protect itself."

Once in the home, Lise Glaser turned to Mrs. Scott and "said, 'It's cold in here.' I said. . . . 'Can you turn on the heat or something.' And she said, 'Yeah,' and then she said, 'It's hot.' It was hot that day, 'why don't we go outside and wrap him up?' "

Mrs. Scott recalled the moment. She told the worried mother, "I will put the heat on," and they went outside to the patio "for about ten minutes, because it was very sunny. I said, 'Let's take him out and get him warm while the house was heated and then we'll carry him back in.' "

Why did she feel the baby needed to be warmed? Talbot asked.

"The one thing in the world that I know about is babies, and I know they need to be warm, if they're not feeling well, they need to be sheltered from chill or cold." She described her confidence with children later during the interrogation: "Prayer is prayer, and it operates different than medicine. Remember, I raised six children. And I had three of them that never missed a day of school because of illness and I, I really don't think many medical families can claim that."

Seth was placed on a mattress in the back yard "and every now and then I would look over, I would see that he was convulsing," recalled

Lise Glaser. Mrs. Scott later said she didn't see the child convulse, and she had been holding him. Lise Glaser said she "couldn't see whether or not he was" convulsing while the practitioner was actually holding the child. "I was not, um, out-and-out, um—it wasn't what this whole case is about ignorance and neglect. I wasn't trying to ignore Seth, but in Christian Science if you're observing something and you're becoming really convinced of it, then it's incredibly difficult to heal."

When the house got warm, Mrs. Scott took the little boy inside, alone. That alarmed Mrs. Glaser. "The fact that she went into the house with him even though she didn't out-and-out say anything to us, told me that she felt that, you know, it wouldn't help us to see his condition even though she didn't say anything and I trusted her, that she knew what she was doing. We had employed her, I mean, even though she didn't charge us, we had employed her to heal."

The Glasers remained in the backyard "for awhile, I remember that," said Mrs. Scott. Then Mrs. Glaser went into the house, "you know, to see how he was doing, if he needed to go to the bathroom," she said. "I saw that he was very limp. He couldn't hold his head up. He couldn't even hold a gaze at all, and his heartbeat seemed slower. I mean, it wasn't rapid any more. But it was, it was down to normal. And she, you know, and she pointed out that the fever wasn't out-and-out terribly cold, but he just, you know we tried to. . . . I said, well, you know, I looked at him and I was, I was scared, and, but he was not convulsing then."

> MRS. GLASER: "I went in, I don't know what time it was, I would probably say about, I don't know, 2:15 roughly. I don't know. I was scared and I told her, I said, 'Gina, this, this frightens me and I don't. . .' "
> TALBOT: "What, what, what was frightening you?"
> MRS. GLASER: "Seth."
> TALBOT: "His condition?"
> MRS. GLASER: "His condition."
> COOPER: "What did she say to you?"
> MRS. GLASER: "She said, she said, 'Honey,' something like, a something in Christian Science. That, 'God is his Life. God can go anywhere. God is right here, taking care of him.' And she said, 'Maybe it would be better for you to take a walk right now.' And I said, 'Maybe it would be.' And I guess then he passed on while we walked."

The reason Mrs. Scott had sent the parents on the walk, Mrs. Glaser said, was to deal with their fear.

> MRS. GLASER: "In Christian Science, one of the greatest things we have to fight is fear, that God is not in control. And if you're afraid of anything, then God is not in control and any thoughts, any fears

you have, it is helpful for the Christian Science practitioner to know. I know this [from] working for myself because bit-by-bit in Christian Science treatment we try and be very specific. Whatever any fear is, we try to negate it mentally and we don't stop till we're absolutely unafraid. That's why you call a Christian Science practitioner if you don't feel that you can handle your fear, your doubts. Then you're being impersonal in helping with the situation."

TALBOT: "Were you looking for reassurance from her?"

MRS. GLASER: "Yes. That's why—"

TALBOT: "Were you—"

MRS. GLASER: "—we do it."

Impersonality is a Christian Science ideal. It is the opposite of the "personal sense of self," which is the very nature of mortal man. "Every trial of our faith in God makes us stronger. The more difficult seems the material condition to be overcome by spirit, the stronger should be our faith and the purer our love," exhorts Mary Baker Eddy.[47] Elsewhere she writes, in the practice of Christian Science "truth cannot be reversed, but the reverse of error is true. An improved belief cannot retrograde. When Christ changes a belief of sin or of sickness into a better belief, then belief melts into spiritual understanding, and sin, disease, and death disappear." Christian Scientists frequently talk about their "radical reliance on Truth." It is a belief that does not admit of error.

*   *   *

The recorded interviews were conducted in interrogation rooms at the Santa Monica Police Station, in the back of the classic art deco city hall building. But several days earlier, on 29 March, officers Talbot and Cooper had conducted an unrecorded interview with Mrs. Scott in the dining room of her Franklin Street home. According to Detective Talbot's report of the meeting, she called Mr. Carnesciali prior to granting the officers an interview.

In Detective Talbot's report, she said she had called Carnesciali not long after the Glasers arrived on the day Seth died. Why? "Because of his severe condition and because of, you know, all about these things, and children in the Sacramento incident.' "

The "Sacramento incident" Mrs. Scott was referring to was the death of Shauntay Walker. Her mother, Laurie Grouard Walker, was, like Lise Glaser, a convert to Christian Science. The four-year-old girl died less than three weeks before Seth, and the case had generated wide newspaper publicity.

There was one significant difference between the Walker and Glaser cases. Shauntay Walker was continuously and obviously ill for seventeen days before her death, and she was physically moved to a secret location after a family member threatened to call medical help. Both a Christian Science practitioner and a Christian Science nurse were involved. The causes of death in both cases were to prove identical.

*   *   *

Seth was face down, lying on a blanket on the floor of the practitioner's office, when he died.

When his breathing, which had been rapid, slowed and became shallow, Mrs. Scott thought her prayers were beginning to have a positive effect. Then he stopped breathing, "and she felt he had passed on." She picked him up, held him, and then placed him on the couch and began mouth-to-mouth resuscitation, which is how Eliot Glaser found her when they returned from their walk.

Even after the child had died, the parents and a practitioner continued their prayers for healing; resurrection remained a hope and promise of their faith. "I'd forgotten," Mrs. Scott told the officers, "but it wasn't a child and I was thinking in terms of children, but I did revive an older woman once. They called from the sanitorium to say she'd stopped breathing, and I continued to pray, and she did revive. So I have had that experience."

In both interviews with the practitioner, the two officers pressed her on one issue: How could she administer artificial resuscitation, a form of medical aid, and yet not call for the obvious source of skilled help, the paramedics? Though medical tests were to show that by the time Seth stopped breathing, irreversible brain damage had already set in, the question is critical. Just what sort of compromise is acceptable from a Christian Science practitioner?

At the first interview, Detective Talbot reports, "We asked Mrs. Scott why she seemed to abandon her prayerful work and begin to give mouth-to-mouth. She indicated that as a result of seeing him pass and being only human, she felt she should render some type of first aid in trying to revive him."

Christian Scientists do resort to other forms of material assistance: glasses, hearing aids, canes. In the second, recorded, interview, at one point Mrs. Scott was trying to explain to the officers why her husband, also a Christian Scientist, was willing to wear an orthopedic appliance for a hernia. His practitioner, "a very fine worker," according to Mrs. Scott, "believes in using the physical supports that you need. He says if you break your leg, you'd use a crutch . . . to cheat at times." She added: "You know, it's just sensible. Somebody said that C.S. stands for common sense, not just Christian Science, and you've got to be sensible." Both

Eliot and Lise Glaser wear eyeglasses.

The officers again raised the issue of why the practitioner had resorted to artificial resuscitation.

> MRS. SCOTT: "It seemed like first aid to me. As I told you, we try to be sensible and I, I don't know much about it but it came to me that I should do it and I felt that it was coming to me through my prayers, that that would be a practical, loving thing to do."
>
> COOPER: "Did you consider at any time at that point when you discovered that Seth had died, calling a paramedic unit?"
>
> MRS. SCOTT: "I considered it. But you see, it wouldn't be my choice. This is something else you have to understand about the difference between practitioners and doctors. Now a doctor is really in charge. He says 'Do this' and you do it. A practitioner does not."
>
> COOPER: "When you discovered that Seth had died and you were applying mouth-to-mouth, did you consider the possibility of calling a paramedic, in that you are attempting to apply first aid—"
>
> MRS. SCOTT: "Mm-hmmm. Yes."
>
> COOPER: "—and I wanted to know if you'd considered calling a professional to try to save this child?"
>
> MRS. SCOTT: "I'd thought about it. I really felt it was up to the parents, because, you see that is taking a medical step and I can't take that for them. I don't have that authority."
>
> COOPER: "But you, you, you did a medical step by applying mouth-to-mouth."
>
> MRS. SCOTT: "Well, I didn't feel that was medical. They also tried it when they came."

Mrs. Scott returned to the example of her Scientist-husband's orthopedic appliance, then rejected it. "That's not a good comparison. I didn't want to call medical people in, certainly without [the parents'] permission. I don't have the right to do that. When they're coming to me as a healer through prayer, I don't have the right to do something else."

Detective Cooper told her he had trouble understanding her reasoning. "Here you apply this, first aid, to try and save the child's life, [yet] you would not make the decision to ask a professional to do that to save his life?"

> MRS. SCOTT: "I understand, I understand. But let me try to put it in a way you can understand it. Believe me, I know why it seems difficult to you. You see, I was still a layman, a Christian Scientist. Now if I called in medical people, I'm lifting that decision out of the parents' hands. What I do personally is not doing that, because I'm still working with them from the standpoint of prayer. If I take on myself to call in the paramedics, I'm not giving them any choice because from

there on the medical takes over, and I did not know that they wanted to do that.

"It was probably, maybe a foolish thing for me to try to do that, because he was really gone. And probably I shouldn't have even perhaps have done it because he was, he was gone. But you, you're never quite sure and I always—"

COOPER: "Well, we're not being critical of you—"

MRS. SCOTT: "I know you're not."

COOPER: "—for applying mouth-to-mouth resuscitation at all."

MRS. SCOTT: "I know you're not. You're being critical of me for not calling the paramedics."

COOPER: "I want— No, we're not being critical of you—"

MRS. SCOTT: "I didn't mean that."

COOPER: "We're trying to unders—"

MRS. SCOTT: "I didn't mean that."

COOPER: "We're trying to understand why—"

MRS. SCOTT: "I know you are."

COOPER: "The thought process—"

MRS. SCOTT: "I know you are."

COOPER: "—is what we're looking for."

MRS. SCOTT: "I know you are."

*   *   *

Mrs. Eddy created some interesting outs. In *Science and Health*, she writes, "If from an injury or from any cause, a Christian Scientist were seized with pain so violent that he could not treat himself mentally,—and the Scientists had failed to relieve him,—the sufferer could call a surgeon, who would give him a hypodermic injection, then, when the belief of pain was lulled, he could handle his own case mentally."[48] These words were written after it became known that Mrs. Eddy resorted to pain-killing shots while passing kidney stones. Elsewhere in the textbook, other oft-cited words evoke exactly what has happened: "During the sensual ages, absolute Christian Science may not be achieved prior to the change called death, for we have not the power to demonstrate what we do not understand. But the human self must be evangelized. This task God demands us to accept lovingly to-day, and to abandon so fast as practical the material, and to work out the spiritual which determines the outward and actual."

To this point, the quotation is often cited in testimonials by Christian Scientists who have resorted to medical treatment. When they subsequently reject medical help for the same or similar afflictions, however, they cite the remainder of the passage:

If you venture upon the quiet surface of error and are in sympathy with error, what is there to disturb the waters? What is there to strip off error's disguise?

If you launch your bark upon the ever-agitated but healthful waters of truth, you will encounter storms. Your good will be evil spoken of. This is the cross. Take it up and bear it, for through it you win and wear the crown. Pilgrim on earth, thy home is heaven; stranger, thou art the guest of God.[49]

There is a third, final, passage often cited as an "out":

If Christian Scientists ever fail to receive aid from other Scientists,— their brethren on whom they may call,—God will guide them into the right use of temporal and eternal means.

Those who see doctors, then are healed later in Christian Science, are apt to add the last sentence of the paragraph: "Step by step will those who trust Him find that 'God is our refuge and strength, a very present help in trouble.' "

*   *   *

Eliot and then Lise also tried artificial resuscitation—it turned out he, too, had learned it. In their interview with the child's father, which exists in Detective Talbot's report only from notes,[50] Mr. Glaser told them he wouldn't do anything beside prayer to alleviate the cause of an illness, but he would take steps to comfort the sufferer, if it seemed right at the time. Talbot recorded that "Mr. Glaser went on to say that he was not averse to the use of first aid, and that he had received training in mouth-to-mouth resuscitation and other methods of first aid treatments as he felt he wished to be a good citizen. When asked why he received the training, he indicated that he felt that he could help others in their suffering." Cooper questioned Lise Glaser on the same point.

> COOPER: "I have another question. Why, why now when you found out that your son had died, did you pursue the mouth-to-mouth resuscitation. Isn't, isn't that sort of an abandonment of your faith?"
> MRS. GLASER: "It's not an out-and-out abandonment. . . . I stopped when Mrs. Scott said, you know. . . . 'That's not really going to help. We are human and we are aware of human's first aid and in a very severe case you do what you can,' and it came to her to do it. She thought about doing it, and then when we came in she suggested it. We didn't think of it right off the bat. She said, 'You might try that and call to him and love him.' Ah, so it's, it's not an out-and-

out abandonment. We did, after I had done it for a little bit, wait a minute, you know, this is kind of compromising it. Let's stick with what we know. It wasn't that we weren't sticking with what we were knowing, but, you know, what, whereas I didn't think out-and-out about going to a doctor or paramedics or something. I didn't abandon Christian Science because we were still praying about it. As, as a mother, I wanted to do everything she can. A . . . and Christian Science seemingly, you know, I mean, I didn't think all these things. . . . We prayed. I called someone else who I knew had revived somebody. We were doing everything we could that we knew how, to keep Seth with us. I guess in an absolute divine sense, we did not abandon Christian Science and take up medical at that point, but—and we didn't break any Christian Science rules either by doing that. But I guess we just all felt that we wanted to [do] what we could."

When resuscitation failed, Lise Glaser still didn't think of calling the paramedics. "I thought of the most available help I had, which was to call my Christian Science teacher." Unable to make contact, she called Mrs. Beverly Bemis Hawks DeWindt, C.S.B., another practitioner and teacher, who told her "over the phone, right then and there, that she had revived a seven-year-old boy and there's also proof of that." She explained that because "Christian Science for us has met every need up to that point," she didn't think even then of calling for medical help. "I rushed to where my sense of most help would be and I called this lady and she agreed to help us."

Mrs. Glaser continued to rely on Christian Science "because [Mrs. DeWindt] had revived people and because I have read testimonies and talked to practitioners who have revived people after many hours of prayer. We stuck with it; we just prayed and we prayed."

Mrs. DeWindt offered help, Mrs. Glaser said, and told the distraught mother a story: "She was asked by someone she didn't even know, a young boy [who] was seven years old that had died in the hospital and the doctors gave up on him and she prayed for him and he . . . was revived. First she told me how her son had swallowed ant poison and all this other stuff and was healed, he was taken care of."

Confronted by death, her religion offered hope. There were tales of Mary Baker Eddy resurrecting a tradesman who had fallen under the wheels of a heavily loaded wagon. There were testimonials in church; lesson-sermons regularly featured the New Testament resurrections performed by Jesus and his followers. Even in the face of the greatest terror, the faithful Scientist holds on to the truth that God is his Life, a Life that cannot die, holds firm to Truth, Principle. The faithful Scientist believes that "demonstration" is inevitable.

Consider too: "I guess in an absolute divine sense, we did not abandon Christian Science and take up medical at that point." In an "absolute divine sense," man is always the perfect reflection, demonstrating the Christ, "the divine manifestation of God, which comes to the flesh to destroy incarnate error."[51]

What might have happened had Seth lingered on, unchanged, Talbot asked. "Might [there] have been a likelihood that you might have sought medical—"

MRS. GLASER: "There might have been. I don't know what percentage it would have been. What would have done it? I don't really know. I've never thought it through before, because Christian Science is preventative as well as curative. I mean, Seth was a very healthy kid most of the time. I know Eliot, Eliot would have never, but he would have respected my [wishes]—we talked about that. Eliot would not have, but if I wanted to, he would have. Absolutely."

Both Eliot Glaser and Mrs. Scott told officers they would have willingly complied with any request by Lise Glaser to seek medical care. But she never thought about it until afterwards.

Mrs. Scott later told Mrs. Glaser that she had called the Committee on Publication when the baby "passed on." "She contacted Mr. Carnesciali again after Seth Glaser's death, later in the afternoon . . . and he advised her to call Mr. Hall at the [House of Hall] Mortuary to make arrangements for the body," wrote Detective Talbot in his report on the officers' first questioning of Mrs. Scott, at her home.

There is little said about the next few hours. At some point, Mrs. Scott gave up: "You understand I was not working on that case later on when it went on for so long. I, I didn't want to attempt that [resurrection?] because I didn't feel I could achieve it."

*   *   *

The first account of the next few hours comes from a document titled "Santa Monica Police Department DEATH REPORT (FIELD)—FORM 3.11.1," and written by Officer Mary Reynolds. By her record the case didn't reach the attention of her department until 2310 hrs—11:10 P.M.—Wednesday. The time of death is listed as "approx 1445," or 2:45 P.M.

Reynolds writes that she had been "detailed to 828 Franklin regarding a 17 month old baby who had died. On arrival I was met outside the residence by Mr. Lawrence Hall. Mr. Lawrence Hall identified himself & said he was from the House of Hall Mortuary. Mr. Hall said that he had been called at approximately 1530 hrs. [3:30] this afternoon by Mrs. Scott, who said that she needed advice & help regarding procedures of what to do about a death that had just occurred. Mr. Hall responded & arrived at approx. 1700 hrs. [5 P.M.]. Mr. Hall said when he arrived, the parents, Mr. & Mrs. Glaser, asked if they could have more time to pray. He agreed & said to call him back whenever they were ready. Mr. Hall said that at approx 2130 hours [9:30 P.M.], Mr. Glaser called him & said they were now ready. When Mr. Hall arrived, he called the coroner to get authorization to remove the body. The coroner denied permission and said to wait for the police."

Here are six to seven hours of prayer by the parents, by Mrs. Scott, by Mrs. DeWindt, by the Committee on Publication, and any others in the church notified of the emergency by the COP.

Mr. Hall, in a subsequent statement to investigators, denies making the first visit. But a statement in Officer Reynolds's report attributed to Mrs. Glaser states that "they did call Hall, who responded.[52] This was when he was first called."

Almost eleven months later, prosecutor Dave Wells called Detective Talbot and requested he reinterview the undertaker. The detective met Mr. Hall at the funeral home on 20 February 1985. According to the officer's typed report, when told the interview concerned Seth Glaser's death, Hall asked if he would have to sign a statement. "I indicated that he did not. He said, 'Good, because I would deny anything or (I?) wrote.' He then laughed and said, 'Go ahead and ask me a question.' " As the two talked, Hall referred to a folder containing documents, newspaper clippings, and a sheet of handwritten notes.

According to Officer Talbot's account, Mr. Hall said he wasn't called until 4:53 P.M. Someone at the house told him they wanted to retain him in a death in the family. "They did not wish him to respond immediately and. . .they would call him at a later time because they wanted to continue their prayerful work." The second call came at 5:20 P.M. By Hall's account, the second call came twenty minutes after the first, and he was at the house within thirty minutes of that. At the house, Mr. Hall was met by Mrs. Scott. The parents were in the room with their dead child. He never made an earlier visit. He had been at the house fifteen to twenty minutes, filling out forms, when he called the coroner. By this scenario, the call was placed to the coroner's office no later than 6:30.

When the coroner's investigator arrived thirty to forty minutes later, the official "was very indignant with Mr. Hall, ordering him from the hall[way]. Mr. Hall left the house and waited in his vehicle until he saw the coroner remove the deceased victim from Mrs. Scott's house and drive away." A Coroner's Investigator's report, which describes its sources as Officer Reynolds and the Glasers, repeats the two-visit version. The report states that "Mr. Hall reported this case to the Forensic Science Center [the morgue] at 2240 hours," 10:40 P.M.

A half-hour later, Officer Reynolds got her call.

It was while they were awaiting Hall's first arrival that Mrs. Glaser decided to contact Mrs. DeWindt for the resurrection effort, according to Reynolds. The parents told her they never discussed taking their child to a hospital. "I don't think I ever did until after the fact," the mother recalled later.

MRS. EDDY'S
MEDIA STRATEGY

The Constitution of the United States does not provide that *materia medica* shall make laws to regulate man's religion; rather does it imply that religion shall permeate our laws. Mankind will be God-governed in proportion as God's government becomes apparent, the Golden Rule utilized, and the rights of man and the liberty of conscience held sacred. Meanwhile, they who name the name of Christian Science will assist in the holding of crime in check, will aid in the ejection of error, will maintain law and order, and will cheerfully await the end—justice and judgment.

—Mary Baker Eddy

Mrs. Scott called Al Carnesciali, Christian Science Committee on Publication for Southern California, before the baby died: "We are taught that if we have a child's case [that] appears as though it's difficult, we must get in touch with him right away to find out what legally is the right thing to do. That is all." She called that day because she felt Seth's case "wasn't the normal thing that I'd worked for him before. I didn't know—I certainly didn't expect him to pass on. I really didn't."

After Seth died, the practitioner called Carnesciali again, who gave her the name of the mortician to call.

*   *   *

Each state has a COP elected by the First Readers of the three largest branch churches in a jurisdiction, as do each of the counties of Great Britain and Ireland. There are four exceptions to this rule: Massachusetts, which is served by the COP of the Mother Church; California, with two (the state is split at the 36th Parallel, between Los Angeles and San Francisco); London, whose COP is appointed by the Mother Church and serves as regional manager for the British Isles; and Washington, D.C., with a special "assistant manager (federal representative)."

There are fifty-one COPs in the British Isles, nine in Africa (three of them in the Republic of South Africa), seven in Asia (including two in India), eight in Australia and New Zealand, fourteen in Continental Europe, ten in Canada, six in South America, six in the West Indies (not including Bermuda and the Bahamas, which have COPs of their own), and one each in Panama and Mexico. All report to the Mother Church COP.

Within each branch church is an "Assistant Committee on Publication," which is responsible for distributing official bulletins from the regional COP, and for extending the COP's reach into the branches to raise support and pass on vital intelligence, e.g., any developments which could pose problems to the church.

The Committee on Publication for the Mother Church in Boston is elected annually by the five-member, self-appointing Christian Science Board of Directors. The COP is charged with correcting "in a Christian manner impositions on the public in regard to Christian Science, injustices done Mrs. Eddy or members of this Church by the daily press, by periodicals or circulated literature of any sort."[53] Mrs. Eddy explicitly decrees: "The Committees on Publication shall consist of men generally."[54]

These are the most powerful figures in the church in many respects. They are Boston's presence throughout the branches, they are in each church and, by sacred obligation, in the practitioner's office as well.

The COP machinery maintained contact with Mrs. Scott during and after Seth Glaser's last moments, and has helped to mobilize financial support to pay the legal expenses for the practitioner and the family.[55] In the hours and days following Seth's death, the COP and officials in Boston were working prayerfully to negate any attempts by mortal mind to destroy the belief that Christian Science heals.

Mr. Carnesciali, COP for Southern California, is a "delightful person," said Mrs. Scott, "and a fine, fine man in every way." The officers wondered why she called him about Seth Glaser before the death? "We're told if you have a case involving a minor, keep in close touch with the COP office," for both legal advice and prayerful support. She said she told Carnesciali that Seth "wasn't holding his head up well. I didn't know what this was and whether there was something else I should be doing."

*   *   *

Professor Gerald Uelmen is dean of the University of Santa Clara Law School and a widely known legal scholar. He came to Northern California from Los Angeles and the law faculty of Loyola University. In L.A., he had an "of counsel" relationship with the law firm of Douglas Dalton, Lise Glaser's attorney. He worked with Dalton on the pretrial appeal.

He encountered two manifestations of the Committee on Publication.

"My sense is that Christian Scientists are the most law-abiding people I've ever encountered in my life. The lengths to which they go to inform their followers of what the law is and what you can do and what you can't do, and the extent to which they go to try to conform to the law, is incredible. It really is. I don't think you can take those cases and lump them together with out-and-out fraud. . . . If you ever encounter a case of good faith attempt to comply with the law, it's the Christian Scientists."

This would be the Committee on Publication as adviser to the field.

Uelmen was also impressed by the church's political sophistication, by "how much clout the church exerted after the 1966 [California] Supreme Court decision in terms of getting the law amended, and how responsive the legislature was. The Christian Scientists went in and got the exemption in the form in which it is now contained in 270."

This would be the Committee on Publication as lobbyist.

Section 270 of the *California Penal Code* is called the "failure to provide" statute, and makes it a crime for parents to neglect the health and well-being of their children.

In 1976, as the result of an earlier state Supreme Court decision, the two California COPs worked with a state legislator, Assemblyman John Knox, and Governor Edmund G. Brown, Jr.'s, legislative secretary to win passage of Assembly Bill 3843. The measure, duly passed by the legislature and signed into law by the governor, specifically exempted from criminal penalties a parent who "provides a minor with treatment by spiritual means through prayer alone in accordance with the tenets and practices of a recognized church or religious denomination, by a duly accredited practitioner thereof."

In researching the appeal, Uelmen turned to the state archives, where the history of laws is preserved in the form of correspondence and other contemporary documents. The legal scholar discovered a highly sophisticated lobbying effort by two California COPs, Robert C. Peacock, C.S.B., of Southern California, and Robert W. Newell of Northern California. The COPs provided extensive legal references and an orange binder full of documentation designed to allay fears that children would suffer from the measure, or that the proposed amendment would open the floodgates to all manner of quacks and crazies.

Legal Rights and Obligations of Christian Scientists in California is the title of a blue, loose-leaf manual available to all members of the Mother Church and branch churches in the state. It is jointly produced by the state's two Committees on Publication, and is revised periodically. When Seth Glaser died, pages sixty-two and sixty-three of the guide contained specific advice for Christian Science parents and practitioners confronted with "certain types of situations involving children," that is, death, serious accident, chronic illness, "if public health or school authorities demand medical attention for a child" and "if a child's condition is given publicity of any kind."[56] In any such case, practitioners should contact the COP "so that he may offer guidance on how the legitimate interest of public authority may be best satisfied." Parents, likewise, should in any child's case "give earnest consideration to engaging a practitioner listed in the *Christian Science Journal*, since state statutes accord recognition to such practitioners. Furthermore, arrangements should be made for a practitioner to visit any child promptly who is being treated for a condition which may be deemed serious and for the practitioner to make such visits frequently if needed."

But the most significant advice is saved for last. It is critical in understanding what role the Committee on Publication plays in cases like Seth Glaser's, and in understanding what procedure may have been followed as the child lay near death in the practitioner's home.

> *Christian Scientists understand that total reliance on God is the safest and most scientific system of healing,* and the rights of Christian Scientists to select Christian Science treatment will continue to be respected so long as inquiries by public officials are not ignored and are answered with genuine concern and *with assurance that effective care is being given the children* (emphasis added).[57]

There is a third role of the COP: To battle any perceived "impositions" or attacks in the media aimed at Mrs. Eddy or her church. Indeed, an attack on Mrs. Eddy *is* an attack on the church, and vice versa. As Mrs. Eddy said, "Christian Science is my only ideal; and the individual and his ideal can never be severed. If either is misunderstood or maligned, it eclipses the other with the shadow cast by this error."[58]

One instance of the committee in action followed the 1929 publication of *Mrs. Eddy, The Biography of a Virginal Mind,* by Edwin Franden Dakin. In the second, "popular" edition of his book, Dakin describes how the church, first through direct contact with publishing officials, then through contact with advertisers in the publication, who might threaten boycotts, mounts effective campaigns against any perceived assaults.[59] The church campaign against the book, made at the height of the Christian Science movement, ultimately failed because it angered writers and editors, who saw it as a naked attempt to suppress freedom of speech. (Their response was not dissimilar to that shown by another generation of journalists following a more menacing attack by another group of believers in the Muslim fundamentalist response to *The Satanic Verses.*)

When the second edition of Dakin's book was released the following February, it contained the following "publisher's note":

The publication of this popular edition of *Mrs. Eddy* marks the failure of an organized Minority to accomplish the suppression of opinions not to its liking.

We published the book on its merits—one of which was its presentation of a highly interesting and significant character, about whom people were entitled to know, in a conscientious and impartial manner. And since a publisher, whatever his personal views of the subject, is required by his profession to publish material of such interest and value, we could not properly have done otherwise.

The book appeared on August 16, 1929. In the ensuing weeks it was reviewed by a score of men of character and of knowledge of the subject, outside the organized Minority, in complete confirmation of our opinion of its importance and fairness.

This enthusiastic reception accorded by nonpartisans was accompanied by so virulent a campaign for suppression that if the issue had been only a commercial one, it might well have seemed the part of practical wisdom to withdraw the book.

But the issue now was that of freedom of speech: if this interested Minority could force the suppression of this book, so any strongly organized minority could force the suppression of any book of which its members did not approve. The situation required us to fight it out and take the consequences.

For many weeks it seemed as if the sale of *Mrs. Eddy* might actually be so reduced that the book could not be kept on the market. Many stores were forced by threats to renounce its sale, and many to conceal it. Others defied those who came to threaten boycott, and in all but a few cities the book could always be bought somewhere. The American book trade recognized the principle at issue, and the moment it gained public support—as it did when the public became aware of the attempt at suppression—it so valiantly rallied against this tyranny that the sale of *Mrs. Eddy* rapidly increased.

Except for the indignant resistance of booksellers and public to the arrogant assumption of a minority that it had the right to dictate the sources of information on a given subject, a precedent extremely dangerous to freedom of the mind would surely have been established.

Grateful acknowledgement is due *The New Republic*, *The Saturday Review of Literature*, the New York *Nation*, the Hartford *Courant*, the New York *World*, the Portland (Me.) *Evening News*, *The Carnegie Magazine*, *Harper's* Magazine, *Plain Talk*, The Author's League, and scores of publications and organizations and hundreds of individuals for their aid in informing the public of the situation.

Dakin and his publisher had run afoul of the Committee on Publication, and its auxiliary arm, the Committee on Business. The duties of the Committee on Business are spelled out in a brief, obscure section of the *Manual*. It is to consist of "not less than three loyal members of the Mother Church, who shall transact promptly and efficiently such business as Mrs. Eddy, the Directors, or the Committee on Publication shall commit to it."[60] According to Dakin, the Committee on Business uses advertiser "muscle" to intimidate editors and publishers who have failed to respond "adequately" to complaints by the Committee on Publication. He describes the process:

Newspapers are not published merely because their editors and owners like to see their views in print. They are published to earn revenue. Mrs. Eddy's own publications were earning approximately $400,000 a year, including advertising receipts, before she died. It thus became wholly obvious to her that a very short and quick route to an editor's heart would be through his pocketbook. And she was right.

If any city editor ever dared ignore a communication sent out by the Committee on Publication, the managing editor would shortly receive a telephone call. He would not find the "committee" talking at the other end of the wire. Rather it would be one of his most valued advertisers. The advertiser would be extremely sorry to have learned that the Unionville *Beagle* was so extremely prejudiced in its news columns. If the managing editor was incredulous, it would be explained that his paper seemed to have a desire to persecute and vilify the religious beliefs of the gentleman who now was speaking. If incredulity was still expressed, the managing editor would be told that he should look at the bottom of column six, on page seven, of his issue last Monday week; that he would find there a news item which was wholly erroneous, unjustified, and an insult to the advertiser who was now expressing complaint. The managing editor would look; would find a stick of type referring to Christian Science as a faith cure; would return to the wire; would try to learn what was the matter. Almost inevitably, before he had hung up, he had promised to print anything the gentleman at the other end wished to have published in the correction.

The result was that the press was strewn with denials that Christian Science was in any way related to common faith cures; denials that Mrs. Eddy was aught but a luminous and vibrant and godly personality; assertions that her discovery was nothing less than a perfectly divine boon to man. So industrious were these various "publication Committees" that editors very quickly came to avoid anything but the most reverent and studied approach to Christian Science, for they learned through bitter experience that the least slip would cause their telephone steady ringing that would not cease until they either had exp regret or had lost an advertiser.

The whole secret of this influence with the press lay not but in organization. Mrs. Eddy's 'committees' were picked with and sagacity; in most instances they combined religious acumen with religious zealotry; and they never rested until they cornered the offending editor with the most influential Eddy disciple in the community. They could pick with unerring accuracy exactly the right individual to assist the editor to revise his expressions of opinion.

It was natural that an editor, finding anything which he published on Christian Science subject to the most careful scrutiny, should reach the conclusion that Christian Scientists must be a remarkably numerous and influential sect; and Mrs. Eddy's 'publication committee' encouraged this idea whenever possible. Mrs. Eddy's own hints concerning the millions who responded to her will, combined with an editor's actual contacts with her disciples, left no doubt in thousands of editorial minds that the lady had untold legions of adherents. Probably few people would have believed, in 1906, that there were not many more than 60,000 Christian Scientists scattered all over the country.[61]

The process of celebrity endorsement—using influential Christian Scientists to impress others with the apparent reasonableness and significance of "the movement"—apparently continues today. Before noted Los Angeles appellate lawyer and Democratic Party political powerhouse Warren Christopher took on a pretrial appeal of one of the California prosecutions, he was placed in contact with many influential Christian Scientists, including the Director of the Federal Bureau of Investigation, William Webster.[62]

In the *Manual,* Mrs. Eddy decreed that COPs examine the last proof sheet of a daily newspaper. Her fiat is beyond the power of influence she can command today. But editors sometimes do hand down unquestionable orders to discontinue or change coverage, or to publish rebuttals by articulate believers, usually COPs or approved authorities and celebrities—the late band leader Kay Kyser was one; others were actors Alan Young ("Mr. Ed"), Jean Stapleton ("All in the Family"), and Ginger Rogers. Favorable articles are then reprinted and distributed, to both insiders and outsiders.[63]

SCIENCE WITHOUT MEASURE

The practical, logistical—and, frankly, spiritual and ethical—difficulties of conducting controlled experimental studies on Christian Scientists' practice would appear almost insurmountable.

—Committee on Publication,
The Mother Church, April 1989

The Sunday following the death (the day before the police interview), the grieving parents went to church. Mrs. Glaser said going "was very hard. We did, and we had a lot of support, just really because they all loved him. When we were at church, we had a lot of support."

One common psychological model describes the process of confronting tragedy. A common reaction is *denial*. You have cancer? No. *No I don't. This can't happen to me. I have things to do, places to go. This is too big a part of my life to let go of. I won't do it.* Only when denial is recognized for what it is can the individual confront and reconcile the changed reality.

Lise Glaser had never confronted mortality firsthand since joining the faith. "This may be hard for you, particularly hard for me, but Christian Scientists don't generally fail," she told the detectives. "You know, in Southern California there are more Christian Scientists than almost anywhere in the world and there are people who through five generations have relied on Christian Science treatment, and their children have been brought up."

Here was a concentrated community of lively, healthy, intelligent people, many young couples like themselves, mutually supportive, sharing the wonderful realization that all causes of human misery—disease, decay, death, deceit—were merely "false claims," inevitably destined to vanish, leaving only eternal, never-boring bliss. There was nothing to prepare her for failure.

Mark Twain describes it thus: "The Christian Science Church, like the Mohammedan Church, makes no embarrassing appeal to the intellect, has no occasion to do it, and can get along quite well without it.

"*Provided.* Provided what? That it can secure that thing which is worth two or three hundred thousand times more than an 'appeal to the intellect'— an *environment.*"[64]

The Glasers were members of Twenty-eighth Church of Christ Scientist in Westwood. Here's how Lise Glaser described it to the officers: "The church I belong to is one of the biggest in the world right now, and it has a very, very strong history, and it's a good service." Trying to clarify a point, she suggested the officers talk to its First Reader for an authoritative response.

Her church, Seth's church, was the largest, most active congregation in the heart of Southern California, the world's largest concentration of Christian Scientists. Westwood is the neighborhood immediately south of the UCLA campus. It is a young, professional, affluent, educated community, surrounded by financial companies, a federal complex, and some of the world's costliest condominiums. The Westwood church reflects its setting. It stands on one of the finest pieces of real estate in an area where real estate goes high. The church is attractive, with a smooth, flowing facade on the concave side of sweeping, well-traveled, elegantly curved Glendon Avenue, UCLA's fraternity and sorority row. It's a show-biz neighborhood, too. Nearby, in the "village," was L.A.'s finest concentration of movie palaces, where movies played to massive audiences in grand old cavernous *theaters,* not "cineplexes." Many major league film deals were consummated in the nearby financial district. Twenty-eighth Church draws its congregation from all segments of this community.

The church interior is soothing, restful, uplifting, modern. The congregation sees not only the readers, soloist, organist, but a panorama of greenery in semi-enclosed gardens behind ceiling-high windows.

The Westwood church has everything: youth, numbers, a strong history, a good service, a comfortable, successful *environment.* And Mrs. Glaser belonged, both to the Westwood church and to the Mother Church. She was conditioned to expect success.

But her experience was atypical. She was a convert, she was a young mother with a Scientist-husband and a child. She had gone directly from Principia to Westwood. She had been twice transplanted into concentrated communities of Mother Eddy's brightest young exemplars and greatest worldly successes.

*   *   *

In reality, Christian Science is a graying, dwindling religion. Churches built for large congregations now often hold thirty or fewer people on a Sunday morning.

Just how many Christian Scientists there are is a well-kept secret. Article VIII, Section 28 of the *Manual*, titled "Numbering the People," directs that "Christian Scientists shall not report for publication the number of members of The Mother Church nor that of the branch churches." She has blocked the press and public from gaining a full picture of her church and its history. Offered instead is literature: testimonies of healing, sanctioned or approved books, and very moral arguments for absolute separation of church and state. One finds everything but the numbers.

This was an inspired stroke on Mrs. Eddy's part. A journalist needs to cite *something* in a story, and must therefore fall back on church propaganda, on the Committee on Publication.

Still, despite the official policy of secrecy, there are ways to judge the relative strength of the movement.

All churches and societies (groups of fewer than sixteen members, or larger groups without a *Journal*-listed practitioner) in the United States listed in the July 1989 issue totalled 1,895—down over 500 in twenty-three years. Many congregations are small, housed in churches built in a day when membership was far larger. The December 1956 *Journal* listed 2,380 churches and societies. The figure for the December 1966 issue was 2,411. Ten years later, in December 1976, the number had dropped to 2,277. By December 1986 the total was 1,997. Figures for California were 355 in 1956, 384 in 1966, 354 in 1976, 314 in 1986, and 302 in July 1989.

A look at the changes in listings shows the church has been transformed from an urban institution into a suburban one, following the pattern of "white flight." The large urban churches have been closing, the buildings sold to denominations with higher proportions of minority members. *Journal* entries for Los Angeles show the church moving from inner city to suburbia, holding its own in "old money" neighborhoods. Branch churches are always given numerical designations for each community, assigned by order of founding. Los Angeles has a First, Second, and Third Church, but the Fourth, Eighth, Fifteenth through Nineteenth, Twenty-second, Twenty-fifth through Twenty-seventh, Thirtieth, Thirty-second through Thirty-fifth, Thirty-ninth, Forty-second, and Forty-fourth are gone. From Thirty-sixth on, all are in affluent suburbs. One Los Angeles church building became the local seat of a church based in San Francisco, the Rev. Jim Jones's Peoples Temple. The First and Second Churches are cavernous shells.

When I attended services there 1975-78, Second Church was an architectural marvel created by a rich and exuberant religion, convinced of its permanence and imminent success, in the heart of a growing city at the start of a new century—a domed, columned, granite and marble Pantheon, complete with a mighty organ to fill the mighty spaces—and vast sweeps of dark, empty pews and a few brave, elderly souls huddled near the front to hear a reader they had brought in from another church. Twenty-sixth Church, where the writer served as reader, was a similar structure, about half the size, but done in brick and wood, with lighter hues and a fruitier organ, and with services almost as small. Today, Twenty-sixth Church is gone, the building taken over by a Korean-language Protestant sect.

A study of other entries in the *Christian Science Journal* reveals still more symptoms of the illness afflicting Mrs. Eddy's movement. The number of practitioners and teachers (practitioners with additional church training) peaked at 11,200 in 1941, according to J. Gordon Melton's *Encyclopedia of American Religions.*[65] By July 1989, the number was 3,028, a plunge of 73 percent. Of these, 2,327 were in the United States—approximately one in four was a Californian.

The ratio of practitioners/teachers to churches/societies has dropped from more than two-to-one in 1956 to 1.22-to-1 in July 1989. That month's ratio for California was significantly greater: 1.9-to-1. When the California numbers are subtracted from the national figures, the ratio for the remainder of the country is 1.1 to 1, an interesting figure, inasmuch as the *Manual* mandates that each branch church congregation must include at least one *Journal*-listed practitioner,[66] and larger church memberships often include several practitioners. In at least one instance, however, a small urban branch church maintained its *Journal* listing as a "church" despite the absence of a listed practitioner.

*   *   *

The church is an English-language church. Despite the massive efforts of the Committee on Publication to claim the true demonstration of a church universal and triumphant, 88.7 percent of the churches and 89.3 percent of the practitioners are in nations where English is the national or principal language.[68] Unlike the Mormons, the Christian Scientists have failed to make significant inroads into the Third World. Only 4.5 percent of the churches and societies are in Third World nations; for healers, the figure is 4.2 percent.

The church has a woman's face. Of the 2,327 U.S. professional healers listed in the July 1989 *Journal*, only 401 names are not prefaced by a "Mrs." or "Miss"—meaning that, at most, 17.2 percent are men.[69] Another indication of gender imbalance appears in the enrollment of Principia College, where Lise Glaser underwent her transformation to Christian

Science. Throughout the school's history, the majority of students have been women.[70]

Though Christian Science looks like a "woman's church," when power is considered, the reality is somewhat different. In her last year of life, at the height of her success, Mrs. Eddy wrote:

> A letter from a student in the field says there is a grave need for more men in Christian Science practice. I have not infrequently hinted at this. However, if the occasion demands it, I will repeat that *men are very important factors in our field of labor for Christian Science. The male element is a strong supporting arm to religion as well as to politics,* and we need in our ranks of divine energy, the strong, the faithful, the untiring spiritual armament (emphasis added)."[71]

Why is this something she only *hints* at?

Christian Science may have been founded by a woman, but like Queen Victoria of England, she was a woman who worked her will through a phalanx of male generals. Statistics reveal that while women outnumber men in the church pews and practitioners' offices, men control the true power centers of the church. Of the 193 Christian Science teachers in the United States listed in the July 1989 *Christian Science Journal*, ninety-seven are men, and ninety-six are women.

The next set of numbers involves the Committees on Publication, which Mrs. Eddy specifically decreed should be given to a woman only if a qualified man couldn't be found. At the time of writing, forty-four of the fifty-one COPs in the United States are men. Worldwide, however, of the 167 COPs, 29.9 percent are women, a figure that rises to 43.7 percent in Third World countries.

Finally, the Christian Science Board of Directors, the five-member, all-powerful, self-appointed guardians of Mrs. Eddy's legacy, began with five men selected by the founder. There has never been a woman majority on the board.[72] This is a perfect reflection of Mrs. Eddy's own mystical feminism, in which the woman exerted *spiritual* force, which in turn controlled the brute power of the male. What man accomplished by sword, muscle, machine, woman accomplished through persuasion and what might be called accommodative magic. "The masculine mind reaches a higher tone through certain elements of the feminine," she wrote, "while the feminine mind gains courage and strength through masculine qualities."[73]

In a poem titled "Women's Rights,"[74] she describes her views:

> Grave on her monumental pile:
> She won from vice, by virtue's smile,
> Her dazzling crown, her sceptred throne,
> Affection's wreath, a happy home.

> The right to worship deep and pure,
> To bless the orphan, feed the poor;
> Last at the cross to mourn her Lord,
> First at the tomb to hear his word:
>
> To fold an angel's wings below;
> And hover o'er the couch of woe;
> To nurse the Bethlehem babe so sweet,
> The right to sit at Jesus' feet;
>
> To form the bud for bursting bloom,
> The hoary head with joy to crown;
> In short, the right to work and pray,
> "To point to heaven and lead the way."

*   *   *

Other interesting statistics from the *Journal* listings:

- Of the twenty-one practitioners listing the nation's capital as their primary location, 10, or 47.6 percent, are men (does the CIA clear William Webster's practitioners? Who cleared Haldeman's, Ehrlichman's?);
- All but 4.2 percent of the identifiable women listed are "Mrs.," indicating a present or past marriage that could be the source of significant non-Christian Science practice household income (either in terms of husband's earnings, estate value, pension funds);
- Though it possesses 24.4 percent of the healers, California has less than 16 percent of the churches and societies.
- Nationally, there is just over one male Christian Science healer (practitioner or teacher) for every five churches/societies; the figure for women is virtually one-to-one (1:.989).
- Teachers constitute only 8.3 percent of the healers; the ratio of teachers is one for every 10.1 churches/societies.

As another gauge of the church's well-being, look at the circulation of the *Christian Science Monitor*. According to a *Los Angeles Times* article by religion writer Russell Chandler, the paper's circulation peaked at 271,000 in 1971; by 1983 it had fallen to 141,000. By 1988, thanks to the efforts of the since-resigned editorial team headed by the highly praised Kay Fanning, circulation had risen to about 170,000, according to the *Wall Street Journal*.[75] (Fanning and other key figures from the *Monitor's* editorial staff resigned to protest the reduction of the newspaper's budget resulting from the inauguration of a nightly cable television newscast under the

Monitor logo.) The circulation figure given in the 1989 *Writer's Market* is 150,000.[76] The newspaper has always attracted a sizable number of secular readers, and it has broad distribution in legislatures, libraries, and class-rooms. All Mother Church members were expected to subscribe: "It shall be the privilege and duty of every member, who can afford it, to subscribe for the periodicals which are the organs of this Church."[77] Other subscribers are Christian Scientists who join a branch church and not the Mother Church, the unchurched attracted to Mrs. Eddy's ideas, and those who buy from the several copies sent to each reading room.

Now that it has dropped advertising, advertisers and their number-hungry agencies won't be asking demographic questions about a publication members are obligated to buy if they can. Considering the newspaper's wide distribution and its avowed missionary role, it is notable that a maximum of half the subscribers are church members. That would give a church membership figure of 85,000. Increase that number by half to account for nonsubscribing members (spouses, children over twelve, the poor), and the figure would be 127,500.

The last time the church issued a number was 1936, when it claimed 269,000 Christian Scientists in "about 2,000 churches." In 1989, there were "about 1900" churches. If the members-per-church ratio remained constant, current membership would be 255,000. If the membership is rapidly aging, however, the membership could be half of that number or less. And the 1936 figure is difficult to gauge: Does it means Mother Church members or branch members? The two figures wouldn't be identical.

Further signs of the greying of Mrs. Eddy's church may be found in the high concentration of congregations and practitioners in states favored by the retired (California, Florida, Arizona, and Texas)—though churches and practitioners are found in all fifty states and the District of Columbia. Many Christian Scientists don't enter the practice until they have reached retirement age, when they are able to supplement their retirement incomes with the small fees they charge for their services.[78] While Mrs. Eddy asked healers to charge rates equal to those asked by physicians, in reality practitioners often charge much less—in the range of seven to fifteen dollars for each day of treatment, according to the church.[79]

Waning membership is also reflected in the decline in attendance of pupils for Christian Science class instruction. The *Manual* limits classes to thirty students per teacher per year. However, when I attended class in 1979, I was one of only fourteen students. The teacher was a popular church lecturer, named the following year to the five-member Mother Church Board of Directors, the governing body of the movement. At the first class session, he noted the small number of students and stated, "What's happening here is happening all over the country. The movement faces a tremendous challenge." There is no indication that this trend has reversed.

Ironically, the dwindling membership is enriching the church. Deaths often mean large bequests to the Mother Church and its branches. Similarly, the collapse of branch churches and societies enriches the Mother Church, which receives their assets.

The decline in the oldest mind-is-all religion in a millennial New Age at first might seem paradoxical. But Christian Science makes exclusive demands which don't fit in with the casual, eclectic attitude of the crystal healers, channelers, psychic surgeons, astrologers, and foot-rubbing reflexologists of the New Age. The sincere Christian Scientist must reject not only medical practice, but all other forms of healing as well. "The Bible, together with *Science and Health* and other works by Mrs. Eddy, shall be his only textbooks for self-instruction in Christian Science, and for teaching and practicing metaphysical healing."[80] The church even forbids members to patronize "a publishing house or bookstore that has for sale obnoxious books."[81]

"THE LAW COULD
BE ADJUSTED"

Christian Scientists are harmless citizens that do not kill people either by their practice or by preventing the early employment of an M.D. Why? Because the effect of prayer, whereby Christendom saves sinners, is quite as salutary in the healing of all manner of diseases. The Bible is our authority for asserting this, in both cases. The interval that detains the patient from the attendance of an M.D., occupied in prayer and in spiritual obedience to Christ's mode and means of healing, cannot be fatal to the patient, and is proven to be more pathological than the M.D.'s material prescription.

—Mary Baker Eddy
(From *Message to the
Mother Church*, June 1901)

What the detectives wanted to know was how Christian Science and its followers dealt with health problems of a child, and on what it based its claims of success. Did the church have a central registry for parents to call when a child exhibited alarming symptoms? Detective Talbot asked.

"That's not the church's purpose," Mrs. Glaser answered. "We are trying to get out of physical diseases. We are trying to see [that] God did not create them, [that] we give them definition. If we have them available for people to know about, that's giving them credence."

Then suppose, Talbot asked, Seth had swallowed rat poison, or a similar poison. Would she stick her finger down his throat to induce vomiting? Mrs. Glaser answered: "I probably would have. I probably would. I would call a practitioner also. I mean the church does not out-and-out teach us to do that. Not out-and-out. It's recognized that, 'Look, we are human,' and I mean most Christian Scientists put bandages on a cut finger."

Some Christian Scientists, Mrs. Glaser acknowledged, do go and learn basic first aid; her husband and her practitioner had. But "in a case like that because I know that poison is out-and-out fatal and I'm dealing with something that is a fatal thing, absolutely life and death, and if I did something as simple as putting my finger down his throat, it might give him more of a chance for his life. I would call a practitioner, but I think I would do that, although some Christian Scientists may not. I don't know if Eliot would, because he's been in it for so long. I mean, I haven't been in it that long, and it's not that after a certain period you're more and more brainwashed, it's just that when you've had years and years and years and years of healing your conviction stacks up."

*   *   *

If medical science has one single "demonstration," it has been in the reduction of infant mortality rates—thanks to the control of a wide range of infectious diseases (smallpox hasn't been found anywhere in recent years, except in laboratory cultures).

As the detectives learned, the church doesn't publicize its failures. There is a reason of course: In divine Science there can be no failures. As Mrs. Eddy wrote, "The practitioner may fail, but the Science never."[82] Anything perceived as a failure is a misunderstanding, and we will be doomed to repeat our "failures" till we get them right, and claim our demonstration.[83]

"Sometimes in a testimony someone will say 'and my husband passed on,' " Mrs. Glaser told Talbot.

The detective continued: "I guess my question is, does it only speak—"

"—of only the good? No. In testimony, as I say, testimony in articles. I read a wonderful article that made me feel better about grief. Someone who had lost someone through Christian Science treatment, or a healing that took forever, like thirty years, that finally came, after thirty years."

Mrs. Scott answered in strikingly similar terms: "You will find healings in the *Journals* and the little weekly *Sentinel* often contain accounts of how people will say for instance, 'I was broken-hearted when my little baby passed on.' They don't claim always to have success or—or I had asthma for forty years and then it was healed."

Mrs. Eddy specifically addressed the question in the chapter of her textbook titled "Teaching Christian Science." She writes:

> If patients fail to experience the healing power of Christian Science, and think they can be benefitted by certain ordinary physical methods of medical treatment, then the Mind-physician should give up such cases, and leave invalids free to resort to whatever other systems they fancy

will afford relief. Thus such invalids may learn the value of the apostolic precept: "Reprove, rebuke, exhort with all long-suffering and doctrine." If the sick find these material expedients unsatisfactory, and they receive no help from them, these very failures may open their blind eyes. In some way, sooner or later, all must rise superior to materiality, and suffering is oft the divine agent in this elevation. 'All things work together for good to them that love God,' is the dictum of Scripture."[84]

From this perspective, even the death of a child offers an opportunity for a blessing.

Now, five days after the event, Mrs. Glaser found herself discussing an unimaginable event with two cops who were having trouble understanding her. Similar frustration showed in Mrs. Scott's statement, "I think you're not hearing what I'm saying." Both practitioner and mother seemed to waver on the issue of the state's role in caring for infants. Lise Glaser said she "would like the investigation to be very thorough. And I would like the law to do what the public wants the law to do. This is a democracy, whether it benefits me or not." Her words echo official church policy. "I believe in obeying the laws of the land," Mrs. Eddy declared. "I practice and teach this obedience, since justice is the moral signification of the law."[85]

Mrs. Glaser started to recall how she explained the same point to her father. Seth could eventually choose his own religion, she had said, but "up to a certain point I am going to do what I feel is best, because he has been placed in my hands."

But then her thought shifted, turning to the present, the interrogation room and the two detectives. "You know, this is a very difficult problem: Are you going to let the state bring up the child or are you going to let the parents do it? I mean, this is difficult."

What does Mrs. Eddy say? "Children should be taught the Truth-cure, Christian Science, among their first lessons, and kept from discussing or entertaining theories or thoughts about sickness. To prevent the experience of error and its sufferings, keep out of the minds of your children either sinful or diseased thoughts. The latter should be excluded on the same principle as the former. This makes Christian Science early available."[86]

"We never knowingly do anything wrong, or withhold what a child needed," said Mrs. Scott. She told Detective Cooper later, "You're aware we're not criminal people. It would be such a sad thing to—well, we have to do whatever we have to do, but it seems to me that those laws could be, ah, adjusted if they need to be, without—well, it isn't my business to tell you your business."

Near the end of the interview, Lise Glaser pointed to an article from one of the Christian Science publications. "This is why this article is very good, because it talks about that very issue. How far is the state going to go in telling people how you are going to run your lives? This is very difficult, because Christian Science failed, okay? But if the state placed the children in the jurisdiction of the parents, at what point can the state step in and say, 'Hey, you're abusing, you're neglecting your child?' Is it when the child is up to a certain age, or what? Are you not allowed to raise them so they have the ability to make that decision anyway?"

The article was written by Nathan Talbot, Committee on Publication for the Mother Church.

*   *   *

Near the end of their interview, when Detective Cooper and Mrs. Scott discussed why a criminal investigation was taking place, the practitioner asked the detective, "What I'm wondering is, and I know it is a silly thing to ask you, you're not the District Attorney, but would it be right for us to be involved in a case of this type when the law presently reads—"

COOPER: "But, you see law—
MRS. SCOTT: "—the way it does?"
COOPER: "—law changes on a daily basis and the change is because of cases like this or other types or—in criminal law it changes by other cases, so it may change, it depends. It might change. If it didn't occur with this case, there might be another case tomorrow in Stockton or somewhere else."
SCOTT: "But of course, what it was on the twenty-eighth of March, which was what we were operating under. That's all I'm saying."

On one point there seems agreement: if the law should be that Christian Scientists routinely provide medical care for infants in their legal custody, Christian Scientists will accede. Not willingly, but they will concede it, as they already have in Great Britain and Canada. In the media and the legislatures, the Committee on Publication will lead the fight against encroachment, the periodicals will provide members with an endless flow of literature on the Christianly scientific line of thinking. It's already happening. The fight may be protracted and costly. But if the law changes, the Committee on Publication will issue a new set of legal guidelines, copies of which are always available to Christian Scientists, and the movement will go on.

Detective Cooper asked Mrs. Glaser a key question: "Your belief actually requires consciousness?"

The response: "Absolutely."

How then, Cooper asked, could a child unable to consciously grasp what was happening make an informed decision?

COOPER: "I mean, you accepted your religion as an adult. You had a chance to evaluate, and tested it and gradually moved your way into it until you felt confident. . . . But how about children who are incapable of—"

MRS. GLASER: "—of making those decisions."

COOPER: "Do you think that they should be subjected to the same conditions that you live by?"

MRS. GLASER: "(B)ut if I was so extremely fearful and I felt a doctor could do better. You know, I hadn't really reached that decision quite yet, but I figured that I would go medical. But as for that decision, I don't know. I think it's out of place for the children in parents' hands and there are lessons to be learned from that. That's hard, it's a very hard question to answer and that's what the law is dealing with right now . . . and the reason why it is kind of moral is because Christian Science is a religion, but it overlaps health like very few other religions do and the Constitution sets up that. You know, we all have the right to be Catholics and Jews or Christian Scientists, but Christian Science and some other religions are different because it's . . . healthier. And because, and the reason why we've gotten this far along is because it has been more successful than, than unsuccessful. As a Christian Scientist, I have to work with that. Look, if I had gone medical, okay, I'm not afraid, even from the beginning, okay, if I felt that this was a dangerous thing and the doctors fail, how could I look at myself as a Christian Scientist? Whereas up to this point I'd had nothing but success in everything."

TALBOT: "Now probably, this is the, probably one of the hardest, could be construed to be the cruelest question that you could be asked. Given the same set of circumstances, what would be your actions?"

MRS. GLASER: "Right now, if the law were repealed?"

COOPER: "No, same set of circumstances."

TALBOT: "Seth's back with you now—"

COOPER: "And you were in the same position, what would you do now?"

MRS. GLASER: "I would rely on Christian Science treatment until I reached a point where I really didn't feel it was benefitting him."

TALBOT: "Okay, so it wouldn't be much different than what occurred?"

MRS. GLASER: "No. . . . That is a very difficult question."

TALBOT: "And I told you it would be."

MRS. GLASER: "I'd love to have him here with me."

TALBOT: "What can you tell other Christian Science mothers about what you've experienced?"

MRS. GLASER: "It'll be hard because he was really loved. What will I tell them? I would say, it works. I know it works. I know he was blessed by being here with us and I know that he was blessed by. . . . See, we feel that Christian Science is helping us get that ultimate goal of just being perfect, okay? And that this experience helped him on his way. Not this experience, this one, but I mean being with us and feeling the love and sharing the love and having the advantage of Christian Science. I see that as an advantage, the advantage of Christian Science treatment and the growing awareness of some of the laws that are timeless and eternal. They apply here just as much as so-called in heaven or before. I would say, I would say it works, and I know it works. And even though we didn't demonstrate it in this instance, you. . . . be true to what you feel is the most right thing in any situation. Don't forsake what you've known just because of this. I'd say, 'Search out. Make sure you know what you're doing because'—you know, if someone isn't as firm as I am, and I'm not as firm as some others, but I am firm. More firm than a lot of people. Then if you're going through a situation where there's going to be any doubt at all, they should go medical."

*   *   *

Since the church won't cooperate in scientific experiments, and since the founder clamped an eternal lid of secrecy on church membership, how can an outsider judge the effectiveness of Mrs. Eddy's science?

William Franklin Simpson of Kansas's Emporia State University discovered ways of answering a question that has long plagued researchers: Do Christian Scientists live longer than non-Scientists?

The first relevant study was conducted by Dr. Gale E. Wilson, based on the records of the King County, Washington, coroner's office for 1949-51. Dr. Wilson, a forensic pathologist, found that records of dead identified as Christian Scientists showed the average life expectancy to be slightly less than the state average, but to a degree below statistical significance.[87]

Dr. Wilson's study was confined to years when antibiotics were few and limited, and before the advent of polio, mumps, measles, and rubella vaccines. Of the deaths in his study, he determined that six percent would have been prevented with the medical help then available.

Dr. Simpson was able to gain a second, more contemporary, fix on believer longevity by charting the deaths of graduates from Principia College and the University of Kansas, both midwestern schools. For his data on the Principia students, he turned to the *Principia Purpose*, the quarterly for graduates—of which he was one.[88] A regular "In Memoriam" column notes the deaths of graduates, giving with the name a year of graduation. Similar data were obtained from the University of Kansas. He compared the data by gender and by year of graduation.

He discovered that both male and female Scientists, who are not allowed to drink alcohol or smoke,[89] were dying at a faster rate than the student population of a state university. His conclusion: "If Christian Science healing methods work as well as medical healing methods, one would expect to see Christian Scientists live as long as non-Christian Scientists. However, this study shows that this is not the case."[90]

There are limitations to all indirect measurements, and some degree of error is inevitable. Still, until better evidence is made available, these are the best indications to be found. The question is, in light of Simpson's findings, and in the light of the refusal of the church to cooperate with scientific tests, just how is a reasonable person, that standard by which the law measures all things, to know that "effective care is being given?"

Other religions embrace the nonsmoking, nondrinking rules of Christian Science and accept medical care. Mormons, followers of one such faith, live significantly longer than the general population, according to a recent study.[91]

* * *

Mrs. Glaser's recorded interrogation ended with discussion of the disease organisms apparently found during the autopsy. When it was over, Mrs. Glaser ventured a question: "One more thing, this is for the protection of my, you know, we're very intent on following the law. The coroner told us it was contagious, but they didn't out-and-out tell us that we needed to do anything about it, contact other people."[92] Talbot assured her that the coroner's staff wasn't upset at the autopsy.

> MRS. GLASER: "Please let me know, because I want to be considerate to other Christian Scientists and other people. We live in a community of—"
> COOPER: "We're concerned, too, because we were present during—"
> MRS. GLASER: "During the what?"
> COOPER: "During the autopsy."

"TO TEACH . . . A LESSON"

> The Cause of Christian Science is prospering throughout the world and stands forever as an eternal and demonstrable Science, and I do not regard this attack on me as a trial, for when these things cease to bless they will cease to occur.
>
> —Mary Baker Eddy

David F. Wells is a deputy District Attorney, and it was Wells who received the evidence from the Santa Monica police officers. Realizing the case was politically sensitive, sure to draw media attention, he initially took a conservative position.

The first stage of the criminal justice process is optional: indictment by a grand jury. Every defendant charged with a felony, a major crime, has a right to ask that the case first be presented to the county grand jury. Indictments are rarely sought in routine cases, either by the defense or the prosecution, since grand jurors hear only what the prosecution chooses to tell them, and issuance of charges is considered a rubber stamp process.

But in complex cases, especially those with political ramifications, prosecutors frequently present their cases to a grand jury. This accomplishes several things. The prosecutor sees how witnesses will present themselves and their testimony in future proceedings, and the transcripts establish a record of testimony that can be used to challenge any contradictions in testimony given later. The use of the grand jury also shows that the prosecutor is making sure the defendants are given all their legal options prior to being charged with crimes.

Wells presented five witnesses to the Los Angeles County Grand Jury: Santa Monica police officers Mary Reynolds and Shane Talbot; physician Irwin L. Golden, a deputy coroner; Gerald R. Greene, associate professor of pediatrics at the University of California, Irvine; and Stephen M. Marcy.

On 20 June 1984, the Los Angeles County Grand Jury returned a "true bill," a finding that criminal charges were merited against both the Glasers and Virginia Scott. Each was charged with two crimes: violation of California Penal Code sections 273a(1), felony child endangerment, and 192(2), involuntary manslaughter.

The next stage in the legal proceedings was announced to the faithful in the July 1984 *Newsletter of the Christian Science Committee on Publication for Southern California*, mailed in quantity for distribution to all members of branch church executive boards. The newsletter, written by Al Carnesciali, noted that:

> All of you are now aware that the parents of Seth Glaser, Eliot and Lise Glaser, and the practitioner, Virginia Scott, were arraigned in Santa Monica Superior Court Friday, June 22, on an indictment of the Grand Jury. The charges are child endangerment . . . and involuntary manslaughter. The proceedings were held over until July 23 for the Glasers and Mrs. Scott to make an entry of a plea.

"There has been no law violated," declared Carnesciali's *Newsletter*, which charged the prosecutor with unjustly and "arbitrarily singling out parents because of their religious beliefs." Then came the argument that the church has raised in every case of this kind of death: "The parents of the hundreds of children suffering from meningitis who receive the most up-to-the-minute medical care—and yet pass on—are not similarly the objects of criminal proceedings. It would be abhorrent to most people to prosecute reasonable, loving parents who lose a child—whether at home or in a hospital—despite everyone's best efforts."

The actions of prosecutor Wells, the *Newsletter* said, were best summed up in a statement of his taken from the 22 June edition of the local CBS television affiliate: "We have to teach Christian Scientists and others a lesson." Carnesciali told the faithful: "With such prejudicial statements as this, obviously there is a great need for effective prayer and love. Remember, it's time for us to be roused, not riled, and our need is to lift the imposition from all mankind."

All the defendants, the *Newsletter* said, "have obtained appropriate legal counsel, and the expenses are expected to be quite high. One fund has already been set up for the Glasers. [I]t is expected that a separate fund will be established for the practitioner, Mrs. Scott."

The "appropriate" counsel for Lise Glaser was Douglas Dalton, Esq., perhaps Los Angeles's most esteemed criminal-defense attorney. With his craggy, care-worn features, dark hair, and lanky build, there is something

Lincolnesque about him, an air that generates attention and respect inside the courtroom. (When director Roman Polanski found himself charged with the statutory rape of a thirteen-year-old girl in Jack Nicholson's home, it was Dalton he hired.[93]) Anthony Murray was hired to represent Eliot Glaser. Though not as well known as his colleague, Murray is an articulate, forceful attorney.

Carnesciali said branch churches could send donations to the defense funds, but recommended that monies come from individual members instead.

> Through its various activities, The Mother Church is offering every appropriate support to the defendants in this case. However, by a precedent established since Mrs. Eddy's time, The Mother Church does not become financially or directly involved for a number of reasons. In addition to the Church itself not being on trial, any direct participation would be seen to indicate that the Church is controlling the defendants and the lawyers involved—just one more example to those critical of Christian Science that the Church seeks to control everything individual Christian Scientists and their families are engaged in. Of course this is absolutely false. Nevertheless, this office working under the direction of the Manager, Committees on Publication, has given and will continue to give all the support that can be given to the defendants within the province of its *Manual*-designated assignment.
>
> It is well to keep in mind that whatever human footsteps are taken, all of these must be preceded and supported by healing prayer. In a letter dated 1903 Mrs. Eddy stated: "Unless we have *better healers*, and more of this work than any other is done, our Cause will not stand and having done all stand. *Demonstration* is the whole of Christian Science and nothing else will save it and continue it with us. God has said this—and Jesus Christ has proved it" (*The Christian Science Journal*, June 1936).

Carnesciali directed all Christian Scientists receiving the newsletter to "review again the Legal Rights book having to do with minors. . . ." He wrote:

> We still retain the basic Penal Code Section 270, which provides that Christian Science treatment by an accredited practitioner is recognized in the law as 'other remedial care.' We should cherish the spiritual basis of this law and trust in God's capacity to bring about healing in spite of obvious opposition to spiritual methods. As the power of God was seen to overcome efforts of the Assyrians to weaken the faith of the people of Israel (brought out in II Kings 18 and 19 in the Lesson-Sermon of July 1), so we should have great trust in this same power to bring about healing quickly and effectively today.

*   *   *

California Penal Code section 270 would be the fulcrum on which the cases of all the California Christian Science child death cases would turn. Originally enacted in 1872, the law states: "If a parent of a minor child omits, without lawful excuse, to furnish necessary clothing, food, shelter or medical attendance, or other remedial care for his or her child, he or she is guilty of a misdemeanor punishable by a fine not exceeding one thousand dollars, or by imprisonment in the county jail not exceeding one year, or by both such fine and imprisonment."

The basic law, cited above, has been amended by the California Legislature through the years to cover such contingencies as Social Security benefits, alimony allotments, and artificial insemination. The words "other remedial care" had been added in 1925. But the addition to which Carnesciali referred was enacted in 1976, and reads as follows: "If a parent provides a minor with treatment by spiritual means through prayer alone in accordance with the tenets and practices of a recognized church or religious denomination, by a duly accredited practitioner thereof, such treatment shall constitute 'other remedial care,' as used in this section."

If the law sounds like it was tailored precisely for Christian Science, that is because it was—and the history of this section, as well as what the legislature intended when enacting into law were to prove key issues in the years to come when the deaths of Christian Science children became issues for the appellate courts.

WHO WATCHES
THE WATCHERS?

Remember, thou Christian martyr, it is enough if thou art found worthy to unloose the sandals of thy Master's feet. To suppose that persecution for righteousness' sake belongs to the past, and that Christianity to-day is at peace with the world because it is honored by sects and societies, is to mistake the very nature of religion. Error repeats itself. The trials encountered by prophet, disciple, and apostle, "of whom the world was not worthy," await, in some form, every pioneer of truth.

—Mary Baker Eddy
(*Science and Health*)

To Christian Scientists, 1984 really was a year with Orwellian overtones. They had reason to believe their faith, their very identity, was under concerted government attack.

Before Seth Glaser's death had occurred the seventeen-day lethal ordeal of Shauntay Walker, the Sacramento four-year-old whose convert mother hid her child from concerned relatives who had demanded she seek medical treatment. On 9 December came the third case, when eight-month-old Natalie Susan Middleton-Rippberger of the northern California town of Healdsburg died following a fifteen-day ordeal.

All three children died of bacterial meningitis, an inflammation of the three-layered membranes that enclose the brain and spinal cord. The disease is comparatively rare; most of the 2,000-5,000 U.S. victims yearly are under the age of five. With prompt, massive intravenous antibiotic treatments, recovery usually follows—though the infection can leave lasting brain damage in its wake.[94]

Other prosecutions were to follow in other states.

In Boston, the seat of Mrs. Eddy's movement, in April 1986, two-year-old Robyn Twitchell died of complications from a congenital bowel obstruction after five days of symptoms. His parents, Christian Scientists, were charged with manslaughter.[95]

On 30 September 1986, Amy Hermanson, a seven-year-old Sarasota, Florida, girl died from complications of diabetes after weeks of suffering. Two Christian Science practitioners had treated the child. By the time a distraught aunt called state child welfare officials, it was too late. The parents were charged with third degree murder.[96]

On 5 June 1988, twelve-year-old Elizabeth Ashley King died of bone cancer, less than a month after Paradise Valley, Arizona, police were called by neighbors concerned because they hadn't seen the child for months.[97] Her parents, both Scientists, were charged with felony child abuse; they had relied on prayer alone to treat a leg tumor that grew over seven months to forty-one inches in circumference, fracturing her leg in two places, according to the prosecutor.[98]

Attorneys in all three of the California cases realized that major constitutional issues were involved. While it was the Walker case, the first of the three 1984 deaths, that reached the California Supreme Court and determined the course of all three, every attorney had filed pretrial appeals. A central legal issue was whether the treatment-by-prayer exemption in section 270 of the *California Penal Code* barred the state from trying the cases under two other sections of the code, manslaughter and felony child endangerment.

Section 270 applies to misdemeanor "failure to provide." The maximum penalty for a conviction is one year in a county jail. Section 273a(1) is the more serious offense, a "wobbler," which can be filed and tried either as a misdemeanor or a felony. Felonies can be punished with state prison sentences, and are the more serious class of crime. The maximum sentence for conviction under section 273a is ten years.

The section reads:

> Any person who, under circumstances or conditions likely to produce great bodily harm or death, willfully causes or permits any child to suffer, or inflicts thereon unjustifiable physical pain or mental suffering, or having the care or custody of any child, willfully causes or permits the person or health of such child to be injured, or willfully causes or permits such child to be placed in such situation that its person or health is endangered, is punishable by imprisonment in the county jail not exceeding one year, or in the state prison [for up to ten years].

Unlike the misdemeanor section 270, there is no specific exemption provided for faith-healing. The question then became: Was it the legislature's intent to provide exemptions for all cases where a child was treated by an "accredited practitioner" of a "recognized church or religious denomination"? Or did it simply intend to exempt cases involving non-life-threatening conditions?

Prior to the 1872 California legislation, an 1868 English common law child death case had acquitted parents of manslaughter because they had acted in "good faith" in turning to prayer for healing.

California's first Christian Science child death case under the 1872 law was prosecuted before a Los Angeles jury in 1902. A diphtheria epidemic had claimed the life of a child who had received no medical care. The arguments raised by the defense in that case were the same the church was to raise in California cases more than eight decades later: Prosecutors were attacking the faith because they didn't understand it, and they weren't prosecuting physicians, who were losing one child in four to the same disease. The jury acquitted the parents.[99]

*   *   *

Two factors were at work in the 1976 amendment to the misdemeanor statute. First was a 1967 decision of the California Supreme Court in the case of another Sacramento woman, a member of the Church of the First Born, whose thirteen-year-old daughter died of complications from an intestinal blockage after an eighteen-day illness.

The mother was convicted of misdemeanor manslaughter, but she was cleared after the state Supreme Court ruled that her confession had been improperly obtained. But the court, which is the highest court in the state, rejected defense arguments that the 1925 phrase "other remedial care" exempted the mother from criminal liability. "The phrase 'other remedial care'. . .does not sanction unorthodox substitutes for 'medical attendance'; it indicates one of the multiple necessities which the parent must decide," the court held.[100]

In the 1970s, two currents of activity converged, one in Sacramento, the other in Washington, D.C.

After Congress enacted the federal Child Abuse Prevention and Treatment Act of 1974, the Department of Health, Education and Welfare issued regulations requiring states to impose a religious exemption clause in child abuse statutes or risk the loss of federal funds.•All states complied.

At the California level, the Committees on Publication were working closely with a powerful Democratic member of the lower house of the state legislature, California Assembly Speaker Pro Tempore John T. Knox of Richmond, California. The result was Assembly Bill 3843, which added the "practitioner"/"recognized religion" language to the misdemeanor child neglect statute.

In a letter of 16 August 1976, the legislator urged Governor Edmund G. "Jerry" Brown, Jr., to sign the measure: "Christian Science treatment is a recognized alternative to medical attendance under Medicare, Medi-Cal, the group insurance for all state and federal civil service employees, and is so recognized by almost every group insurance company in the United States whenever so requested by the employer."

The arguments Knox used were raised in a letter sent to him and the governor's legislative secretary 23 June 1976 by the state's two Committees on Publication, Robert W. Newell for Northern California and Robert C. Peacock for Southern California. The concluding paragraph of the letter declared: "We sincerely feel that the only possible reason for an objection to this bill would be because of a lack of knowledge of the recognition and effectiveness of Christian Science treatment."[101]

Knox's bill was passed by a 65-2 vote in the Assembly and 28-1 in the Senate, and was duly signed by the governor. There were no prosecutions for Christian Science deaths until the three children died eight years later.

*   *   *

While Al Carnesciali's *Newsletter* said the Mother Church couldn't appear to be controlling the parents' cases, the church has, in fact, played a major role. The church retained its own lawyers to file friend-of-the-court briefs, it footed the bill for research for the defense lawyers, and it conducted an "ardent" media and public relations campaign.[102]

It took the Walker case four years to reach the state Supreme Court. Along the way, the state Court of Appeal, Third District, had rejected defense motions for a prohibition against prosecution on the grounds that Laurie Walker was protected by section 270, the United States Constitution First Amendment freedom-of-religion protections, and the California Constitution requirement that citizens receive fair notice of a law before they can be tried for its violation.

Walker was represented by some of California's finest legal talent. Warren Christopher, a leading figure in state and national Democratic politics, had handled the appeal. He was joined by a host of other lawyers. But the primary attorney was Thomas Volk, a Sacramento defense specialist who would defend the mother in the trial should the court deny her appeals.

The court gave its answer in a forty-four-page decision handed down 10 November 1988. The seven-member court held unanimously that Laurie Walker could be tried for involuntary manslaughter. One justice, Allen Broussard, dissented from a majority decision by the other six to also allow Laurie Walker to be charged with felony child endangerment.

The first issue the court took up was the implications of section 270 for the counts charged, felony child neglect and involuntary manslaughter. Reversing its decision in the Sacramento case, the court ruled that the "other remedial care" language inserted in 270 in 1925 *did* bar conviction of anyone under that misdemeanor section administering treatment by prayer alone. Nonetheless, wrote Justice Stanley J. Mosk in the majority opinion, "there was no legislative intent to exempt prayer treatment, as a matter of law, from the reach of the manslaughter and felony child-endangerment statutes."

One key reason for the decision was a five-word phrase in the 1976 amendment: prayer was acceptable as " 'other remedial care,' *as used in this section*" (emphasis in decision). Thus, the exemption was limited to 270, and did not apply to the charges at issue. The court also held that the main purpose of 270 was to hold parents financially responsible for providing care.

What, then, is the basis for a parent's criminal liability in a death where the parent sincerely believed he or she was providing the best possible care? Here the court cited a definition of criminal negligence it had handed down in 1955:

> We have defined criminal negligence as "aggravated, culpable, gross, or reckless," that is, the conduct of the accused must be such a departure from what would be the conduct of an ordinarily prudent or careful man under the same circumstances as to be incompatible with a proper regard to human life.[103]

The legal structure of the state, the court said, "reflects not an endorsement of the efficacy or reasonableness of prayer treatment for children battling life-threatening diseases but rather a willingness to accommodate religious practice when children do not face serious physical harm. Indeed, the relevant statute(s) suggest that prayer treatment for gravely ill children is sufficiently unreasonable to justify the draconian step of depriving parents of their rights to custody."[104]

Turning to the claims of constitutional protection, the court cited a case state deputy Attorney General Clifford K. Thompson, Jr., used in his argument for prosecution: the 1944 U.S. Supreme Court decision in *Prince* v. *Massachusetts*,[105] where the court ruled, "The right to practice religion freely does not include liberty to expose the community or child to communicable disease, or the latter to ill health or death." Parents, the court held, "may be free to become martyrs themselves. But it does not follow they are free, in identical circumstances, to make martyrs of their children before they have reached the age of full legal discretion when they can make that choice for themselves."

The state court agreed, incorporating language from the 1944 U.S. Supreme Court decision:

> Imposition of felony liability for endangering or killing an ill child by failing to provide medical care furthers an interest of unparalleled significance: the protection of the very lives of California's children, "upon whose healthy, well rounded growth . . . into full maturity as citizens" our "democratic society rests, for its continuance."

While the judges expressed concern for the conflict between religious rights and the state's duty to protect children, they pointed out that Christian Scientists are permitted by the church to seek medical care, and that members who do so are not stigmatized or subject to divine wrath or punishment.[106]

*   *   *

Gerald Uelmen, who worked on Mrs. Glaser's appeal with Douglas Dalton, is dean of the University of Santa Clara Law School, and one of California's most respected legal scholars.

In an interview conducted for this book he said: "The real problem I have with Mosk's opinion in Walker is how it deals with that due process issue of lack of notice to the parents, that this could be treated as criminal conduct." This was the state constitutional ground cited by Walker's attorneys. The parents believed they were acting legally, and the state had made no effort to inform them that it was operating under a new interpretation of the statutes. Certainly they were acting within the guidelines laid out by the Committee on Publication, which had been instrumental in the passage of the "practitioner" provision of section 270. Even after the indictments were handed down and the parents and practitioner arraigned, the Committee on Publication was telling the faithful that "there has been no law violated."

The Glaser defense arguments submitted to the state Court of Appeal in Los Angeles were based primarily on statutory rather than constitutional grounds, the legal expert said. "I honestly don't think that there's much future in the constitutional argument that the right of parents to select prayer healing over conventional medical treatment is protected by the First Amendment—I don't think that's going anywhere. But I think the existence of the statutory exemption should provide a defense to criminal prosecution."[107]

Uelmen raised another, more philosophical issue. "My whole experience and career has been in the criminal justice system. I see it as such a crude tool in terms of formulating public policy and carrying it out. It really has no place in this debate. And whatever else the parents are—call them deluded, call them misguided, call them zealots—they're not criminals. I think that there is very much of a concerted position that is being taken by prosecutors across the country that is really challenging the exemptions that traditionally have been given to Christian Scientists. The confrontation is very real. I don't think it helps to impugn anybody's motives in that confrontation, but I really question whether it's appropriate for that confrontation to be in the context of a criminal prosecution of parents. If they want to fight that battle in the legislature and even in the courts and redefine what the obligations of a parent are, that's fine. But it shouldn't be done on a kind of a post hoc basis in which the parents face criminal penalties. I don't have any First Amendment problems in saying to them, 'You're free to abide by your beliefs, but when it comes to children, the state has an interest in intervening and we may initiate proceedings to take the decision out of your hand and exert ultimately control over what kind of medical treatment is appropriate for children.' But I think it's a whole different dimension to turn around and say, 'We're going to prosecute you for criminal homicide for the death of a child.' "

*   *   *

On 19 June 1989 the U.S. Supreme Court declined, without comment, to consider Walker's case, and the way was paved for trial in all three California cases. The first to reach court was the case of the Healdsburg couple.

Mark Rippberger was thirty-five when their trial began 19 June 1989; his spouse, Susan Middleton, was thirty-nine. On one side was Deputy Sonoma County District Attorney David Dunn, the prosecutor; on the other was David Mackenroth of Sacramento, law partner of Thomas Volk, the defense attorney in the Sacramento Laurie Walker case.

Among the expert witnesses called by the state was Dr. Birt Harvey, president of the American Academy of Pediatrics, which almost two years before had called for an end to religious exemptions from child health protection laws.[108] The physician testified that 95 percent of similar child meningitis patients survive with antibiotic treatment.[109]

Mackenroth successfully fought an effort by the prosecutor to keep the parents' religious beliefs from the jury, maintaining they had no relevance to the simple issue of whether or not the parents had allowed their child to die without medical care. He argued that failure of Christian Science treatment to heal one disease victim was not grounds to condemn the religion or its followers.

The jury returned a verdict at the end of the trial's seventh week. The parents were guilty of child endangerment, but not guilty of involuntary manslaughter. Prosecutor Dunn praised the jury for showing "remarkable intelligence in handing down this verdict." Mackenroth said the parents would appeal.[111]

On 2 November 1989, the couple was placed on probation and fined over $10,000. As a condition of probation, the court ordered medical care for the couple's five surviving children—a provision defense attorney David Mackenroth said he would contest.[110] Parents in the Florida case had already been convicted of child endangerment, and the Arizona case had been resolved in a plea bargain to a similar charge.

The Glaser case would be the next to go to trial, scheduled for late 1989 before Santa Monica Superior Court Judge Robert W. Thomas. Virginia Scott was not on trial. All charges against her were dismissed early in the proceedings; there was no evidence she was acting outside the constitutionally protected bounds of her religion.

Laurie Walker was scheduled for trial in Sacramento early in 1990.

Gerald Uelmen was optimistic for the Glasers: "I think each of these cases is a little different. The Glasers had less than twenty-four hours, and when a parent is pushed into that corner and ultimately has to choose, I think that element of time is a very significant factor."

Prosecutor David Wells agreed, and said that winning a conviction would be difficult.

As Uelmen explained it, "the strongest defense the Glasers have really is based simply on the causality issue; that even if at the point at which the symptoms appeared serious they had sought conventional medical treatment, it probably wouldn't have made any difference. I don't think they're going to be able to prove beyond a reasonable doubt that at that point if they had sought medical treatment the outcome would have been different. It was a very virulent case of meningitis."

The Glasers simply didn't have the weeks that were available to the parents of Natalie Middleton-Rippberger or Shauntay Walker. Seth Ian Glaser was dead within thirty hours of showing the first alarming symptoms. "According to Justice Mosk's opinion in *Walker*, the test is that of the reasonable parent, the objectively reasonable parent who does not have these religious beliefs," Uelmen said. In this case, it may not have mattered.

If the Glasers lost at trial, Uelmen said, their case would continue. "All of the challenges were pretrial challenges, motions to dismiss the indictment. So now that the issues raised on those motions have been disposed of, we'll go to trial and then it will work its way up again," he said.

TWO MARTYRS

The oppressive state statutes touching medicine remind one of the words of the famous Madame Roland, as she knelt before a statue of Liberty, erected near the guillotine: "Liberty, what crimes are committed in thy name."

—Mary Baker Eddy (*Science and Health*)

Both sides in the Glaser case had concluded that subjecting the couple's fate to the whims of a jury would be in nobody's interest in a case where an appeal was likely, whatever the verdict. There was only one real issue in *Glaser* different from any of those in the other cases: Would the child have been saved even had the parents taken him to physicians instead of a practitioner? That was an issue best left to a judge.

By law, every criminal defendant has the right to a trial by jury, to have guilt or innocence decided by fellow citizens. But in this case, a jury would receive limited, inflammatory evidence: descriptions of tragic death, pictures of the dead child, religious claims in conflict with beliefs of the jurors, and the constrained but passionate arguments of attorneys skilled at playing on reason and sentiment.

Juries can be fickle. In the same building a decade earlier, a juror in a child rape-and-mutilation murder case who had voted to convict changed her mind when it came to voting on the death penalty because she'd been communing with the spirits of the dead children in the jury bathroom, and they said the man was innocent.[112]

If the Glasers, their attorneys, the prosecutor, and the judge agreed, the case would be heard by a jury of one, a professional student of the law who knew what evidence could and could not be considered, and who, presumably, had seen enough of tragedy to enable him to focus on facts rather than feelings.

The judge both sides accepted was Robert W. Thomas, a former prosecutor who became, in turn, a municipal then a superior court judge in Santa Monica. Thomas is a pragmatist, with a relaxed, personable style on the bench; he is well-liked and considered honest and fair by attorneys.

Thomas would give a clear, well-reasoned verdict, one that wouldn't be clouded with peripheral issues when it reached the appeals courts. The case came before him for trial on 8 December 1989, a bright Southern California winter's day, with the mercury in the 70s. Pedestrians outside were clad in shorts and wore sunglasses.

Before Judge Thomas called their case, there was a jury to instruct in another criminal trial.

Lise and Eliot Glaser took seats in the second row of the audience, directly behind me. Eliot wore a grey suit with a bright blue-grey tie with day-glo pastel hues. He had retained his beard. Lise was dressed like a Catholic schoolgirl, with a blue-green-and-white-plaid jumper and a high-necked white blouse. Though her driver's license described her hair as red, it appeared dirty blonde. Both sat erect, whispering occasionally, listening closely as Judge Thomas instructed the jury. As he told the jurors that legal"evidence" is "anything presented to the senses," Lise Glaser nodded, whispered to her husband the single word, "Sense!"

Their case was called promptly at 10 A.M., after the prosecutor and two defense attorneys conducted a final meeting in the prosecutor's office.

In a criminal trial, the burden of proof is on the prosecution, which must prove the crimes charged "beyond a reasonable doubt and to a moral certainty." Because the prosecutor carries the burden, David Wells would have the first and, if he chose, last words to the court.

When the case was called, Wells, the Glasers, and their lawyers all stood. To establish a record that all legal requirements had been met, Wells began a lengthy recitation of the understandings that had been reached, establishing that the Glasers understood and agreed to each item.

The Glasers gave up their rights to a jury trial and to hear and cross-examine prosecution witnesses. They agreed to the submission of the preliminary hearing transcript and exhibits. They retained their right to present a full-blown defense, with witnesses and exhibits.

When Judge Thomas gave his assent, Wells declared, "People at this time rest."

Then Douglas Dalton rose to his feet and asked the judge to dismiss the case under Section 1118 of the *California Penal Code*, which reads:

In a case tried by the court without a jury, a jury having been waived, the court on motion of the defendant or on its own motion shall order the entry of a judgment of acquittal of one or more of the offenses charged in the accusatory pleading after the evidence of the prosecution has been closed in the court, upon weighing the evidence then before it finds the defendant not guilty of such offense or offenses. If such a motion for judgment of acquittal at the close of the evidence offered by the prosecutor is not granted, the defendant may offer evidence without having first reserved that right.

Now the defense and the prosecution would raise what both sides agreed was the central legal issue of the case: whether or not the prosecution's evidence supported its contention that Seth Glaser's death resulted from the parents' failure to act reasonably.

"The facts will determine that at that point the seriousness was recognized, that there's nothing medicine could have done to save this child," Dalton said. "The critical issue is one of agency," said Anthony Murray. "If [Eliot Glaser] had sought medical attention when beyond a reasonable doubt he should have, would that have saved the child?

"The child had previously been ill and had had a fever and had a flu-like syndrome a week or two weeks before and had recovered from it. Not at all unusual. This is a seventeen-month-old child, and in the course of seventeen months, a child is going to have those kind of cold- and flu-like symptoms. [Prosecution witness Dr. Gary Overturf] says that the best he can give the child's chances as of March 28, the last day, early in the morning, were fifty-fifty. And that's all by itself, that is not beyond a reasonable doubt.

"Finally, what [prosecution witness Dr. Gerald R. Green] called the point of no return was reached when they put the child in the car [on the way to Mrs. Scott's house], and that as I have indicated is around twelve-thirty or one o'clock, approximately one and a half to two hours before the . . . death. I submit to the court that [the evidence shows that] before that, the symptoms were classical flu-type symptoms. I would submit, and these doctors agree that at that time when they put the child in the car, the child could have been in the Mayo Clinic and it wouldn't have made a bit of difference."

The parents' motives were irrelevant and their actions were not criminal, the defense argued, because by the time they—or anyone else, for that matter—reasonably felt urgent help was needed, medicine couldn't have done anything for the child.

Wells opened his argument with an explanation: "What we're talking about here is involuntary manslaughter. There's no intent to kill. There's no question in my mind and in this court's mind and in anybody else's mind that first of all that you can't punish a parent any more than they already have been punished if their child died. That's irrelevant to the charges here. The charges here are based on a violation of law wherein the state is the victim in a case like this, and the state has a motive in protecting its citizens from other citizens, and that's exactly what we're talking about.

And to not pursue a case like this in essence puts an imprimatur on the conduct of the defendants in a case such as this. What we're talking about in this case, your honor, is *negligence*, acts which are so aggravated and reckless and gross that it constitutes a disregard for the human life or an indifference to the consequences."

Wells contended that the evidence showed that symptoms were severe enough the day before the death that a reasonable parent would have sought medical help. "All of these symptoms we got from the defendants themselves," he said. "They're not something we got out of the air. So the only evidence of the child's symptoms were through the eyes of this child's parents."

Judge Thomas listened to arguments and set 12 January for his ruling on the defense motion, to be followed by the defense case if he determined the prosecution had made a case.

*   *   *

Throughout the December hearing, sitting near the rear of the courtroom was a small band of dedicated Christian Scientists, their faces intent and somber. One was Al Carnesciali, C.S.B., Committee on Publication for Southern California; another was Nathan A. Talbot.

After the hearing, the Glasers met with the church officials in the hallway outside. "Well, I guess we have our work cut out for us for the next month," Lise Glaser told Talbot. "Yes, we do," the COP answered. They talked for a few more minutes, before walking out in front of the cameras. "I guess we can give the press our usual 'no comment,'" said Lise Glaser as they began their journey out of the court.

They had become two martyrs, steadfast in their loyalty, standing on the side of almighty Truth, divine Principle, knowing that, as Mrs. Eddy wrote, "any so-called law, which undertakes aught but sin, is null and void."[113]

*   *   *

On 16 February 1990, Judge Thomas made his decision. The Glasers were not guilty.

The ruling, he said, was not about Christian Science; only about whether or not the Glasers might have been able to save their child at the moment any other parents would have determined the child's health was in danger. That, he said, had not been sufficiently established by the prosecution.

There was no appeal from his ruling.

The case was over.

"HIS TRIAL WAS A TRAGEDY"

In her chapter "Christian Science Practice" in *Science and Health*, Mrs. Eddy presents Christianly scientific treatment through the analogy of a trial.

Suppose a mental case to be on trial, as cases are tried in court. A man is charged with having committed liver-complaint. The patient feels ill, ruminates, and the trial commences. Personal Sense is the plaintiff. Mortal Man is the defendant. False Belief is the attorney for Personal Sense. Mortal Minds, Materia Medica, Anatomy, Physiology, Hypnotism, Envy, Greed and Ingratitude, constitute the jury. The courtroom is filled with interested spectators, and Judge Medicine is on the bench.

The trial commences, with the prosecution calling its first witness.

I represent Health-laws. I was present on certain nights when the prisoner, or patient, watched with a sick friend. Although I have the superintendence of human affairs, I was personally abused on those occasions. I was told that I must remain silent until called for at this trial, when I would be allowed to testify in the case. Notwithstanding my rules to the contrary, the prisoner watched with the sick every night in the week. When the sick mortal was thirsty, the prisoner gave him drink. During all this time the prisoner attended to his daily labors, partaking of food at irregular intervals, sometimes going to sleep immediately after a heavy meal. At last he committed liver-complaint, which I considered criminal, inasmuch as this offence is deemed punishable with death. Therefore I arrested Mortal Man in behalf of the state (namely, the body) and cast him into prison.

At the time of the arrest the prisoner summoned Physiology, Materia Medica, and Hypnotism to prevent his punishment. The struggle on their part was long. Materia Medica held out the longest, but at length all these assistants resigned to me, Health-laws, and I succeeded in getting Mortal Man into close confinement until I should release him.

The next witness is called:—

I am Coated Tongue. I am covered with a foul fur, placed on me the night of the liver-attack. Morbid Secretion hypnotized the prisoner and took control of his mind, making him despondent.

Another witness takes the stand and testifies:—

I am Sallow Skin. I have been dry, hot, and chilled by turns since the night of the liver-attack. I have lost my healthy hue and become unsightly, although nothing on my part has occasioned this change. I practice daily ablutions and perform my functions as usual, but I am robbed of my good looks.

The next witness testifies:—

I am Nerve, the State Commissioner for Mortal Man. I am intimately acquainted with the plaintiff, Personal Sense, and know him to be truthful and upright, whereas Mortal Man, the prisoner at the bar, is capable of falsehood. I was witness to the crime of liver-complaint. I knew the prisoner would commit it, for I convey messages from my residence in matter, *alias* brain, to body.

Another witness is called for by the Court of Error and says:—

I am Mortality, Governor of the Province of Body, in which Mortal Man resides. In this province there is a statute regarding disease,—namely, that he upon whose person disease is found shall be treated as a criminal and punished with death.

The Judge asks if by doing good to his neighbor, it is possible for man to become diseased, transgress the laws, and merit punishment, and Governor Mortality replies in the affirmative.
Another witness takes the stand and testifies:—

I am Death. I was called for, shortly after the report of the crime, by the officer of the Board of Health, who protested that the prisoner had abused him, and that my presence was required to confirm his testimony. One of the prisoner's friends, Materia Medica, was present when I arrived, endeavoring to assist the prisoner to escape from the hands of justice, *alias* nature's so-called law; but my appearance from the Board of Health changed the purpose of Materia Medica, and he decided at once that the prisoner should die.

The testimony for the plaintiff, Personal Sense, being closed, Judge Medicine arises, and with great solemnity addresses the jury of Mortal

Minds. He analyzes the offence, reviews the testimony, and explains the law relating to liver-complaint. His conclusion is, that laws of nature render disease homicidal. In compliance with a stern duty, his Honor, Judge Medicine, urges the jury not to allow the judgment to be warped by the irrational, unchristian suggestion of Christian Science. The jury must regard in such cases only the evidence of Personal Sense against Mortal Man.

As the Judge proceeds, the prisoner grows restless. His sallow face blanches with fear, and a look of despair and death settles upon it. The case is given to the jury. A brief consultation ensues, and the jury returns a verdict of "Guilty of liver-complaint in the first degree."

Judge Medicine proceeds to pronounce the solemn sentence of death upon the prisoner. Because he has loved his neighbor as himself, Mortal Man has been guilty of benevolence in the first degree, and this has led him into the commission of the second crime, liver-complaint, which material laws condemn as homicide. For this crime, Mortal Man is sentenced to be tortured until he is dead. "May God have mercy on your soul," is the Judge's solemn peroration.

The prisoner is then remanded to his cell (sick bed), and Scholastic Theology is sent for to prepare the frightened sense of Life, God,—which sense must be immortal,—for *death*.

Ah! but Christ, Truth, the spirit of Life and the friend of Mortal Man, can open wide those prison doors and set the captive free. Swift on the wings of divine Love, there comes a dispatch: "Delay the execution; the prisoner is not guilty." Consternation fills the prison-yard. Some exclaim, "It is contrary to law and justice." Others say, "The law of Christ supersedes *our* laws; let us follow Christ."

After much debate and opposition, permission is obtained for a trial in the Court of Spirit, where Christian Science is allowed to appear as counsel for the unfortunate prisoner. Witnesses, judges, and jurors who were at the previous Court of Error are now summoned to appear before the bar of Justice and Eternal Truth.

When the case for Mortal Man *versus* Personal Sense is opened, Mortal Man's counsel regards the prisoner with utmost tenderness. The counsel's earnest, solemn eyes, kindling with hope and triumph, look upward. Then Christian Science turns suddenly to the supreme tribunal, and opens the argument for the defence:—

The prisoner at the bar has been unjustly sentenced. His trial was a tragedy, and is morally illegal. Mortal Man has had no proper counsel in the case. All the testimony has been on the side of Personal Sense, and we shall unearth this foul conspiracy against the liberty and life of Man. The only valid testimony in the case shows the alleged crime never to have been committed. The prisoner is not proved "worthy of death, or of bonds."

Your Honor, the lower court has sentenced Mortal Man to die, but God made man immortal and amenable to Spirit only. Denying justice to the body, that court commended man's immortal spirit to heavenly mercy,—Spirit which is God Himself and man's only lawgiver! Who or what has sinned? Has the body or Mortal Mind committed a criminal deed? Counsellor False Belief has argued that the body should die, while Reverend Theology would console conscious Mortal Mind, which alone is capable of sin and suffering. The body committed no offence. Mortal Man, in obedience to higher law, helped his fellow-man, an act which should result in good to himself as well as to others.

The law of our Supreme Court decrees that whosoever *sinneth* shall die; but good deeds are immortal, bringing joy instead of grief, pleasure instead of pain, and life instead of death. If liver-complaint was committed by trampling on Laws of Health, this was a good deed, for the agent of those laws is an outlaw, a destroyer of Mortal Man's liberty and rights. Laws of Health should be sentenced to die.

Watching beside the couch of pain in the exercise of a love that "is the fulfilling of the law,"—doing "unto others as ye would that they should do unto you,"—this is no infringement of law, for no demand, human or divine, renders it just to punish a man for acting justly. If mortals sin, our Supreme Judge in equity decides what penalty is due for the sin, and Mortal Man can suffer only for his sin. For naught else can he be punished, according to the law of Spirit, God.

Then what jurisdiction has His Honor, Judge Medicine, in this case? To him I might say, in Bible language, "Sittest thou to judge . . . after the law, and commandest . . . to be smitten contrary to the law?" The only jurisdiction to which the prisoner can submit is Truth, Life, and Love. If they condemn him not, neither shall Judge Medicine condemn him; and I ask that the prisoner be restored to the liberty of which he has been unjustly deprived.

The principal witness (the officer of the Health-laws) deposed that he was an eye-witness to the good deeds for which Mortal Man is under sentence of death. After betraying him into the hands of your law, the Health-agent disappeared, to reappear however at the trial as a witness against Mortal Man and in the interest of Personal Sense, a murderer. Your Supreme Court must find the prisoner on the night of the alleged offense to have been acting within the limits of the divine law, and in obedience thereto. Upon this statute hangs all the law and testimony. Giving a cup of cold water in Christ's name, is a Christian service. Laying down his life for a good deed, Mortal Man should find it again. Such acts bear their own justification, and are under the protection of the Most High.

Prior to the night of his arrest, the prisoner summoned two professed friends, Materia Medica and Physiology, to prevent his committing liver-complaint, and thus save him from arrest. But they brought with them Fear, the sheriff, to precipitate the result which they were called to prevent.

It was Fear who handcuffed Mortal Man and would now punish him. You have left Mortal Man no alternative. He must obey your law, fear its consequences, and be punished for his fear. His friends struggled hard to rescue the prisoner from the penalty they considered justly due, but they were compelled to let him be taken into custody, tried, and condemned. Thereupon Judge Medicine sat in judgment on the case, and substantially charged the jury, twelve Mortal Minds, to find the prisoner guilty. His Honor sentenced Mortal Man to die for the very deeds which the divine law compels him to commit. Thus the Court of Error construed obedience to the law of divine Love as disobedience to the law of Life. Claiming to protect Mortal Man in right-doing, that court pronounced a sentence of death for doing right.

One of the principal witnesses, Nerve, testified that he was a ruler of the Body, in which province Mortal Man resides. He also testified that he was on intimate terms with the plaintiff, and knew Personal Sense to be truthful; that he knew Man, and that Man was made in the image of God, but was a criminal. This is a foul aspersion on man's Maker. It blots the fair escutcheon of omnipotence. It indicates malice aforethought, a determination to condemn Man in the interest of Personal Sense. At the bar of Truth, in the presence of divine Justice, before the Judge of our higher tribunal, the Supreme Court of Spirit, and before its jurors, the Spiritual Senses, I proclaim this witness, Nerve, to be destitute of intelligence and truth and to be a false witness.

Man self-destroyed; the testimony of matter respected; Spirit not allowed a hearing; Soul a criminal though recommended to Mercy; the helpless innocent body tortured,—these are the terrible records of your Court of Error, and I ask that the Supreme Court of Spirit reverse this decision.

Here the opposing counsel, False Belief, called Christian Science to contempt of Court. Various notables—Materia Medica, Anatomy, Physiology, Scholastic Theology, and Jurisprudence—rose to the question of expelling Christian Science from the bar, for such high-handed illegality. They declared that Christian Science was overthrowing the judicial proceedings of a regularly constituted court.

But Judge Justice of the Supreme Court of Spirit overruled their motions on the ground that unjust usages were not allowed at the bar of Truth, which ranks above the lower Court of Error.

The attorney, Christian Science, then read from the supreme statute-book, the Bible, certain extracts on the Rights of Man, remarking that the Bible was better authority than Blackstone:—

Let us make man in our image, after our likeness; and let them have dominion.

Behold, I give unto you power . . . over all the power of the enemy;

and nothing shall by any means hurt you.

If a man keep my saying, he shall never see death.

Then Christian Science proved the witness, Nerve, to be a perjurer. Instead of being a ruler in the Province of Body, in which Mortal Man was reported to reside, Nerve was an insubordinate citizen, putting in false claims to office and bearing false witness against Man. Turning suddenly to Personal Sense, by this time silent, Christian Science continued:—

I ask your arrest in the name of Almighty God on three distinct charges of crime, to wit: perjury, treason, and conspiracy against the rights and life of man.

Then Christian Science continued:—

Another witness, equally inadequate, said that on the night of the crime a garment of foul fur was spread over him by Morbid Secretion, while the facts in the case show that this fur is a foreign substance, imported by False Belief, the attorney for Personal Sense, who is in partnership with Error and smuggles Error's goods into market without the inspection of Soul's government officers. When the Court of Truth summoned Furred Tongue for examination, he disappeared and was never heard of more.

Morbid Secretion is not an importer or dealer in fur, but we have heard Materia Medica explain how this fur is manufactured, and we know Morbid Secretion to be on friendly terms with the firm of Personal Sense, Error, & Co., receiving pay from them and introducing their goods into the market. Also, be it known that False Belief, the counsel for the plaintiff, Personal Sense, is a buyer for this firm. He manufactures for it, keeps a furnishing store, and advertises largely for his employers.

Death testified that he was absent from the Province of Body, when a message came from False Belief, commanding him to take part in the homicide. At this request Death repaired to the spot where the liver-complaint was in process, frightening away Materia Medica, who was then manacling the prisoner in the attempt to save him. True, Materia Medica was a misguided participant in the misdeed for which the Health-officer had Mortal Man in custody, though Mortal Man was innocent.

Christian Science turned from the abashed witnesses, his words flashing as lightning in the perturbed faces of these worthies, Scholastic Theology, Materia Medica, Physiology, the blind Hypnotism, and the masked Personal Sense, and said:—

God will smite you, O whited walls, for injuring in your ignorance the unfortunate Mortal Man who sought your aid in struggles against liver-complaint and Death. You came to his rescue, only to fasten upon him an offence of which he was innocent. You aided and abetted Fear and Health-laws. You betrayed Mortal Man, meanwhile declaring Disease to be God's servant and the righteous executor of His laws. Our higher statutes declare you all, witnesses, jurors, and judges, to be offenders, awaiting the sentence which General Progress and Divine Love will pronounce.

We send our best detectives to whatever locality is reported to be haunted by Disease, but on visiting the spot, they learn that Disease was never there, for he could not possibly elude their search. Your Material Court of Errors, when it condemned Mortal Man on the ground of hygienic disobedience, was manipulated by the oleaginous machinations of the counsel, False Belief, whom Truth arraigns before the supreme bar of Spirit to answer for his crime. Morbid Secretion is taught how to make sleep befool reason before sacrificing mortals to their false gods.

Mortal Minds were deceived by your attorney, False Belief, and were influenced to give a verdict delivering Mortal Man to Death. Good deeds are transformed into crimes, to which you attach penalties; but no warping of justice can render disobedience to the so-called laws of Matter, disobedience to God, or an act of homicide. Even penal law holds homicide, under stress of circumstances, to be justifiable. Now what greater justification can any deed have, than that it is for the good of one's neighbor? Wherefore, then, in the name of outraged justice, do you sentence Mortal Man for ministering to the wants of his fellow-man in obedience to divine law? You cannot trample upon the decree of the Supreme Bench. Mortal Man has his appeal to Spirit, God, who sentences only for sin.

The false and unjust beliefs of your human mental legislators compel them to enact wicked laws of sickness and so forth, and then render obedience to these laws punishable as crime. In the presence of the Supreme Lawgiver, standing at the bar of Truth, and in accordance with the divine statutes, I repudiate the false testimony of Personal Sense. I ask that he be forbidden to enter against Mortal Man any more suits to be tried at the Court of Material Error. I appeal to the just and equitable decisions of divine Spirit to restore to Mortal Man the rights of which he has been deprived.

Here the counsel for the defense closed, and the Chief Justice of the Supreme Court, with benign and imposing presence, comprehending and defining all law and evidence, explained from his statute-book, the Bible, that any so-called law, which undertakes to punish aught but sin, is null and void.

He also decided that the plaintiff, Personal Sense, not be permitted to enter any suits at the bar of Soul, but to be enjoined to keep perpetual silence, and in case of temptation, to be given heavy bonds for good behavior. He concluded his charge thus:—

The plea of False Belief we deem unworthy of a hearing. Let what False Belief utters, now and forever, fall into oblivion, "unknelled, uncoffined, and unknown." According to our statute, Material Law is a liar who cannot bear witness against Mortal Man, neither can Fear arrest Mortal Man nor can Disease cast him into prison. Our law refuses to recognize Man as sick or dying, but holds him to be forever in the image and likeness of his Maker. Reversing the testimony of Personal Sense and the decrees of the Court of Error in favor of Matter, Spirit decides in favor of Man and against Matter. We further recommend that Materia Medica adopt Christian Science and that Health-laws, Mesmerism, Hypnotism, Oriental Witchcraft, and Esoteric Magic be publicly executed at the hands of our sheriff, Progress.

The Supreme Bench decides in favor of intelligence, that no law outside of divine Mind can punish or reward Mortal Man. Your personal jurors in the Court of Error are myths. Your attorney, False Belief, is an impostor, persuading Mortal Minds to return a verdict contrary to law and gospel. The plaintiff, Personal Sense, is recorded in our Book of books as a liar. Our great Teacher of mental jurisprudence speaks of him also as "a murderer from the beginning." We have no trials for sickness before the tribunal of divine Spirit. There, Man is adjudged innocent of transgressing physical laws, because there are no such laws. Our statute is spiritual, our Government is divine. "Shall not the Judge of all the earth do right?"

The jury of Spiritual Senses agreed at once upon a verdict, and there resounded throughout the vast audience-chamber of Spirit the cry, Not guilty. The prisoner rose up regenerated, strong, free. We noticed, as he shook hands with his counsel, Christian Science, that all sallowness and debility had disappeared. His form was erect and commanding, his countenance beaming with health and happiness. Divine Love had cast out fear. Mortal Man, no longer sick and in prison, walked forth, his feet "beautiful upon the mountains," as of one "that bringeth good tidings."

Neither animal magnetism nor hypnotism enters into the practice of Christian Science, in which truth cannot be reversed, but the reverse of error is true. An improved belief cannot retrograde. When Christ changes a belief of sin or of sickness into a better belief, then belief melts into spiritual understanding, and sin, disease, and death disappear. Christ, Truth, gives mortals temporary food until the material, transformed with the ideal, disappears, and man is clothed and fed spiritually. St. Paul says, "Work out your own salvation with fear and trembling." Jesus said, "Fear not, little flock; for it is your Father's good pleasure to give you the kingdom." This truth is Christian Science.

Christian Scientists, be a law unto yourselves that mental malpractice cannot harm you either when asleep or awake.[114]

*   *   *

I come from a "privileged" perspective: I was once a Christian Scientist. I was sincere, worked hard at the practice of my faith, and assumed progressively more responsible positions in my branch church. I received class instruction, the prerequisite for becoming an authorized healer. I had been called on for healings by other believers. I was convinced of the righteousness and invincibility of my cause. I left the church when I failed to gain a healing of crippling rheumatoid arthritis.

"We cannot serve two masters," Scientists are admonished, and I left because I felt I must. If I was to seek healing through drugs, I must give up Science. It would be hypocritical to have done anything else. Perhaps someday, I told myself, I would return.

When I left the Mother Church, my teacher phoned to tell me the clerk of the Mother Church had informed him I was resigning. He said I didn't need to leave the church if I submitted to medical care. I couldn't be treated by a practitioner, but I could continue to read and study, to attend services, to maintain my membership in the Mother Church and my branch. And even if I quit the Mother Church and the branches, I would still belong to his association, and could attend the annual meetings. But he would prefer I didn't come if I were somehow incapacitated or forced to use "an obvious medical appliance of some kind. You can understand."

My rheumatoid arthritis had developed slowly. Before I finally sought medical care, the pain in my feet had become so intense that it took me ten to fifteen minutes to lever myself out of bed every day, and every morning's first steps were like walking barefoot on broken glass. I would limber up as the day went on, but my arms were drawing up at the elbows into a permanent contracture, and my hands collapsing as the disease consumed the cartilage in their joints. Though twisting off a car gas cap could bring tears of agony, I still worked to deny the aggressive mental suggestion that material sense is anything other than an impotent false claim about God and His ever-harmonious, divine idea, man. I didn't walk so much as hobble out to the platform on Sunday mornings.

But by then, almost my entire circle of friendships and working relationships centered on fellow Scientists. I put on a good, stoical front, and no one in my church ever asked me why I couldn't straighten my arms or walk smoothly out to my seat on the stage. I was an actor in a musical drama scripted by Mary Baker Eddy, a star before an adoring audience who saw not me but the role I we had both chosen.

We were all working mightily, doing our Christianly scientific best to reject any sensation of mortal error, any lie that would claim to attach itself to the revelation and the revelator: She who discovered the True

Science, founded the Mother Church, and, through her writings and her will (both literally and legally), was forever the leader of the movement. Because of my relative exposure to malpractice as both First Reader and a journalist, I must understand that I was like a lightning rod to error's thunderbolts. Error, personal sense, was attacking the movement through me, suicidally demanding to enthrone itself in matter.

Mark Twain was right. Mrs. Eddy had created something far more valuable than sweet reason. She had indeed created an *environment*, which is easily worth, to the average consumer, far more than something so limiting as life confined to the evidence of material sense.

We all fought to defend her *environment*.

*   *   *

Did Christian Science influence my professional decisions?

Yes. While a Christian Scientist and a newspaper reporter, I discovered that a man arrested for sexual abuse of young boys was a Christian Science Sunday school teacher. He had taken Polaroid pictures—no risk of a phone call to cops by an incensed commercial film developer—of young boys nude on his bed, *Christian Science Sentinels* clearly visible on a bedside table.

I asked the deputy district attorney handling the case if there was any evidence he had abused any of the children in his Sunday school class. I was told "no." I was the only reporter who worked the courthouse regularly, and I knew that no other reporter was likely to stumble onto the Christian Science angle. I discussed the matter with a practitioner, who suggested an "out": Since none of the victims came from his class, there really wasn't any reason to mention it, was there? Thus relieved, I omitted a significant fact from a story, priding myself for thus denying error's efforts to attack the church.

I also notified the clerk of the branch church to which the man belonged, and told her both of the details of the arrest, including the photographs, and that I did not intend to include the fact of his religion in my report.

I don't like today what I did then. But I was convinced of the rightness of my actions. My intentions were honorable; my motives, the best I could imagine.

NOTES

Nathan A. Talbot, Committee on Publication for the Mother Church, was gracious enough to grant a lengthy interview on the current challenges confronting the church. To present his views in their entirety, I am placing them in an Appendix, found on page 337.

1. Bernard DeVoto, ed. (New York: Perennial Library), pp. 15-16.
2. One factor in the rise of Islam was its promise to males of a heaven filled with compliant, nubile houris, unfailing virility, and endless orgasms.
3. In a letter she wrote to the *Boston Post*, published 5 June 1882.
4. "Retrospection and Introspection," from *Prose Works*, p. 31.
5. Ibid., p. 32.
6. Dagobert B. Runes, ed., *Dictionary of Philosophy* (Totowa, N.J.: Littlefield, Adams, 1962), p. 320.
7. Mark Baker Eddy, "Pulpit and Press," a sermon delivered in the Mother Church 6 January 1895, from *Prose Works*.
8. "The First Church of Christ, Scientist and Miscellany," pp. vi, vii, in *Prose Works*. Hereafter abbreviated as *My*.
9. See Edwin Frandin Dakin's *Mrs. Eddy: A Biography of a Virginal Mind* (New York: Charles Scribner's Sons, 1930), p. 530.
10. According to Dakin's biography, drawn in large measure from an earlier work by Georgine Milmine.
11. Dakin, op. cit., pp. 165-169.
12. *Rev.* 10:2.
13. Emphasis in original, op. cit., p. 317.
14. By Mary Baker Eddy (Boston: Christian Science Publishing Society).
15. Mary Baker Eddy, *Church Manual of The First Church of Christ Scientist* (Boston, Mass., 1908), pp. 64-65 (hereafter *Manual*). The following section, "A Member not a Leader," mandates that no one but she shall be "called Leader by members of this Church, when this term is used in connection with Christian Science."
16. See "Reply to Mark Twain" in *The First Church of Christ, Scientist and Miscellany*, pp. 302-303.
17. Last revised in 1906 (Boston: Christian Publishing Society); henceforth authorized editions carry uniform page and line numbering.
18. In *Christian Science* (Minneapolis: Bethany House, 1957), pp. 7-13.
19. "Christian Scientists shall not report for publication the number of members of The Mother Church, nor that of the branch churches. According to the Scripture they shall turn away from personality and numbering the people." *Manual*, Art. VIII, sect. 28.
20. *S & H*, p. 494.
21. The soloist in the Beverly Hills church for many years was a Mormon.
22. *Manual*, Art. XVI, Sec. 1.
23. Others are doubtful. One Hollywood actress once said she went to testimony meetings to practice her craft: to tell a story and judge her effect on the audience. The actress was Talia Shire, according to a Christian Science teacher, the late David W. Rennie, C.S.B.
24. This is also a fair description of my own class experience. Students were supposed to keep the fact of their going to class secret, to prevent mortal mind from grabbing at them. While teachers can instruct no more than thirty pupils a year, enrollments tended to be half that a decade ago, according to my teacher.
25. *Manual*, Art. IV.
26. Ibid., Art. VI, Sec. 2.
27. In my own class instruction there were only two points clearly stated by my teacher not made repeatedly clear in the open writings. First was that Jesus didn't rise from the

dead, because he didn't die on the cross; he only seemed to die to the personal sense of those watching. The second teaching was that the Roman Catholic Church is the Antichrist, the Beast of the Revelation of St. John; but, we were told, "don't make a big deal of it."

28. Op. cit., p. 42.

29. *Manual*, Art. III, Sec. 6.

30. *Manual*, Art. I, Sec. 9. The next longest entries are a pair to be found in the article on COPs.

31. *S & H*, 59: 8-11.

32. The Church, following in this vein, does not celebrate Easter or Christmas—the *spiritual* Christ was never born into matter, and nor could he die. Neither are the birthdays of Scientists celebrated.

33. *S & H*, 69:26–30

34. Dakin, p. 503.

35. *Boston Post*, 5 June 1882.

36. His first unauthorized title was *Practical Scientific Christianity* (Santa Rosa, Calif.: Meadow Book, 1983).

37. *Manual* Art. XXXI, Sec. 2.

38. One notable rebellion of the Trustees of the Christian Science Publishing Society and the Mother Church Board of Directors found its way into the courts in the mid-1920s in *Eustace v. Dickey,* producing reams of scathing insider gossip for the press, but leaving the Mother Church Board in control. An earlier challenge by one Mother Church Director against the others who had ousted him resulted in what Oxford sociologist Brian R. Wilson called a "protracted and sordid lawsuit" upholding the majority's action. (From his article "Christian Science" in the *Encyclopedia Britannica Macropedia*, V. 4, pp. 562-564, 15th ed., 1982.)

39. Copies of all publications are recirculated by branch church literature communities. Got too many back issues? Give them to the branch church, and they'll pop up in laundromats and literature boxes in front of reading rooms and in an occasionsal unexpected site, a restaurant, laundromat, or gas station, perhaps. Hospital waiting rooms are favorite targets, too.

40. From the writer's own experience, practitioners often advise converts to tread gently when dealing with non-Scientists, to protect the unfolding of the divine idea in the new believer's consciousness. This saves the student from any threatening encounters before belief is firmly established to the point where "appropriate" responses are automatic.

41. From Mrs. Eddy's "spiritual sense of the Lord's Prayer," the culmination of the first chapter of *Science and Health.*

42. *S & H*, 468:9–15.

43. *S & H*, 414:32–415:1.

44. At the time of my son's birth, Dr. Hale, the obstetrician, required parents to take a natural childbirth class, particularly if the husband was to attend the delivery.

45. *S & H*, 251:1–6.

46. Dr. Hale, who attended at my son's birth, also attended at Seth's.

47. *S & H*, 410:15–17.

48. *S & H*, 464:13–18.

49. *S & H*, 254:16–32.

50. The tape recording was ruined when the tape twisted while the machine was running.

51. *S & H*, 583:10–11.

52. "Responded" is part of the loaded language of the police world. "Responded" is shorthand for "responded to the scene," or, in non-cop talk, "in response to a call, I went to the place where it happened." The officer, writing the day of the event, specifically adds that Mr. Hall responded "when he was first called."

53. *Manual*, Art. XXXIII.

54. *Manual*, Art. XXXIII, Sec. 4.

55. See Carnesciali's July 1984 *Newsletter.*

56. *Legal Rights and Obligations*, p. 62. Interestingly, the section immediately proceeding the directive on child cases involves practitioners called to testify in court about a patient or the practice. Any practitioner in such a fix "should contact the office of Committee on Publication before giving such testimony."

57. *Legal Rights and Obligations*, p. 63.

58. *Miscellaneous Writings*, p. 104.

59. *Mrs. Eddy, The Biography of a Virginal Mind* (New York: Charles Scribner's Sons), pp. 392–395.

60. *Manual*, p. 79.

61. Dakin, op. cit., pp. 393–395.

62. According to Nathan A. Talbot, Mother Church Committee on Publication, in an interview with the writer.

63. A recent, relevant example is *Freedom and Responsibility, Christian Science Healing for Children*, assembled by the COP and published in late 1989 by the Christian Science Publishing Society, the media arm of the movement—a copy of which was given me by Nathan A. Talbot.

64. Mark Twain, *Christian Science* (1907, reprinted in 1986 by Prometheus Books, Buffalo, N.Y.), p. 54.

65. Cited by *Los Angeles Times* religion writer John Dart in "Healing church shows signs it may be ailing," 20 December 1986, Part 8, page 1.

66. *Manual*, Art. XXIII, Sec. 7.

67. The since defunct Twenty-sixth Church of Christ Scientist, Los Angeles, during the author's term as First Reader and President.

68. Of the 2,289 English-speaking national based churches and societies, 1,895 are in the U.S., 206 in the British Isles, 79 in Canada, 68 in Australia and New Zealand, and 30 in the Republic of South Africa. The remainder are scattered throughout Puerto Rico, the Virgin Islands, and former outposts of the British colonial empire. The figures for healers are 2,703 congregations in English-dominated lands: 2,327 in the U.S.; 211 in the British Isles; Australia/New Zealand 65; Canada, 59; South Africa, 32, and other North American, 9.

69. A dozen of the remaining names are traditionally female: two "Elaines," and a "Virginia," "Ginny," "Marie," "Susan," "Patricia," "Helen," "Elizabeth," "Beverly," "Roberta Ann," and "Alene Faith." They are included in the non-Mrs./non-Miss total because I have met a male "Shirley" and a male "Beverly."

70. Graduating student totals from the school quarterly, *Principia Purpose*, as reported by William F. Simpson in the *Journal of the American Medical Association*, 22–29 September 1989, 262:1567–68.

71. *My.* 355:6–14.

72. At this writing two of the five are women.

73. *S & H*, p. 57.

74. Reprinted in *Miscellaneous Writings*, pp. 388–389.

75. 15 Nov. 1988. p. B-7, in a report by David Stipp.

76. *Writer's Market* (Cincinnati: Writer's Digest Books, 1989), p. 330.

77. *Manual*, Art. VIII, Sec. 9. The section's continuation—"and it shall be the duty of the Directors to see that these periodicals are ably edited and kept abreast of the times"— is a clear rationale for the Board's new, electronic *Monitor*.

78. To complement the mental healers, Mrs. Eddy created the position of Christian Science Nurse. These individuals fulfill the mechanics of sick room care, including cleansing and dressing of wounds, bathing, and assisting in movement. They are graduates of Mother Church—recognized courses held at "benevolent associations" (church parlance for nursing homes). The nurse does not play the role of practitioner or spiritual healer, but is required to maintain a spiritual view of the patient in their own thought. Practitioners and nurses work together on cases. The July 1989 *Journal* lists 490 nurses in the United States, many of whom work only part-time. The largest number, 133, or 27 percent, is found in California. Second is Massachusetts (home of the large church-founded Chestnut Hill Benevolent Association, housed in one of Mrs. Eddy's former homes) with 38, followed by Florida with 37. Together, these three states account for 42 percent of the nurse listings. There are no nurses listed in 14 states and the District of Columbia (the one nurse listed for the Capital carries a "See Annandale, Virginia" note). The Church once maintained two Benevolent Homes, convalescent/old age residences, one at Chestnut Hill (the former Eddy residence), the other in San Francisco. These have since been disestablished and are now private institutions which, along with many other non-profit "sanitoria," serve the aging community.

79. From amicus brief submitted in *People* v. *Walker*.

80. *Manual*, Art. IV, Sec. 1.

81. *Manual*, Art. VIII, Sect. 12.

82. *My.*, p. 205.

83. See, for instance, *S & H* 240:18–26.

84. *S & H*, 443:14–444:6.

85. *My.*, p. 220.

86. *S & H*, 237:15–22.

87. G. E. Wilson, "Christian Science and Longevity," *Journal of Forensic Science*, 1965, 1:43–60.

88. According to a Reuters dispatch quoted in the *Sacramento Bee* 30, September 1989, Scene-10.

89. *S & H*, p. 454.

90. "Comparative Longevity in a College Cohort of Christian Scientists," *Journal of the American Medical Association*, 22/29 September 1989, pp. 1657-1658.

91. Janny Scott, "Mormon ways shown to be healthy," *Los Angeles Times* wire service story in the *Sacramento Bee*, 6 December 1989, p. A-5.

92. The county Health Department was later notified and the room sterilized, according to Mrs. Scott's testimony.

93. Polanski fled the country after completing half the 90-day time the judge insisted he spend in state prison. Earlier in the proceedings, I was called by Dalton to testify on Polanski's behalf, to correct an erroneous wire service photo caption that had led the judge to demand Polanski immediately commence his sentence.

94. *American Medical Association Encyclopedia of Medicine*, p. 675.

95. See Doris Sue Wong, "Judge keeps manslaughter charge against Christian Scientist parents," *Boston Globe*, 23 April 1989.

96. See Jeffrey Good, "Dying for their beliefs," *St. Petersburg (Florida) Times*, 9 April 1989, p. 1-B.

97. J. W. Brown, "Parents of girl who died of cancer charged with negligent homicide," *Phoenix* (Arizona) *Gazette*, 10 August 1989, p. 1.

98. Tamra Jones, "Child Deaths Put Faith on Trial," *Los Angeles Times*, 27 June 1989, pp. 1, 16.

99. Herb Michelson, "Prayer healing—when is it legal?," *Sacramento Bee*, 18 August 1985, p. A-19.

100. *People* v. *Arnold* (1967) 66 Cal.2d 438, 452.

101. Laura Sessions Stepp, "Doctors decry faith healing for kids," Washington Post story reprinted in the *Sacramento Bee*, 10 January 1988, p. A-14.

102. Tamara Jones, "Child Deaths Put Faith on Trial," *Los Angeles Times*, 27 June 1989, pp. 1,16.

103. *People* v. *Penny*, 44 Cal.2d, 861, 879.

104. The reference is to the state Welfare and Institutions Code.

105. 321 U.S. 158, 168 (88 L.Ed. 645, 653, 64 S. Ct. 438).

106. The source for this information was an article by Nathan A. Talbot, manager of the Committee on Publication, in the *New England Journal of Medicine*, 1986, 26:1641–42.

107. Not even Justice Broussard, who dissented from the decision to allow Laurie Walker to be charged with felony child endangerment, agreed. His dispute with the charge under section 273 was that section 270 covered the possibility of "great bodily harm or death" resulting from lack of medical care, while section 273 concerns, not medical care, but "willful active conduct causing harm or endangering the child's health or person." Therefore, 273 could not be charged against Laurie Walker because of the 1976 amendment. She could, however, be tried for manslaughter, an unrelated statute.

108. Committee on Bioethics, American Academy of Pediatrics, *Pediatrics*, vol. 81, no. 1, January 1988, pp. 169–170.

109. Associated Press, "Christian Science Pair Convicted," *Sacramento Bee*, 5 August 1989, p. 4.

110. Associated Press dispatch, "No jail for Christian Science couple," *Sacramento Bee*, 3 Nov., p. B-5.

111. Associated Press dispatch, reprinted in the *Sacramento Bee*, 5 August 1989, p. A-5.

112. *People* v. *Zimmerman*, a case covered by the writer while at the *Evening Outlook*.

113. *S & H*, p. 441.

114. *S & H*, p. 430–442.

PART II

WHEN FAITH HEALING IS FRAUD

Got stomach cancer? Liver disease? Suffering from abdominal pains and afraid to go to a doctor? Just been told you're going to have to take dangerous medications for the rest of your life?

Then talk to Brother Joe.

He'll rub you down with eucalyptus oil a few times, then plunge his bare hands right into your gut and pull out a bloody mass of tissue, the source of all your troubles. You'll be healed. There won't even be a scar. No insurance claims, no anesthetics, no infections, no incapacitation, no pain, no metastases reaching deadly fingers into the brain, the lungs, the sexual organs, the gut, gnawing away at your life, your dignity, your humanity.

No, none of that. Bother Joe, Jose Bugarin, is the master of an arcane art. He doesn't use a knife, because he doesn't need one. He has the Power, the Power from God. When he reaches inside you, molecules part before his fingers . . . the Red Sea before Moses's wand.

He's a psychic surgeon.

KNOCK THREE TIMES AND ASK FOR BROTHER JOE

For Jerry Smith, it began with a note. Frank Garcia, a lawyer on the Sacramento County Counsel's staff, had called and left a message about a Filipino, Brother Joe, who "operated" on folks with his bare hands.

Garcia's wife, Stephanie Doran, had gone to see Brother Joe after her physician recommended surgery for a breast growth. Doran is a professional psychic who advertises herself as a crime-solving specialist consulted by federal and local law enforcement agencies and insurance agencies. According to her ad in the Fall 1988 issue of *Evolving Times*, a Sacramento-based New Age periodical, she "is especially unique in her field of psychometry by being able to hold a personal item, such as a weapon or a piece of clothing belonging to either the victim or suspect, and with the energy transmitted by the item, describe with amazing detail and clarity how the crime was committed, the weapon used, location, hair and eye color, initials and sometimes names. Stephanie is recognized by other psychics and law enforcement as 'The Psychic's Psychic.' "

Smith is a burly, bearded, mountain of a man, standing six feet one inch tall. He wears a size forty-six coat and weighs in at 250 pounds. He'd been a cop for ten years: three of them as a deputy sheriff in nearby Yolo County, two as a California Highway Patrolman, and the last five as an investigator for the state Board of Medical Quality Assurance (BMQA)—the agency charged with regulating health care professionals. As he read over the note, he scented a crime.

Garcia had learned about Brother Joe from one of his clients and had passed the information on to his wife. Brother Joe, Garcia was told, had apparently removed a cancerous tumor from the throat of the client's sister-in-law. Garcia and Doran contacted Helene Athena Mellas, a minister ordained by the mail-order Universal Life Church (which makes a minister of anyone who sends cash, a check, or a money order), who was promoting a weekend series of treatments with Brother Joe. Mellas was a New Age healer who professed to "read" and treat the auras of her clients, led chanting sessions, and had recently branched out into crystal healing. Doran knew Mellas: They had met three years earlier, at the home of another member of Sacramento's psychic community.[1]

On 6 March 1987, Garcia and Doran went to a home on the expensive, exclusive shores of Lake Tahoe on the California-Nevada border and shelled out $165 for four sessions with Joe, each of which lasted less than two minutes. Garcia said Brother Joe, a short, dark-skinned man who spoke broken English, pulled a few "tumors" from Doran—one "looked like a chicken gizzard," another "like a piece of curly salad pasta."[2]

Doran was impressed, but Garcia smelled fraud. On 10 March, the lawyer called the BMQA. He reached Nancy Kraemer, the agency's local representative. "Mr. Garcia's wife, who is a very intelligent individual, believes she has been cured of the growth by Brother Joe," Kraemer quotes Garcia as telling her. "However Mr. Garcia is going to insist that she see her physician for follow-up." Garcia also told Kraemer that he estimated Brother Joe and associates pulled in $5,000 that day from the thirty or so patients who had responded to Mellas's announcement. The healer would be back in the area the first weekend in April.

Smith launched an investigation, beginning with a 10 March interview with Garcia at his county office. The lawyer said he was worried not only about his wife, but about his client's sister, who "now feels that she is 'cured of cancer.' "

A week later, Smith took his information to Chuck D'Arcy, supervising deputy district attorney for Sacramento County. After a verbal report by the investigator, D'Arcy gave him written authorization to make secret recordings. Later that afternoon, with a tape recorder running, Smith's supervisor, Lynn Thornton, phoned Mellas.

LYNN THORNTON: "Hi, my name is Lynn Bowman, and I am trying to make an appointment to see Brother Joe."
HELENE MELLAS: "Who referred you, please?"

When "Bowman" gave Doran's name, Mellas softened. "I just have to be a little cautious about this," she said.

Bowman told Mellas her brother, Dave Cooper (actually Investigator Dave Thornton, Lynn Thornton's real-life husband) had just been diagnosed with lung cancer. "Is he getting any kind of chemo or anything like that?" Mellas asked. When told that treatment hadn't begun, Mellas said, "Good, because the healing is far more effective before that kind of energy hits the body."

Mellas told Bowman she had been working with Brother Joe Bugarin "for nearly three years," and recommended that Cooper "have as many appointments as possible, and the most he can have is four a day," at least two hours apart. Eight appointments were scheduled, four for each of the two days Bugarin would be in town. "It's $45 for the first one and $40 for every one after that. . . . It's better to have more than not any," she said.

Then, at Bowman's request, Mellas described the process of psychic surgery: "The hands of the healer become electromagnetic in energy, and they attract whatever is foreign to the body. And depending on many, many different things, at times they can see better than others. But at least they do sense—through, they say through spirits, and they say 'stop' when the body has all of the energy it can stand at the time."

Indeed, Mellas said, the healer may say the patient doesn't need any more treatments, or that he or she should come back at a later date. Mellas said she had been doing healing herself "through my hands" since 1978. "Joe started that way, but he is now blessed with the ability to enter the body. His hands go in as if your hands go through water. So that is what he does. That's why we have to be very careful about this kind of thing because we don't want to lose the blessing of having him come and do this kind of work, [which] is really frowned upon [by the American Medical Association]. And he would be in terrible shape, you know, so you have to be very careful."

Mellas also offered some pre-surgery suggestions: "Joe recommends that one has no liquor and no red meat the day before and the day after the healing . . . and have him shower before coming because we ask that he does not shower when he gets home that evening. This keeps from disturbing the energy of the healing and could be more effective."

Then came this: "The other thing is that the donations must be in cash, because Joe has no way of handling checks." Mellas told Lynn Bowman to tell her brother to "bring a robe and put it in a discreet bag or something because I'm not trying to wave flags at my neighbors of what is going on."

The next day, Garcia called Smith to say that his spouse had gone back to her physician, who took an X-ray, which revealed that the supposedly healed tumor had grown in size, requiring immediate surgery.

*   *   *

The stage was set. Jerry Smith—now Dave Bowman, Lynn Bowman's husband for the sting—and his two fellow officers were about to witness what was either a medical miracle or a sleight-of-hand scam. Their investigation would lead to the prosecution of Jose Bugarin and Helene

Mellas, and would uncover their links to a travel agent who had been a key player in a landmark federal regulatory action.

The case would raise two key questions: When is the act of healing itself a crime? And is the cover of religion sufficient to protect a criminal preying on the weak and helpless?

STAR-POWERED
MIRACLE

It's the New Age, that bastard child of the Acid and Me generations. LSD tickled some cells that squirted some chemicals inside the skull, setting off a literal brainstorm. While the drug experience often shattered old perceptions of the world, what acid didn't do was provide any lasting answers. The tripper always came down, always to the same world. But for many, the answer to acid was to be found in doctrines of mystical surrender, which is what the New Age is all about.

Not all acid-heads became mystics. But for many, the answer to acid was to be found in doctrines of mystical surrender, which is what the New Age is all about.[3]

*   *   *

If any single figure has come to embody New Age beliefs for the celebrity-loving media, it is Shirley MacLaine. In a series of semi-autobiographical books—she admits to some altering of reality—she had described her transformation from actress and political activist to activist and spiritual seeker to professional spiritual guru and to actress/non-guru-guru.

But more than that, she is a "great communicator" whose theatrical skills make her a powerful and eloquent advocate for her beliefs, which turn out to be a typical New Age collection of folklore and superstition. She's the movement's hottest publicist.

In May 1989, Bantam Books published *Going Within: A Guide for Inner Transformation*, in which she tells of some truly remarkable people and events she had witnessed, including one South American guru who could urinate a stream of light.[4]

But the most remarkable event of all, the final miracle recounted in a miracle-laden book, is an event that happened at her home in Malibu, California, apparently during the 1988 Christmas season, when she played host to a Filipino healer who claimed to be able to thrust his hands through bare skin, remove diseased tissue, and pull out his hand without leaving a scar, despite the considerable blood in evidence.

The healer's name is Alex Orbito.

MacLaine first saw Orbito in action in a film, then in person in Las Vegas, where he extracted "negative energy clots" and "negative stress clots" from her abdomen. She was so overwhelmed that she broke down and cried. Then she brought him to Malibu, when "nearly one hundred came on Christmas Day and the day after."[5] From there he went to a "New Thought" church in Ojai, a small community north of Los Angeles, long a haven for Theosophists and other mystics.

MacLaine profited spiritually and financially from her encounter with Orbito. She learned about a marvelous New Age art, and she garnered a chapter for her best-seller.[6] Orbito profited as well: He gets about a hundred dollars a minute for his services, according to magician James "The Amazing" Randi, who is the premier authority on pseudoscientific fraud.[7] Thanks to MacLaine, Orbito presumably collected a hundred $100-a-minute offerings in two days, and was able to return home to the Philippines with a large amount of cash and publicity.

*   *   *

In her book, MacLaine claims that Orbito enabled her to plunge her own hand "up to the wrist" into the abdomen of a friend. Experiencing an event which, if true, was utterly miraculous, she explained it in almost the same words Helene Mellas used in her interviews with investigators. MacLaine writes:

> I can accept the concept that psychic surgery is performed through a spiritual connection with the Divine by separating the living atoms one from another with an energy that doesn't violate, but simply and gently slips *through* the physical, much as a hand slips gently, without violation, through liquid. I don't need a scientist to tell me if it's true or false. I know it because it happened to me. (emphasis in original)[8]

Psychic surgery has won supporters on the fringes of the academic community as well. The best known is Stanley Krippner, who holds a doctorate in psychology and directs the Center for Consciousness at Saybrook Institute in San Francisco. Krippner and Alberto Villoldo, an adjunct professor at California State University, San Francisco, have written sympathetically of the Filipino healers and their counterparts in Brazil,

Mexico, and the United States.

In *The Realms of Healing*,[9] the two academics adopt a paradoxical stance: They acknowledge that sleight-of-hand tricks may be a part of the healer's repertoire, but hold that patient skepticism may inhibit the healing process. Krippner, the (relatively) more skeptical of the two, agrees that no scientific study of the art can be conducted without the assistance of a magician, a professional in the ancient art of deception.

But the evidence is overwhelming: Psychic surgery is a fraud, one of the oldest on the books, and has never been successfully performed under scientifically controlled circumstances.

Developed in ancient or prehistoric times and used by primitive cultures, it was a means to cope with sickness and death. The shaman would palm bits of one thing or another and pretend to pull them from the patient's body. But the idea was that the "miracle" was a focus for relieving anxiety— that of the patient and those close to him or her.

Though the desperately ill still comprise a large share of those who fly to the Philippines for treatment, today's patients are apt to be New Age devotees seeking to master the art for themselves. For them, psychic surgery confers another kind of relief: In its "proof" of the miraculous, it provides an escape from the anxieties of living in a world that is merely material.

As Orbito tells MacLaine: "Westerners especially feel they need that kind of *physical* proof. . ." (emphasis in original).[10]

THROUGH THE EYES
OF A BELIEVER

Then they began to tell me about the Philippines. They had been there a time or two already. I was very excited about it. I felt such a pull toward it that I thought, that, well, maybe this is what I'm supposed to do next.

—Rev. Helene Mellas

The Rev. Helene Athena Mellas was born in McAlester, in East-Central Oklahoma, a small town founded in 1870 as a trading post in what was then the Choctaw nation of Indian Territory, at the juncture of the Texas and California trails. Today a county seat, McAlester's two major local institutions are the Oklahoma State Prison and the U.S. Navy Ammunition Depot. A railroad town since 1872, it has produced coal, gas, clothing, and processed food.

McAlester also has a strong mystical heritage. Located here are the headquarters of the Scottish Rite Masons, a quasi-religious fraternal lodge with strong mystical underpinnings and complex initiation rites. Here too is the affiliated International Temple of the Order of the Rainbow for Girls.[11]

Both of Helene Mellas's parents were deeply religious. Her mother was a minister's daughter, and her father had been a lay minister in the First Christian Church. But he was not a conventional Oklahoma Christian. He was also a Rosicrucian for thirty years, his daughter said.

"And so I grew up with a metaphysical background, too, and I believe very strongly in reincarnation and many of the things that came with that," she would later say.

She and her brothers were closer to their father than their mother.

Her father, she said, "was very good at making me feel better. In fact, I think all through childhood I never, never called for mother if I were hurting. Neither did my brothers.

"For the first year I was very healthy," she said. After that, however, she suffered from an ongoing variety of disorders. As a result of tonsillitis, both she and a brother had emergency surgery on the dining room table; the local hospital was closed. The school years brought one illness after another, and finally she contracted rheumatic fever. The agonizing chest pains she suffered afterwards weren't diagnosed as angina until several years later.

She married young. Her husband was in the military, and in 1948, at the age of seventeen, she was on her way to Japan, where she lived four years. Their only child, a son, was born the year after they returned to the states. "We almost lost him," she said.

A year later, the Air Force sent her husband on a special mission to Ecuador. A stateside assignment followed, then it was off to Venezuela for three years. It was 1964 when the family finally settled in Sacramento, a city that then had two major Air Force bases.

Her heart continued to plague her. Military doctors put her on a variety of medications, including digoxin and nitroglycerine. She carried an oxygen bottle for visits to higher altitudes. "I can remember thinking of Lourdes, and thinking, 'Oh my goodness, I wish I could go there.' "

But there was no clear consensus among the physicians she saw as to what, precisely, her condition was. "One doctor would say, 'It's this,' and the other would say, 'It's not,' and it was back and forth, back and forth all the time." At several points, surgery was suggested, but she always refused.

By 1977 her health had progressively deteriorated, but she was refusing hospitalization. If a heavy attack occurred, "if I could stay very still and could stay perfectly calm . . . and not exert myself in any way, I could kind of sneak through." But sometimes the attacks came with such frequency she was forced to stay in bed for several days at a time. She would require constant attention, allowed up only for short trips to the bathroom.

While in South America, she had become associated with the Lutheran Church and learned of healing by laying on of hands. "I talked with the pastor about it, and we began the practice." Whenever she was sick, she would call the pastor, and he would come and perform the healing rite. She was seeking divine, miraculous intervention.

It was 4 A.M. when she had her miracle. Her mother, her husband, and her best friend were with her, in her bedroom. She lay under an oxygen mask. She was forty-five years old, she remembers.

"I had had all of the medication I could take, and it wasn't doing any good. The nitrate was poisonous. You can only take so much. The pain persisted and reached such a peak that it was just almost unbearable.

"And then I remember thinking, 'But I'm not hurting any more.' And that oxygen was blowing on my face. And I felt myself leave my body and look down on it, and I had a tremendous, tremendous spiritual experience, and [had] seen Christ and having him touch me, and I felt— there's no way I can describe it. It's beyond that. Just kind of a blessing."

With the vision of Jesus came a conviction that everything, "just the way it was, was perfect." She awoke, smiling. People screamed. Her husband ran from the room. "I said, 'It's so beautiful, it's so beautiful.'[12]

"And I was totally changed from that time on and began really trying to see what I was sent back for, and watching for it, meditating, praying all the time and asking for guidance. Very shortly after that I heard about healing, and I thought, 'This is what I'll do.'

"By the time I went to the Philippines in 1980, I hadn't had any attacks for months."

*   *   *

Mellas's continuing poor health and her father's death had already inclined her toward intense mysticism, she said. The night she saw her vision, she was seeking release, some image she could focus on, could surrender to. Her recovery wasn't instantaneous. By the time of her Philippine trip in 1980, she had been free of the attacks for a matter of months. Her miracle, her Near Death Experience came in 1977. "I knew after the death experience everything was going to change. I had known for a long time I needed to get a divorce and change a lot of my life, and I just needed a little bit of a boost, I guess, to get myself aligned in the material sense and be sure of what I was doing, because I wasn't very sure spiritually."

Her first step out of her conventional world was to attend Lifespring, one of a variety of quasimystical self-awareness disciplines that grew out of the "human potential movement" of the late 1960s. She took two Lifespring courses, then went on to take the Silva Mind Control course, which promised, among other things, to help students develop psychic powers. It was in the Silva course she met the young couple who told her about psychic surgery.

"It's like any circle dedicated to a certain thing. If you get in with the people who play tennis, you hear all the names, and you get into this kind of thing," she explained. One introduction led to another, as she picked and chose among the various New Age offerings she encountered.

The young couple came from out of town, and she invited them to stay with her whenever they came to Sacramento. It was during a visit at her home in 1979 that they told her about the miracle workers of the Philippines. They demonstrated the art of laying on of hands as they had learned it, treating both Mellas and her mother. They told of another trip, the following March. Helene Mellas decided to join them.

The decision seemed a natural one. Her networking with other New Age believers had led to the formation of a group that met at her home. "There were so many others [i.e., groups] like mine," she said. "What can we do? Where can we go to talk about this? We need to get together. And there were several in the group in a group who were quite good at different things. One man was a European-trained graphologist, reading of handwriting. One girl was into astrology, and somebody into something else. As so each month when we met, I would have one of the others present their kind of thing, and then I would present things too in between. And shortly after that my classes got started. This from people saying, 'Please, would you teach this?' "

Gradually her teaching led her to create something she called Heart Center. She had brochures printed, describing herself as a minister, teacher, speaker, and "facilitator," leading classes offering "a full spectrum in exploring metaphysical, spiritual, and practical approaches to wholeness." Services offered included "Counceling [sic] & Readings, Meditation, Instruction, Crystal Awareness, Hypnosis, Healings." According to the brochure, "Her awakening as a Healing Channel was spontaneous and continues to develop as does the ability to scan the body both physically and psychically to determine and correct energy imbalances. After years of illness, a Near Death Experience totally changed Helene's life. It has become her mission to pass on to others what was and is given her that they, too, may awaken to new life."[13]

On 17 September 1985, she began an ongoing class, "Awakening and Awareness," which promised to teach students about "Psi-energy and life energy to teach you to reach your highest potential." The classes touched on meditation, *chakras* and other Eastern concepts, hypnosis, and healing.

An all-day seminar, "Introduction to Crystal Energy," was presented 21 September of that year, "a basic workshop to acquaint you with the finest natural tool our universe provides—the QUARTZ CRYSTAL." Students learned how to "select, clean and clear your crystal," how to use the crystal "to enhance meditation, concentration, centering & balancing," and how to "program your crystal for specific purposes," "attract your needs & desires," and "balance the *chakras*."

The crystal-energy class was repeated 15 March the next year, followed the next day by an all-day session called "Crystal Consciousness," where students learned to use "pulse breath for clearing and programming your crystal," "channeling of healing energy through crystal and hands," "healing with your crystal," as well as pendulum diagnosis, radiesthesia, and radionics—systems of healing that have been discredited by science and medical testing.[14]

*   *   *

By the time of the March 1980 trip to Tony Agpaoa's *ashram*, Helene Mellas was already convinced she could literally feel healing energy in her hands. The Near Death Experience had brought one conversion; the Philippines was to bring a second.

"Even though I didn't have the heart problem to . . . any degree that I was aware of," Mellas would say. "When I was on the table, Tony did something here [pointing], operated right over the heart. And I said, 'What are you doing? My heart's fine now, isn't it?' And he said, 'Oh, little thing in the arteries, no problem.' " Agpaoa also treated her for chronic nasal obstruction and pain from surgical scars in her abdomen, both of which helped make her feel better, she said.

Later Tony was to call to her to stand with him as he operated. "I was just thrilled to pieces with it," she said. "I think it's important, too, to say that the whole thing was more than just phenomena. . . . What they did that impressed me so much was the spirituality of the thing. To go around Tony and some of the healers was an amazing experience because they absolutely radiate power."

At one point, while Mellas was on the table for treatment by one of Agpaoa's assistants, she yelled out to the healer. Other healers were called from another room, and as Mellas lay on the table, six of them stood around her and placed their hands on her body. "It was so powerful that I never forgot it," she said. "Tears just started going down my face." Agpaoa's uncle, one of the six, asked her why she was crying. Did she have pain? "I said, 'No, just joy.' I spent the rest of the day and the evening in the chapel just trying to orient myself . . . and at the time, when we were ready to go, if my mother hadn't been living with me, I would have stayed there."

Mellas later offered some illuminating statements about experience with the Filipinos. "I never experienced the actual removal [of diseased tissue], even with Tony. He would reach in and cut the root of the tumor with his finger and you could see a big tumor move like that—one on a man's leg. I remember watching. "Then he would say, *through your faith in your own soul's work, you know, this will go away or it won't* [emphasis added]. And many times it did and other times, I guess, it didn't."

*   *   *

No doubt, this "psychic surgery" seemed to have both an individual and a social benefit. The "placebo effect," after all, is quite real. Anything perceived as a treatment will bring a relief of symptoms to a large minority of patients. This is perfectly in tune with New Age attitudes. "Sometimes it works."

But sometimes it doesn't work. The placebo effect doesn't occur in the majority of subjects. Another critical fact is this: four out of five medical problems are self-limiting. Either they will go away on their own, like a cold or a tension headache, or they will stabilize. Indeed, most diseases will resolve themselves with or without medical intervention, and a significant percentage of patients suffering from all types of disease will be helped by anything they believe is a treatment.

Historically, because of the relative ignorance of "medicine," a whole range of healing practices has flourished. And except where the healers prescribed harmful potions or actions, one form of treatment was as likely to be effective as any other.

By imparting hope to the sick, healers helped the patient. By imparting hope to friends, family, clan, healers helped society. There was a natural blending of the healing and religious functions. If the healing appeared to fail, the physician became a priest, and prescribed rituals for the departed—which were, in fact, rituals for the living, conveyed in myth and symbol.

"... ANYTHING BUT THAT SURGICAL KNIFE"

It was through Helene Mellas that Mary Armstrong[15] discovered Brother Joe. Sunny Tucker, Armstrong's sister and a friend of Mellas, tells the story: "We were at the Medical Center[16] and I asked my sister, 'Would you like to go by Helene's house and we'll pray.' My sister had cancer of the larynx, and that happens to you, you do things that you wouldn't ordinarily do. You get desperate for anything, you start reaching out—anything but that surgical knife.[17]

"Helene spent like an hour with my sister, and she was very loving, and my sister was very touched with her prayer and holding her hand on her throat," Ms. Tucker said. They sat in a room filled with hundreds of crystals, each bearing a price tag. A sign was on the wall:

Donations
for
Spiritual Services
———
Counseling, Reading
Chakras, Hypnosis
$50.00 per hr.

Healing—
Present—$40 per hr.
Absent—$10 per sess.
$50 per mo.

"And then Helene suggested this Brother Joe meeting—I don't know what they called it." There was an invitation to a healing weekend with this Filipino wonder-worker in Lake Tahoe. So the two sisters went.

The sessions were held in a private home, a million-dollar property with an indoor pool on the shores of Lake Tahoe. An orientation was held downstairs, featuring Mellas and some graphic, bloody footage of "operations" in the Philippines. Mellas was comforting, and the tapes seemed to show miracles.

Armstrong stripped to her underwear, donned a robe she had brought, and took a numbered ticket that marked her place in the treatment order. When her turn came, she entered an upstairs bedroom, where Mellas and a small, dark-skinned man were waiting. She underwent the oily rubdowns, and the holy-man thrust his hand into her throat and pulled out some disgusting-looking tissue saturated in a strange brown fluid, supposedly her afflicted blood. She was healed, he told her. The cancer was gone. Wait six weeks to go to the doctor and he'll be amazed that you're healed.

Psychic Stephanie Doran was also present in the room. She later told investigators "Brother Joe put his fingers into Mary's throat where she had been diagnosed as having cancer" and pulled out a small "tumor." When it was over, she said, "she heard Brother Joe tell Mary that her cancer was 'all gone.' She also heard Brother Joe tell Mary that she should drink a special tea Brother Joe would sell to her. Brother Joe told Mary not to go back to the doctor for approximately three weeks and, when she did go back, the doctor will be surprised that the cancer is gone."[18]

Armstrong finally did see her doctor, confident he'd find a miracle. Instead the disease had spread, and when it came time for a biopsy, she had a heart attack under the anesthetic. She had to wait two more months before the surgeons would finally operate. When they did, complications ensued. Today she speaks only with the aid of an electronic device, and problems following surgery have left her weak and chronically ill.

When Mary Armstrong suffered her heart attack, the complexion of the "Brother Joe" case changed. Were she to die, Investigator Smith figured he would have a murder case on his hands. Under California law, if a crime, even a "non-violent" crime like cancer quackery, leads to the death, it is legally murder.

David Druliner, a senior officer in the Sacramento County District Attorney's office, looked at Smith's evidence and filed three charges against Brother Joe and Helene Mellas: cancer quackery, practicing medicine without a license, and conspiracy.

"TRAVEL KING"

On 8 January 1974, the Federal Trade Commission filed a complaint against three West Coast travel agencies engaged in massive promotion of psychic surgery junkets to the Philippines. Two months later, a fourth travel agency was named in the action. The regulators charged the firms with "misleading, deceptive, and unfair acts and practices" in promoting "non-existent 'operations' " costing victims "large amounts of money" and, in the worst cases, hastening the deaths of their clients.[19]

Psychic surgery tours were big business, said Randall Brook, one of four FTC attorneys who handled the 1974 case. "They were taking millions of dollars in ticket sales over a year. There were thousands of people involved. . . ."

The commission conducted hearings from 9 to 24 September, taking testimony from forty-eight witnesses and reviewing 134 exhibits. The resulting transcript, 2,388 pages long, provides the most complete look ever at psychic surgery by a governmental body. The result was an FTC order forbidding the agencies not only from conducting advertising or promoting the tours, but even from using the words "psychic surgery" in any future promotions.

The FTC had determined that psychic surgery was "pure fakery and a fraud."[20] The travel agencies were ordered to send a notice to all future would-be patients, declaring psychic surgery "fraud and fakery," involving "sleight-of-hand and other tricks and deceptions." As a result of the Travel King case, Brook said, "Anyone promoting trips for psychic surgery is in violation of the law. If someone promotes a trip for psychic surgery as a cure or as a treatment, then that violates the law."[21]

One of the companies named in the action was Phil-Am Travel Agency Inc., a San Francisco firm that began selling the healing tours in August 1973. The marketing and sales manager for Phil-Am was Victorino P. Mapa.[22] He also testified at the FTC hearing that ended with the ban on psychic surgery tours.

When officers hauled Helene Mellas and Brother Joe off in handcuffs from Mellas's home in 1986, they didn't arrest a third person found in the house, a Filipino who had come in with Brother Joe, carrying a paper bag. This man had spent some of his time that day selling psychic surgery tours to the Philippines, operating out of a San Jose travel agency.[23] The man was Mapa. Brother Joe identified him as his agent. He was the recipient of most of the cash collected from the surgeries.[24]

Bugarin said Mapa brought him to the United States in 1976, two years after the start of Travel King, "to help people."[25] Mapa was not charged with any criminal activity in connection with the psychic surgeries, although according to both the "surgeon" and the woman whose house he used, Mapa profited both from his share of Brother Joe's earnings and from sale of tours of precisely the sort that had been banned in the landmark, nationally publicized case in which he had testified.

Moreover, Brother Joe's surgeries were promoted virtually the same way Mapa's old company had used. Mapa mingled with the patients before and after the surgeries, hustling his tours, this time arranged through Japan Air Lines, which also provided the brochures.

Brother Joe wasn't the only magic-fingered Filipino healer working the underground U.S. circuit, nor was he the highest paid. That honor goes to the previously mentioned Alex Orbito. A third well-healed healer was Placido Palatayan, who collected seventy-five dollars for his operations, and was arrested in Oregon in February 1989.[26] A fourth, "the Rev. Monsignor Gary G. Magno," charged seventy-five dollars for the first operation and fifty for each thereafter—except for those clients who signed up for his $2,000 one-payment lifetime treatment plan.[27]

THE SETUP

She talked to us about healers, referring to herself as a healer and also
to Brother Joe as a healer. I believe she said she had a heart attack and
actually died, went up, saw Jesus Christ—had a spiritual experience, I
guess she referred to it as, during this death, then came back with the
power that she had. She had come back to life.

—Investigator David Thornton
on Rev. Helene Mellas[28]

On 19 March 1987, Jerry Smith, posing as Jerry Bowman, called Helene
Mellas to ask if he and his wife, Lynn Bowman (really Lynn Thornton,
Smith's supervisor) could attend the pre-surgery orientation for Lynn's
brother, Dave Cooper (really investigator Dave Thornton, Lynn's real-
life husband), who was to be operated on for lung cancer. Smith played
the role of a concerned relative, and Mellas agreed to let him come. "I'm
kind of fascinated by this," he explained. Mellas said the orientation would
answer most of his questions. "I know that many, many people have heard
very negative reports about this kind of thing," she said. "It just has always
been a good thing for me when I feel that I have a good group that
really wants to hear the truth and have a good look at it."[29]

Smith said he would be delighted if his wife's brother didn't have
to return to the conventional medical care provided by the in-law's insurance
plan.

"We don't promise any more than the doctors promise," she said. "But
one thing about [psychic surgery], it cannot harm. It has never done any
harm, and it does do good on many levels because it's a powerful spiritual
influence, too."

Mellas also told Smith that "even working with people in hospitals . . .-
which we have to be very discreet about," even when patients die, "they

do it in such peace."

> SMITH: "It's got to be better than dumping a bunch of chemicals into your system, too."
> MELLAS: "Right, right. At least, you know, to give us a chance to try these things first. This is what I feel is needed here, and even they can work side-by-side, as we feel sure they can."
> SMITH: "Oh, what is the success rate? Do you have a percentage, or—"
> MELLAS: "No—"
> SMITH: "Oh, you don't keep stats or anything?"
> MELLAS: "No, we can't because it's not—well, how many people do you see again, right?"

Mellas told Smith that normally she only worked with Brother Joe when he was in the Sacramento area, although "I may accompany him to Mexico this year. He goes all over the country and . . . Canada and so forth, and there's just not time to set up that kind of statistical reporting on these things."

*   *   *

For would-be patients who had passed the referral test, the next stage was an orientation seminar. The next day's mail contained a letter to Dave Cooper. Inside was a single sheet of paper, a map to Mellas's home.[30]

The three state undercover officers attended Helene Mellas's offering 2 April, the evening before the scheduled surgery. A fourth officer, Ronald D. Olson, sat outside in a car, monitoring signals from the transmitter Lynn Thornton had concealed in her purse.[31]

The investigators arrived at 7:15. Taped to the front door was a note card, reading "Please Come In (If You Have An Appointment)."[32] They entered. Walking through the front door, they came to the kitchen, where two women were checking names against a pair of notebooks. Smith wrote in his report: "I told the lady that I was Jerry Bowman, and that I was here with my wife and brother-in-law. The lady located our names on the binder list and asked for $5.00 each, for the orientation."[33]

The trio was directed to a room off the kitchen, a garage converted into a family room, or what one close friend of Mellas described as a "prayer room."[34] There, three rows of chairs had been placed facing a television and desk. There were forty others there, and the three investigators were among the last to appear. They seated themselves next to a wall. At 7:40, Mellas entered the room and began her presentation.

According to the investigator's report, "Mellas said that as a little girl, she had rheumatic fever, which caused her to live with heart problems. Mellas said in 1977 doctors told her she needed surgery to repair her heart. Mellas did not want to have the surgery, so one night she was on her death bed in her home and she was in tremendous pain. Suddenly the pain went away and she felt very peaceful. Mellas said that next she knew, she raised above her body and looked down. She could see that her body looked almost black and her family members were crying. Mellas then saw a bright light and started into the light. She then saw Jesus Christ and said she was elated, but Jesus raised a hand and stopped her. Jesus told Mellas that she was to return to her body and become a healer. Mellas said that she returned to her body and woke up and had no more pain."[35]

Mellas told the patients that she could see into bodies and locate problem areas, which she would then work to heal by channelling energy through her hands. "Mellas then pointed out that she was a minister; otherwise she would not be able to touch the body," Smith wrote.

She led her audience through a guided meditation, described by Lynn Thornton during a 10 June 1987 pretrial hearing on the legality of the search warrant.[36] "[She] asked everyone to do some mental imaging about a ball, a light, being above you, and you taking the light into your hands, and everyone was kind of meditating on this, and that you were moving your hands while you were meditating, and this ball was going through your body, or something like that." (The technique Lynn Thornton describes is very similar to a practice called *agni yoga*, espoused by Ralph Metzner, Harvard colleague of Timothy Leary and Richard "Ram Dass" Alpert.[37] The process also might be considered a form of trance induction, i.e., hypnosis, and could help make the audience more receptive to what was to follow.)

"She pretty much tried to tell us how the whole thing would occur during our treatment," recalled David Thornton.[38] "There would be the laying on of hands by both her and Brother Joe, and this was in order to channel the energy, as she put it. And then when he felt the need to go in and remove an object, that he would 'go in'—that was the term she used—would be to go in and remove the object. It may not have been the thing that we had complained about. If we were complaining about cancer, and Brother Joe happened to find something else, he would also go in and remove that."

Mellas talked about the surgery itself using the same analogy she used in the phone call with Lynn Bowman: The healer's electromagnetic hands part human flesh the way ordinary hands pass through water. Sometimes, she said, a healer may choose not to remove a large tumor, because the resulting loss of energy would harm the body. In those cases, the surgeon "would just cut the 'roots' of the tumor" and prolonged treatment might be required.[39] Similarly, while Brother Joe might extract a tumor—macaroni-shaped lumps were common in the throat, she said—

he might not. He might simply rub them down with oil; the lack of blood didn't mean a healing wasn't taking place. The magic was in his hands. If he did pull out a tumor, though, patients could look, but not touch.[40]

Another of Brother Joe's talents was his ability to "enter the stomach and swish his hands around like a wash(ing) machine, which cleanses the blood"; and he could also heal hemorrhoids. But his most exciting gift, she said, was restoring sight to the blind and hearing to the deaf. David Thornton recalled her saying, "The only thing he probably couldn't cure was warts."[42]

Mellas made another vital point. She said that in addition to complicated disorders requiring multiple treatments, "another reason for patients having to come back to the psychic surgeon was they return to their bad life style and the illness returns."[43]

Some of the discussion revolved around the previous month's sessions at South Lake Tahoe, which many in the room had attended.[44] David Thornton recalled hearing others there talking about how "they hadn't seen each other since Lake Tahoe."[45] Even though the orientation was billed specifically as an "introduction/orientation into the fascinating phenomena of spiritual Healing & Psychic Surgery," many of those present apparently had already been through at least one previous session. They had returned for reinforcement, for reassurance that the miracle was real.

"During the orientation Mellas paused three or four times. Mellas said her guider spirits were contacting her," Smith wrote. "When Mellas was contacted by her guider spirits, she would close her eyes, smile, and move her head in an up-and-down manner."

Then Mellas showed two videotapes. One was a documentary about Alex Orbito, the other about one of her own pilgrimages to visit "Brother Virgilio," Virgilio Gutierrez, Jr. Both healers were included in Phil-Am's tours in the days when Mapa was putting together packages for that agency.[46]

The Orbito tape, produced by TAO Video of Los Angeles,[47] is smooth, impressive to an untrained eye, and full of gore. His most shocking trick seems to be plucking leech-like bits of tissue from the nostrils. Many of his patients appear to be Japanese, who constitute a major market for the tour packagers. Orbito is seen not only in surgery, but at his own private, sacred cave where he goes to meditate and recharge his spiritual energies. The narration is good, the music appropriately New Age, and because of its news documentary format, the tape conveys an air of objectivity. But there are other messages, too: Viewers are told that Orbito will sell them a tour through his own company, Manila-based Orbit Tours, and they can obtain a video of their very own surgeries through the healer's very own Orbit Photography Services. The tape tells viewers that much of Orbito's work is charitable; nothing is mentioned of his hundred-dollar-a-minute surgical swings through the United States.

But it is the second tape, while technically inferior, that is most significant, because two of its "stars" are Victorino P. Mapa and Helene Mellas, and the end credits express "Special Thanks" to two healers, Sister Josephina Sison and Brother Joe Bugarin. According to the opening credits, the film was produced by the Brotherhood of Spiritual Pathfinders Inc. (BSPI) and Romano Scavolini Productions. BSPI, viewers are later told, was founded by Virgilio Gutierrez in 1974.[48] The narrator is "Atty. Rebecca D. Gutierrez, BSPI Training Directress."

The tape opens with a scene aboard the tour bus of arriving tour members. The camera captures views of the passing countryside, then the bus pulls up in front of a hotel/resort. The sign on the bus is difficult to read, but seems to say "Rajah Tours." (What is apparent is a number painted on the right front of the bus, a sure omen to any fundamentalists in the lot. This is bus 666.) Tour members are shown leaving the bus. One, a woman, is carried from the bus by a male and placed in a wheelchair. Next, the screen shows the large group clustered around tables on the open terrace of the resort, animatedly talking or quietly meditating. Cut to a quick shot of another woman, on crutches, but not seeming to rely on them that much. Another man, reclining in a chaise lounge, seems deep in contemplation. The narrator's voice drones on—she's obviously reading from a script she hasn't rehearsed too well. Now the patients are seated first at a table, raptly listening to Virgilio, a small, handsome man who is talking with obvious solemnity. Virgilio takes them outdoors and casts solar reflections off a spherical mirror onto some kind of fabric held by a tour member. We aren't told what is to be seen in the reflection, but it has something to do with an "ancient Japanese prophecy."

Now the camera is inside. A plain-looking woman with dark, short page-boy hair, heavy-framed glasses and a striped blouse stands, microphone in hand, next to a simple portable public address system. Next are scenes of the group in an idyllic forest glade, with grass meadows, palms, and plenty of shade. Virgilio sits in a circle with the others, who are fixed on his every word. Other groups have split off and sit by themselves.

Then the tape cuts to a man wearing a short-sleeved shirt open at the collar, sitting at a table, his face to the camera. With her back to the camera is a woman "reporter." The man has a round, pleasant face, relaxed and expressive. He is wearing a traditional Philippine shirt. He appears to be about fifty years of age. His name is spelled out on the screen:

VICTORINO P. MAPA
Travel Professionals, USA

Mapa tells the "reporter" that Virgilio and Tony Agpaoa "were the two best known of all the healers." She asks "[Do] you have a lot of stories to tell us about the experience of getting healed by Virgilio?" This question appears to be a lapse on her part, as Mapa arches his eyebrows, rolls his eyes in response, then gives his answer slowly, deliberately. "I wouldn't. . . . but these tourists would." The reporter appears flustered, half turns to the camera, touches her hair. "Ah, 'these tourists' I meant to say." Mapa is putting the onus for the claims not on himself, but on his clients.

The reporter asks Mapa whether this is his "first time to lead a group of people here?" Mapa answers yes. The reporter adds, "To study about psychic phenomena?" "I have been bringing them here for the past fifteen years," he answers.

REPORTER: "Fifteen years? On the same kind of trip?"

MAPA: "Before I would conduct strictly nothing but healing trips. I would take them straight from the USA, put them to hotel, bring three healers there, closet them for twelve days and then get them back to the USA. There was no attempt at trying to find the power source, trying to learn the ways where one can become a healer, trying to find out where the healers get their power from. This one has become unique because I take them from the beginning. Not only do they get to meet the healers, but, ah, I take them on a pilgrimage to one of the psychic centers of the world, Mount Benahow."

REPORTER: "So we can say this is more of a study tour?"

MAPA: "Study—study and healing."

Then come scenes of some actual surgery, which prove to be very unimpressive compared to the scenes in Orbito's film.

The first woman patient wears a bra and large bikini panties. She has dark, full, shoulder-length wavy hair, and a comfortable layer of fat on her abdomen. She is lying on the "operating table," head to the upper left corner of the screen, thighs bottom-right. Virgilio is standing on the far side of the table, assisted by a woman whose arms and torso are seen. Virgilio wears a long-sleeved white shirt with epaulets and two flapped pockets (the flap of the left pocket being up), and dark slacks, held up by a belt with a fair-sized buckle. The belt sags, as though not worn too tightly. There appear to be two clip-type pens in his pocket. The music is fruity-fluty, saccharine.

The second woman patient has short wavy blonde hair. She is slim, with a prominent nose and a lively face. She wears a short-sleeved, form-fitting blue blouse with epaulets. Moving out of camera, she removes her blouse. The camera cuts to Virgilio, panning past the first patient, standing, her back to the wall, with a deeply sober expression. Virgilio is looking down, his head slowly moving as his patient, beneath the plane of the camera, lies back on the table. He turns toward her, and now the camera shows the upper part of her head as she is reclining. Virgilio reaches out with his right hand, picks up a small white towel, opens it, and draws it across her breasts, momentarily laid bare. Her shoulders are drawn up and lips slightly parted.The camera pans down her body, She is wearing the same practical, high-waisted panties as the first patient.

Virgilio now moves his hands to her left hand, which is outstretched along her side, palm up. An open Bible sits beside the patient. The camera moves to her face. Virgilio and his aide, a heavy woman in a sleeveless burgundy sundress, maneuver small wads of cotton over the woman's face, stopping here and there over her forehead and eyes. He rubs the patient's forehead with a small piece of cotton, then caresses her hair backward, resting his palm on the locks above her forehead. This pose is held as the music switches to a faster, more urgent, twangy beat. Virgilio withdraws his hands and briefly touches each of the patient's hands, as the assistant raises her hands above the patient, where they hover at a height of three or four inches. Now the woman is smiling ecstatically, her eyes beaming at Virgilio with a childlike joy. She sits up, as the assistant's hands reach out for the towel. We see her naked back as she sits and faces Virgilio, who has been hunched over his Bible. He places the open Bible on her lap, and she reaches down to turn the page, her upper arms clenched to her side, holding the breast-covering towel. The camera moves on to Virgilio, who has been holding his hands clasped together, grasping a small towel, over his groin. The hands part, the towel remaining in the right hand.

Now the woman is shown from the side, Bible in lap. The camera pans up, and sweeps to include Virgilio, who extends his right hand to the left side of the woman's face, out of the camera's view. Virgilio is shown from the abdomen up, his belt and left arm out of camera range. He raises his eyes from hers, says something to his assistant. (The viewer hears nothing of the healer/patient interchange.) Lips move, but the only sound is the relentless New Age music. Now she rises. Lower back and panties move out of range, as Virgilio's eyes follow her, smiling.

Next comes a close-up, hands working on soft flesh. It is the third patient. As the camera pulls back, Virgilio and his assistant are working the "love handles" of a dark-haired woman who is lying on her side, her back to the camera. The assistant holds a cup of a milky-looking fluid in her left hand, cotton in her right. Virgilio's fingers are held together as he reaches his left hand toward the bowl. His fingers work the fluid, which turns red. The right hand moves to the bowl now. He also appears to take something out with his right hand twice before the procedure is done. We have seen blood, but no tissue. The woman looks grateful after the "incision" site is wiped clean. Her panties are momentarily lowered slightly by the assistant over the right buttock, and Joe touches and prods momentarily. Briefly, the assistant raises her hand, blocking the scene from the camera. Why? There is no apparent reason—no blood, no tissue, nothing immodest revealed. The panties are restored, and the patient rises from the table, looking first anxious, then relieved.

Now comes the first male patient. A young, dark-haired man, with heavy eyebrows and hairless chest is lying back on the table. Virgilio dabs at the man's forehead, reaches for the assistant's bowl, which is no longer bloody. The surgeon dips his right hand in the fluid and anoints two small areas on the man's breasts, apparently painting small crosses with the fluid between the nipples and sternum. Then he brings his fingers together and describes a rotary motion over the heart. A cross is briefly made over the larynx and over the abdomen midway between the navel and genitals. The assistant pulls the man's pants downward, momentarily exposing a glimpse of pubic hair. The patient's eyes are closed, his shoulders drawn up.

Now Virgilio works the small layer of fat. The camera pans up to the patient's face, which is smiling hugely as he says something to the assistant, off-camera, playfully arching his eyebrows. The camera pulls back to the original position, and we see the assistant holding the bowl outstretched over the young man's abdomen. Then the tape jumps abruptly. The woman's hands have moved, and the fingers of Virgilio's right hand are cupped together, their backs to the camera, thumb out of sight as though concealing something in a conical cavity created by the cupped palm. The fingers, still together, pulse rhythmically, bring the liquid in contact with what, if anything, is concealed in the palm. Now we see the clearest evidence that something has been "palmed." The right hand, still concealing something, if merely a cone of air, moves to the soft fleshy covering of the abdomen and is prodded against the flesh. As Virgilio extracts his hand, the fingers can be clearly seen to have been curled up into a fist. The assistant has also constructed a small cotton "dam" on the belly that prevents the camera from recording whatever Virgilio has been doing with that mysterious right hand. Now a glimpse of something red—is he about to "extract" tissue? No, he does not. We only see the cleanup of some red fluid by the assistant's right hand. Now the camera pans up to Virgilio's hands, which, out of range of camera, had moved up to the upper chest. The right hand is cupped.

Virgilio has been playing his cupped hands over the patient's heart, and as he pulls back, there appears to be a little bit of something sitting on the chest. The assistant quickly moves in to remove it.

Now comes the assistant with her little cotton dam, the quick swabbing up of the whatever-it-was, the mopping up by Virgilio and his aide, and the young man rising, smiling like a man on whom the gods had found favor. Virgilio uses a small white towel or washcloth to wipe the red fluid from his hands.

The camera pans down to the Good Book, open on the table.

*   *   *

After several more operations come the testimonials.

The first comes from a man identified as a "Shiatsu therapist." He wears a *dashiki*, a loose-fitting shirt of African origin, and sports a beard. His speech is rigid, but sincere. His interview is taped outdoors, in an informal setting.

The massage therapist tells how he discovered psychic surgery when he attended a session in the United States, where a healer named "Joe" was operating on his girlfriend. Wanting to see what was happening, he tried to enter the room where the "surgery" was happening, but he was turned away. A minute later, "Joe" came to the door. "He just said, 'Come.' And when I walked up to the door, when he opened it, when I walked up to the door, he says to me, 'Spirits call. I know you're here.' And I was, uh, you know, you know I was like, shocked, to say the least. I was watching Joe starting to perform his surgery. And he looks up at me and he says, 'You're going to the Philippines.' And I, I sort of went like, 'Yeah, sure,' you know. I wasn't even thinking. I was just, you know, sure, why not, you know. I said yes anyway."

At first the Shiatsu therapist suspected fraud. "I started saying to myself, 'This guy is doing quackery. He's taking chicken necks, chicken gizzards, out of this person.' I didn't believe it. I just said to myself, 'No, this isn't it at all. This is not real. I don't like this—this guy's a magician. He's good, you know.' So anyway, I decided to watch a little longer."

"Within about I'd say half an hour, my mind started, my head started filling up with pressure, confusion. I was starting feeling dizzy."

On the way home from the session, he became lost, driving in circles. Finally he had to stop for a drink, he says. The next Friday he was back with Joe. "And I walked in and so they opened the door to let me in. No problem this time. And then Joe looks up at me and he says, 'Well, have you decided? You are going, I know.' And I looked at him and I said, 'Yes, I'm going.' I started working that day, the following Friday, I started working with Joe. Working with him I meant working standing next to him and he was doing the surgery and he would rub my hand and put it right in the area where he was working on, and he opened up the person. And I saw him, I felt him use my finger and so that was leaning me a lot more toward what I originally saw the first time."

The next interview subject is a woman. She is dressed in a peach-colored blouse with collar high on the back of the neck. Her dark auburn hair is meticulously groomed. Her voice is calm, constrained, and she speaks as though slightly swallowing the words. She looks up and to her left, as she recalls. Small gold hoops hang from her ears. At the end of the segment, she gives a nervous smile.

WOMAN: My first experience with the Philippine Islands was in 1980. I came here—

TITLE/CREDIT:

REV. HELENE MELLAS
Spiritual Counsellor, USA

—and attended the healing at the ashram of Tony Agpaoa and was indeed very impressed with what occurred there and with the work that was there. And I was allowed to help some with the healing at that time, which also was I felt a tremendous privilege. I am not acquainted with anyone in Mexico or the other countries where these things are done, so I guess I simply followed the path of what I was already acquainted with. And I felt too that this, this Philippine healers, I always feel a tremendous spiritual . . . ahmm, yes, between myself and them on occasion that is very, very strong. But also I feel that this is so much a part of them, of them, and of their work, and I like this. Again, not phenomena alone; it is part of their being-ness, and I think they are addressing what I myself feel drawn to—that it must come from above, and they all will tell you that they are guided by spirit, by holy spirit, and they feel that without this they cannot do anything further. And since this is my direction also, perhaps that is part of the strong attraction for me. Let me put it this way then, insofar as learning to enter the body is concerned, developing this ability—my belief is that it would have to be at the feet of a practitioner here in the Philippines because I know of no one else who has attained that, and so far as the ability itself is concerned, again, it must depend upon the person. I find that simply in magnetic healing, there are those who take to it right away or those to whom it comes spontaneously. There are others who develop it and work at it and work at it and it comes. I, in my talking with many healers, have found that each one has a different concept of how long it would take me to learn to enter the body if I chose to pursue that. And it's anywhere from "Any day now, mum," to "Ten years," you know. And it doesn't bother me, I might add right here that I am not seeking that. My path in life is already surrendered to the powers that be, and if I am to do psychic healing, or psychic surgery rather, the entering of the body, then I will also be given a way to use it, and it won't be in the United States at this time. I do hope I live to see the time when doctors and alternative healers can work in cohesion and do so happily. That I—it certainly is not happening right now."

*   *   *

The next testimonial comes from another male massage therapist, whose name also appears on the client list seized from Mellas's home after her arrest. He too first met a psychic surgeon in the United States—Brother Joe. He describes how he turned to religion after his son was killed and he had suffered burns.

There is a final testimony, a woman this time, and then the camera cuts to the Rev. Virgilio Gutierrez, Jr., displaying the model of a healing center he hopes to build on a hill overlooking the China Sea with contributions from the faithful.

"Since the 1950s," he says, "there is a man who introduced psychic phenomena in the Philippines. Not only in the Philippines, but it is around the world, and his name is Eleuterio Terte, which you can see in this picture. He died in 1979. So he has a dream also to build up something that he can, that somebody can follow his footsteps. And maybe I am one of the lucky ones who have his support, support his dreams and ideas." (Terte was the first of the healers. Physician-researcher William Nolen was told he "discovered" the art in 1943, then shared it with a gifted student, Tony Agpaoa, several years later.[49])

Indeed, the Rev. Gutierrez tells the camera, he and Terte were born in the same village, which is also to be the site of the healing center, where "those who are interested to know and to learn psychic phenomena in the Philippines, especially healing, they can come to us and we can learn together what the learning that we can share with them is the experiences that we have [sic]." The healer also claims "there are several doctors, medical doctors, who are working under me. They are seeing people here to come before the healing and after the treatment."

Then come the credits.

*   *   *

After the tapes, Helene Mellas took questions, mostly from those in the audience who wanted to become healers themselves. Mellas told the attendees that they could purchase a booklet for one dollar. There was a stack of documents on a table in the dining room (as well as a large display of "healing" crystals, each bearing a sticker: prices ranged from $15 to $250).[50] Photocopied and with a blue cover, the sixteen-page booklet was apparently written by a Florida man in 1973 and is titled *A Guide to Spiritual & Magnetic Healing & Psychic Surgery in the Philippines*. In question-and-answer form, the booklet tries to make a solid case for psychic surgery. There isn't a single comment critical of the practice. (This same booklet was sold to prospective clients by Phil-Am Travel Agency Inc. at the time the FTC moved against the tour packagers. Victorino P. Mapa testified to that fact.[51])

Also available at the orientation, at no cost, was a flyer entitled "Psychic Exploration and Easter Tour to the Philippines," departing 8 April 1987. Prices started "from $1,799.00."

> Travel, live and study with the leading healers and psychics of the Philippines during HOLY WEEK—a time of the year when the energy level and spiritual consciousness of the people are at their highest. The blend of traditional Roman Catholic Devotion and the even deeper commitment to Spiritualism and Mysticism makes for fascinating and powerful experiences during this special week. . . . This is the much-awaited Easter Tour that is running well into its fifth year.[52]

Under a section entitled "COST DOES NOT INCLUDE," prospective buyers are told that price does not cover "love offerings or donations to psychic healers, mediums and any services connected with them." Inside, printed just above the itinerary in a box bordered with a thick, dark rule is this:

> IF YOU WOULD BE HEALERS. . . .
> During Workshop and Seminar days we will observe, research and study the "Psychic Surgeons" at work. We will study questions like: "The Psychic Surgery controversy," "What really happens in Psychic Surgery?" "What is the subtler Body?" Workshops on healing will include "Developing your own natural healing Ability," "Psychic Diagnosis and "Self-Healing."

Tour members are promised an opportunity for "sessions and consultations" with two psychic surgeons, "Sis. Josephine" and "Bro. Virgilio Gutierrez." The brochure, printed on a Japan Air Lines "shell," directs prospective travelers to send $200 to Travel Professionals, 31881 Alvarado Boulevard in Union City, California. A copy of the firm's stationery gives the name of the company as M.W.M. Travel Professionals. (The company was still there in 1990. According to documents on file with the California Secretary of State's office, M.W.M. Travel, Inc., was incorporated 12 May 1982. Two annual officers' statements were available, for 1983 and 1984. No subsequent forms were filed, nor were the requisite annual fees paid. On 1 May 1984, California Secretary of State March Fong Eu suspended the "corporate powers, rights and privileges of said corporation."[53] In the 1983 statement, the chief executive officer and the individual who signed the form is Victorino P. Mapa. Mapa also signed the following year, listing himself as an officer and legal agent for the firm.)

*   *   *

The next day's surgical patients were told to bring a written list of the conditions they want treated, which they were to give to the healer before their "operations." The session ended shortly before 10 P.M. Patients were told to come back at their appointed times and to bring a bathrobe concealed in a paper bag "because she didn't want her neighbors upset by seeing a lot of activity around her house."[54]

*   *   *

The three undercover officers and Ron Olson held a brief meeting at a nearby 7-Eleven store. Over sodas, they learned that the tape recorder had been working, and they confirmed their plans for the following day. They went home about 10:30.

"NEXT TICKET-HOLDER PLEASE"

A day or two before the orientation, Jerry Smith had met with Lt. Max Davidson, watch commander for the Sacramento Sheriff's Department. The meeting had two purposes: Law enforcement agencies routinely notify each other when making arrests in their jurisdictions. Smith also wanted two uniformed officers as backup.[56] They were going to be making arrests in a house full of believers, some of them *desperate* believers; the precaution was routine.

Smith and the lieutenant agreed that at 10:30 the morning of the operation the state investigators would rendezvous with the two officers at the home of another BMQA staff member who lived close to the Mellas home. "I didn't see any need for them to be there during the first treatment time," Smith would say later, "and I figured that after the first treatment we could get together and discuss what happened and go from there."[57]

The same day Smith met with Lt. Davidson, he received a call from Mike Leury, a reporter for KCRA-TV, Channel 3, the NBC affiliate in Sacramento. Leury told the investigator he "was going to send through one of his undercover people from the TV station to do a story on it." Smith hung up and talked with Lynn Thornton, then called Leury back to make "a deal with him that if he didn't send through an undercover operator and risk our operation, we would tell him the day we were going to do our operation and he could stand by."[58]

The next day, the television reporter came out to the BMQA offices and met with Smith and Lynn Thornton, who drove him out to Helene Mellas's neighborhood and showed him where he could park his car to be able to spot the uniformed officers when they swept in to make the arrests.[59] The same day, Lt. Davidson assigned two deputies to work with the BMQA officers, according to Deputy James Basden, one of the pair.[60]

The morning of the sessions, the state undercover officers and Sheriff's Deputy Simms met at the house of the BMQA employee at eight o'clock.[61] Also present were BMQA agents Lorin E. Hays and Ronald E. Olson (again monitoring the transmitter) as well as Vernon A. Leeper, the agency's chief of enforcement. Because of relatively poor radio reception the night of the orientation, Olson was to park nearer the house. The deputies and other BMQA agents were to wait at a defunct fast-food restaurant within a minute's drive and monitor a special "operations channel," a radio frequency reserved solely for the day's events.[62]

The stage was set for the arrests.

*   *   *

The three investigators pulled up outside the Mellas home at 8:45 for "Dave Cooper's" (investigator Dave Thornton's) first surgical appointment. He was carrying a brown paper bag with a bathrobe inside. The sign on the door bid those with appointments to enter without knocking. The trio walked in.

Inside, a blonde woman seated at a counter in the dining area was checking patient names against a spiral-bound appointment book. Jerry Smith walked up to her and said he was there with Dave Cooper. He gave the woman forty-five dollars in marked bills, which she put in a small accordion-style folder. Cooper's name was the tenth of fourteen scheduled in the 9:00-10:00 A.M. period. The woman entered "45" next to the name in a column headed "Pd".[63,64]

Dave Thornton was given a "small ticket like you would use on a carnival ride, and it had five or six numbers, and you used the last two numbers, and my number was seventy."[65] Thornton was the sixth of eight patients to arrive, according to the appointment book; five others scheduled for the hour were eventually marked "NO SHOW." Near the appointment log was a sheet of paper, reading:

INSTRUCTIONS FOR SIGN-IN ASSISTANTS

The first appointment donation should be $45 ($40 plus a one-time registration fee of $5). If other private appointments are requested the suggested donation is $40 for each one.

Please request each person to sign the mailing list so they can be notified of future visits. Check their writing/printing and ask for spellings if you cannot easily read their writing. Check each one also for: ZIP codes, Area Codes and request a Post Office Box number on all South Lake Tahoe, California or Zephyr Cove and Stateline, Nevada addresses.

> *Tell them that in order for "Brother Joe" to be available to as many people as possible, it is important that they remove all jewelry (except tight finger rings), and wear only robes, slippers and underpants (please, no bras or T-shirts or socks or pantyhose). Glasses and contact lenses should be removed, unless their removal causes an unusual problem. This saves time for everyone.*

> *If there are special instances that are not able to comply, let "Brother Joe's" assistant know so the person's special needs can be accommodated.*

Male patients were directed to the family room to change, female patients in a bedroom. Dave Thornton went to the family room, the scene of the previous night's orientation, where he stripped to his shorts, placing his clothes in the bag he had used for the robe.

Back in the dining area, "They had set up a couple of chairs, and there was two elderly lady standing around these chairs." Elderly, to Thornton, meant mid-fifties. "And these people were known as 'openers.' What they would do, they described it as opening you up. They placed their hands on my shoulders, neck, in the head area to open me up, as they described it, to the healing process that Brother Joe . . . and Mrs. Mellas would be performing."[66]

They were also "closers," he said. "Apparently if you were going to leave the house for a period of time, you were supposed to go back and have them do the same thing, which would close you up. To be honest with you, I don't know what this accomplished or what they—what this was supposed to accomplish. I assume that whatever the healing powers— Brother Joe's healing powers would have, they would close up so it wouldn't spill out."[67]

The morning of the surgery was the first time David Thornton had heard of the process. His spouse watched the "opening," in which one of the women spent several minutes "moving her hands over areas of his body, basically from head to toe."

Patients had been told the night before to write down the condition to be treated. "It could be one thing, or it could be as many as you wanted," Dave Thornton said. "Some of us didn't have a list, so we were allowed to write it down that day. I wrote on mine that I had lung cancer and indicated it had just been diagnosed." They were told to give the paper to Brother Joe or Helene Mellas when they entered the "treatment room."[68]

As they waited for the healer to arrive, the investigators saw several hand-scripted signs posted around the house. One bedroom carried a brisk notice: "Off Limits—Do Not Enter." "Prayer and Meditation will enhance your healing experience," declared a second. A third read:

After your healing . . .
Refrain from alcohol Today.
Wait to take a shower
until tomorrow.
Nothing strenuous, remain calm.

One last sign had been typed, framed with neat black lines.

Please refrain, as much as you can, from:

- Eating meat
- Drinking alcohol
- Smoking
- Bathing
- Activities that tire you

—at least until tomorrow—to allow your body, mind & Spirit to absorb the marvelous Spiritual Healing energies you have received.

Quiet and rest are recommended for everyone and are essential for those who tire easily. Do that which you know is best for you.

Some individuals feel that these energies can continue to do their healing work for as long as three weeks or more.

So remember to be good to yourself.

---

*   *   *

Brother Joe didn't arrive until 9:30. He entered the house accompanied by a woman, later identified as his female companion of two years, and Victorino P. Mapa. Mellas escorted Bugarin into the rear of the house. They were followed by Mapa, who was carrying a brown paper bag.[69]

Helene Mellas returned to the dining room alone, and announced that Brother Joe was ready to begin. She asked everyone present to hold hands around the table in the center of the room, which was covered with dozens of quartz crystals. "Mellas had us close our eyes and she talked about bringing energy into the room. Mellas then asked all the persons to recite the Lord's Prayer."[70]

The holders of the first two tickets were directed down the hall toward the master bedroom, designated the "treatment room" for the day. The first patient was to go inside, while the second was to wait on a chair that had been placed in the hall next to the door. "They would keep a procession of people being treated going into the room without having to look for you. Once you got seated in that chair, then you gave up your number. They took your ticket," recalled Dave Thornton.[71]

As the patients began to file in for surgery, Victorino P. Mapa circulated between the surgery and through the rest of the house, talking to patients and Mellas's assistants.[72]

PORTRAIT OF A SCAM

This is how it's done.

The Travel King case was nothing less than a trial of psychic surgery. For the travel agencies to be acting wrongly, there had to be evidence that the practice of psychic surgery was a fraud. If the healers really were removing tumors, no wrong would be involved. But if there was clear evidence of fraud, then the tours could be barred.

When Federal Trade Commission attorneys summoned an Iowa couple to the witness stand, they provided Administrative Law Judge Daniel H. Hanscom with clear, convincing evidence, cited at great length in his findings of fact.[73] What follows is the only description of the psychic surgeon's "art" as related by (disillusioned) practitioners.

Donald F. and Carol Wright started out as believers. An interest in ESP led them eventually to psychic surgery, and they made two trips to the Philippines in 1973. They saw dramatic operations, but strangely, none of the patients seemed to show any marked improvement. Among the healers they visited were Vic Mapa's old friend, Virgilio Gutierrez, Alex Orbito, and Romeo Bugarin (possibly a relative of "Brother Joe," as Mellas later said he came from a whole family of healers).

Despite the lack of miraculous healings, the Wrights were convinced *something* was happening, so they decided to stay on when the rest of their companions returned to the United States at the scheduled end of the second visit, in July. Though they studied with several healers, only one is named in the Travel King decision, Virgilio Gutierrez.[74] "While working as assistants to a number of different 'healers,' the Wrights discovered 'psychic surgery' did not consist of 'surgery at all,' but was being performed by sleight-of-hand. Donald Wright noted objects falling from the healers' hands onto the bodies of the patients before the 'operations,' and Carol Wright had the opportunity to examine a 'tumor.' As an assistant, one of her jobs was to dispose of the 'extracted' material at the end of an operation."[75]

Carol Wright eventually saved a "tumor" from destruction. She testified about what she found: "I took the membrane and pulled it back and found that this was a tumor, a membrane that had been stuffed with cotton and blood clots and it appeared very much like a tumor, but it was not. It was just a flat piece of membrane that had been stuffed with cotton and blood clots to look like a round tumor."[76]

Concluding finally that psychic surgery was a trick, and that the patient's body was never entered, the Wrights confronted their teacher, who admitted that, yes, the surgery was all trickery. Because the Wrights had established a relationship of trust during several months of working with the healer, they were inducted into the secrets of the art, ultimately joining the Union Espiritista Christiana de Filipinas, the healers' association that Mapa's former employer had exclusive rights to represent in the United States.

The secret of psychic surgery, they were taught, was something the surgeons called a "bullet," formed either from animal tissue or a clot of blood mixed with cotton.

They were shown how to shop for the necessary animal parts, how to prepare and shape the bullet, how to hide it, how to drop it on the patient's body. "The Wrights were taught where to hide the prepared bullets, for example, on their persons, inside cigarette packs, in their stockings, in their belts, etc. They were taught the techniques of palming so that no one would see the bullet, planting the bullet on the patient's body, moving the bullet if it were necessary, using continuous kneading action in an indentation on the patient's body (which appears to be manipulation but allows the 'psychic surgeon' to open his bullets), the importance of such an indentation in the patient's body, the addition of water obtained from saturated cotton balls often passed to the 'healer' by attendants, which mixes with a small bullet of animal blood and is used to make the appearance to the uninitiated of human blood issuing from an opening in the body, the spreading of an animal membrane in the blood in the indentation in the human body to look like an opening therein, and the bringing 'out' of the hidden animal membrane so that it seems that material from the body of the person being operated on is being removed. The Wrights were shown how to end an operation, how to clean up the area being 'operated on' and to dispose of all the bullets."[77]

Carol Wright described the specific steps in making a bullet, and then using it in the surgery:

Q. Where were the materials for these operations obtained?
A. In an open market.

Q. What kind of materials were obtained?
A. Blood clots, blood, from the blood of a cow, which was congealed, and also materials from pigs and cows. Liver was used. We were shown how to look in the intestines to pick out small glands and cysts that could be used, for example, in an adenoid operation or thyroid operation. We were shown what to look for and how to prepare the material so that it would very closely resemble the human body as you would bring out a piece of tissue.
Q. And how were these materials prepared before the operation?
A. Before the operation they would be prepared, for example, taking a small piece of blood clot, perhaps the size of a marble, and placing it into a square of cotton, a small piece of cotton—they always used Red Cross cotton, for some reason—rolling it up very tight and then placing it into a cigarette pack so it would not be noticeable when it was carried.
Q. How were these carried to the scene of the operation?
A. Inside these cigarette packs, empty cigarette packs. They were also secreted on the person of the healer, the psychic surgeon, perhaps in his socks. We were shown that if you wear socks like a man would wear, to put these inside the elastic at the top. They could be put inside the belt, they could be under the collar, they could be—I observed one of the female psychic surgeons take one from her bra—any place on your body which would be or could be a hiding place.
Q. And in the operation you were shown, how were the materials which were prepared then used to create the appearance of the operation?
A. Taking one of the bullets, which is the blood clot inside the cotton, it would be palmed and held in such a manner that it would not be seen by the patient or by relatives or whoever was around, have it in here like so [demonstrating how to palm], and would be planted on the patient's body somewhere and then, after a moment, it would be brought to the area wherever they were going to do the operation and they would begin kneading and they would also make a pressure indentation into the patient's body if it's on the abdomen. If the person was very, very thin, they would often bring the legs up in order to make it softer so that the hands could go down further. And then, through kneading, through pushing, then adding some water, this blood that is in the cotton would begin to mix with the water and appear red and begin to run all over the body and be kind of messy and dramatic and then, if there was also wrapped inside the bullet a piece of tissue, then, while the psychic surgeon's hands are down in, with the hands folded underneath, then it could be—they would break that open and bring these pieces out bit by bit, always keeping one hand in. This was one thing they would say, if they took both hands out, the opening would close, but there was always one hand down and the fingers would be bent under like so, and this is how I was taught to do this.

*　　*　　*

The Wrights stayed in the Philippines until April 1974. They tried to expose the fraud before they left to return to the United States, and continued their crusade back in the U.S. by making appearances on local television stations.

The Wrights testified that they spotted the same sleight-of-hand surgery practiced everywhere they went in the Philippines. One of those they named specifically as a fraud was Shirley MacLaine's wonder-worker, the Rev. Alex Orbito. Gutierrez was a fraud as well, they testified, as were Terte, the man who started it all, and his prize pupil, Tony Agpaoa. Also named by the Wrights as fakes were Placido Palatayan, Romeo Bugarin, and eight others.[79] "They concluded that the techniques used by the 'psychic surgeons' were all essentially similar and all were fake."

LUNG CANCER AND EUCALYPTUS OIL

Clad only in his underpants and a bathrobe, Senior Special Investigator David Thornton sat on a chair in a hallway in a comfortable suburban home, waiting for a pair of criminal suspects to do a number on his bare flesh. He admitted later to being "a little nervous. Whenever you do an investigation you get nervous. But I didn't feel my life was in danger."[80]

He wasn't alone. Fellow officers Jerry Smith and Lynn Thornton, David Thornton's wife and supervisor, were right there, armed and ready, and backup was less than a minute away. Still, an awful lot can happen in sixty seconds.

Finally, Thornton's number was called. "They said, 'It's your—it's time to sit in the chair. So he went," recalled Lynn Thornton.[81]

Jerry Smith and Lynn Thornton walked into the room with him. Earlier they had asked the woman who had given David Thornton his ticket if they could watch as Brother Joe operated. The response: "Oh, you might be able to. Just ask Brother Joe."[82] What they saw was a master bedroom, with the bed against the opposite wall. To their right, two people stood next to a portable massage table. There, behind the table and with his back to the wall and facing the door, was Brother Joe. Helene Mellas stood nearby.

"I handed my slip of paper to Mellas, who read a diagnosis of 'lung cancer' to Brother Joe. I was told to take off my robe and glasses and lie on my back," David Thornton said.[83]

Thornton removed his robe and glasses, placing them on the bed. He walked over to the massage table, passing a smaller, metal table, covered with bottles of what seemed to be oil, and a wastebasket, with bloody-looking cotton in the bottom.[84] He lay down on the padded table, his feet facing south, toward the wall opposite the door. Behind his head was a second door, to a bathroom. There was a woman standing there in the doorway, attractive, dark-haired, slim, the one who had come in with Brother Joe and Vic Mapa. She was out of Smith's range of vision.[85]

Against the wall, between the bathroom and hallway doors, was a dresser with a lamp. Atop the dresser Thornton saw small cups (apparently filled with water), a number of plastic bags, and some cotton balls.[86]

The psychic surgeon seemed to dislike something—Smith's presence in the room. "Brother Joe stopped doing anything and just stared at me . . . I felt I was making him uncomfortable, suspicious, so I left the room on my own accord not to arouse any more suspicion," Smith said.[87] He took up a position in the hall next to the door, which was left a few inches ajar.

David Thornton asked if he could have his "sister" or "brother-in-law" in the room with him. Bugarin said nothing; Mellas said no. The room was too small.[88]

As he lay on his back, Brother Joe and Helene Mellas anointed their hands with something that smelled to Thornton like eucalyptus oil (there had been sprigs of the plant for sale on the table, Lynn Thornton said[89]). Mellas had taken up a position to his left, and began rubbing his left leg—she called the process "laying on of hands." Brother Joe was rubbing his upper torso, stomach, and right leg. As they massaged, they talked to the patient. Bugarin "asked me how long I have had the lung cancer, and I told him it had just been diagnosed," Thornton said.[90] Mellas gave the answer at the same time.[91] Brother Joe then asked if anyone else in his family had suffered from cancer; "My father had lung cancer," the agent responded. Then the healer asked him if he exercised; the agent said he jogged.[92]

As the two healers continued to rub him with the fragrant-smelling oil, Thornton said Helene Mellas told him their massage was "energizing the body, channelling the energy—by doing this, this was helping the cancer, and it was also helping him to channel the energy prior to him, meaning Mr. Bugarin, going in later on."[93] Then, at some point during the treatment, Thornton said, Bugarin told him he did, in fact, "go in," although nothing was extracted.[94] During the rubdown, Smith said Bugarin would throw occasional glances toward him at his post behind the open door, but he continued with the rubdown.[95]

Helene Mellas asked David Thornton how many visits he had scheduled with Brother Joe. "I told her three today and three tomorrow," he said. Brother Joe told him to roll over on his stomach, and they continued their rubs, noting a growth on the investigator's back, wondering aloud between themselves if it was a cyst (which it was).[96]

Finally, after five to seven minutes, it was over. Helene Mellas told him they had channelled his energy, which "does as much . . . as if he actually went in."[97] Brother Joe would probably "go in" on his next visit, at 11 o'clock. Dave Thornton returned to the family room, dressed, and left with his two companions. The time was 10:07.[98]

*   *   *

The officers headed back to the nearby rendezvous house—"to collect ourselves," was how Jerry Smith phrased it.[99] The investigator wasn't sure if they'd bust the pair after the second surgery or not, but since Brother Joe might "go in" at that time, it was a possibility.

The undercover officers entered the psychic surgery house again at 11:05 A.M. Smith paid the money—$40 for this, the second visit, and the assistant marked "Dave Cooper" "Pd". He was the eighth patient to arrive for the 11 o'clock session. Only one patient arrived after the agents, Jay Tucker, in the company of his wife, Sunny. (There were three names marked "NO SHOW," and one that appeared to have been partially erased and crossed out. This was Stephanie Doran, whose "surgery" had originally brought in the BMQA agents.[100])

"I was there with my husband, who's legally blind, and we went there for his blindness," Sunny Tucker said. Her sister, Mary Armstrong, did not come. She had waited out the two weeks and gone to a doctor in her home town, outside Sacramento. "The doctor told [her] that the cancer was still present and that she should go back to her specialist . . . as soon as possible," Sunny Tucker was later to tell Jerry Smith. "Mrs. Tucker said that [Mary Armstrong] was devastated because Brother Joe said that he removed all the cancer. Mrs. Tucker said she and [Mary Armstrong] contacted Helene Mellas and told her that the cancer was diagnosed as still being present . . . Mrs. Tucker said Ms. Mellas asked [Mary Armstrong] to go back to Brother Joe on 4/3/87 and 4/4/87 for further extensive treatments. According to Mrs. Tucker, Ms. Mellas said the hospital and surgery will always he there, and they should give Brother Joe and her another chance."[101]

But Mary Armstrong couldn't wait it out. Before the 3 April sessions, she went in for the biopsy and suffered the heart attack, which was to cause still further delays in her surgery. Despite that, Sunny Tucker had still come with her husband. The reason again: desperation. When Jerry Smith eventually interviewed Jay Tucker at his home: "Mr. Tucker said in April, 1969, he had a rare disease that made holes in the retinas of his eyes. To keep from losing the fluid in his eyes, he had to go to Stanford Medical Center where they used a laser to seal the holes on the retinas. As a result, Mr. Tucker developed scar tissue on the retinas of both eyes and he has lost all central vision. Mr. Tucker said he is legally blind. He cannot read or drive, but he has enough lateral vision to shave, make coffee, etc.

"Mr. Tucker said that his condition is extremely frustrating because he is so close to being able to see. He has exhausted all known medical techniques of today and wanted to try an alternative method. Mrs. Tucker's wife made appointments for him to be seen by Brother Joe."[102]

Sunny Tucker still maintained an element of her faith, despite her sister's experience. Later she realized she had had serious misgivings about what she had seen at the Lake Tahoe sessions. "The truth was,"she said, "that I saw it at the time. When they showed the cup with the supposed blood in it, it wasn't quite the shade that I had remembered blood to be, whichever the last time I'd seen blood. It was a little too watery. They pulled this lump of stuff out, and it didn't look real to me, but the truth was, I wanted to believe it so bad I just didn't say anything."[103]

Unlike Mary Armstrong, Jay Tucker had nothing to lose except his money. Medicine had already tried and failed. Why not try something new? They paid their forty-five dollars, and Jay Tucker was given a ticket. He was to follow Dave Thornton into the surgery.

*   *   *

As the Tuckers waited their turn, Sunny Tucker watched Vic Mapa "working" the other patients. She recalled him doing the same at the Tahoe session. "I did not blame them for what happened to us because we had a choice to go there or not go there, and that's exactly the way I felt about it, I took full responsibility for what we did. But there was an old man, an old woman from [a foothill community], and I was within earshot, I wasn't really listening, I just heard it, I was within earshot of them talking them into this trip to the Philippines which I believe now is another scam. And they were going to have to—their home was paid for, and for some reason I can just picture it—an old home, maybe that's because the people were so old. In [the old mining town], I pictured them old homes up there. There was nothing said how old the home was, but somehow I figured it was paid for. And they talked them into like taking a second mortgage or hocking their home to take this Philippine trip and I knew they were making arrangements for it; and I felt sorry for them because the result would be the same: nothing."

About Mapa, Lynn Thornton had this to say: "Well,'I did not know what the role of Mr. Bugarin's assistant was, the man who came with him that day. You know, I—I never really was too clear on what his role was."[104] She did talk about the other people there in the dining room, waiting for their personal miracles. "There were quite a few people I overheard discussing their—the fact that they had cancer and different ailments, and that they were there to be treated and I did overhear—

and I would consider those people quite desperate, looking for alternative means to save their lives."[105]

Prior to the second session, Dave Thornton walked back to the family room, stripped to his shorts, and donned the robe again. When he rejoined his two companions, they asked the ticket-giver and Vic Mapa if all three could be in the room.[106] The answer again was no. When they went back to the treatment room with Thornton, Helene Mellas "met us at the door and said that we could watch through the door," which was left further ajar this time, Jerry Smith said.[107]

"We pressed it a little harder this time to try to get at least one other observer in to the room to observe the treatment," David Thornton later testified, "and Brother Joe had more or less a fixed stare, like an untrusting stare is what it appeared like to me, watching us. He didn't say anything one way or the other about anybody coming into the room, but gave the impression that he didn't want anyone."[108]

After laying his robe and glasses on the bed, the patient was directed to lie face down on the treatment table. "I asked them if they remembered what they were treating me for, and Mrs. Mellas said they were treating me for lung cancer, and I said, 'Good, I'm glad you remember me.' "

The second treatment was similar to the first, oily rubbing of the body, rolling over, more rubbing; no blood and gore, "except on this occasion he would stop and look out the window of the bedroom, like he was looking for somebody or someone, then he would start again on the treatment, and stop, look out. He did this about three times, like he was looking for somebody outside the window."[109] He did something else, too. He "appeared to be feeling for something under my shorts near the top of my leg," Thornton said. "I felt he was looking for a body transmitter."[110]

Jerry Smith reached a conclusion. Joe was alert and on guard. If he'd "made" the three investigators, there wasn't any point in continuing the charade. Because the house was empty of all but the Tuckers, the healers, and the assistants, there would never be a better time to make the arrest. "It wasn't really a pre-planned thing," he said later. "It was just when [David Thornton] got off the table, I looked at him because he was still in his shorts, and I kind of [indicating, with a sharp nod meaning] 'are you ready to make the arrest,' and he nodded 'yes,' and we went in."[111]

"I felt that if we waited any longer. . .if we waited to come back. . .to the next appointment at two o'clock, that evidence could be destroyed [and] he may not be there."[112]

Smith was edgy, but he didn't feel threatened.[113] But his partner, Lynn Thornton, did. She struggled for words when asked to testify about her feelings as they walked into the room: "There was an indication that the people were very, very—believed very much in what was going on there. And I have had direct experience in—in types of cases where individuals who believe very strongly about—who have real strong beliefs in these types of areas, tend to be quite protective of the individuals who are, quote, healing them . . . and have been violent."

*   *   *

"Peace officers! You're under arrest!" Smith yelled, clipping a previously concealed badge to his sports coat and marching into the room, followed by Lynn Thornton.

Smith pulled out his handcuffs and walked over to Brother Joe. "I told him it was okay. He had locked his hands down, like straight down to his body, and because he had oil on his hands, I couldn't get a grip on him, and Investigator David Thornton then helped me to put his hands together to handcuff."[114]

Inside the bathroom, Lynn Thornton encountered Bugarin's companion, the Massachusetts woman who was later to tell investigators Brother Joe had removed a tumor from her throat. "I asked her what her role was in the treatments and healings and she—she seemed to be a little alarmed. She said, 'All I do is flush the contents given to me in the styrofoam cup down the toilet.'" Other patients later confirmed that extracted tissue was first displayed, then dropped into a cup and passed to the bathroom.

When the agent peered into the toilet bowl, she saw material floating on the surface. It looked like chicken skin, she said. In addition, "there were some red clumps at the bottom of the toilet bowl that looked like some kind of real dark red tissue, and what they were, I have no idea."[115] She took a paper cup from the front room, scooped up the material on the surface of the water. She made no effort to get the red clumps from the bottom, believing them out of reach.

Outside in an undercover car parked one house away from the Mellas residence, Ron Olson hadn't heard Smith when the officer announced the arrest. What sparked him into action was the sharp metallic clicks of handcuffs being snapped into place. "At the time I didn't know if the handcuffs were being used on our suspects or on our officers," he would say later. Grabbing the handi-talkie, he barked for backup. "I told them that the arrest was happening, was coming down, and that I was responding to the house now. Immediately."[116]

He flicked on the car's emergency blinkers, gunned the engine, made a sharp U-turn, and pulled up in front of the house. Two other BMQA agents parked further down the street saw him and drove up seconds later. The agents were close behind as Olson sprinted to the front door and knocked.[117] In the vacant parking lot, radios barked, five engines raced, rubber squealed. The two marked sheriff's cars were in the lead, followed by two BMQA undercover cars and the TV crew.[118]

Smith had asked the Filipino whether he had any identification. When he didn't respond, "I asked him again, and again there was no response. So I reached—I felt the back of his pockets to look for a wallet and felt a—what felt like a wallet in his left rear pocket." When Smith pulled it out, he found he was holding the bottom half of a plastic hand lotion bottle, full of a dozen soggy, red-colored cotton balls.

Jerry Smith had found Brother Joe's magic bullets.[119]

CHAOS AND COLD CASH

The scene inside the house was chaos. When Olson first appeared at the door, Louise Nielsen[120] tried to head him off, but another assistant beat her to it. "I couldn't get there in time," she testified.[121]

Olson identified himself as a police officer, and asked if he could come in. Do you have a warrant? she asked. Olson answered, "I don't need a warrant. I have officers inside and I'm coming in."[122]

The woman opened the door, and Olson took two or three steps, saw people "standing around in the hallway, and in the kitchen to my left. I again identified myself as a police officer, and I ordered everyone into the dining room where all these crystals were on the table. And I said, 'Everybody into that room,' and I went looking for my investigators, my officers."[123]

When Olson entered the house, only one patient was still waiting for treatment, Jay Tucker. His wife, Sunny Tucker, who was also present, recalls what happened: "I was just standing looking at the crystals. She's got a large crystal collection, I just look at all of them. Three men knocked at the door, and they said, 'Helen,' [sic] and they said, 'She's in the bedroom.' They said, 'Police, everybody stay where they are.' "

Olson took off down the hall, opening and closing doors as he searched for his three comrades. When he finally entered the treatment room, he found Mellas handcuffed and standing by the door and Bugarin, also handcuffed, beside the treatment table. When the officers in the room told him they had everything secured, Olson walked back toward the front of the house, where BMQA Investigators Martin A. Machado and Jack Miller were keeping things under control.[124]

Olson was detailed to locate and question Vic Mapa, and when he walked into the kitchen, he was looking for the travel agent. "Before I had a chance to contact him, I observed Investigator Hays in the back yard motioning to me. So I walked over and let him into the house."[125]

BMQA Investigator Lorin E. Hays was in the first unmarked car to pull up behind the sheriff's units. During the meeting of officers between the two sessions, Hays had volunteered to secure the rear of the home while the other officers took the front.[126]

There were two doors at the back of the house, and he found both locked. He could look into three windows, but he could see activity behind only one, the rear dining-room window. He waved, hoping to attract the attention of one of the officers inside "to let me in. Obviously they didn't see me." So he stood at the window for several minutes, observing what was happening inside. He saw a woman sitting at a breakfast counter, with a BMQA agent standing nearby. As he watched, the investigator left the woman's side and vanished from Hays's sight.

"Then I observed the woman make what I thought was a—an unusual move," he said. "She reached and got what appeared to be some papers [from the counter top], and turned, and may have got out of the chair a little bit, I don't recall how far. But she opened the refrigerator, looking around to see if anyone was watching her was what I thought she was doing—and she put the papers in the refrigerator and closed the door and stepped back. And subsequently she did the same thing."[127]

Another person who saw the woman's actions was Sunny Tucker. "When they said 'Everybody freeze,' the girl that was taking the money threw it in the refrigerator," she said.

Louise Nielsen had been the registrar for the surgeries, taking money from patients, marking off the amounts in the "Pd" column of the ledger. It was she who had taken money twice that day from Jerry Smith. It was she who hid the money and the appointment book in the refrigerator.[128]

At a later court hearing on the admissibility of evidence seized in the arrest, Sacramento Superior Court Judge John Boskovich twice questioned her about her motives in hiding what would be critical items of evidence in a criminal trial. She insisted she didn't stash them in the refrigerator to hide them from law enforcement.

> JUDGE: Young lady, may I ask a couple questions? You indicate that you put those things in the refrigerator?
> WITNESS: (Affirmative nod.)
> JUDGE: You didn't put them in there to hide them from law enforcement or anyone else?
> WITNESS: No.
> JUDGE: Why did you put them in there for?
> WITNESS: Because they scared me. They came like a SWAT team, and it just frightened me, and I didn't know what to—
> JUDGE: You knew they were officers, didn't you?
> WITNESS: Well, I knew that the first two were, but I had closed the door because the dog was loose, and then some other people opened the

door and there was about ten of them that they just busted in the house.
JUDGE: Okay. Thank you.
WITNESS: And it scared me.
JUDGE: Thank you.[129]

Hays finally managed to get the attention of Investigator Ron Olson, who had been the first to enter the house. Olson opened the patio door, and Hays told him what he had seen. He went over to the refrigerator, opened the door, and found what turned out to be the appointment ledger and a brown folder.[130]

The folder proved to be the day's receipts, $1,174 in now literally cold cash and a $45 check.[131] Included in the cash were four twenty-dollar bills and a five-dollar bill that Jerry Smith had marked with his initials and the date before paying them to Louise Nielsen. Their serial numbers matched those he had recorded.

The appointment ledger turned out to be a standard student seventy-page narrow-ruled spiral notebook. The book listed ten days of psychic surgery sessions, held 13 and 14 September 1985, 13 through 16 December 1986, 5 through 7 March 1987, and 3 April 1987. For those ten days, payment entries—virtually all untraceable cash—totaled $15,930. The largest single day's take was $2,425 for 6 March 1987 at Lake Tahoe. Next to two patient name entries, one each on 15 and 16 December 1986, was written the word "child."

At some point Investigator Ron Olson produced a Playmate ice chest, into which the toilet findings and "bullets" were placed. "We went to the crime lab ahead of time and they said if you take any biological substance, any substance you think is a biological substance, put it on ice immediately," Smith said. The chest the crime lab personnel gave to Olson before the raid was a small one-person lunch-size chest just large enough for the two evidence baggies.

Brother Joe—in a new, white, short-sleeved shirt tucked into dark, pleated, belted trousers—was escorted handcuffed from the house by Sheriff's Corporal Simms, past the waiting camera of Channel 3. He offered no comment to Mike Leury, only a scowl. Helene Mellas came out moments later in a pale grey belted jumpsuit, gold hoop earrings, neatly permed auburn hair, poised and erect. She was handcuffed, arms behind her back, her left upper arm gripped by Deputy Basden. She gave a "no comment" to Mike Leury, looking at the reporter directly, frankly.

Brother Joe and Helene Mellas were driven off to Sacramento County Jail, where they were fingerprinted, photographed, and booked.

CONFLICTING INTERESTS

Legal disputes are adversarial proceedings. Jose Bugarin and Helene Mellas were alleged to be partners in crime, but what was in the interest of one was not necessarily in the interest of the other. Hence, each defendant had an attorney. It wasn't a two-sided issue; it was subtler than that, more complex.

Jose Bugarin picked an attorney in many ways his exact opposite. Ray Simmons is a former Sacramento County Sheriff's Deputy. Big, burly, mustachioed, he's a tough fighter, outspoken. Representing Helene Mellas was William Hale, whose home and work phones appear on Mellas's computerized mailing list, HEALPHO, and whose name also appeared as a patient on one of the psychic surgery session lists.

Representing the People of California was David P. Druliner, assistant chief deputy district attorney for Sacramento County, head of the agency's thirty-three-prosecutor Felony Bureau.

Brother Joe and Helene Mellas were charged with two crimes. The first, "Unlawful practice with serious injury," is defined in Section 2053 of the *California Business and Professional Code:*

> Any person who willfully, under circumstances or conditions which cause or create risk of great bodily harm, serious physical or mental illness, or death, practices or attempts to practice, or advertises or holds himself out as practicing, any system or mode of treating the sick or afflicted in this state, or diagnoses, treats, operates for, or prescribes for any physical or mental problem without a valid medical license can be punished with time in state prison or county jail.

The second charge was violation of Section 1714 of the *California Health and Safety Code*, which states, in part:

It is unlawful for any person, with the intent to defraud, to falsely represent and provide for compensation a device, substance, method or treatment as effective to diagnose, prevent, or cure cancer.

To prove this crime, the state must show that the alleged criminal knew the treatment was fraudulent, and that the treatment was provided for money.

*   *   *

The attorneys first met head on at the Preliminary Hearing, conducted before Judge Jack V. Sapunor in Sacramento Municipal Court. Only three witnesses were called: Lynn and David Thornton and television news reporter Mike Leury.

The investigators testified about the orientation and healing sessions, as well as the arrest itself. Leury was called because Ray Simmons wanted to know who had tipped him to the arrests. Leury came into court, accompanied by a TV camera operator. Leury told the court very little: He started the investigation in March, he kept his story notes at the station, and he interviewed several witnesses.

When Simmons asked whether he had talked to law enforcement officers, the reporter responded, "I'm sorry. I can't answer that question. I refuse to divulge my source."[132] Leury similarly refused to say whether he had provided any information to law enforcement as the result of his investigation, or even if he had made videotapes of interviews.

Patrick McFarland, the station's attorney, argued that the reporter couldn't be forced to reveal anything that might lead to identification of a confidential news source—protected by the California "Shield Law." (Incorporated as Article I, Section 2 of the state Constitution, the law prohibits courts from forcing journalists to divulge confidential sources or issue subpoenas for unpublished/unbroadcast notes, tapes, and film. The law is further buttressed by Section 1070 of the California Evidence Code.) The court sustained McFarland's motion, and the reporter's brief moment on the stand was over.

At the end of the hearing, Simmons asked the judge to dismiss both counts, based on the testimony of the two officers. "Mr. Bugarin did not participate in any practice of medicine, and there's only been two witnesses that testified that, for the most part, Mr. Bugarin rubbed some eucalyptus oil on one of the investigators, which . . . appeared to be (his) total involvement." Not only that, Simmons said, but there was nothing on the record to show that Jose Bugarin "did in any way cause or create risk of great bodily harm or serious mental illness." Since he wasn't practicing medicine anyway, there was no need for a license.

As for the "cancer quackery" charge, the record offered nothing to show that Brother Joe "attempted to defraud anyone of any money. The witnesses have testified that Mr. Bugarin spoke infrequently, if at all, to them. There was no mention of money demanded by him. He received no money." Additionally, "There's no indication here that he falsely represented that he could cure cancer. In fact, the testimony of David Thornton is that Mr. Bugarin at no time said he was going to cure any cancer whatsoever. Nor was there any device or substance used, other than eucalyptus oil, and it wasn't used to—to cure cancer; nor did he arrest, prevent, or cure cancer in any way. Therefore, we ask that all charges against Mr. Bugarin be dismissed."

The court also had the option, Simmons said, of reducing the crimes from felonies to misdemeanors.

Then came William Hale's turn. He, too, asked for dismissal of both charges. As to the first count, unlicensed practice of medicine, "The only evidence before the court, presented by two witnesses in oral testimony, tends to prove that she was engaged in the laying [on] of hands to help heal people who voluntarily came to her and sought help as part of her religious beliefs and her religious practices through her church. There's no evidence that any great bodily harm, or serious mental illness, or death would have occurred because of her act of laying on hands through her religious beliefs."

As for the charge of cancer quackery, "There's been no evidence provided that anyone was defrauded, period, much less the specific intent on the part of this client to defraud someone. There's no evidence that she received any money in this transaction," Hale said.

Prosecutor Druliner countered Hale by noting that no testimony had been introduced establishing Mellas as a minister; therefore, Hale's argument had no basis in the limited evidence presented at the hearing. As for the lack of any proof of great physical or psychological harm, any action, done wilfully, "under circumstances which cause or create a risk of great bodily harm. I would submit that common sense indicates—and the court obviously can use its common sense in analyzing the evidence and the law in this case—common sense indicates when someone comes in to someone, as did David Thornton, and tells them specifically, and writes it down, 'I have lung cancer, recently diagnosed,' then that person or persons engage in a form of treatment with the person who has represented that they have lung cancer."

And if the patient actually had lung cancer, "that would have undoubtedly created a risk and would have resulted in literally . . . great bodily harm occurring by the representations of the defendants," Druliner said. Further, after Helene Mellas told Brother Joe about the written diagnosis, "Mr. Bugarin engages, on both occasions, in what I would describe as a false, phoney medical history . . . obtained when they weren't licensed to be doing that. They both held themselves out to being able to practice this form of treatment for cancer, and it did, in fact . . . create a risk of great bodily harm."

The prosecutor argued that the law did not require "that we have a cancer victim, a person actually afflicted with cancer." Were that the case, the law "would have been changed long ago," he argued. "There's no way in the world that we can police the medical profession and people who take advantage of victims, and be restricted to only sending in undercover officers who have cancer."

As for the defendants receiving money, Mellas herself stated the cost of treatments at the orientation. Regardless of who ultimately received what monies, Druliner said, the evidence clearly established a fraud in which both Mellas and Bugarin were the central players. Central to this argument was that "one of the first questions by Miss Mellas, in the presence of Mr. Bugarin, is 'How many treatments are you scheduled for?' "

Druliner speculated that the question indicated Mellas and Brother Joe wouldn't be performing "their grand finale act" until the sixth and final treatment.

"I think the intent to defraud has been established," Druliner said, "and what has been established is that there are other people involved in this operation who are probably less culpable than these two, but nonetheless involved in what, I would submit, would be a conspiracy to defraud people with grave ailments."

Hale countered: "How can you create a risk of harm when you give a massage and laying on of hands when there's nothing wrong with the person? Where are the victims that the District Attorney alleges that were injured or defrauded? Why don't they come forward and file their own complaint?

"They didn't come forward because they were here on behalf of Helene Mellas. A third of these people were ready to testify at this moment, that they were actually there the day of this arrest. They were not defrauded, but benefited by the spiritual laying on of hands and her praise.

"There are no victims. The only victim is the entrapment had by this office. There was no circumstance or conditions which would cause bodily harm or death. The man was perfectly healthy."

As for the money, "they are all donations. No one testified that they saw Helene Mellas take money."

Simmons raised a final point on behalf of Brother Joe. "There was no indication whatsoever that Mr. Bugarin, if Mr. Thornton had lung cancer, indicated to Mr. Thornton that he should stop medical treatment." But Druliner reminded the court that the officers had testified that Helene

Mellas had told one woman at the orientation that delaying medical treatment would help the psychic surgery process.

*   *   *

Judge Sapunor ruled immediately: "The court finds that there is sufficient evidence to show that the charged offenses have been committed as to each defendant, as to each count." As to whether or not the court should hold the crimes felonies or misdemeanors, the judge had this answer: "I don't think there's anyone in this courtroom who hasn't been touched by cancer. This horrible disease defies the efforts of men to cure it, or even to arrest it. Because of the terrible nature of the disease, people are driven to people like the defendants in search of a cure. These defendants prey on the desperate and direct them away from treatment that has proven to be effective. These people's lives are at stake.

"For that reason, the court will deny the defense request to deem that this case be tried as a misdemeanor."[133]

*   *   *

At 5:36 that evening, BMQA investigators Jerry Smith, David and Lynn Thornton, and Martin Machado went to Helene Mellas's home, armed with a search warrant. Now that the court had bound the defendants over for trial in Superior Court, the investigators wanted to strengthen their case.

Search warrants must pass a judge's scrutiny, and must specify precisely what is being sought. Jerry Smith had prepared a 14-page affidavit, complete with a photograph of the house and a map of its location. The warrant specified six types of evidence to be seized: healing crystals with individual price tags, the two videotapes, pamphlets and other literature describing psychic surgery and faith healing, bank records in the name of either defendant, and "items which appear to be tissues from a previously living animal, to include fluids which appear to be blood."[134]

When Smith arrived at the home, "I observed Ms. Mellas standing inside by the window that overlooked the front door." The curtain was quickly closed, and Smith stepped up to the front door and knocked, announcing that he was a peace officer, armed with a search warrant. There was no response. Smith waited a few seconds and knocked again, with the same result. Meanwhile other officers tried the home's other doors, finding them all locked.

After five minutes of knocking, "Ms. Mellas was observed through the kitchen window to move quickly from the kitchen area to another part of the residence. Fearing that evidence might be destroyed and concerned about the safety of the officers, the front door was forced at 5:41 P.M.[135]

The search lasted until 8:07 P.M. Soon after the officers broke in and Smith read the warrant to Ms. Mellas, her attorney arrived on the scene, staying throughout the search, taking photos of the officers as they worked. Shortly before the officers left, Smith wrote, "Mr. Hale called me and the other three investigators together. Mr. Hale then apologized for us having to force [the] door open." The lawyer explained that his client had called him when the officers arrived, and he had forgotten to tell her to let them enter.

"He said he would pay to have her front door repaired," Smith added.

The officers seized thirteen videotapes (including one of Mike Leury's broadcast of the arrest), financial records, seventeen "healing crystals," tickets, pamphlets, business cards, mailing lists, and a large roll of blue "ADMIT ONE" tickets. Not seized but photographed were hundreds of other crystals, a briefcase piand kit of "Bache Herbal Remedies," a variety of books offered for sale, two boxes of cotton balls, and one bag of cotton puffs.

One of the most interesting items taken into evidence was an inexpensive twenty-page photo album, apparently the same one seen by some patients at Lake Tahoe. This is Mellas's collection of photographs of her own trips to the Philippines. While many of the photographs are undated and unlabelled, some bear stamps from the developers. The earliest of these date to June 1980, and show a Filipino woman performing psychic surgery on two patients. There are some "routine" psychic surgery shots, including six of one woman, topless, being worked over by a female surgeon.

Some of the most interesting items taken were business cards and magazine article reprints featuring the Rev. Joseph Martinez, a self-proclaimed psychic surgeon from San Francisco. It was the Rev. Martinez who was indirectly responsible for first bringing Helene Mellas to BMQA's attention two years before the Brother Joe case—and for bringing BMQA to the attention of the Rev. Helene Mellas.

Saul Silverman, a Sacramento physician whose specialty is treating cancer patients with radiation, had seen an ad for Martinez in the May 1984 issue of *New Ground*, a New Age newsletter.

Dr. Silverman complained about the Reverend Joseph Martinez to the BMQA, a small agency with a small budget and a small staff. Most of the BMQA efforts are devoted to regulating the practice of licensed health care professionals—physicians, psychologists, nurses, chiropractors, even acupuncturists. It wasn't until 17 December 1984, half a year later, that Investigator Lynn Sullivan called the number listed for information on the Sacramento psychic surgeries of the Rev. Martinez.

When Sullivan called, the person who answered identified herself as

Helene Mellas. She told "Sandy Wilson," Sullivan's undercover name, that Rev. Martinez had stopped coming to Sacramento, and could be reached at his healing center in San Francisco. According to the report, Mellas then "stated she is also a healer and performs her healing by scanning the body with her hands and has cured such illnesses as cancer and menstrual problems."

Sullivan told Helene Mellas she was suffering from physical ailments, and booked an appointment for 11 A.M. January 8. When Sullivan asked what Mellas charged for her services, she was told "the amount of money depended on the patient and how much they wanted to pay."[136] The 8 January appointment was cancelled "due to surveillance problems," and another made for 16 January 1985. Mellas was now the focus of the investigation, which was assigned case number 2-03450.[137]

There is no record of any follow-up until a year later, 29 January 1986, when Investigator R. V. Keszler interviewed Mellas at her home and described for her the laws governing unlicensed practice of medicine and psychology, and told her about the undercover calls by "Sandy Wilson."

Helene Mellas told the investigator she was a licensed minister of the Universal Life Church, "and conducts metaphysical and spiritual help. She does not diagnose or prescribe" and "she encourages ill people to continue seeing their physician and has never taken anyone off their medication or guaranteed to cure them."

(Stephanie Doran was to tell Smith that about this same time, she had met with Helene Mellas at the home of a fellow psychic, where they discussed the potential legal problems associated with healing. Mellas said the solution she had found was to become a Universal Life Church minister. "It only costs ten dollars," Doran said she was told.[138])

Mellas told the investigator that her practice consisted primarily of "scanning" the patient's body, observing the "aura," and praying with the patient "to correct any break or deformity in the aura." Keszler wrote that Mellas claimed success with her art. "'Good results in cancer and female problems have been reported to me after I observed their aura and prayed with them,'" he quotes her as saying.[139]

Mellas also told the investigator she was also a student of "crystalology," another popular New Age belief, reflected later in the massive display of crystals offered for sale at the time of her arrest. "The crystal has been used for many years by many different people," Keszler records her as saying. "The crystal contains properties that are still misunderstood today but have proven themselves over many years." In a brochure, Mellas listed herself as a student of Marcel Vogel, a retired IBM researcher who claims, among other things, that crystals can heal thyroid growths[140] and age red wine instantaneously.[141] One of Vogel's videotapes was seized at the time of Helene Mellas's arrest, and Mellas appears to be in the audience at the seminar where the tape was made.[142]

Keszler wrote that he explained to Mellas "the possible areas of conflict of interest between the practice of medicine and psychology in regard to her lack of formal training in religion," and of the danger of "unscrupulous people who would take advantage of old persons under the guise of religious beliefs." Mellas agreed that charlatans do exist, but assured Keszler that she neither diagnosed nor prescribed. "She believes the human spirit and mind can be a tremendous aid for helping people in dealing with their own illnesses and can even help in the cure."

Based on his interview, Keszler recommended the case be "closed with merit." His supervisor, H. B. Keener, agreed. On 4 February 1986, the first investigation ended. Mellas had been warned. An agent of the state had told her what she could and could not do almost fourteen months to the day before her arrest.

HELENE MELLAS'S CHURCH, BROTHER JOE'S MEMORY

The case was back before a judge, this time in Superior Court, 10 June 1987, for the start of a hearing on a defense motion to invalidate the arrests on the grounds that the officers entered Mellas's home improperly on the days of the orientation and surgery. The court heard ten witnesses over three days of testimony, most notably Jose Bugarin, Helene Mellas, and Louise Nielsen.

What the defense lawyers hoped to show Judge John J. Boskovich was that the two healers were engaging in the constitutionally protected practice of their religion and were essentially no different from, say, Christian Science practitioners. If that were the case, then the officers had no legal basis for entering the home and taking property three different times, twice without a warrant.

"Had Brother Joe and Helene Mellas been practicing a religion, then they very possibly would have had a very complete defense or excuse for what they were doing," Druliner said.[143] The problem was, in part, that *Helene Mellas did not ask the psychic surgery patients to become members of her church.* Nor did she ask them detailed questions about their religious beliefs. She told them about psychic surgery and led them through a guided meditation. There was even a recitation of the Lord's Prayer. But Sunny Tucker hadn't come for a religious experience; neither had Mary Armstrong or Stephanie Doran. They had come for healing, and they were not expected to practice a religion.

When it was his client's turn to testify, Hale walked Mellas through a recitation of her religious education and the founding of her own church. The first questions focused on training she had received from the pastor of the Grace American Lutheran Church in Rancho Cordova, near her home.

"I was certified as a teacher after two years of intensive training. We were required, absolutely required, to study at least eight hours every day or we couldn't possibly complete the course," she said. The course makes the student a "teacher of the Bible and its messages." (According to a letter later received by Smith from the current pastor of the same church, the class Mellas took is a lay study course that gives an overview of the Bible; it does not prepare its students for ordination in the ministry. There is one classroom hour per week for six twelve-week periods.[144])

The defendant said she had been ordained a minister in the Universal Life Church in August 1980, and had received a charter for a congregation at her home address. As part of her ministry, she practices "faith healing by prayer."[145]

By testifying on direct examination, she was now available to Druliner for cross-examination. The transcript of his questioning is nearly three times longer than her testimony for Hale. First, the prosecutor got Mellas to agree that the Lutheran Bible course "literally had nothing to do" with her ordination in the Universal Life Church.

Q. "Ms. Mellas, isn't it true that you can obtain an ordination, if you will, with the Universal Life Church, just simply by asking for it from the Church?"

A   "It's my understanding that that's possible, yes."

(Indeed it is true. As part of his work on the case, Investigator Jerry A. Smith became an ordained man of the Universal Life cloth.)

Druliner's questioning established that the Rev. Mellas headed a very informal church. There is a board of directors, headed by herself, the minister. The board has no set number of members. "In other words," she explained, "we have so many at this time and they change later." There are three officers: secretary, treasurer, president. At the time of her testimony, the secretarial post was open.[146]

As far as meetings and services, "We conduct our congregation as we choose. We have our prayer meetings and gatherings as we choose. It may be with different titles, different purposes. And there isn't that kind of set routine I feel you're implying," she told Druliner.[147]

As for healing, Mellas said: "Our belief is to—to simply be instruments of God in prayer healing. And it doesn't matter to me or any other minister I know what the diagnosis of someone else may be. Diagnosis doesn't enter into it. I neither know nor am concerned with whether it's cancer."

Why, then, Druliner asked, did she have her patients write out their afflictions on a piece paper, which she then read to Brother Joe? "I did this because we have found that many people come with their complaints listed. They feel better if they—if they let the healer know what they feel is troubling them. And we read it and let them know that we have, and we put it aside and that's it. There is no way that we are concerned with what they're diagnosed to have. That is the least of my concern."[148]

Mellas acknowledged that the Universal Life Church itself neither condemns nor condones faith healing. "I can tell you that their tenet is that they believe. . .in what is right for each individual, and that there are circumstances that govern that in every case."[149] She knows of nothing in the parent church regulations prohibiting members from seeking medical care.

Did she know to what, if any, church David Thornton belonged? No, she did not.

Then came questions about money. Wasn't David Thornton required to pay before he underwent his healing sessions? "The answer is no," Mellas said. "We treated many people—or rather channeled healing to many people who hadn't paid."

Why then was the notation "Pd" included in the appointment book, instead of donation? "I really don't know," Mellas said. "It was 'contribution' or 'donation,' nothing more. I repeat, we have worked with many, many who have not been able to donate or able to donate much less than was suggested." (These contentions were not readily apparent from the appointment ledger, which lists full payments beside most appointments where a sum has been entered. In at least one case, there appear to have been treatments given without payments entered, but these were to the woman who hosted the sessions at Lake Tahoe.)

Mellas acknowledged that she did tell Lynn Thornton that the first session was forty-five dollars and that all subsequent ones were forty dollars, with the additional five dollars for the first session for registration and expenses. She did not tell Lynn Thornton that the sessions could be had for no cost. "I was not asked. I would think it's usual" for the client to ask, she said.[150] "We do not charge. No sir. We do not charge them. It's not a charge. Never has been."[151]

*   *   *

Then came Brother Joe's turn. Simmons's examination of his client produced a mere fifty-six words of testimony. Jose Bugarin recognized David Thornton from Mellas's home. He had treated him twice. Asked to describe the first session, he said,"I lay my hand and doing [sic] the spiritual healing." And the second session? "I do the same thing, laying my hands and do [sic] the spiritual healing." Was he a member of a church? "Yes sir." Which? "Union Estiritista [sic] Cristiana de Filipinas." Where is the church located? "In Manila, Philippines." How old is the church? "I believe that is about two hundred years old." How long had he been a member? "About twenty years old." And that was that.

But Druliner had questions, too. Hadn't he asked David Thornton for his family's history of cancer? "I ask the history of the family," he said. But the healer said that *he* never said the patient had cancer. Mellas had read the diagnosis from the slip of paper, and Thornton had told him how many sessions he had scheduled (three each for both days).

As for the healing itself, Jose Bugarin said he put oil on his hands, then placed them on the patient's body. "I move my hand from different way," he said, "but I don't slide my hands over the body."[152] Was Mellas doing the same thing at the same time? "I don't remember, sir, because I'm doing the spiritual healing." How long did the first treatment last? "I don't—I don't recall because I'm doing the spiritual healing."

During the first treatment, did Helene Mellas tell David Thornton that Brother Joe probably wouldn't enter the body then? "I don't remember because when I'm doing the spiritual healing, I'm not—I'm like unconscious . . . by doing prayer."[153] Did Helene Mellas ask Thornton if he belonged to any church? "I don't remember." Did Helene Mellas tell Thornton anything about Brother Joe's membership in any church? "I don't remember when I'm doing the healing because I'm like unconscious."[154]

"I don't intend to heal cancer," he said. But wasn't he attempting to heal David Thornton's lung cancer? "No sir. I just do the spiritual healing." But didn't Thornton complain *only* of having cancer? "I don't—I don't remember."[155]

Druliner tried to ask Brother Joe whether he had given similar sessions in other cities of the United States. Simmons objected; the question was clearly outside the bounds of the case before the California court. Judge Boskovich agreed, and the psychic surgeon was allowed to step down.

Druliner's arguments carried the day. The religious exclusion did not apply, the judge declared. The evidence was properly seized and could be used in the trial.

A MATTER OF CLAIMS AND EVIDENCE

As the investigation continued, Jerry Smith looked for witnesses. The most logical place to find them was from among those who had also gone to the orientation and healing sessions.

His first call, to a couple through an intermediary, was rebuffed. His second was to Dora Lewis (a pseudonym), who told him "she was having a bad day" and asked him to call back the following the week. It was Lewis who called Smith, five days later, to tell him: "When I went to see Brother Joe, the cancer had already been removed from my breast. I went to Brother Joe and Helene Mellas for religious reasons only." Smith told her she sounded "like she had been coached." Lewis responded, "I'm testifying for the other side," then hung up.

Cheryl Blanchard received a call. She refused to cooperate, telling Smith that he "was doing a terrible thing by stopping Helene Mellas and Brother Joe from continuing with their work."

The next call was to Dora Allen. She had learned about Brother Joe through a friend, contacted Helene Mellas, and booked an appointment with Brother Joe the morning of the arrest. She came from out of state to be treated. Allen sought healing "for hay fever, sinus problems, backaches, thyroid problems, and digestive problems." She didn't see what happened during her treatment; her eyes were closed. "She did not remember what took place except she received some type of massage." She told Smith she considered herself a religious person, but had no idea what beliefs Mellas and Bugarin held, "because they never discussed religion."

Another call was to a woman who had attended the orientation but skipped her scheduled surgery appointments. She had gone out of personal interest—she is a practicing psychic—but she skipped the surgery because "she had nothing wrong with her."

A man who was marked as a "no show" for a surgical appointment the morning of the arrest told Smith he'd never heard of Helene Mellas or Brother Joe. Another man said simply, "I have nothing to do with that any more" and hung up.

One of the calls produced a glowing testimonial. Mark Fengler (a pseudonym) told Smith he and his spouse had attended sessions in Tahoe and at the Mellas home. He was the first patient for the 11 A.M. session. He was being treated for knee pain, his wife for allergies.

During his Sacramento session, Mellas massaged him with oil while Brother Joe worked on his knees, extracting "white stringy pieces of tissue." Fengler said the treatment was "hard to describe because it's hard to believe," and insisted he had been helped, "because he can now play tennis." A Christian, Fengler never discussed religion with the two healers, had no idea of their religious beliefs, didn't know Mellas was a minister.

Then came interviews with Sunny and Jay Tucker, Mary Armstrong, and Stephanie Doran.

Doran provided Jerry Smith with a graphic image of the Tahoe sessions. Doran and her spouse, Frank Garcia, didn't attend the orientation the night before her first "operation," so she didn't know quite what to expect. When she entered the living room, she found herself in the middle of a "carnival-like" atmosphere. "There were approximately seventy-five persons present with approximately thirty to thirty-three patients in a row waiting to see Brother Joe and Helene Mellas." She was directed to a card table, where she signed a mailing list, was told the surgery would cost forty-five dollars. She paid in cash and was given a ticket. She was then told to go to the ladies' changing room, take off everything except her panties, put on a robe, and wait for her ticket number to be called.

Near the card table, displayed for all to see, were photo albums of psychic surgery and a brochure from a travel agency for trips to the Philippines.

After Doran changed, "the whole group joined hands and Helene Mellas talked about uniting energy, and she said the Lord's Prayer." Then came the surgeries. Doran witnessed Mary Armstrong's treatments as well as her own. She heard Brother Joe tell the woman her cancer was "all gone."

Sometime after her Tahoe sessions, after she discovered her own growth was still there, Stephanie Doran said she called Helene Mellas. According to Doran, Mellas told her that "because Brother Joe's hands are so electromagnetic, maybe what he grabbed were small tumors and not the larger one." The solution Doran said she was offered was to return to Brother Joe for more treatments when he came to Sacramento in April.

Convinced by her husband and the doctor's prognosis, she resorted to medical treatment instead. The growth was surgically removed. It proved benign.[156]

*   *   *

Less than a week after the court heard the defense motion to suppress evidence, the BMQA investigators received the first of two lab reports on the tissue samples seized in the arrest. Meridee C. Smith, criminalist with the District Attorney's Laboratory of Forensic Services, said the "bullets" were "twelve cotton balls saturated with blood. Enclosed with each ball is apparent fatty tissue. The blood was determined to be neither of human nor fowl origin." Ms. Smith also tested the liquid from the toilet, but not the stringy tissue. The liquid was neither human nor fowl in origin.[157]

California law affords defendants a very important right: *discovery*. Anyone charged with a crime is entitled to see everything in the prosecution's hands. All investigative notes, recordings, pictures, physical evidence, statements, and lab tests must be available to the defense. (There is no similar obligation on the part of the defense.)

Knowing what will confront them when the case comes to court, the defense attorney and client may decide to "plea bargain" with the prosecutor. The process is a compromise, but a realistic one. Trials cost a great deal of money. Lawyers are expensive, and a lengthy trial can consume a fortune. For both sides, there are investigators to pay, expert witnesses (who charge up to $500 an hour, sometimes more), costly lab tests. The state, the prosecution, and ultimately the taxpayers, are paying salaries for a judge, a court clerk, a bailiff, jurors (though they receive a pittance), and all the other overhead it takes to run a court.

The prosecution already had a strong case.

But then there were the magicians . . .

There was a local group, the Society for Rational Inquiry. Composed largely of academics and other professionals, including several amateur magicians, the society had an unusual standing offer: they would give $10,000 to anyone who could demonstrate *any* miraculous power at all—faith-healing, mind-reading, future-event-prediction, mind-over-matter. All the applicant had to do was pass a test under scientifically controlled conditions jointly agreed upon beforehand.

It was my involvement with the Society for Rational Inquiry that led me to the Brother Joe case. I was editor of the group's newsletter, *Psientific American*, and a partial sponsor of the reward. On learning of the arrests, I met with David Druliner and Jerry Smith at Druliner's office to tell them about two magicians who had made psychic surgery a special study. One was an accountant, Robert Steiner of the San Francisco area, who was also president of the Society of American Magicians.

The other was James Randi. A grey-bearded, fiery-eyed professional conjurer, Randi had just been awarded a MacArthur Foundation "Genius" fellowship in recognition of his role in debunking other faith-healers, as well as the indefatigable "psychic" huckster Uri Geller. Randi had a $10,000 offer of his own, predating by two decades the skeptics' offer. But his offer wasn't the oldest. Erich Weiss, the great Houdini, had offered his $10,000 up to his dying day. None of the offers had ever paid out.

Both Steiner and Randi had been following the Philippine psychic surgeons for years. Randi had amassed a substantial library of videotapes, and he'd gone on "The Tonight Show with Johnny Carson" three months earlier with a demonstration of this chicanery. Both Steiner and Randi would be willing to testify that they had thoroughly investigated the art of "psychic surgery" and found nothing but sleight-of-hand artistry.

Independent of ours, another skeptic's group made contact with the prosecutor. Bela Scheiber of the Colorado-based Rocky Mountain Skeptics reported that his organization had been instrumental in running Brother Joe out of their state, with the help of a Denver TV station. The TV report estimated that Brother Joe may have taken in as much as $17,000 in one weekend—a figure that seems very high, compared with the take from the Mellas sessions.

Scheiber, a systems analyst for telecommunications firm U.S. West, managed to sneak a sample of the blood, which turned out to have come from a chicken. He appeared on television with the lab report. There was one significant variation from the Tahoe and Sacramento sessions. Would-be patients were required to sign disclaimers that they knew Brother Joe was only providing "spiritual assistance" and was not licensed to practice medicine.[158] All this information regarding Brother Joe's m.o. would be available for a trial.

*   *   *

Sometime during the summer, a mailing had gone out, headed:

CRUSADE
for
SPIRITUAL JUSTICE
Pick Up Your Faith and Join With Us

The brochure reveals something of Helene Mellas's own feelings about her plight; it also conveys an urgent plea for money and volunteer help. Excerpts:

> On April 3, 1987, I was arrested in my home by officers of California State Medical Board of Quality Assurance [sic]. Also arrested was a Philippine healer. We were charged with two counts of practicing medicine

without a license. . . . Both are felony charges.

At the time of this invasion of my home and my right to privacy, we were involved in spiritual healing. I am a minister and healing is a strong part of my ministry. I also conduct crystal workshops and offer quartz crystals for sale to raise funds for my church.

Subsequent to the arrest, the BMQA agents returned to my residence on May 5th with a search warrant which gave these agents the right to seize every crystal in my house that had a price tag on it. The District Attorney's Office intends to use these as further evidence in the prosecution of my case. Since crystals are an 'alternative' means of healing, it seems obvious they will attack all those who use them in this manner.

The case against me is obviously one of religious persecution. I believe in the right of everyone to practice any form of spiritual healing within his or her religious beliefs and to choose the kind of healing to be practiced upon his or her body, I also know these rights are being threatened and that this case will set a precedent. If this case is won, it will open the doors more widely to all natural forms of healing. If the case is lost, our persecutors will go on to close more doors.

Because of the way our legal system works, even when one is innocent, the cost of defending yourself is devastating. An attorney who believes as we believe has already donated approximately $15,000.00 of his legal time and advice. He has advised me that this case may continue from three to five years before it is settled. The legal costs and attorneys' fees will be in excess of $60,000. *We need financial help.* Donations to the Legal Defense Fund should be made payable to William E. Hale in trust for Helene Mellas . . .

Included with the appeal was the announcement of the "soon to be formed Association of Natural and Spiritual Practitioners," which would offer business and administrative consulting, networking, legislative and legal counseling to New Age healers of all stripes. With the announcement was a questionnaire for prospective members.

There is no evidence of how her fund plea fared. Faced, however, with the prosecution's evidence and the threat of devastating legal expenses, by 8 February 1988 Helene Mellas made a crucial decision.[159] In exchange for no jail time, she would enter a plea of "no contest" to the charge of practicing medicine without a license—and she would give her full cooperation to the prosecution.

Helene Mellas had rolled over on Brother Joe.

The plea was reasonable from the prosecution's standpoint. Druliner was convinced that Helene Mellas was sincere in her belief in psychic surgery. She was not a confidence artist; she had been conned as well. These were *friends* she was bringing in for treatment. She was a believer. And her testimony could be invaluable in trial. If she had damning things to say about Brother Joe, there was a good chance the jury would believe her.

From Helene Mellas's perspective, the plea was also reasonable. She wouldn't have to go to jail, and a "no contest" plea couldn't be used as evidence against her should she be sued by some of the patients in a civil proceeding. She would also avoid the agony and expense of a trial.

The triangular relationship between the prosecution, Helene Mellas, and Jose Bugarin had shifted. Now Brother Joe's own codefendant was making a statement to Jerry Smith, a statement that would be made available to Brother Joe through the pretrial discovery process. His ally had become his enemy.

*   *   *

In 1981 Helene Mellas had seen an advertisement for Joseph Martinez, the San Franciscan who healed through pulling-and-tugging channeled "spirit psychic surgeons." She called in relation to an eye problem; "I also just wanted to meet him," she said. When they met, "I was interested in some of the concepts that he offered and so we made an agreement to begin teaching at my house." So the two began working together. Martinez "never touches. He doesn't even do the laying on of hands. No, never anything like this."

She remembered BMQA Investigator Ron Keszler's visit. "I actually have a date on that." The investigator came one afternoon at five. "It was a very pleasant visit," she said. "We sat in the living room and talked. He asked me questions about what I did, about some of my beliefs and practices. Then I suggested that we go into my workroom as I call it, so that he could see where I worked, and we just continued to talk for a while. And he was a very amiable person."

What, Jerry Smith asked, had she concluded from Keszler's visit? She gropes for an answer: "My feeling, well, what he tells me was, he left me with the feeling that what I was doing was fine so long as I didn't step beyond those bounds."

It was someone she met through Joseph Martinez who led her to Brother Joe. "I can't remember her saying that Vic told her or Vic asked her to, you know. I was called and asked if I would like to sponsor a healer, and I told the person that I would have to call them back. And I did a lot of praying and asking God, 'Is this what you want me to do? Is this what I am to do?' And the feeling was so strong I went with it. And Vic [Mapa] set it up and he and Joe came in the evening and met us. We had dinner together and then the next morning we went to work."

As a sponsor, she understood it to be her duty "simply to get some people in. And it wasn't any trouble at all. I had students who were climbing all over each other wanting to help and wanting to experience it." Volunteers were assigned as greeters and hosts. A registration list was started, with names, addresses, telephone numbers. "He also told me how he wanted the room arranged that night. Fortunately I had a massage table that belonged to a friend of mine and we put that up and used it."

Smith asked her what she believed Mapa's role to be. "The term that I heard both him and Joe use all the time was Joe's agent. He made the bookings for him when he went," she said.

Before their September 1985 meeting at her home, Mellas had spoken to Mapa;[160] he had called her to say "they would work from this time to that time, so many hours a day. And how many people he could see in an hour. That sort of thing. Vic would say what he thought the donation should be, because I had no idea of anything like that. And I did ask him about people who couldn't afford to pay, and he said, 'Then you simply tell Brother Joe and ask him.' And at any time I did, he said, 'No problem. Let them come.' "

At first, Helene Mellas said, she received nothing for her time and expenses in hosting the sessions. She was footing the bill for postage, long-distance calls—"there were a lot of people would call from out of town, out of the country even—and I got nothing in the beginning for it." Later, the five dollar surcharge was added to the first session "donation" to cover Mellas's costs. By late 1986, she had stopped giving her own classes.

In the operating room, she was the assistant, attentive to Brother Joe's every need. "He just told me what to do, and that was it." But the "telling" wasn't always verbal. "I had to learn to watch which way his head was going to land, because I never knew which to pick up, the oil or the cotton."

And when she gave him the cotton, *it wasn't dry*. "There was a teeny bit of water so that the cotton would be moist when he rubbed it on the body," she said. All the healers use oil too, she said. "They say it grasps the energies better or something, makes it easier on the body . . . I don't know why, but that was what I was doing."

After the surgeries, patients would often ask to see the tissues, and Mellas would hold them up. Only two patients asked to take the gore with them, and both times Brother Joe said "no." Mellas never asked why.

"If you listened to Joe and some of the other healers explain it, it's as though the negative energies that are in the body sort of congeal and form something that you can look at and something that your mind will set off. 'There's the thing that was wrong,' and that's all.

"Tony always said that it was because the people would not believe if they didn't see something. He said you could stand there and wave your hands over them all day long, but his spirit protector said, 'You take something out and tell them "That's the bad, it's gone," and they're going to believe it.' "

"It's just a manifestation. It doesn't necessarily have to be a piece of an organ or something like that." In the Philippines, she said, healers in rural areas extract banana leaves, stones, and other foreign objects.

"That's why I said manifestation. It wasn't actually in there. I cannot explain this part. I can only say that there is, because through what Christ did and what he taught, I believe that the Holy Spirit, working with mine, working with consciousness, can do all kinds of things."

Mellas displayed the tissue, then passed it to the bathroom to be flushed down the toilet. "We didn't want it. Some of it smells horribly, especially if they've been smoking."

Helene Mellas said she was never told explicitly that psychic surgery was illegal. The term "be careful" was used, and participants were urged not to tell people who were opposed to it. Once, Mapa called and asked her to help another woman host a session in Gardnerville. The woman had heard about Brother Joe and tracked him down in New York or Boston, seeking treatment "for a cyst on her ovary or something of the kind" that had been causing her pain. After the treatment, the pain stopped, and the woman told Mellas she had called Mapa and asked Brother Joe to her home to help her ex-husband and others. "I believe that it was Vic then that let me know about that, and said that he'd like me to help her because she didn't know anything about it."

Mellas assisted with other out-of-town sessions, including the ones at Tahoe. "A whole lot of times people were picking me up and taking me there." The last one was held at her home, "simply because there was one woman who asked Joe to come. . . before he left the area, because of his heart, he could not go in to the altitude [at Tahoe]."

There had never been any complaints "until this last time," when she had heard from Stephanie Doran and Sunny Tucker, she said. But then, she acknowledged, "a lot of them I never saw again."

In talking of the Tahoe sessions, Helene Mellas disputed some of the statements made by Sunny Tucker and Stephanie Doran. She said she didn't believe Brother Joe had told Doran that he had removed her growth. "Usually he says, 'That's all. Bye-bye, see you next time.' " According to Mellas, Doran "kept saying, 'Oh, look at that. My tumor is out.' I said, 'That's not what it is, look.' And I had to keep telling her, 'This is tissue,' because you can't say that's the tumor."

"Sunny called the first time in tears, telling me that Mary wasn't feeling well," she said. "I was devastated by that. I really liked Mary." But she did not recommend that Mary Armstrong postpone any tests. Indeed, Mellas said, Sunny Tucker had said that the physician had approved putting off tests while Armstrong tried spiritual healing.[161] Neither had she ever told Mary Armstrong or her sister that Tucker had been healed. "I said, 'We never told you it would be.' "

Because she was preparing for her Easter trip to the Philippines, Mellas originally agreed only to "just a little bit of time on a Sunday morning, and that's it."Mapa called her later to tell her, "'Since Joe's going to come, I fixed it so he has time enough he can see people for two or three days.' I remember telling him I'd never get packed, and he said, 'Oh, you can pack overnight. Don't worry about it.' And so it stretched out into a big one, which I had not wanted at all."

When the arrests came, Helene Mellas told Smith she didn't see him pull the packet of bullets from Brother Joe's pocket. "I didn't even know you did that. I was so frightened about Joe because if you could see you and him from where I was standing, I thought you were going to crush him against the wall. He is so little. I thought, 'What are you doing to him?' And then I thought you were just checking him for—in fact I heard him [Thornton?] say, 'Does he have anything on him, a weapon?' or something like that.

"When I saw that stuff on TV, I thought it was the biggest set-up anybody could ever pull. I did not believe anything like that came out of my house. I didn't know what it was until my attorney told me. And I couldn't believe it, that there was any kind of cotton balls or fakery stuff on him. I was floored."

Rather than believe Brother Joe had committed fraud, she chose to think that he had been set up by a state agency controlled by the medical establishment. Only when her attorney, a fellow believer, told her that Joe was carrying concealed bullets did she finally admit the possibility of deceit. "How could he ever have done it," she asked herself. "Never had I seen him do this."

She did recall that Joe used to stand with his thumbs down in his pocket, and walk in a peculiar manner during the surgeries, as though stretching his shoulders. She also remembered that both men always brought briefcases to the surgeries, and "sometimes Vic would come in carrying a bag with cotton and oil and things like that. This last time he did bring the baby oil. Also the small bottles of the oriental oil or whatever it is that they added to the baby oil. He always supplied that. I don't know where they got that, because I certainly have never found it anywhere other than the Philippines." The oil, which apparently contained a strong scent, was never tested.

She said she finally conceded some deception had been committed when first Brother Joe and then Mapa admitted it to her.

She said Brother Joe made his admission during a face-to-face meeting of only the two of them in the office of Brother Joe's attorney. "He was very, very apologetic, and he said, 'I am so sorry. Vic prepares these for me,' he said. And I said, 'Why? Because I know you can heal and you know you can. You don't need these things. What was it for?'

"And he said when you work on so many people in a day, he would get so tired that he couldn't open a channel strong enough. I said, 'Then you should just refuse to work on so many people,' and I was really angry. And he said nothing, and I walked out."

*   *   *

Mellas encountered Mapa on the Easter Philippines pilgrimage she made after the arrest. She said she was "left with the impression" that Mapa prepared the bullets for Brother Joe. "He tried to give me a song and dance about, 'Well, all the healers do that, you know, when they get tired.' And I said, 'That's not true; I don't believe it. I've watched too many, and I've watched them . . . on the Holy Mountain. It's very primitive there.' "

She remained convinced that Brother Joe was a genuine healer. "I don't know why he would have had to do it if the excuse was because he was really fatigued later on. My feeling was that what he did that morning was legitimate, up to that point," she said. "I never, ever believed that he was doing anything that was other than honorable, absolutely did not. Never did I see him do anything that was questionable to me.

"I still think the man has tremendous healing powers and I think that he has great abilities in that direction, and I think that it was a tremendous mistake for him to allow himself to do something like that, whether for gain, whether to please . . . Vic, whatever reason, it was a dreadful mistake. And I'm just really disappointed."

Those were her last encounters with the two men, she told Smith.

Mellas remains to this day a firm believer in psychic surgery. Lynn Thornton asked her what she would do if her son were a child again, "a boy who had cancer or some operable condition—appendix, let's say. He needed an operation; what would you do with him?"

MELLAS: "If I were told it was about to rupture, I'd take him to the nearest hospital. And if I were told it was a condition [that] was growing, I'd take him to the Philippines.
THORNTON: "When he was grown?"
MELLAS: "Well, like if he had a tumor, and they said, 'If this gets any bigger, he's really going to have a problem and this should come out,' but it's not an overnight threat, like an appendix."
THORNTON: "Why would it matter?"
MELLAS: "Because I would want to try the other first, before being cut upon, before doing that. Because I think that our bodies have all their parts and pieces for a purpose."

THE CHURCH OF DIVINE MAN

Brother Joe's most outspoken defender was a church that practices channelling and whose leaders promote tours to Philippine psychic surgeons. According to officials of the Church of Divine Man, Brother Joe is the victim of a conspiracy by the medical establishment.

The church was founded in Berkeley, California, in November 1973, "to disseminate its faith as given in its Creed and Holy Books; to conduct religious services, to conduct, charter or affiliate with churches, congregations, societies, libraries, schools, colleges or institutes for the advancement of its Faith and the development of religious education, to teach and practice the healing of the sick and suffering by means of prayer and other spiritual remedies without the use of remedies or material aids, to found and conduct within itself such orders, divisions and companies as may be deemed necessary for its operations, to accept fees, contributions and donations, to publish, promote and sell or donate its publications."[162]

A state tax-exemption followed.

The church created a seminary, called the Berkeley Psychic Institute, begun in that San Francisco Bay city, which now has affiliates in San Jose, Santa Rosa, Sacramento, Palo Alto, Pleasanton, San Anselmo, and Concord in Northern California, and Los Angeles and Carlsbad in Southern California.

The church first created a monthly publication, known today as *Psychic Reader*, "The Only Newspaper By Psychics For Psychics," and which receives extensive free distribution through bookstores and New Age businesses in Northern California. The paper is the product of Deja Vu Publishing Company, "a religious corporation . . . affiliated with The Church of Divine Man."[163] In its present incarnation, *Psychic Reader* is an attractive, graphically sophisticated tabloid, full of articles and columns. Readers will find a full range of New Age services in the advertisements.

You can find, for example, a veterinarian who gives not only rabies shots but "pet readings" that describe the animal's past lives, *karma*, health, and goals, among other things, and who'll give a taped reading by mail. Another offers "professional performance readings" for those with "past lives as a performer, performance anxiety, and burnout." Others offer past-life regression classes, "a Chinese life-extension mushroom," "spiritually focused psychotherapy," computerized horoscopes, acupressure, the stones that "would help you most," a "medicine teacher/shamanic practice apprentice program for women," "clairvoyant numerology readings," "the Japan Life Sleep System," "wholistic aura evaluation," a mail-order guide titled *California's Nude Beaches*, and the services of the Reverend Joseph Martinez and his "unique variation of the Philippine Psychic Surgery."[164]

The president and founder of the church is The Very Right Reverend Lewis J. Bostwick, whose main public exposure, other than church publications, has been a regular monthly public lecture entitled "You May Be Psychic, Not Crazy." The Very Right Reverend Bostwick and his spouse, *Psychic Reader* Editor Susan Hull Bostwick, also write monthly for the newspaper.

*   *   *

The first sign of the church's interest in the Brother Joe case came in January 1988, when the paper reported that an unnamed minister, during a church New Year's Eve mass channelling, had predicted "a psychic surgeon would be prosecuted." There was no mention of where or when. The "prediction" was made eight months *after* the arrests, and reported in an issue carrying an ad for the Reverend Joseph Martinez. The paper subsequently linked the prediction with the Bugarin case, and claimed it as a clairvoyant "hit."

In March 1988, attorney and Church of Divine Man Bishop Michael J. Tamura wrote a column appearing in the paper under the caption "Are You Above the Law?"[165] Tamura was then assembling a book, based on his past columns, to be titled *Jesus Was Not an M.D.—Or How to Handle the Medical Inquisition*. Psychics performing healings are "truly above the law," he wrote, because the place where healing occurs is beyond space, time, and human law. He advised every psychic to learn "what laws, religion and churches have to do with being psychic." He used the analogy of buying car insurance, with the additional factor of the Board of Medical Quality Assurance investigators, whom he likened to government agents "hired to deliberately seek you out and crash into your car and sue you just because you don't have insurance."

But perhaps the strongest *Psychic Reader* article appeared in the August

1988 issue in a column by bishop/attorney Tamura, headlined: "Psychic Surgeon Charged/Innocent Until Proven Guilty?"

In the article, Tamura reports—accurately—that Brother Joe was given the offer of avoiding all jail time if he would plead guilty to the practicing medicine without a license charge and agree to provide the government with information about psychic surgery and the business of importing healers into the United States.

Tamura asks: Who did Brother Bugarin kill, injure, rob, or steal from? Each time the answer is "No one." It is no crime to be a psychic surgeon and minister of churches in the United States and the Philippines. What, then, he asks, is happening?

It is, Tamura says, the "Medical Inquisition," which consists of the American Medical Association and the rest of the doctor-drug-hospital industry, operating through its law enforcement representatives in California, the Board of Medical Quality Assurance.[166]

There is also a hint of what is to come. How can a healer, Tamura wonders, bear up under the huge expense of "allowing the State to prove you are a criminal?"

The November edition reported: "Filipino Faith Healer Jailed."

Indeed, he had been.

After back-and-forth negotiations with the District Attorney's office, Bugarin entered a "no contest" plea in August 1988, which he then sought to withdraw. Finally, on 27 September 1988, Jose Bugarin agreed to be sentenced. Druliner, Simmons, and Bugarin appeared before Sacramento County Superior Court Judge James L. Long.

Simmons noted in court that Bugarin had not pleaded guilty. "He entered a plea of no contest."

"—of no contest," the judge interposed, "which has the same force and effect if guilty, which I think I told him when his plea was taken."[167]

Bugarin agreed to be sentenced, asking the court for a thirty-day delay before the start of his jail term. Simmons then made a plea for leniency. Jose Bugarin still claimed he believed he was practicing a religious art, not medicine. But "as a result of personal feelings, he has decided not to go forward with the trial in order not to jeopardize other people who share the same beliefs that he does." While he was willing to take whatever punishment the court meted out, his lawyer asked the court to note that Helene Mellas, who had appeared for sentencing less than three weeks earlier, had received only a fine and an order to donate 100 hours of community service time. Brother Joe was employed, and anything he made from his surgery was duly reported to the federal and state tax agencies. He has agreed not to perform any more surgeries.

Then came the prosecution's turn. David Druliner first maintained that the cases of Jose Bugarin and Helene Mellas were very different.

Ms. Mellas, he said, "at a relatively early stage in the proceedings agreed to cooperate with the prosecution and provide us with a good deal of information" on Bugarin and the psychic surgery "scam that is being used by the defendant and others like him."

The victims of psychic surgery, he said, "are people who are extremely defenseless, and in a very, very awkward position in their lives" and have exhausted avenues of medical help. "They, for the most part, are people who have been diagnosed with problems such as incurable cancer. People such as Mr. Bugarin simply prey on them and take advantage of them. He can claim anything he would like" about practicing the tenets of a religion. "I would submit to you he's not. He knows he's not. He knows he's not helping these people," only "giving them false and misleading thoughts and hopes in taking money from them." Druliner asked the judge to impose the maximum sentence under the plea bargain, a year in County Jail.

Simmons was quick to respond. Brother Joe had many witnesses he could have called to testify to his "good will and kind heart, and all the help that he has helped them with regarding their problems. Mr. Bugarin has opted not to place those people in jeopardy." In fact, "he martyred himself on behalf of those people." Simmons started to say something else, but the judge interrupted: "He martyred himself with money, [didn't] he?"

"I wouldn't agree with the court regarding that at all," Simmons replied.

With these comments, the judge passed sentence: "I note that in the crime that you committed, basically what you did was, you took advantage, despite whatever good faith belief that you had as a psychic surgeon in representing to people—desperate people—you could remove tumors from their bodies and cure them of possible deadly illness.

"And I noted also, that despite what your lawyer says, that you are not doing it out of charity and good wishes to assist those persons who were physically ill, but you were charging money for people who were really emotionally involved in . . . their own specific sicknesses and disabilities in reaching out . . . for any possible cure," including " 'phoney' ones."

[Although Jose Bugarin said he was only religiously motivated], "I do note that despite that, there was a significant monetary interest on your part, and what you did was to bill persons who were in a desperate situation."[168]

Judge Long gave Brother Joe nine months in County Jail and ordered him to pay a $400 fine. The thirty-day delay in commencing sentence was denied, and Brother Joe was ordered to begin serving his term on 3 October 1988, eighteen months to the day after his arrest.[169]

A story in the November *Psychic Reader* portrayed Jose Bugarin as a selfless martyr, who had elected to go to jail rather than bring any harm or unwanted exposure to his clients. Simmons is quoted: "His religious belief and his choice of the loss of personal freedom guaranteed that other people would get to enjoy theirs."

NOTES

1. *Board of Medical Quality Assurance Investigative Report*, Cases 2–04556 & 04568, p. 24. (Hereafter abbreviated *BMQA*.)

2. *BMQA*, Case 2–04556, p. 3.

3. M. A. Lee, and B. Schlain, *Acid Dreams*, p. 29.

4. MacLaine, *Going Within*, p. 206.

5. MacLaine, op. cit., p. 227.

6. Entitled "My Body as Atoms of Ultimate Awareness," op. cit., pp. 213–39.

7. Personal communication.

8. MacLaine, op. cit., p. 232.

9. San Francisco: Celestial Arts, 1986.

10. Ibid., p. 230.

11. *Encyclopedia Britannica Macropedia*, (Chicago, 1982) VI:427.

12. Helene Mellas has described a classic near-death experience, an NDE. Ronald K. Siegel, a psychologist at the University of California, Los Angeles, is considered the world's leading authority on hallucinatory experiences. He has done extensive research on mind-altering drugs and other hallucinogens. A close comparison between NDEs and chemically induced hallucinations shows no significant difference between them. NDEs, he writes, are "hallucinations, based on stored images in the brain. Like a mirage that shows a magnificent city on a desolate expanse of ocean or desert, the images of hallucinations are actually reflected images of real objects located elsewhere." There is no scientific evidence in the reports to justify any claims of reality for the images seen, no hidden information disclosed that was not already known or believed. Siegel makes one additional observation. "Even if the experience of life after death doesn't lead to a 'real' other world, the belief may very well change behavior in this one." For Helene Mellas that was certainly to be the case. See Ronald K. Siegel's "Life After Death," in *Science and the Paranormal, Probing the Existence of the Supernatural*, George O. Abell and Barry Singer, eds. (New York: Charles Scribner's Sons, 1983), p. 184.

13. Heart Center brochure.

14. For example, see Martin Gardner's classic *Fads and Fallacies in the Name of Science* (New York: Dover Books, 1957).

15. A pseudonym.

16. The University of California, Davis, teaching hospital, located in Sacramento.

17. In an interview with the writer.

18. *BMQA*, pp. 23–24.

19. This and all subsequent quotes from the action are drawn from the *Initial Decision in the Matter of Travel King, Inc., et al.*, (hereafter *Travel King*) Federal Trade Commission Decisions, 86 FTC 715.

20. Ibid., p. 764.

21. Telephone interview, 5 July 1989.

22. From a declaration of 8 August 1974 by the firm's owners, Adeline C. and Emile H. Heredia.

23. M. W. M. Travel Inc., incorporated in California 11 May 1982. Victorino P. Mapa and Flordelisa T. Mapa are two the six corporate officers listed on filings with the California Secretary of State, and Victorino P. Mapa is listed as president in 1983 and executive vice-president the following year. On 1 May 1984 the company's right to do business as a corporation was suspended by the state for failure to pay an annual fee.

24. Jose Bugarin in Probation Report, 30 August 1988, p. 6.

25. Ibid.

26. "Deal lets 'psychic surgeon' escape charges," Associated Press story in the *Portland Oregonian*, 4 March 1989, p. C–4. He was found to be using cow organs. His business cards carried an ad for a company offering package tours to the Philippines. See Carollo, Russell,

" 'Psychic surgery' defended by some, scorned by others," Spokane, WA: *Spokesman-Review/ Spokane Chronicle*, 5 February 1989, pp. 1, 12.

27. "Bleeding them dry," *Arizona Republic*, 11 August 1986, p. A-1.
28. *Preliminary Hearing*, transcript (hereafter abbreviated *PH*), p. 54.
29. All quotes are taken from a transcript included in the *BMQA*.
30. *BMQA*, p. 6.
31. *Motion to Suppress*, p. 399. (Hereafter abbreviated *MTS*.)
32. The sign was seized at the time of the arrests.
33. *BMQA*, p. 7.
34. *MTS* hearing transcript, p. 371.
35. Ibid.
36. *MTS* hearing transcript, p. 110.
37. Ralph Metzner, interview with author, 1972.
38. *PH*, pp. 56–57.
39. *BMQA*, p. 8.
40. Ibid.
41. Ibid.
42. *PH*, p. 55.
43. *BMQA*, p. 8.
44. *PH*, p. 54.
45. *PH*, p. 103.
46. *Travel King*, p. 715.
47. Copyright 1985.
48. Agpaoa has his own group, the Philippine Church of Science and Revelation.
49. Nolen, William M.D., p. 172.
50. Lynn Thornton, *MTS*, pp. 15, 76; Jerry Smith, *Affidavit for Search Warrant*, 30 April 1987, p. 7.
51. *Travel King*, pp. 729–730.
52. An associate of Mapa told me in January 1990 that a similar trip was planned for that year. Mapa subsequently denied this, telling me he hadn't conducted a trip for "two or three years."
53. Certificate of Filing and Suspension.
54. David Thornton, *PH*, p. 72.
55. David Thornton, *PH*, p. 106.
56. *MTS*, pp. 234–235.
57. Ibid., p. 251.
58. Ibid., pp. 253–254.
59. Ibid., p. 255.
60. Ibid., pp. 326–328.
61. Because of an unrelated court appointment, Deputy James Basden arrived late, at 9:30. Motion to Suppress, p. 327.
62. *MTS*, p. 328.
63. Jerry Smith, *MTS*, pp. 220–221.
64. Photocopy of appointment book.
65. *PH*, p. 63.
66. Ibid., p. 61.
67. Ibid., p. 126.
68. Ibid., p. 65.
69. *BMQA*, pp. 9–10;.
70. Ibid. p. 10.
71. *PH*, p. 46.
72. Ibid. p. 66, Sunny Tucker interview.
73. Unless otherwise noted, the material for this section is drawn largely from *Travel King*, pp. 744–48.
74. *Travel King*, p. 744
75. Ibid.
76. Ibid.

77. Ibid., p. 245.

78. Ibid., p. 746.

79. Tony Rumbo, Tony Alcantara, Juanito Flores, Tony Santiago, Jose Mercado, Felicia Irtal, Rosita Bascos, Marcello, and Rudy Paltayan. Ibid., p. 715.

80. *PH*, p. 110.

81. *MTS*, p. 28.

82. Ibid. p. 28.

83. Affidavit for Search Warrant, 6 April 1987, p. 2.

84. *PH*, p. 149.

85. The woman, who identified herself as Brother Joe's girlfriend, was never charged. She faithfully accompanied Bugarin to court the day he surrendered for his jail term.

86. *PH*, p. 138.

87. *MTS*, p. 275.

88. David Thornton, *PH*, pp. 64, 144.

89. *MTS*, p. 27.

90. Ibid., pp. 145–146; *PH*, p. 154.

91. Ibid., p. 147.

92. *PH*, p. 154.

93. Ibid., p. 162.

94. Ibid., p. 153.

95. *MTS*, p. 277.

96. *Affidavit for Search Warrant*.

97. *PH*, p. 67.

98. Ibid.

99. *MTS*, p. 279.

100. Appointment ledger.

101. *BMQA*, pp. 19–20.

102. Ibid., p. 20.

103. Interview with writer.

104. *MTS*, p. 119.

105. Ibid., p. 110.

106. Ibid., p. 33.

107. Ibid., p. 286.

108. *PH*, p. 9.

109. David Thornton, *PH*, p. 75.

110. *Affidavit for Search Warrant*, p. 4; *PH*, p. 195.

111. *MTS*, p. 291.

112. Ibid., p. 234.

113. Ibid., p. 292.

114. Ibid., p. 223.

115. Ibid., pp. 120–122.

116. Ibid., p. 405.

117. Ibid., pp. 405, 409.

118. KCRA TV-3 News tape of the arrest, broadcast on "Channel 3 Reports" 5 p.m. the day of the arrest.

119. *MTS*, p. 224.

120. A pseudonym.

121. Ibid., p. 380.

122. Ibid., p. 413.

123. Ibid., p. 408.

124. Ibid., p. 410.

125. Ibid., p. 411.

126. Ibid., p. 344.

127. Ibid., pp. 349–351.

128. Ibid., pp. 385–394.

129. Ibid., pp. 393–394.

130. Ibid., p. 353.

131. *BMQA,* "Evidence List."
132. *PH,* p. 174.
133. *PH,*pp. 211–223.
134. *Affidavit for Search Warrant,* p. 2.
135. Sec. 1531 of the *California Penal Code* allows officers serving a valid warrant to force entry when admission is refused.
136. *BMQA,* 27 December 1984.
137. Ibid., 4 February 1986.
138. Ibid., p. 24.
139. The "aura" is another Indo-Tibetan concept popularized by the Theosophists. It is declared to be a sheath (or series of sheaths) of light energy enveloping the body and representing a subtle, "etheric" or "astral" body invisible to the spiritually unenlightened. No substantial scientific evidence has ever been offered for its existence, but it is an integral part of most New Age beliefs.
140. As seen in a videotape, produced by his nonprofit foundation, seized from Helene Mellas's home the day of her arrest.
141. This is one of many interesting claims made in his regular column for the New Age magazine *Magical Blend.*
142. Shirley MacLaine claims that a crystal, placed atop a television set, "draws in the radiation that the color TV emits." Be sure to "cleanse" the crystal in sea salt every three months, she advises, and you might even throw in some apple cider vinegar just to be on the safe side. Be sure only to handle the thing with a cloth; "otherwise, you are absorbing radiation from the TV into your body." See MacLaine, op. cit., pp. 137–138. (Note that this would be easy to verify, thanks to all sorts of modern radiation monitoring technology. Then, of course MacLaine might be talking about *spiritual* energy . . .)
143. Interview of 29 May 1989.
144. Letter of 17 June 1987 from David C. Curtright, pastor, to Jerry A. Smith.
145. *MTS,* pp. 443–448.
146. Ibid., p. 454.
147. Ibid., p. 455.
148. Ibid., p. 457.
149. Ibid., p. 460.
150. Ibid., pp. 464, 467.
151. Ibid., p. 468.
152. Ibid., p. 425.
153. Ibid., pp. 427–428.
154. Ibid., p. 437.
155. Ibid., p. 439.
156. *BMQA,* Cases 2–04556 & 2–04568, pp. 17–21.
157. Lab No. A87–172, report of 10 June 1987, received by *BMQA* 19 June.
158. Conversations with TV reporter Ward Lucas and Bela Scheiber; Scheiber's account, "Psychic Surgery Comes to Denver" in *The Rocky Mountain Skeptic,* September/October 1986, pp. 1, 3.
159. The date of a letter of agreement between Mellas's attorneys and the District Attorney's office. Cf. Mellas statement, p. 1.
160. Mapa was in charge of two of the tours Helene Mellas took to the Philippines. "I think he worked with—oh, I'd better not say that, that's just 'think.' It's not that I know that he worked with anyone else before, but I do know that he knows a lot of healers." One tour, in January 1986, Helene Mellas booked directly through an organization in the Philippines, "called the Christian Travel something." (This would be the Christian Travel Center, which Mapa had represented exclusively in the United States while he served with Phil-Am Tours, and which has a relationship with Brother Joe's church, the Union Espiritista Cristiana de Filipinas, Inc., which was also the church of the Wrights—who had testified to the fraudulent nature of every healer they had seen.)
161. He did not, and sent her a certified letter 6 March 1987 warning her that "delay in treatment may cause the tumor to become incurable, and eventually become a fatal situation." From a copy in writer's files.

162. *Articles of Incorporation*, California Secretary of State's corporate filing number 692604, filed 8 November 1973.

163. *Articles of Incorporation*, California Secretary of State corporate No. 1090195, filed 15 September 1981.

164. A sampling from the August 1989 edition.

165. Op. cit., p. 11.

166. Druliner ridicules the charge. "There was no influence of any sort put on us by anyone at all." Nobody called him from the AMA. (From interview with the writer, 24 May 1989).

167. Court transcript, p. 4.

168. Ibid., pp. 10–11.

169. This writer tried to interview Bugarin before he surrendered himself to begin his sentence. His only comment was, "You'll get yours someday."

PART III

A MATRIX
FOR CHANGE

I am a clinical psychologist. I first read about LSD in Life. *Then I heard that a friend of mine was to do an experiment with LSD. I offered to help, with the proviso that I be one of the subjects. The experience so impressed me that I felt that LSD had therapeutic possibilities, so I tried it therapeutically on myself, with such extraordinary results that Dr. [Sidney] Cohen and I felt that a therapeutic study should be done. The study turned up some quite remarkable phenomena.*

My work with LSD, while extremely interesting therapeutically, uncovered the possibility for research into psychodynamics and into the unconscious. Even more exciting than the therapeutic possibilities of LSD are its potentials, and those of similar drugs, for helping us to answer the many questions we have about what makes us what we are as human beings.

—Dr. Betty Grover Eisner
The Second Josiah Macy, Jr.,
Foundation Symposium on LSD
(Covertly funded by the CIA)
Princeton, New Jersey, 1959

"SHE SEEMED TO BE IN CHARGE"

Although he'd answered some 3,100 calls as a fire department paramedic, as he stepped into the living room of the spacious Spanish colonial home William Michael Curtis realized this one was different. There, on what looked like a physician's examining table, lay the blanket-draped body of a man, face down, being worked over by two muscular men. They were performing the outmoded lift-the-arms-and-press-the-chest form of artificial resuscitation. On the floor near the head of the table was a wastebasket; inside were bloody tissues.

But the strangest thing was the group. "Approximately fifteen or twenty people were standing in a circle around the patient. They were holding hands and had interlocking arms. They weren't doing anything except standing there." Curtis looked from the stricken man to the group and asked what had happened. There was no response. He asked again, and again no response. Finally an older woman stepped forward and began to answer. "She seemed to be in charge," Curtis said.

The call had come in at 8:38 P.M., and six minutes later the paramedic was pulling up in front of the house, located on La Mesa Drive in Santa Monica, the most exclusive street of one of Southern California's most exclusive neighborhoods. As he entered the house, he passed a foyer filled with coats, sweaters, purses, and shoes.

It was a Friday night, 18 November 1976. Curtis was witnessing the start of what was to become a landmark California case, the costliest, lengthiest, most complex licensing action ever undertaken by the state against a psychologist.

*   *   *

Curtis and his partner positioned themselves on either side of the table and turned the man over. The body was hot, especially the chest, but there was no sign of breath, no pulse, and the pupils of his eyes were fixed and dilated, a sign that his brain had been deprived of oxygen for some time. Tissue around the nose and ears had turned blue—another sign of oxygen deprivation.

Under his questioning, Curtis later said, the older woman said that the man hadn't been breathing for fifteen minutes, and that he had earlier taken a dose of Ritalin, a nervous system stimulant used mainly for treatment of hyperactive children.

The paramedics began cardiopulmonary resuscitation (CPR), using closed-chest heart massage and oxygen. Curtis set up two-way radio contact with emergency room physicians and, under their direction, set up an IV, administered emergency drugs, including sodium bicarbonate, epinephrin (adrenalin), calcium chloride, and dopamine. He attached electrodes to the man's body, to send readings on electrocardiographs at the scene to the hospital.

"He was straight-line, no rhythm," Curtis recalled. As the CPR was continued, the paramedics managed to evoke a fast, irregular heartbeat interspersed with moments of normal activity. "We never really got a good rhythm after that because he went into ventricular fibrillation," a condition associated with heart attack, drowning, or electrocution.[1] The heart was beating rapidly, irregularly, inefficiently.

The paramedics managed to keep the heart fluttering for almost an hour. "We were never able to get a rhythm that was very hopeful," he said, "so the hospital instructed us to bring him in."

*   *   *

Noel Ronald Kramer was pronounced dead on arrival at the hospital.[2] For Betty Grover Eisner, the older woman Curtis said appeared to be in charge, his death would threaten to end her career. For her patients, it was the beginning of a nightmare that would force them to reveal their innermost secrets—from sexual relationships to childhood traumas—to the harsh glare of publicity and the rigors of courtroom cross-examination.

What unfolded was almost a California caricature, a tale of psychedelic drugs, seances, communes, sex, and, ultimately, death.

This story is told largely in the words of the participants, harvested from transcripts, court declarations, police reports, and the writer's own interviews. Dr. Eisner and her attorney declined to be interviewed for this book; it was, the attorney said, not in Dr. Eisner's best interest to be interviewed, nor to have others interviewed about the case.[3] However, I have been able to find Dr. Eisner's statements on almost all aspects of the case and have included them. I hope she will tell her story someday. She is a remarkable person who was in a remarkable place at a remarkable time. Her story is important.

TO THE STARS
THROUGH DISCIPLINE

She believed that our bodies have pretty much evolved into a static form. . . . Our next evolutionary change or development must therefore be psychic and her group was making that change. To her, the group represented humanity's leading edge of psychic change.[4]

—Bill Sturgeon

Noel Kramer worked as an engineer with TRW, a high-tech aerospace electronics firm in Redondo Beach that had once cultivated so hang-loose a structrue that it was penetrated by two kids in the pay of the KGB. Kramer had movie-star looks and a child's shyness. He drew a good salary, and he lived a pleasant lifestyle in a beachside L.A. suburb south of Santa Monica. Those who came to know him in Dr. Eisner's therapy group described him as a quiet man, maybe too quiet. Recalled one fellow patient, "He had trouble expressing his feelings. He never seemed to be angry, never seemed too emotional."

But then he got into therapy with Dr. Eisner. He found himself "in relationship with" another patient. They had a child, a daughter.

Though friends say he never outgrew his painful shyness before he died, he had become part of Group, part of a new universe.

*   *   *

For Betty Grover Eisner, Group was everything: a matrix of forty to fifty individuals "dedicated to the removal of barriers which stand in the way of the fulfillment of our potential. . . . a matrix for rapid change."[5] Professors, engineers, physicists, physicians, and students in the chaotic years of the 1950s, '60s, and '70s were entranced by her message of hope and immense potential.

Dr. Eisner and her attraction cannot be understood outside the context of her experience, and how it meshed with the turbulent decades in which she practiced, when post-war euphoria dissolved in the wake of assassinations, nuclear phobia, civil upheavals, and an incomprehensible war half a world away—and most of all, without an understanding of a chemical isolated from a deadly poison that had ravaged Europe for centuries.

Lysergic acid diethylamide-25 (LSD) was the discovery of Albert Hofmann, a chemist for Sandoz Pharmaceuticals, a Swiss drug industry giant. Hofmann was studying the ergot fungus, cause of St. Anthony's fire, a deadly ailment produced by eating contaminated rye. The ergotamines offered great promise in treating migraines, because of their ability to constrict headache-dilated blood vessels in the brain.

Hofmann had first synthesized the chemical in 1938, but not until the afternoon of 16 April 1943, during the Second World War, did he accidentally touch the powder he'd made. A few thousand molecules passed through the skin of his fingertips, and the Swiss chemist was off on the world's first acid trip: "As I lay in a dazed condition with eyes closed there surged up from me a succession of fantastic, rapidly changing imagery of a striking reality and depth, alternating with a vivid, kaleidoscopic play of colors. This condition gradually passed off after about three hours."[6]

Three days later, thinking it was probably too little to have much of an effect, he took an incredibly small dose—250 micrograms (a quarter of a thousandth of a gram)—and was off on another full-blown trip. It was quite an adventure, beginning with a bicycle ride that has become legendary among drug initiates.

Fascinated and delighted, Hofmann shared his discovery with other scientists, and once the war had ended, the world was ready for his mind-bending discovery.

*   *   *

How to describe an acid trip? Thousands have tried. A few molecules brush momentarily over the synapses, and the brain erupts. Senses fuse: Colors are tasted, smelled; smells are felt, heard. Ordinary objects melt and transform; the imagery of dreams breaks through into waking consciousness. Colors take on new intensity; music acquires incredible depth and nuance. Words come slowly, rapidly, or not at all. Feelings burst into the moment, from hellish agony to orgiastic ecstasy. Time becomes a dimension of incredible richness and variety; experiences that seem to consume hours turn out to have lasted seconds, and the birth and death of a universe can seem to be encompassed within the span of a breath. Revelations, insights, memories take on tangible momentum. The tripper may know, in the space of minutes, tears, laughter, shudders, and catatonic physical and mental immobility.

In the early days, LSD, psilocybin, and mescaline were called "psychotomimetics" (psychosis imitators), a label hung by the Freudians on drugs they believed produced artificial psychoses. But Britisher-turned-Los-Angeleno Aldous Huxley and the Canadian psychologist Humphrey Osmond finally agreed on another term that best described (and still does) the effects of the drugs: "psychedelic," literally "mind-manifesting."

Acid came to L.A. early, through UCLA physiologist and psychiatrist Nicholas Bercell. "He was a Hungarian, and he went back for some sort of conference in Europe very early, and [W. A.] Stoll, who was in the laboratory at Sandoz at the time and had worked with Albert Hofmann, reached into his waistcoat pocket and gave him a couple of vials and said, 'You might want to try this,' " recalls Oscar Janiger. Bercell did, and was quick to share the drug with colleagues.

A psychiatrist himself, Janiger was fascinated by the drug, as were other psychiatrists and physicians—most clustered in Westwood, then a small, picturesque collection of offices, shops, and theaters near the main gate of the UCLA campus.

One of those especially interested in the drug was Sidney Cohen, an internist on the UCLA faculty with an appointment to the Veterans Administration Hospital in Westwood. Tall, elegant, silken-voiced, and sharp-featured, Cohen moved in exclusive circles. One of his acquaintances was publisher Henry Luce. Luce and his remarkable mate, Clare Booth Luce, exerted a powerful influence on American culture through their magazines, *Time, Life,* and *Fortune.*

One memorable day in the mid-1950s, Sidney Cohen gave Henry Luce a dose of acid. More trips followed for the publisher and his wife, who both found the drug magnificent, but something to be reserved for the social elite.[7] But *Life* carried decidedly pro-drug stories, introducing psychedelics into the mainstream culture.

"I first read about LSD in *Life*," she told fellow researchers at a 1959 conference.[8] "Then I heard that a friend of mine was to do an experiment with LSD. I offered to help, with the proviso that I be one of the subjects. The experience so impressed me that I felt that LSD had therapeutic possibilities, so I tried it therapeutically on myself, with such extraordinary results that Dr. Cohen and I felt a therapeutic study should be done." Another source, author W. V. Caldwell, dates Eisner's first psychedelic experience at 1957, and says that it was Cohen who administered the drug, from the first batch Sandoz supplied to the Los Angeles area.[9] The man who provided it was Harry Althouse, the West Coast representative of the Swiss firm. The drug came in small, robin's egg blue, lens-shaped tablets, under the brand name "Delysid."

As an LSD researcher, Dr. Eisner soon found entree into that amazing circle of English eccentrics who found stimulation in what Janiger called "the raw, exciting, fermenting climate of Los Angeles." The two most influential of "these cultured upper class Englishmen" were Huxley and essayist Gerald Heard. Huxley chose to live in a white house (so painted because of his atrocious vision) in the L.A. hills, almost literally in the shadow of the HOLLYWOOD sign.

Their mutual enthusiasm for psychedelics brought Huxley and Eisner together. Another mutual acquaintance, author and diarist Anais Nin, wrote of a spring day in 1958 when she lunched with the Huxleys at their home and met the psychologist, apparently for the first time: "He had invited Dr. Betty Eisner, who wanted to meet me. She brought a liveliness and naturalness to an otherwise formal Huxley. We discussed my LSD experience." Nin's account of her acid trip in Oscar Janiger's office in 1955 is a classic account of the effects of the drug on a creative mind in a comfortable, reassuring setting.

> At first everything appeared unchanged. But after a while, perhaps twenty minutes, I noticed first of all that the rug was no longer flat and lifeless, but had become a field of stirring and undulating hairs, much like the movement of the sea anemone or a field of wheat in the wind. Then I noticed that doors, walls, and windows were liquefying. All rigidities disappeared. It was as if I had been plunged to the bottom of the sea, and everything had become undulating and wavering. The door knobs were no longer door knobs, they melted and undulated like living serpents. Every object in the world became a living, mobile breathing world. . . .
>
> My body was both swimming and flying. I felt gay and at ease and playful. There was a perfect connection between my body and everything that was happening. . . .
>
> My senses were multiplied as if I had a hundred eyes, a hundred ears, a hundred fingertips. The murals which appeared were perfect, they were Oriental, fragile, and complete, but then they became actual Oriental cities, with pagodas, temples, rich Chinese gold and red altars, and Balinese music. The music vibrated through my body as if I were one of the instruments and I felt myself becoming a full percussion orchestra, becoming green, blue, orange.[10]

Nin was clearly impressed with Dr. Eisner and her "tremendous fervor" in describing her work.[11] Nin and Huxley clashed on the need for psychedelics, with Nin contending that training in meditation, dream awareness, and art and music appreciation would eliminate the need for drugs. Huxley contended that, with few exceptions, only the psychedelics could allow access to the unconscious.

Dr. Eisner promised to send Nin copies of some of her papers. When her *Observations on Possible Order Within the Unconscious* ultimately arrived, it carried the dedication, "To Anais Nin, who knows more about this than any of the scientists do."[12]

This is consistent with Nin's own perceptions. "I reached the fascinating revelation that this world opened by LSD was accessible to the artist by way of art. . . . All the chemical did was to remove resistance, to make one permeable to the image, and to make the body receptive by shutting out the familiar landscape which prevented the dream from invading us."[13] Creativity, she felt, was preferable to chemical intoxication. Dr. Eisner agreed, citing the artists and other creative personalities as the least desensitized among men.[14]

Later, Nin describes what may have been the same or another afternoon when she "had lunch with the Huxleys and a woman doctor, Betty Eisner, who believes LSD will cure the neurosis of the world." Eisner and Huxley told the writer they both felt the drug "not only opens up the unconscious but that you understand and are aware at the same time."[15]

Another of Janiger's remarkable Britishers was Alan Watts, an Anglican cleric turned chain-smoking, drug-tripping Eastern metaphysician. Watts, in his self-assigned role as interpreter of Eastern thought for Western minds, may have been nearly as influential as Huxley in preparing American culture for the psychedelic onslaught.[16] Janiger was his personal physician.

Watts and Nin were both to figure in Dr. Eisner's later career, appearing as guests at the regular Friday evening social gatherings held at the psychologist's home for her patients.

*   *   *

There is little documentation available on Dr. Eisner's history prior to her therapeutic work. She was raised in Kansas City, Missouri, daughter of a successful attorney.[17] Her first exposure to Bohemian culture may have come at Stanford University on the San Francisco peninsula, where she won a B.A. in political science "with great distinction" in 1937. In her junior year she was elected to both Phi Beta Kappa and Cap and Gown, the women's honor society. Her education was interrupted by the war years.

Between her graduation from Stanford and the resumption of her education at UCLA, she spent "thousands of hours" in volunteer work for the Red Cross, as a visiting nurse, at a hospital, and for a blood bank.[18] She travelled to Europe, and there met Carl Gustav Jung, an apostate disciple of psychoanalysis founder Sigmund Freud.[19] She also told patients about meeting Mohandas Gandhi.

She married an engineer, Will Eisner, who joined the staff of the Rand Corporation, a Santa Monica-based "think tank" with strong ties to the Defense Department. The couple had a son and a daughter.

Sometime in the 1940s, she discovered two major influences: Jiddu Krishnamurti[20] and Jung, who had founded his own mystical "depth analysis" school of therapy based on myth and archetype.

"She said the two things that influenced her most in her life were LSD and Krishnamurti," recalled one former patient. A remarkable Indian, Krishnamurti had taken up residence in Ojai, a Bohemian coastal community north of Los Angeles, where he would hold occasional talks. Krishnamurti was close to Huxley and many of the other pre-War Bohemians. His tale was fascinating. At an early age, he was taken up by the Theosophists and proclaimed as the Avatar (God-incarnation) of the age. He renounced the mantle, and became a Vedantic philosopher, teaching an austere view of the world. He would remain an influence throughout Dr. Eisner's career.

In 1952 she was enrolled at UCLA. "She was certainly the best student in our class," said Dr. Philip Oderberg, a classmate who would later rally to her side. "She's bright. She's creative. She's clinically perceptive."[21] She received her M.A. in 1955, and her doctorate the next year with a thesis titled *Some Psychological Differences on the Rohrshach Between Infertility Patients and Women with Children.*[22] She entered private practice the same year.[23] She shared a two-office suite with the now-Dr. Philip Oderberg.

*   *   *

Dr. Eisner's work with LSD was to win her international recognition. She published her first major paper, with Sidney Cohen and a fellow psychologist, Lionel Fichman, in July 1958, based on their experimental work at the Veteran's Administration Neuropsychiatric Hospital in Westwood.[24] The paper details experiences with five of thirty subjects, none of whom had ever had intensive psychotherapy or psychiatric hospitalization. Most seem to have been professionals drawn from the local community. The researchers' conclusions were tentative, but the paper did note that all patients experienced a drop in IQ scores under the influence of the drug, with the greatest losses in the ability to reason abstractly. The drug also appeared to disrupt psychological defenses, impair contact with objective reality, and distort efforts to deal with demands of the environment.

In her next paper, published in December 1958[25] and co-authored with Cohen, she described the results of the use of LSD in psychotherapy. Rather than the single-session approach used in the earlier, nontherapeutic study, these subjects were neuropsychiatric patients, and were given an average of four to five weekly sessions, with dosages progressively building up in 25 microgram increments from 25 to as much as 250, the average last-session dose being 125.

These sessions clearly bear the hallmarks of another remarkable individual, Capt. Alfred M. Hubbard, a self-made millionaire who became a wandering evangelist for the psychedelic cause, discovering new drugs and travelling the world with them, to share with researchers. "I remember old Al Hubbard coming up to the house with his leather pouch," recalled Oscar Janiger. "You know, he rode the circuit. . . And he would train you up. . . . We'd say, 'What do you have for the month, Al?' [and he would say], 'Well, we've got this and that. Something new's coming up, how'd you like a little of that?' Oh God, we were waiting for you. We were waiting for you like a little old lady on the prairie waiting for her Sears, Roebuck catalog."26 Hubbard was a hard-core Catholic and once even convinced his archdiocese to give the drug a friendly endorsement.

It was Hubbard who spread the gospel of "set" and "setting," the premise that the outcome of a psychedelic drug experience derived from a combination of the tripper's mental condition (mindset), and the physical environment in which the session occurred. Give people acid in a psychiatric hospital around disturbed patients and in a condition of obvious confinement, and people who act psychotic, well, that was their "set": a bad trip is practically guaranteed. But give it, say, in a chapel, with beautiful music and inspirational pictures on a day of great religious significance, and people might—and did—respond with joyous rapture.27 Another part of Hubbard's message was that the drugs were *sacraments*, reserved for use by an elect inner circle of initiates.

*   *   *

By 1958, Dr. Eisner was established both as a respected researcher and as a therapist using "cutting edge" techniques to work with difficult patients. Her listing in that year's membership directory of the American Psychological Association describes her as a clinical psychologist specializing in psychotherapy, drug therapy, group therapy, psychosomatic disorders, crime, and sexual inadequacies and dysfunctions.

On 2 January 1959, she became the recipient of license number PL591 when the State of California began a separate psychologist licensing program. Dr. Eisner was "grandfathered-in," automatically given a license because she had been successfully practicing before the licenses were required. (A "grandfather clause" is a provision in professional certification/ registration programs which provides that when it is unrealistic to require current practitioners to meet new standards, they must be given the certification.) Even had the grandfather clause not been in effect, Dr. Eisner was certainly likely to meet any standards: she had a doctorate from a top school and was a published, respected researcher and clinician.

The same year, she attended the second Josiah Macy Foundation Conference on the Use of LSD in Psychotherapy, held at Princeton, New Jersey, 22-24 April.[28] The foundation, then a conduit for Central Intelligence Agency research funding,[29] had brought researchers together once before, in 1955. The second conference differed from the first in several respects, not the least of which was the presence of a large Los Angeles delegation— a Westwood delegation, really, since it included, besides the venerable Sidney Cohen, Betty Grover Eisner and two of her fellow Westwood acid therapists. Dr. Eisner described her therapy (working up from small doses), said she rarely saw paranoid delusions in her subjects, and remarked to colleagues that she had once stayed high for three days (a good experience).[30]

THE EARLY DAYS

Prior to the time the FDA declared LSD to be "illegal" I had many therapy sessions with Betty during which I was given the drug. In those days the letters "LSD" were meaningless and arbitrary. I hadn't seen anything in print about it. . . . *Life* hadn't discovered it yet.

—Bill Sturgeon

Soon after she started practice, Dr. Eisner began giving LSD to her private patients. One was a troubled engineer from the Lawrence Berkeley Laboratories, Bill Sturgeon. He describes himself as he was then: "Oh, I lied, I was a shop-lifter, I had very destructive habits, self-destructive habits, and these were what we worked on in my early LSD sessions."

Sturgeon had been "an army brat." His father ran a crew of Italian stone masons who built bridge towers, moving from project to project in Pennsylvania and Ohio. The boy was able to form few friendships. "I went to six high schools. And my father was away a lot, so I was raised by two older sisters and a mother and a grandmother, all females. So I learned how to relate with women, to women." With women playing such a dominant role in his life, it would later prove natural for him to find a woman therapist.

"I got drafted in '52, spent two years in the Army, got out in '54," he said. He married an English nurse he'd met in the service. They returned to the United States. A year later she was pregnant. The baby was born retarded. The pregnancy also turned out to have masked the symptoms of the mother's unsuspected, now-fatally advanced cancer. She was dead within two years of their marriage. The child was adopted out. Then came a chance meeting with an attractive woman and, thirty days later, marriage. Within a year, however, the relationship was falling apart.

Sturgeon's father-in-law was a pharmacologist who had met Dr. Eisner at a conference on LSD earlier in the decade, and had referred his daughter to her for drug therapy before her marriage. When the marriage grew shaky, Sturgeon said, "we went to see Betty. We drove down to Santa Monica and stayed there for about two weeks, and during which time each of us had about three LSD trips with Betty."

Sessions were all-day affairs, conducted in a pleasant convalescent hospital room, the expense covered by Sturgeon's medical insurance. Prior to treatment there was an initial office visit "where we just talked, where she learned some of my dynamics and some of my problem areas." Dr. Eisner was originally skeptical of Sturgeon's suitability for the drug. She saw him as deeply conflicted—which he was. But ultimately she decided to go ahead with it.

Sturgeon was referred to a physician for authorization to receive the drug (which, as a psychologist, Dr. Eisner could not prescribe). He still has the physician's original authorization, scrawled on a prescription pad, framed on his wall.

He reported to the convalescent hospital on 30 July 1959. He took the drug in the form of Sandoz tablets. "Robin's egg blue, little flattened spheroids about two or three millimeters in diameter."

Sturgeon was placing himself in the hands of a highly trained therapist for a form of treatment completely new to him. It was the first time he had even heard of LSD. It was medicine, good enough medicine that his father-in-law had sent his own daughter to receive it. Now here he was, burdened with grief and looking for release. "My first trip was with twenty-five gamma (micrograms, millionths of a gram). She started low and worked up till she found a comfortable dose for each patient. I turned out to be quite sensitive to LSD. I was getting imagery at that small a dose.

"So I would take the twenty-five gamma of LSD and I'm lying in the hospital bed and she's sitting in a chair next to me. I would put on one of these masks you go to sleep with—covers your eyes. And she would pick out a record and play it. So the record would go fifteen, ten, fifteen, twenty, thirty minutes, whatever, and when it finished, I would take off my mask and sort of come back into the here-and-now, into the room environment from wherever I'd been, and report to her what I'd experienced. And she would—a lot of what I reported was in unconscious symbolic forms like you might see in dreams. And she would interpret the meaning of this stuff in terms of my own personal dynamics and explain to me what she thought it meant to her, and most of the time it sounded right on to me. And after the session was over, I was instructed to write a report and submit that before I had my next session."

Sturgeon keeps a large box full of session reports, correspondence, and other documents of his years as a patient of Dr. Eisner's. The stack of papers is fourteen inches thick, filed in chronological order. He also has the recordings made of his earliest LSD sessions and the psychologist's own personal records (at one point Eisner gave her old files back to patients). From these Sturgeon is able to vividly reconstruct those early years with Dr. Eisner.

*   *   *

A biomedical engineer/inventor, today Sturgeon lives on the grounds of an old sawmill, his home the bunkhouse, on the banks of the Mattole River. The mill, a skeleton of massive redwood beams, still stands; it had once been Sturgeon's dream to turn it into a house. The property, at the end of a narrow, treacherous-in-the-winter pair of back-country tire ruts, is in the heart of one of Northern California's most inaccessible regions, the heart of the "Lost Coast." He calls his home Cambiamos, Spanish for "we are changing."[31]

There is a burnished aluminum trailer next to the house, filled with electronic gear, all meticulously arranged, as well as a bed. The trailer doubles as the guest room. Here he works on various inventions. He is currently marketing two biomedical devices: a fast in-the-mouth heating device for solidifying rubber implanted in root canals, and a portable, compact electronic device for performing safe, rapid vasectomies both in the field and in clinics (he hopes to provide it to Third World nations).[32]

The walls of his home are lined with books. There are two desktop computers; one his, one his mate's. A combination study-workroom boasts a ham radio outfit, and the livingroom-bedroom contains stereo, television, and VCR. Outside, beyond a vast sweep of lawn, are fruit trees, and a huge garden, with food plants, flowers, and herbs to keep out gophers and other pests. Speakers are mounted in trees and on buildings, so he can have his music outdoors. In front of the house sits a wheeled erector-set-like steel skeleton with a plywood top and a folding chair. It is his portable desk, which allows him to take his battery-powered computer to a scenic outdoor setting to write, surrounded by trees, river, flowers, music pouring from the speakers if he chooses.

Some of the music he listens to today he first heard lying on the hospital bed, mask on, flowing with the acid, Dr. Eisner at his side. What did she play to spark the trips? "Sibelius symphonies, Chopin piano concerti. All the music was selected by her to elicit stuff from the unconscious. Some of my favorite music I first heard under LSD."

His voice is deep, resonant, pleasant. Sitting on a folding chair at a card table, his box of documents close at hand, Sturgeon recalled his first trip, and how Dr. Eisner used the drug. "I got visual imagery—with the mask on it makes it a lot easier to see the imagery because you don't have photons coming into your eyes. I would see colors and geometrical patterns. I came back from one of these musical episodes and told her I was getting imagery of holly, holly plants with red fruit, little red things, and sharp green leaves. And she interpreted that to me that I was perceiving my sexual identity in this plant. The red was my female side of my psyche, and the green was the male side of my psyche. This was a typical interpretation she would make of the imagery I would come back with."

In a few short hours, LSD had changed his life. "I felt like I was opened up to a whole new domain of myself or the world that I'd never seen before. I remember leaving the hospital late that afternoon, and my vision was different. I remarked that my visual acuity, that my color perception was greatly enhanced. I was seeing colors that looked alive to me, and things were very clear to me visually. I would get kinesthetic perceptions. With the mask on and lying down and listening, I would feel my body shrink or grow or shrivel or things like that. I didn't know quite what to make of what had happened, except it was new to me; it was different from anything I'd experienced before. I was quite excited by it; felt that there was a lot of fruitful stuff going on for me."

If he didn't know what to make of the experience, Dr. Eisner did. The interpretation, valid or invalid, was further reinforced by the act of preparing a "session report," an account of the experience written by the patient, which was then turned over to the therapist, who had made her own notes, which were then filed away. One of Sturgeon's reports, involving a later session with another chemical, goes on for nine single-spaced typewritten pages.[33]

During the same interval, Sturgeon's wife was having her own drug sessions with Dr. Eisner, at the same hospital on different days. Both partners were impressed with the therapy and the therapist. They returned to Northern California, where Sturgeon was crunching numbers on a computer for the late Dr. Luis Alvarez, a physicist who was to win the Nobel Prize. Therapy continued by correspondence, punctuated by Dr. Eisner's occasional trips to Northern California, where she would administer therapy to the Sturgeons.

"After a while," he says, "I found out that she had what she called a research group, and they were experimenting with group activity and LSD, and we went down and attended one of these group sessions. And after attending a few of these group sessions every six weeks approximately, I decided that this was something I wanted to get closer to, so I left my job at the Berkeley Radiation Laboratory and went down to UCLA and started work at the physics department at UCLA, exchanged jobs so I could move down to West L.A. and be part of this therapy group."

The Group was an LSD therapy group, and it met on weekends for sessions. Like Sturgeon, many of the men were engineers. Dr. Eisner has written that, with few exceptions, men in contemporary society are un-feeling to some degree. The problem, she said, is especially pronounced in professionals (physicians, attorneys, accountants), reaching its greatest extent in mechanical engineers.[34] Both her mates were engineers, as was her closest male friend, say former patients.

Sturgeon describes the group sessions: "[There were] a lot of couples. I can't remember an individual married person who was in the group and the spouse was not in the group. Betty had a tendency to draw your spouse and children into the group. I think it would be against her flow to have one member of a married couple in therapy with her and not the other one, because she couldn't control the situation that way."

Group drug sessions consumed the whole weekend. Friday night was the social gathering. Saturday came the session. Sunday was to be kept clear for integrating the experience and preparing the session report. Typical drug sessions involved fifteen to twenty participants. "And if there was a routine, it was that the group would gather on a Saturday morning and we would spend all day Saturday with a group session. Typically one person would take a high dose of LSD and the rest of us would take a minimal dose of LSD. The minimal dose most of us got, plus the contact high that we got from the person with the high dose, would put everybody into an LSD experience. And the dynamics of the person on the high dose—whatever they were working on—became the theme of the day for the rest of us."

A high dose was "250, 300 (gamma). I never had over 150 myself. A high dose might typically be 250 and everybody else might have 25 or 50 or 75, something like that."

But they didn't leap immediately into the drug experience. "Before we took the drug Saturday morning, we had a thing called 'reservations.' Reservations consisted of sitting in a circle and going all the way around the circle. Each person in turn would state any reservations they had about anyone else, about themselves, anything left undone, anything they were hung up on, so that we could go into the drug session without any of the residue of this stuff. Everything in the personal dynamics of everybody was pretty much examined and cleared. Sometimes this reservations period would take half the damn day. Once that was over we'd take the drug, put on some music, and sort of lie down and see what happens."

*   *   *

Most of the early sessions focused on interpersonal dynamics between group members, often dealing with specific problems of individual patients. In Bill Sturgeon's early years with her, "the first half, two-thirds of my experience with her," he and the therapist worked on his destructive behavior patterns, his lies, his crime. "I remember asking her, 'What's wrong with shoplifting?' She said, 'Oh, it offends your sense of orderliness.' And somehow that reached me and that made sense to me and I understood that there was a good reason to stop this. I can't explain it any better than that, but it made a lot of sense to me at the time. So I cleared up all my self-destructive—well, the ones that were worked on—behavior pattern things and that changed. I guess any therapist could have done this. I think with LSD it happened faster. I've always described LSD as psychic penetrating oil.' It loosens up the wheels in which you—it evokes unconscious material for you to work on, to deal with, to confront and figure out what it means and change your life in accordance with what you find.

"A lot of the time the dynamics between two people at the group session would prevail. And what would happen would be that these two people would sit facing each other. Often they would be instructed to scream at each other or express verbal hostility by Betty. Sometimes not. Sometimes that would happen. And the rest of us would stand or sit in a circle around the couple, facing each other, and watch what happened, just put our energy into it. And we called this process 'eyeball-plunging.' Where these two people would sit and stare at each other's eyes, just watch their face without losing eye contact, sometimes for twenty minutes. And the most extraordinary thing about this to me was that under LSD I could look at somebody's face and the face would change. It would appear to change, I mean. I would see a different face there. I might see somebody change into a wizened old Chinese face or atavistic savage or any face from any point in time in history.

"Now a lot was going on in these sessions that didn't get verbalized, a lot of perceptions were made by people which didn't get talked about at the session. And these perceptions would often find themselves into the written reports by the people afterwards. One of Betty's rules was that you had to write a report, and you had to have read everybody else's report before we could have another session, which was a remarkably wise thing for her to be doing. And I would read other people's reports about what they perceived during somebody's eyeball-plunging, and I was astonished to read that they were seeing the same faces I was seeing at the same time I was seeing them. They weren't my hallucinations any more. I didn't know what they were, but I couldn't claim them as hallucinations because it was a shared experience. And after a few of these LSD sessions where I was puzzled by what I was perceiving, somebody handed me a book by a woman named Gina Ceminara, and it was called *Many Mansions,* and it was about Edgar Cayce, and reincarnation as understood by people who study Edgar Cayce's readings. When I read that book I suddenly had a model into which I could put all these bizarre perceptions that people were sharing. I understood—I had a model that explained what I was seeing, and it was explained by the whole idea of reincarnation. *We were seeing past life images.* And I still hold this model to be what I call the truth. I knew nothing about reincarnation before I met Betty, but I sure learned about it during the experience with her."

Eyeball plunging, later shortened simply to "eyeballing," was to remain a vital part of Dr. Eisner's therapy. She would "eyeball" the patient herself, sometimes calling in other group members to "eyeball." Sometimes the eyeballing was directed—the patient was told whose face to see; sometimes it was free association.

*   *   *

As Group evolved, Dr Eisner began to focus the group acid sessions on single themes. Sturgeon remembers: "Very often, at least—not in the early days so much but later on themes would develop for the Saturday drug sessions. I remember one session where the theme was licenses. We had to—we were talking about licenses, license to do things, and everybody had to take a license and put it in the center of the circle and relinquish it somehow to the group. And it turned out that most people used their driver's license. [A physician] was at this particular meeting and there was a big flap with him and Betty because Betty wanted him to write a prescription for LSD and he refused to do it. She demanded that he write a prescription, and she said, 'We may burn it, we may—I may keep it, I'm not saying what we'll do with it. I just want you to do it.' And he refused to do it and he walked out of that session.

"She was I think asking people to trust that she wouldn't misuse the licenses that they put in the circle or the prescription for LSD or stuff like that."

Another themed LSD session was conducted on a sun-drenched hillside where stoned patients used modelling clay to make statues of themselves, into which they were then to project their hostilities and negative feelings about themselves. There is a picture of the group, standing proudly together, their dolls on a blanket before them.

Still another communal trip convinced Group members they had come into psychic contact with extraterrestrials. "There was a session where we were meeting space people, space entities," Sturgeon recalled. "I don't know what to say about that, except that it was very convincing and very intriguing."

There was considerable, almost religious, ritual at sessions. "One of the LSD sessions we were at a beach house and I was put in charge of ritual. And I lit incense and passed a loaf of homemade bread around and [we all] fondled it and smelled it and things like this. So she's very much into sensory experience and she talked—I remember her talking about the Catholic church and all the sensory experiences that they create in the mass, with the incense and the stained glass windows and things of that nature. And she talked about the value of that in therapy, and we had a lot of that emphasis during the LSD sessions. I had taken a glass goblet and gotten a wide variety of colored acetate sheet and I cut the colored acetate sheet into small shapes, triangles and rectangles and glued them on this glass and made it look like a stained glass chalice. And I brought that to many of the LSD sessions, and we drank the water from this glass, passed it around the circle. I still have that somewhere."

Along with the weekend drug sessions, Dr. Eisner soon began holding informal group socials at her house Friday evenings. Patients would bring food—Bill Sturgeon took on the regular salad-making assignment—and they would gather, eat, dance, laugh, and, once a month, celebrate group member birthdays. "Betty would often have somebody interesting come to one of the Friday night parties and talk to the group about something. Alan Watts was one of them who came over. John Lily came over one time and talked to us. I remember meeting John Lily up at Esalen a few months later, sat down beside him at dinner and told him I was one of Betty's patients and reminded him where we'd met. And he looked at me and said, 'Tell me, is she still the queen bee?' "

Sturgeon also recalls meeting Anais Nin at one of the parties. Sid Cohen came, as well as Oscar Janiger. Both Bill Sturgeon and Leo Breiman, a fellow Group member, recalled the night Al Hubbard showed up with a tape recording. Breiman tells it this way: "He said, 'I had this guy I gave some acid to,' and he said, 'I want you to listen to this.' And he played us a tape of Bob Dylan singing 'Hey Mr. Tambourine Man.' It was long before the record appeared with 'Mr. Tambourine Man' on it. God, I thought that was the loveliest song I'd ever heard, I mean, even with Bob Dylan's voice and all, it was just terrific. It was like this guy had had a real LSD experience."

Group members recall other LSD researchers dropping by. A South American psychiatrist came by with a jungle drug supposed to foster visions of jaguars. Group members took the drug, but there were few feline hallucinations. Another evening, who should drop in but the man who coined the term "Spaceship Earth," geodesic dome inventor R. Buckminster Fuller, a friend of one of Dr. Eisner's patients.

*   *   *

To be part of the group was to be part of something exciting, stimulating, adventuresome, daring, innovative. They were explorers. Bill Sturgeon's description: "She felt that society at large was mentally ill. That's the only way I can describe it. That the collective unconscious was full of violence and warfare and all manner of horrible stuff and that the only people that were really sane were those in the group. Maybe a few people on the outside were not psychotic, but *most* people were, in her view. She had the notion that the world is full of psychopathy and we were learning how to outgrow these aspects of human personality. I think she pictured having—well, she was greatly into personal achievement. She had people going out, going to medical school, and she pushed on me to get my registered professional engineer certificate. She pushed on me to work hard to graduate from college. She was pushing her people into achieving all these things, which is part of achievement of their potential, and once she had accomplished these things, I think she pictured people going out and changing the world by becoming the next generation of leaders that was going to show the world the way out."

*   *   *

In *LSD Psychotherapy*, W. V. Caldwell has written that Dr. Eisner "brought into play all the expressions of hostility such as yelling, clay throwing, pounding, destruction of pottery, throwing eggs, and even spitting. The latter, she reports, has relieved hostility blocks when all other methods failed."[35]

Bill Sturgeon recalls the origin of the spitting in therapy this way: "She had a patient, one of her violent patients in her office that Philip Oderberg had to come drag off of her. She had this Irish fellow, I've forgotten his name, small wiry Irish fellow who was probably borderline schizophrenic, and he tended to get violent. And she was in her office in a session with him once and she said that she could tell that he was on the verge of becoming violent. They were eyeballing, and she suddenly got an insight. She said, 'Spit. Spit at my face.' And he started spitting into her face, and this discharged his hostility, so he didn't have to get violent, and this is a surrogate for violent behavior. And so she used this as a tool whenever, very often whenever one of her patients she perceived to be on the verge of violence, she would say spit, and I always thought there was an element of masochism in there for her. To spit at her, right in her face. She would just stand there and say, 'Spit. Spit. Spit.' And her face would be drenched with saliva.

"This is one of the tools she'd developed for controlling violent behavior. I did it to her. A lot of people did it to her. It wasn't rare. I've been the spitter and the spittee both. They're both kinda weird."

There were other unconventional practices, apparently improvised on the spot and often reported as helpful by the patients. Bill Sturgeon recalled one such incident: "At one of my earlier sessions which was held in my wife's parents' home in San Francisco, Betty was leading a session with me and another woman there—I didn't know her, but it was another of Betty's patients and she was giving us both, we were both having—was it LSD together? I don't remember if we had LSD this day or not. At one point in the day, Betty had me sitting in her lap—there was a lot of body contact in this group—Betty had me sitting on her lap, and after a while she, she was picking stuff up on an intuitive level and she took out her breast and had me nurse it. And the other one, and whatever I was going through, I was going through some kind of a weird reliving my infancy I guess, and I didn't think much about this. I thought Betty was pretty open and nonrigid to think of creative things like this—well, if I can label it that—to do in a therapeutic session."

"What Betty's whole emphasis on through all of her therapy that I remember, is teaching people how to express anger without hurting anybody physically. Pounding boxes, pounding punching bags, screaming, eyeball-plunging and yelling, spitting, all these things were okay. Physical violence was not okay."

*　*　*

Dr. Philip Oderberg, who shared a professional suite with Dr. Eisner at 1334 Westwood Boulevard, described Dr. Eisner's approach to handling hostility: "She's a woman with a lot of guts. I think she's been described as a sensitive person. She is a sensitive person. She is also tough. One of her theories has to do with hostilities being at the base of a lot of pathology. She's helped to try to deal with that hostility, try to work with it . . . so that people who carry it and who find themselves unable to function in life are able to function better. We shared an office for many years. . . . Many times I used to have to break through the waiting room area into her office because someone was beating on her. She tended to orchestrate hostility deliberately as a way of trying to get the anger out."[36]

"Lethal hostility" was a key phrase in Dr. Eisner's language. Society had become fossilized, dangerously rickety because its systems and habits were impossibly complex, inflexible, discordant. Humanity had passed the point where transformation could occur harmoniously and peacefully. Change could come only through radical, creative revolutionary means.[37]

There was one common element in the thinking of Mary Baker Eddy and Betty Grover Eisner, and that was a profound "knowledge" that the universe is an orderly, rational place, and that dedication to higher purpose would automatically resolve matters of money and supply.[38] Both also shared a conviction that children were spiritually more receptive than adults, and that spirituality was lost as the result of what the founder of Christian Science called "mortal mind," and what Dr. Eisner called "interlocking neuroses."

For the psychologist, cultural neuroses were programmed at the earliest level, in the distortions of relationships with siblings and parents. Only by re-creating the environment in which development was arrested and distorted could the original emotions be released and rechannelled in a loving, creative way. To reach that level, the patient had to work through hostility and sexuality, and the group was a perfect matrix for working out those primitive relationships.

In *The Unused Potential of Marriage and Sex*, Eisner identifies the four qualities she believes necessary to maintain a therapeutic sexual relationship: openness, warmth, casualness, patience.[39] These were also characteristics ascribed to Group, which was committed to exploring the patient's darkest hopes and fears in an uplifting, energizing, loving environment. It promised the sense of *family* they craved.

Here, in the context of Group, patients could experience and thus liberate themselves from their own quite reasonable but misdirected hostility. But, as Dr. Oderberg's experiences showed, hostility could turn dangerous. Limits were needed, Eisner realized, and to set them, she created something called the "commitment." As her practice evolved, the "commitment session" was the first of all drug therapies given a patient admitted to the group. "Before anybody had a session, at least in the later years, they had to make a commitment to non-violence," Sturgeon recalls. "The commitment was very specifically worded. It was a precise, it was a recipe. And you would say [his voice becomes deeper, firmer, slower] 'I'—and you'd say your name—'I, Bill Sturgeon, will not hurt myself or anyone else physically during this session.' Those were the words. It was fascinating to watch people try and say these words, because their unconscious was holding back on making this commitment. So a word would come out wrong, something would be left out, or a word be substituted or something like that, and we might spend hours just getting a commitment out of someone right. They would leave out the time frame. They would leave out the word 'physical.' All kinds of distortions would come up in saying this commitment, but it was a commitment she insisted on before somebody was starting into a session. Just to define the line which you must not cross. And up to that line you could do what you wanted. You could tear towels apart or kick the bed—but you couldn't break your foot during it, though, because that's hurting yourself. You couldn't scratch somebody—that was hurting them. Physical harm was forbidden, and it was very clearly stated to everybody. Everybody understood that. And that was the one rule that was almost ubiquitously applied at the beginning of the session. Everybody had to say it."

The peculiar power of the commitment session was described by other former patients. All agreed that somehow Dr. Eisner was able to create a powerful vehicle for allowing aggression and hostility to be expressed within physically safe limits. It worked. The violent physical attacks Oderberg had seen in the early days stopped. The commitment became an integral part of therapy, repeated before individual drug sessions, and before the Wednesday evening therapy groups.

One permissible expression of hostility was screaming, yelling, or growling at another. This was called "blasting," and was considered a powerful, helpful psychological tool. While the ideal would be full vocalization, necessity intervened and forced Dr. Eisner to devise an alternative. The problem: Neighbors who had heard the screams had called the police. So, Dr. Eisner figured out a way to blast at a quieter level. Patients would roll up dry washcloths and clench them between their teeth. This muffled the sound enough to avoid most problems, and Dr. Eisner prefaced at least some meetings with a phone call to police, alerting them that loud or unusual noises reported at her address were simply sounds of a therapy session in progress.[40]

*   *   *

Bill Sturgeon spent twelve years with Dr. Eisner, ten of them as a member of Group. The beginning of the end came when his second marriage collapsed. "My wife left with one of the other people in the group. They're married now. They were living together. My wife was living with this guy for several months as man and wife in the group, and finally they both resigned together, both from therapy and from the group. And they did this when everybody else was in Mexico."

Mexico, Puerto Vallarta, played a major role in Group. Dr. Eisner and her husband owned a minority interest in property there, the Bucanero, a combination ice plant—producing *Diamante Jelado,* the only ice then made in Mexico from purified water—and retreat for Group, where Dr. Eisner and many of the patients spent summer and Christmas. Group eventually created a volunteer school for a nearby village, which would fill the summers of many of the younger, college-age patients. "And this summer we were all down there except for my ex-wife and the fellow she was living with. For some reason they couldn't go with us. And it was when they were away from the group that they were able to leave the group, because they didn't have Betty manipulating them to stay in the group. I don't think it could have happened otherwise, that they could have left the way they did."

The couple's daughter went to the custody of her mother. The girl later drowned in a swimming pool accident.

"My wife left me and left Group at the same time. That's when I should've left Group, because the attitude about Group and about Betty changed toward me after that. It was as though somehow I had failed, and the respect for me went down about thirty-five notches, and I was put into the Wednesday group. I got taken out of what they used to call the Research Group and put into the Wednesday group, which was the therapy group, with the younger people. And the reason they gave for doing this was because everybody else in the Tuesday group was coupled and I was no longer coupled with anybody. But I felt like I'd been demoted. The Tuesday group was the therapy group—consisted of her long-term patients that she'd been with a long time. They'd had LSD or the equivalent with her before, so they were considered trustworthy, reliable. The Wednesday night group, therapy group,was the newer people, the younger people, typically students who came to her sometimes through other therapists."

"Research Group" eventually changed its name, Sturgeon said. "Somebody laid—came down on her for that, because when you do research, you're not paying patients, for therapy. They're mutually exclusive. And so she changed the names Research Group and Therapy Group to Tuesday Night Group and Wednesday Night Group. She simply changed the labels."

By whatever name, the group experience was a kaleidoscope of ever-changing, overwhelming experiences. "Everything in relationships changed. Once you got into her group, Betty would shuffle people like a deck of cards. I don't mean the whole group, but one at a time. She would send a husband off to live somewhere else, or she would send somebody in a relationship off, or she would send somebody who was not in a relationship to go live with somebody else. She had me living with Naomi Feldman for a couple months. It was horrible—for me. The purpose of this was to put you into a situation that would goad you. She would put you in a situation that would evoke whatever you needed to grow. If she perceived you to be hung up in some area, she would find out how to confront you with that in the fastest way. She was doing this all for enhancing the growth experience. This is her way of doing it.

"All these groups were one big family and they were almost interchangeable parts in this family. The kids would be assigned to different parents sometimes. If the parents—if the husband and wife in a family were having interacting dynamics that took all their energy, then she would take the kids and send them off to live with someone else for a while."

With Dr. Eisner's therapy the goal was not for the patient simply to adapt to a society that was neurotic, violent, and dangerously repressed. The goal was *transcendence*, evolution to a higher state of consciousness, which could only be attained within the context of Group. Thus, anyone who left betrayed the group ideal. "Over the years occasionally somebody would get up in a therapy session, in a group meeting, and they would announce that they felt that their psyche was cured and they wanted to leave therapy. And Betty would come across as receptive to the idea and not get upset over it, but then she would always say, 'But you've got this one issue in your life that hasn't been resolved yet; why don't you stick around until it gets resolved.' And so the person would say, 'Okay, that sounds reasonable.' And the person would never leave Group. This was her way of hanging on to her patients—I saw this as her way of hanging onto patients. And I have never in my experience remembered a patient leaving her without a cloud, without being under a cloud of some kind. The patients who left her would—she would talk about them and say, 'This person has left Group and they've done it invalidly and they're gonna get screwed up by it. They're still a little bit crazy and they're not ready to leave and they left anyway, so don't get—don't talk to that person, don't associate with them.' She had a way of encapsulating the group from contact with outside influences. I think there was one patient—Charlotte Riegel[41] I think was the only person I remember leaving therapy with Betty that was not under a cloud. One person out of several dozen."

What ultimately led to Bill Sturgeon's separation from his therapist was a psychedelic drug session at her house where he confessed he had been smoking marijuana as well as growing two plants in his backyard to provide a supply of the drug. "Her thing about marijuana was that if you were a Tuesday group member that could be trusted, and you went up to her and said, 'I'd like to have a marijuana experience,' she would query you about certain things and then give her blessing or not as to whether you could go ahead with it; and I did this several times. And after about four or five or six times of doing this, I saw a pattern in her questions. She would say, 'Is it safe?' She would make sure that you did it under safe conditions, safe from the law and safe from society. And I saw this pattern, and so after a while I stopped asking her for permission, just went ahead and did it on my own. And this escalated, and pretty soon I found myself smoking a lot of marijuana without her knowledge. But it felt okay to me because I was using the guidelines that she had given me in checking me out for the first five or six times I'd done this. So I felt okay with it.

"I think she suspected I was doing this, and it was okay with her. But I don't know that for sure; I'm guessing. Until I had the LSD session and I decided it was—I had a lot of help from my unconscious when I took the LSD and I literally made, I literally exaggerated the amount of involvement I was having with marijuana just to provoke her.

"I had the 'big session'[42] . . . on a Saturday. The following Wednesday was the group meeting and she opened up the group meeting with the statement that we have the most serious problem to deal with we've ever had, and that's what I've been doing. And she outlines to the group what I—what I'd reported to her that I'd been doing, which was smoking marijuana without her permission. And she talked at great length about this and how devastating, what a devastating betrayal to the group she saw this as. And then she had—the structure was that we sit in a large circle for one of these meetings and we'd go around the circle and everybody talks. And so she set the theme for the evening, which was my invalid behavior and what it meant to the group. And after she finished, everybody went around and they contributed their piece of what a shithead I was, and I just sat there and I listened for about two hours to this stuff, and then they—the meeting ended and I left and I was told to go to Ojai to live with her. I was told to go back home; I was told to communicate only with Bob Daniels.[43] They had a long talk about what I should do. I should go out in the desert, I should go work outdoors as a forest ranger or surveyor or something like that. Get away from people. And it was set up at the end of the evening that I was only to communicate with Bob Daniels, nobody else, not even Betty. And after a few days. . . . Leo [Breiman] called me and said I wasn't to talk to Bob Daniels any more because he was getting hooked into me. I was only to talk to Leo. And Leo told me that they had decided that I had to leave for some months, and I said, 'Well how long is that?' And he said, 'Well, you tell me.' And I said 'some months' means—that's plural, so that means two months. He said, 'Okay—two months.' And that's when I packed my car and took off and left my tropical fish and everything, God knows what was going to happen to them, and I went up to live with Pam.

"She had me leave—she had me get a prescription for Thorazine before I left. A hundred Thorazine, huge prescription. She said, 'You're gonna need these.' I took two of them once about a month later—two of them just to see—I'd never had it before—took two of them to see what happened, and my God, it all but immobilized me. I know what they mean by chemical straightjacket. Horrible stuff.

"So I went up to Ojai and I moved in with Pam and I gave a lot, of course I gave a lot of thought to what had come down in my life, and I was puzzled by some, by much of it. I didn't understand really what was going on here. I felt pretty clearheaded, but I was pretty shaky in my own—my belief that I was—I had such a strong suggestion implanted in my mind that I was on the edge of a psychotic break that I felt very shaky about that. On the other hand, my mind was working quite clearly. So I didn't understand a lot of this, and when Pam came back one week later from—she drove from Ojai down to Santa Monica and attended the subsequent Wednesday meeting one week after the one where I got booted out. She came back and gave me an account of what happened.

"She told me that during the break that she was in the kitchen with Betty and Betty asked her, 'What's Bill's attitude?' And Pam said, 'He doesn't want to burn any bridges behind him.' And I don't remember what all they talked about, but the thing that was most important to me was when Betty said, 'Give him Thorazine if he starts to talk funny.' And Pam said, 'Well, what does that mean?' And Betty said, 'If he starts to talk about me.' Pam told me this and I thought about it, and all of a sudden I realized that Betty was afraid of me. I wasn't aware—I didn't have that insight until that moment. I had no idea that Betty was afraid of me. So once I realized Betty was afraid of me, all I had to do was look and see why, and it didn't take very long for me to figure out that at the beginning of that big session when she gave me the LSD, she told me it was LSD, she told me who gave it to her, who her source was, and I knew then that this was the information that she was afraid that I would reveal to people. And this is why she isolated me from the group, and this is why I believe that she loaded me with the heaviest suggestion imaginable that I was going crazy. And she did this—in my mind she did this to discredit anything I might say about her.

"But when I pieced all this together and I realized that she had sent a patient away forbidden to contact her and telling that patient that he was about to go crazy, this was—this didn't track. And that gave me what I needed to write a letter of resignation with no uncertainty about what I was doing. I was no longer puzzled by it all. It was coming—the pieces were starting to fit together into a pattern that I could understand."

*   *   *

Sturgeon's letter of resignation produced a scathing response from the psychologist. In a letter of 12 December 1971, Dr. Eisner predicted that he had started to go insane, and that he bore a justifiable burden of guilt for exposing Group to danger. Growing marijuana was violent, treacherous, monstrous, she wrote. Moreover, he bore a great measure of blame for a spot that had appeared on Beatrice Lowenstein's lung.

"I was in relationship with Beatrice on Betty's instruction and I was beginning to like Beatrice a lot," Sturgeon remembers. "I thought she was a fine person, and Beatrice—I don't know how she came to have a chest X-ray. Maybe it was a routine physical exam. But there was this spot on the X-ray. Nobody knew what it was.

"But . . . Betty was having problems with me. This is towards the end of my stay with her, so she started looking to build a case against me. And so she, I think more for effect in the group than anything else, she was—Okay, this is already after the marijuana flap. I told her I was doing the marijuana thing. And so therefore she concluded that the spot on Beatrice's lung was my fault because I was messing around with something you inhale."

Sturgeon's response to Dr. Eisner's letter was relief. The ties had been severed. He was in a good relationship, one which has continued to the time of this writing, almost two decades later. But he does not reject the past, nor much of what Dr. Eisner believed. "I think she's very creative and very dedicated but she's not committed to her own growth, as I see it. And that's her downfall. And she got wackier and wackier, like I mentioned, I see a point in time when she made a decision to back away from the process of her own self-exploration during a carbogen [gas-inhalation therapy] session [in 1965], and she's gotten wackier and wackier ever since, less accurate. I think up until that point in time she had, I could see her becoming one of the world-renowned practitioners of new, creative forms of psychotherapy. But she has her personality problems in dealing with authorities. She couldn't accept anyone else's authority. She had to be the head honcho. She would allow no colleague, nobody who would say 'I know better.' She wouldn't allow that, whether it was a doctor or a psychiatrist or what.

"She was convinced that there was so much psychopathology 'out there' that in spite of the fact that she was only one and out there were millions, they were still wrong."

ACID GOES UNDERGROUND

In 1963, under a new amendment to the Cosmetic, Food and Drug Act of 1938, the psychedelic drugs became "investigational new drugs." This is a standard label under which a large number of new, unproven medications are now classified. It means in practice that every user of these drugs is required to submit special reports to the [Food and Drug Administration] involving complex tests, records, and data. Most private therapists and clinics, though they might prove acceptable, cannot afford the time and expense involved.[44]

—W. V. Caldwell

Group sprang into being at the height of the LSD's Golden Age. The drug was legal. For patients, there was no cultural backlash, no stigma beyond any already attached to seeking help from a "headshrinker." For professionals, here was a chemical microscope for exploring the innermost reaches of human experience. These were exciting, euphoric times. But then several things happened.

First came the outrageous behavior of Drs. Timothy Leary, Richard Alpert, and Ralph Metzner of Harvard University's Psychology Department, where turning on had become an everyday, highly visible event. "Drug" is a highly loaded bit of language, and a sign of cultural schizophrenia. There are "drugs," "cigarets," "drink," "medicine," and "food." The first is disreputable, the second and third rapidly becoming so. Leary had transgressed the boundary between "medicine" and "drug." He had become a revolutionary. He issued a call to the barricades and the government had to respond. He was taking drugs to the streets.

Leary, Alpert, and Metzner were the first of the researchers to openly break ranks with conservatives like Janiger, who feared what might happen if the drug leaked out of the professional suite and hospital ward. Leary's outrageous experiments sent shock waves through the staid Harvard faculty, and soon all three were out of work, living it up in an acid-drenched paradise named Millbrook, preaching a gospel of "Turn on, tune in, drop out."

Leary's egalitarian stance was disavowed by the "elitists" like Huxley, Cohen,[45] and Janiger, who believed that drug use should be held in tight professional control, and designed to produce breakthrough experiences, almost sacramental initiations into the further realms of consciousness. They never wanted it to hit the streets. Still, there was obvious affection among all the researchers. Janiger made a videotape of one of their gatherings. Leary, ever center stage, Cohen, Janiger, Hubbard, and all the others are smiling and laughing. They are still initiates; they differ on a matter of policy.

*   *   *

In 1962 stories broke about an epidemic of deformed babies being born in Europe after their mothers took a supposedly "safe" sleep-inducing drug called Thalidomide. The medication had only been blocked from entry into the United States by an obstinate federal researcher. The resulting furor, including heart-rending photos in *Life* and a mother's tragic headline-punctuated quest for an abortion, led Congress to pass the Kefauver-Harris Drug Amendments, requiring manufacturers to provide painstaking proof of a drug's safety and effectiveness before they could sell it. The Food and Drug Administration, the federal agency regulating the pharmaceutical business, announced that it was not satisfied that Delysid would meet the necessary safety/efficacy standards. Henceforth, the drug was to be considered experimental—making it off-limits to all but agency-approved research. The golden days of acid were over.[46]

It was 21 November 1963, a day before John F. Kennedy's assassination, when the CIA pulled the plug on its last research project, a tragically, sadistically misguided effort at brainwashing that employed a combination of massive doses of acid, enforced confinement, and endless playing of tape loops featuring the patient's own voice talking about emotionally charged subjects. The victims were unsuspecting institutionalized mental patients in Canada (CIA policy barred experiments on unwitting U.S. subjects). The victimizer was a world-respected U.S. psychiatrist who was also analyst for the wife of legendary CIA Director Allen Dulles. Dulles had been forced out a year earlier after the Bay of Pigs.[47]

*   *   *

In California, Bill Sturgeon accompanied Dr. Eisner to a meeting in a home in the hills of Berkeley, California. He recalls: "Betty and I and a couple other of her patients, [another researcher] and his wife, Aldous Huxley and maybe half a dozen other people met and we had a discussion about what do we do now, we can't use LSD any more."[48] Dr. Eisner's initial response, according to Sturgeon, was to take the group to Mexico, where it was still legal to administer the drug. "There was a session in Tecate that took place the same weekend I think Tim Leary was down in Mexico and somebody got killed or murdered in Tim Leary's group. I think this was the same weekend. And we had an exorcism. The group session was going on and at one point Betty said, 'Don't anybody move.' Nobody could move and there was a period of time, it must have been forty minutes, where nobody could move. I remember getting up; both my legs were asleep. We were talking about experiencing really bizarre things, like force, I don't know how to describe it—it gets into the occult. We had to be still because there was a malevolent force looking for us. And it couldn't see us if we didn't move. And that malevolent force, she said, went down and got Tim Leary, and killed one of the people he was working with—and this was her interpretation. And I was convinced at the time. Maybe I still am. I don't know—that was one of the most bizarre things I remember, but that wasn't atypical either."

The controversy is over what happened next in the United States, where Dr. Eisner no longer had legal authorization to use the drug on her patients. She had already used other drugs in conjunction with LSD. Ritalin, a stimulant similar to the amphetamines, could produce emotional arousal that could enhance the effects of other drugs, including LSD, or by itself be used for psychotherapy.[49] She found a physician who would authorize her patients to receive Ritalin injections, administered by his nurse. Marty Goldstein[50] was a later patient, who recalled what was his first drug experience: "When we had our first sessions with Ritalin, we went to [the doctor's] office and then were driven to the therapy sessions at Betty's house. So you tend to remember all of—with some really good clarity—the way you felt on the way before the shot, right after the shot, on the way in the car having that rush hit you and realizing that everything was going to be fine no matter what went on. And then just sitting down nestled up to Betty and beginning what was going to be a trip for the next four hours."

Dr. Eisner has applied the lessons learned with the psychedelics to drugs legitimately available under a physician's direction. She spoke and wrote about her therapies. All the former patients agree that she was able to manipulate set and setting to greatly enhance the power of what would otherwise be considered very small doses of the drugs. Her use of surrogates, having herself and other patients "stand in" for vital figures from the patient's past and present, developed during the legal acid days, was carried over to Ritalin. Music and blindfolds were also used, along with a variety of other techniques.

Physical contact played a major role in the sessions—individual and group. Dr. Eisner provoked feelings in various ways, including blasting and other forms of physically safe "hostility release." Ex-patient Hank Walker has described an early Ritalin session in which various patients lay fully dressed on top of him one at a time, with Dr. Eisner encouraging him to express the feelings this evoked. Even though he was in intimate physical contact with women and men, separated only by clothing, the resulting feelings weren't sexual. Another technique described repeatedly was "piling on" or "containment," in which patients literally "piled on" the subject, causing complete physical immobility. The pinioned patient was instructed to struggle with all available energy. The concept was that final acceptance of the sense of entrapment would produce a psychological breakthrough. These intense intrusions on the normal bounds of personal space were highly emotionally charged, and produced dramatic results.[51]

Both Walker and Goldstein were attracted to Dr. Eisner's emphasis on "bodywork," a term that embraces conventional rubdowns, chiropractic, various forms of exercise and yoga, and the deep muscle massage called Rolfing. But each had first been attracted to Dr. Eisner because of W. V. Caldwell's *LSD Psychotherapy.*

Caldwell describes Dr. Eisner as a practitioner of "anacyltic psychedelic therapy". This is defined as "involving an even deeper, more primitive, and less understood level of communications and response, it has recently been recognized as a vital determinant in the healthy development of the emotions. . . . The only adult relation practiced at this 'gestural' and physiological level is sex. But psychedelic patients discover a rich and varied range of asexual expressions such as caressing and patting, tearing, biting, spitting, and throwing and a host of others of more ambiguous and complex intent. For these primitive movements of the psyche they can find no adequate substitutes, and the rationalization that there are other, more adult methods of healing damaged minds now is being questioned. . . . [O]f all the psychedelic therapists, Betty Eisner of Los Angeles has shown the greatest awareness in discovering, understanding, and making use of these nonverbal biological communications of the psyche. Possibly she is in the vanguard of an exciting new theoretic and therapeutic movement, which may fundamentally alter our understanding of the mind and our capacity to avoid and repair its neurotic disabilities."[52]

On 18 May 1966 possession of LSD by anyone other than an FDA-approved researcher became a federal crime, under the Drug Abuse Control Amendments to the Federal Food, Drug and Cosmetic Act. The following year, Nevada became the first state to enact legislation following the federal lead. California followed, soon joined by the other states. When Caldwell published in 1968, the number of federally approved research centers could be counted on the fingers of one hand.

Between the FDA action in 1962 and the crackdown, LSD dwelt in a state of limbo. Physicians couldn't use it unless they had designed and funded an FDA-approved experiment; yet possession was legal, or, rather, not illegal. It was during this era that Leo Breiman joined Group.

ACID AND THE BOHEMIAN

> I saw her constantly changing, from a therapist—which she still pretty much was when I first came to see her—into more and more a sort of prophetess, an unquestionable leader/authority figure. It was like a steady erosion of her role as therapist and assumption of this new mantle of cult leader. . . . When Jonestown happened, I thought, "There but for the grace of God go I."
>
> —Leo Breiman

It was acid that brought Dr. Leo Breiman to Dr. Betty Eisner. A world-renowned statistician, author, and then-professor at UCLA, he was known as a Bohemian, friends say. At the time he met Dr. Eisner, he was just back in the United States from a year overseas, where he had been working to help build the educational system of a Third World country. Then a friend pulled an Al Hubbard number on him. He describes how he entered Dr. Eisner's fold: "I believe it was 1965 I decided to take a sabbatical from UCLA and I didn't want to just go to another university and teach or do research. So I went to UNESCO and I said I want to go to another country, but I don't want to just go to a university. I want to do something different. And finally they said, 'Okay, we've got a job in Liberia for an educational statistician for the year. How about it?' I said, 'Well, I'll probably be as close to an educational statistician as they can get, so OK.'

"I finally arrived over in Liberia, and spent a lot of time hiking around the backwoods and trying to locate schools. At the same time there was about only a hundred paved miles in the whole country, and it was a real problem finding out where schools were, because a lot of them were started by missionaries—nobody knew where they were. All told it was just a great time. I loved it there. I really loved being there.

"On the way back I had a message from a guy I'd been in therapy with in Berkeley much earlier—I'd done my graduate work there. And he said, 'I've discovered some fantastic new stuff. Be sure and stop by Berkeley on your way back from Africa.'

"So I stopped back, and he gave me an LSD session. I don't even think I knew what LSD was at that point. But it was an incredible session. I mean, I just laughed and cried and saw visions, and it was probably the most incredible thing that had happened to me up to that time. Under this drug, all of a sudden I was seeing things I'd never dreamt I could see. This was crazy. This was a metaphysical experience. I was talking to God. God was talking to me. I was [seeing] things coming out of what I could only interpret as thousands of years out of the past and into the future. It was just an extraordinary experience. There was classical music, there were also spirituals. I remember one woman who had such a marvelous [voice]—Mahalia Jackson or someone—singing spirituals. They just sent me off.

"Anyhow, for somebody who was until then pretty much in the everyday world and never worried about mysticism, anything of that sort, this was—" he pauses, searches for words, shrugs, laughs.

Is there anybody in L.A. who knows how to use the stuff? Breiman asked his friend. "He was kind of hesitant, but finally he said, 'Well, I know of this one woman named Betty Eisner.' So I went down to see her, and that's how I got hooked." He was to remain with her for twelve years, a member of Group until nearly a year after Noel Kramer's death, through two marriages.

*   *   *

Leo Breiman was considered a major figure in the San Francisco Bay Area Bohemian community, at a time when San Francisco's counterculture was a major cultural influence. In the '60s, Berkeley was the center of the action. It was in Berkeley where Leo Breiman earned his doctorate in mathematics. He returned there once as a visiting professor (a post he also held at Yale) during his years at UCLA. It was while he was there that Noel Kramer died.

He is back in Berkeley today, living in a spacious, comfortable house of his own design in the shade of three massive redwoods at the end of a cul-de-sac high in the hills. He is recently married. He describes the experience of joining Group in 1968: "When I came into the group it was much different than the group" at the time of Noel Kramer's death. When he first met Dr. Eisner, "She came across as a person who knew a great deal about drug work, had given many people LSD. She'd done some of the early LSD experiments with Sidney Cohen, so it seemed to me she had a lot of credentials.

"There was also this feeling that she gave off, by all the things she said, some of which were right on the mark, of being able to see into the occult, mystical part of one's soul."

Group was well-established by the time Leo Breiman joined, six years after Bill Sturgeon. And many of the processes Sturgeon had watched evolve had become firmly entrenched rituals: the commitment and reservations had become routine. This was the "research group," what later patients were to call the Old-Timers, the *Viejos*. Breiman relates: "Basically the group consisted of Betty's patients. Nobody was living in communes, or anything of that sort. By Betty's patients, I mean people who might see her once or twice a week. They were a very odd mix of people, and I think a lot of them had been brought there, like me, not because of a great need for serious therapy, but for the adventures under the drug experience. And they included a number of very enjoyable and very bright people whom it was a pleasure to be around—people who later dropped out of Group. The people in the original group are almost disjoint from the people in the group" when Kramer died.

"Basically what we had in common was that once a week, or once every other week—I can't remember which—there would be a party at Betty's house on Friday night, where we'd all get together. About every two or three months an LSD session would be held, in various places where we could be private. Sometimes in a beach house; I think one time we rented a mountain cabin. There was an effort to get into a beautiful natural surrounding."

*   *   *

Breiman, Sturgeon, Marty Goldstein, Hank Walker, and all the other former patients I interviewed said they were given psychedelic drugs by Dr. Eisner at therapy sessions. When Breiman, Goldstein, and Walker joined the group, the drug was banned for all but federally approved research. Sturgeon and Walker still have session reports employing euphemisms for the drugs. Once the FDA restrictions came down, Sturgeon says, Dr. Eisner continued to use either LSD or another psychedelic. Acid was known initially as "propellant," apparently one of the first of many code words for drugs so outsiders wouldn't catch on. "She had LSD that had been•pipetted onto methamphetamine tablets. So you take the methedrine tablet and you're getting both methedrine and LSD," Sturgeon recalls. "It took different forms depending on what was currently available in terms of LSD. Sometimes it was a piece of blotter paper with something on it. Sometimes it was a few drops of something colorless," says Breiman.

At the time Breiman joined, the group sessions followed a routine: "The whole group was involved, and at that time the group was considerably smaller, perhaps twenty people all told. Betty would pass out a dose which she had tailored to the individual; she would be the only one who would not take the dose. At the beginning, we would lie there on the floor, some of us with cushions, some with blankets, letting the drug take us over.

"Sometimes there'd be groups of two or three, and so on. Generally, it was just free-form drifting. Then after a while usually, Betty would spot somebody with some sort of a problem, and she would muster everybody to help this person who had the problem try to understand it and get through it in some way or other.

"I could never tell with Betty. Sometimes out of nowhere, she'd begin yelling for what she sensed you were doing wrong in your session. Here you are deep under the influence, and here's this woman yelling at you for something you're 'doing wrong.' My theory is that one way she managed to establish dominance is by working people over emotionally when they were deep under the influence of this drug. It was just like somebody asking a patient who's under open heart surgery whether they're going to do what you want them to do or not. I don't know if that's true, but it's my theory."

The group drug sessions were generally pleasurable, however, and were frequently followed by long periods of general merriment. "There were a lot of fun people in Group, a lot of very sparkling people who were very witty, and particularly after LSD sessions when everybody was still somewhat high, we'd have absolutely hilarious times. We'd go on for three or four hours telling jokes. God, we would just wipe each other out. And those were the good days. Betty rarely partook in those; the kids were just acting up and having fun."

The bonds formed at the drug sessions weren't solely platonic. After the acid, after the good humor, partnerships formed, Breiman said. "There was to the best of my recollection no sex at these group sessions. I don't remember any at all. Now, certainly afterwards people could go home with perhaps somebody they'd had a revelation with in the group session, something of that sort. But there was no sex at the sessions themselves."

He also recalls individual sessions involving psychedelics and other mind-altering chemicals. "She would invite generally two or three or four other group members to come for the purpose of assuming roles that the person having the session could project on or interact with. A good idea, I think."

*   *   *

In 1967, Breiman resigned his tenured position at UCLA to become a writer/consultant. "I had wanted to do this for many years, as I had felt that I was becoming too abstract and removed from real-world problems," he said in a 1977 court declaration. "In the next five years, I wrote three books on probability and statistics. The advanced graduate book on probability" became the first or second most widely used text in the field, and his undergraduate volumes on probability and statistics were to be adopted in most of the nation's major universities.[53]

He became "one of the three or four most successful fulltime statistical consultants in the United States," with clients ranging from two major Santa Monica "think tanks" to the California Department of Transportation (he helped design pioneering freeway traffic and air quality monitoring systems), the federal Environmental Protection Agency, and the U.S. Department of Justice.

During his time as a patient with Dr. Eisner, he was offered tenured faculty positions with Yale, Purdue, and Carnegie-Mellon universities and two campuses of the University of California, Berkeley and Santa Barbara. He took several "visiting" academic assignments, at Berkeley, Stanford, and Yale, and was elected to the sixteen-member governing council of the professional association for statisticians, the Institute of Mathematical Statistics. At the time he wrote his 1977 declaration in support of Dr. Eisner, he could confidently state, "If there is any question as to my credentials in the fields of probability and statistics, I suggest the statistical staff of any major university be consulted."

*   *   *

His twelve years with Dr. Eisner would bring Breiman through two relationships, as well as the career change. He would also become an elected public official, a member of the Santa Monica Board of Education, after winning a campaign run by fellow Group members in the months following Noel Kramer's death. He was a key participant in the School for Learning, the Group-sponsored volunteer school for the children of a rural Mexican commune, and provided educational opportunities for some of those children in the schools of Santa Monica.

He left Group a year after Noel Kramer died, and was to wind up testifying against Dr. Eisner when the state moved to revoke her license.

GROUP AND SEX

Today society is an interrelated network of rigidities of behavior. It is an intricate and restrictive structure of complicated institutions and outworn customs and traditions. The resulting grand rigidity is so much a part of behavioral problems that evolutionary change is impossible; institutions and mores must be shattered in order to be escaped.[51]

—Betty Grover Eisner

Dr. Eisner's perspective was in harmony with the radical, acid-washed explosive euphoria of the 1960s and early 1970s.

She called for a violent destruction of the old order. Old perceptual patterns were to be "blasted" loose by intense bodywork, overwhelming drug experiences, angry confrontations, "piling on," explosive discharges of feelings.

She was a revolutionary pragmatist, evaluating every experience from its potential as a means of shattering the arthritic, teetering old world order. Highly charged emotions were sought out; no area of life was off-limits. No neurotic old-order restrictions were to be tolerated. The only valid limits were those imposed by the authority of reality, as embodied in Group itself.

Taboos concealed paths to the transcendent place beyond mere reason and mortality. Sexuality was a central focus, and the topic of Eisner's first (and thus far, only) published book, *The Unused Potential of Marriage and Sex*, which dates from 1970.

For Freud, sex was everything, the core experience around which personality took form. Normal psychological development was arrested by highly charged events in early childhood at the anal and oral stages. To the Freudian, psychological balance wasn't possible without a re-experiencing of the original trauma, accompanied by a discharge of psychic energy. And to this extent, Dr. Eisner was a Freudian.

As the most highly charged emotional encounter between two human beings, sex was the most potent tool for self-discovery. According to Eisner, "Sexual expression of any and all forms should be explored, experimented with, and developed by anyone who desires to develop himself and his relationship to the fullest. The only constraint is that whatever is done be acceptable (as a minimum) to both partners. Or perhaps one should say *all* the partners."[55]

Sex was a tool for shattering interlocking neuroses, for breaking down "double binds," the knots that entangled human relationships. And while she called for sex practices acceptable to both partners, she also called for covert relationships: "Solutions of double binds in sexual blocking differ: sometimes it requires a discreet affair of one member; sometimes a visit or two to an attractive call girl; sometimes interaction with another warm and loving couple; sometimes a menage a trois; even an orgy could be helpful."[56]

In *The Unused Potential of Marriage and Sex*, Dr. Eisner set forth a view of sexuality similar to that of the *tantrics* of Tibet. More than a mere animal urge, sexuality was a process for mystical unification—first with another, then with humanity in general, and finally with the cosmos.

She prescribed three marriage types, or "committed ongoing relationships," rather than the traditional single, supposedly lifetime commitment. First would be a "sex-union-marriage," a pairing, often short-term, to develop sexual expression in the context of a loving, mutually supportive relationship. Next, would come a "growth-union marriage," which is either a lifelong pairing or a shorter-term relationship based on the attainment of mutual goals. Finally is the "procreation-union-marriage," where a couple commits to staying together until children are raised to self-sufficiency, and which could be continued longer.[57]

Relationships in Group were heterosexual, homosexual, and multiple. "Three-ways" and "four-ways"—sexual encounters with three and four patients participating simultaneously—were described to the writer by several patients. Marriage partners experimented with other individuals, and at least four former patients have said that these experiments were encouraged and even suggested by the psychologist.

Intercourse, while pleasant, wasn't the most important part of sexual activity. What *was* important, what kept things safe, was the presence "of some sort of guide or mentor who can offer unbiased perception about the reality of the difficulty and the necessities of the situation."[58]

Dr. Eisner's theories about sexuality make a fair amount of sense, and certainly conform to today's real world where lifelong monogamy has been replaced by serial marriage, open same-sex partnerships, and a variety of other relationships. In the context of Group, however, the constant state of sexual flux was a powerful tool for insulating members from the outside world, where many might disapprove. Sexual freedom among a selected few enhanced Group bonding.

There's no doubt Dr. Eisner and Group were indeed on the cutting edge. What happened inside Group would happen to the rest of American culture later: "We shall see more and more of variations in sex and multiple sex experiencing in they years to come—like it or not. Within a decade the various practices will probably be more or less acceptable means of working out difficult sexual problems for living and committed partners (and as a basis for sexual relearning for individuals with difficulties), whether church and state give formal blessings or not."[59]

PSYCHOLOGICAL MYSTICISM

It would be interesting to see how she saw herself in terms of a fairy tale character. Because you know, I think that I guess the Snow White character or the shepherdess character as being as much an archetype as the wicked witch. Now everyone can see her as a wicked witch. But how many can get her as one who tends the flock?

—Marty Goldstein

"When I started going down there we had a project of creating a school for children who lived in an *ejido* [a rural village] five kilometers away," recalls Marty Goldstein. "And we were all putting in time, coming out, going down there, putting in time and teaching little kids. We taught English, there was some music, there was some math, whatever we could do to eventually insure that they had jobs in the city."

When Marty Goldstein first went to Mexico, the ice plant Bill Sturgeon had helped install was up and running, and life pulsed between the two poles of the School for Learning and the *Bucanero*, a magnificent adobe building in the old, cobblestone street area of Puerto Vallarta then seldom visited by tourists. He describes the structure: "Physically it was like a square with a courtyard in the middle. Rooms around the upper patio, rooms underneath the patio. The first floor was the gathering area with soft lights and straw off by the side. Inside areas in the courtyard. White with black shutters and things like that. It was terrific."

It was at the Bucanero, in a land where Goldstein didn't speak the language, that his mysticism and a chronic, potentially lethal disease were to meet in a confrontation that was almost to cost him his life.

*   *   *

To several former patients, their first encounter with Dr. Eisner in the presence of Group proved powerful enough to lead to an immediate commitment. Such was the case with Marty Goldstein, who met her in 1969, through a distant relative, Naomi Feldman, another Eisner patient: "Naomi said to Rachel [Goldstein's spouse] and I one day, 'I know that you think everything is fine, but how are you going to go through life together without becoming your parents? And reflecting in your behavior together what your parents do to each other?' I listened to that, I heard that loud and clear, and I didn't think at that point that there would be anything that life could offer that would change my course, and I didn't like that. I think I originally got into the group because of that and because of my own feeling that I had for a long time that I could deal with my diabetes by really questioning a whole lot of things concerning the administration of diabetes care more than anything else."

Marty Goldstein was distressed. His life had reached a crisis point. Until now, he had done everything his parents wanted. Music was his first love, and though he had won a scholarship to attend music school, he bowed before the will of his parents and became a lawyer, working for a government agency. He married not the woman he cherished, but the woman his parents approved. Moving to California was the first thing he'd ever done on his own in his life.

But distance alone wasn't enough. He couldn't flee from the diabetes, and he couldn't cope with the anguish conditioned by his childhood. He had come from a strong, unhappy family; he was looking for a strong, happy family, and the promise of a happy, healthy tomorrow.

Like Bill Sturgeon, he came from a home where the father was distant, and like Sturgeon he had never taken a psychedelic. While Sturgeon had been haunted by death, Goldstein had been haunted by a controlling disease. Diabetes is a serious disorder, impossible to ignore. Doctors told him his condition required daily shots of insulin for the rest of his life and ordered a restricted diet, restricted activities, constant monitoring of the sugar spilled in his urine, and frequent blood tests. He had to live with the fear that something as simple as an ingrown toenail could quietly turn into an infection that might cost a leg. There are other problems: many serious, some fatal. Interference with the medical regimen could mean death. Diabetes was as much a way of life as a disease.

He was receptive when his own relative shared her zeal for this wonderful therapist she had discovered. So he and Rachel accepted Naomi Feldman's invitation to come to her house for a Saturday party. It was Marty's birthday, after all, and they'd only been in California for a couple of weeks and they needed to unwind, and Dr. Eisner and Group would be there.

"I loved her immediately," he says. "I mean, first of all she was surrounded by everybody. I think I felt a magnetism before I felt a control; she was controlling the situation. She was like Loretta Young coming down into a room—she swept in like a queen. But she was really nice when she spoke to me. She could see my good points immediately." It was as though she could read his mind, he thought. When I asked him if Dr. Eisner, rather than employing telepathy might have already heard about him through his cousin, he paused, then laughed. "I'm sure. I'm sure," he said. "I really haven't thought about that. But now that you mention it, it couldn't be anything else but that way. We were in fact 'fished.' But that's okay. Because I think if it had conflicted with the way that I was feeling, I wouldn't have gone. But it was right in line with where I was going, and I really liked Betty.

"Betty saw something in me that my parents really hadn't been able to be free to see. I think my creative potential. And she really made me feel good about it. She basically said, and I think she said it to everybody, 'Wow, you know, you're really something. You don't know you're really something? Oh, wow! God, what potential you have.' You know, things that are truths. But she made it real personal. She was wonderful doing it and I felt wonderful about that. I mean it's like if all of a sudden you're feeling pain, she says, 'Hey, isn't it great to cry. You ought to feel good about your ability to cry, that's terrific.'

"Even at that point I could tell that she was dealing with feelings. It was a happy circumstance at the party, very happy party. Because all of a sudden I was surrounded by people who were hugging, and I really liked that—magnetized. It was magnetized, it was like 'Wow!' And I really liked hugging Betty."

*   *   *

His meeting came at a unique juncture in Group history. Young People's Group, Thursday Group, was being formed. It would meet for the first time the next week.

Tuesday Group, Old Group, sometimes known as Research Group, after the group's origins, was composed of veteran acid initiates like Bill Sturgeon and Leo Breiman. There was a second group which met Wednesday night for what has been described as a fairly traditional group therapy session. Thursday Group was different. They would have a special destiny. As Keith Lowenstein, once a member, describes it, they were "the bright young people who were going to lead a better life than anyone had ever lived because they were going to work through their problems while they were young." Marty Goldstein recalls: "We immediately met the group of people. It just happens that they were forming another group composed of some of these people and some of Betty's more recent patients to begin like that next week. And I think we were allowed to come in, even though we weren't seeing Betty at the time.

"We met everybody and went around the circle, did some sharing. I don't remember exactly what we shared about. I think it was probably like a drop-in encounter would have been. It was the beginning of this group and they were toasting it, like we were a ship leaving port on a voyage that other groups had gone down before and Betty was the expert at piloting. And we wanted to do that because only by recreating the early family could we create an environment where we would not replicate our parents."

Goldstein's parents fit a stereotype. His father's income as a manufacturer of women's coats and suits—the *schmata* business—earned them a good home in a good neighborhood, what he called a nice insulated suburban Jewish ghetto. As a freshman in college, called on to describe his father in the mandatory freshman English autobiography, "the only thing that I could write about him was that he was a provider. But I couldn't capture anything else." He and his father were in constant competition. His knew his mother as a manipulator. She played the role of mediator between austere, aloof, father and bright, naturally exuberant children, controlling both by emotional rather than physical force.

The parents were conflicted, a classic case of what Dr. Eisner would call "interlocking neuroses." According to his father, his mother was limiting his success by refusing to give him the support he needed, including her refusal to open the home to social functions for his business. She, in turn, felt he had shoved her out of his business because of his jealousy of her college education (he had only gone to high school), and then put her at demeaning tasks while constantly criticizing her abilities—to the point where she had lost all self-confidence.

"One of the things that happened, if I can take that one step further, is that my mom nurtured my creativity since I showed talent in that direction, and found different places—that being one—to stand up to my father." She projected herself into her children's lives. Marty Goldstein, being the eldest by five years, got it first and longest. When the children did well, the mother "gained a lot of pleasure." But should they fail to meet her expectations, "We'd feel very, very guilty." Then came the punishment, prefaced by " 'This hurts me more than this hurts you,' and all sorts of things."

She controlled the children's relationship to their father, or, as Goldstein said, "in some way protected my father from us covertly as overtly she protected us from him." There were constant cues. " 'Don't be noisy around your father; he's had a terrible day at work.' You know, 'Go up and kiss him at the door, I don't care how you feel.' I think it's not an atypical Jewish family. Lot of loving, but there's so much guilt in there that the loving comes tinged with rapier—it's like love till you die, love till you hurt. . . .

"I think I came out of a family where I was in my own way pretty much the pawn of all my family life, between my parents. I remember a couple years before my father died hoping that he would die first because it was easier for me to accept my mother's reality as something I really think happened, as against my father's reality which I know was not what happened—I'd have to change the truth."

Another important factor attracting him to Dr. Eisner was W. V. Caldwell's book. "When I first went to her, I went in response to the book, and I think she knew that right away," he said. "I never had any doubt that Betty was tremendously accomplished, enough to be written about."

*   *   *

Dr. Eisner's writings, as well as her public and private statements, reveal her mystical nature. Acid, rightly used, transported the user to the integrative experience, "that curious sunlit place in the mind where the conflicts disappeared."[60] Drugs were not something to be casually used; only peril lay in that direction. But drugs, in conjunction with group confession, release from "unacceptable" hostility, and a highly controlled authoritarian environment offered a way into the higher levels of consciousness where the individual gained progressive freedom from the limits of the material plane.

One of the most revealing documents from her early years is a speech she delivered in Rome on 13 September 1958[61] entitled "Observations on possible order within the unconscious," which was reprinted in *Neuro-Psychopharmacology*, a respected, international professional journal. She proposed a hierarchy of three levels within the unconscious mind, each separated from the other (in most individuals) by a layer of symbolic imagery.

The third level is an archetypical account of the mystical experience, in which opposites are united, conflicts resolved, eternal ideals recognized, and the sense attained that one can give and receive love freely, endlessly, unconditionally. Attainment of this integrative state provides substantial, tangible stress reduction. Not only does it feel wonderful, but it confers lasting, healing, psychological benefit.

If the promise was immense, so was the price. Dr. Eisner's therapy required enormous self-discipline. The term used in Group was "structure." Patients had to have a routine, an order in their life, pivotal points that would become fulcrums of power for the expression of creativity.

And creativity wasn't something to be compartmentalized; it touched all levels of the individual's life.

The enforcement side of "structure" was "authority." Here Dr. Eisner's work parallels that of another therapeutic group community, Alcoholics Anonymous and its clones, in which each participant has a "sponsor" to report to.[63] Dr. Eisner's patients were assigned an "authority," usually in regard to a designated area of behavior. You reported your conduct to your authority—a fellow Group member—and confessed when you had failed to live up to your commitment. You recorded it all in your diary, which Dr. Eisner might or might not read in a private therapy session.

The "structure"/"authority" system was ultimately enhanced by its application in "group houses," communal homes—the day-to-day therapeutic communities in which patients relived and exorcised the traumas of childhood, learned to break free of the interlocking neuroses.

What happened was not dissimilar with what happens in a monastery, a convent, or a temple community—and for similar reasons. Eisner's therapy, with its profound alterations of consciousness, belief that the traumas may lie in previous lives, communal living, meetings with hugging and kissing, confessionals, regular, ritualized venting of unacceptable feelings, and its large vocabulary of loaded language, was so unique and intense that patients could only fully express themselves to other patients.

It was Group, El Groupo, a collection of uniquely creative individuals ready to spark the revolutionary changes that would overwhelm the ossified institutions of the old order. They would go forth into the world and show what a truly free human could do. They were both missionaries and revolutionaries, providing the models by which humans could become more creative and more loving.

Reincarnation is critical to an understanding of Group. It gave them perspective: This life's anxieties and sufferings aren't accidental or senseless; they come from your karma, payback from the deeds of countless past lifetimes. The traumas and pains of this life serve a noble purpose: to expiate bad karmas from the past and to raise consciousness in this lifetime and in incarnations to come. Reincarnation—an ancient concept—is also a perfect balm for the Atomic Age of Anxiety, promising that however bad it gets, there's more to it all than this. Belief in reincarnation focuses attention on the self and its relationships to the small group of cobelievers with whom your life is karmically entwined. Bill Sturgeon recalled Dr. Eisner making a passing jest, "I must have done something bad in a past lifetime to have earned so much karma with you people."

Dr. Eisner was the guru. At first, it was regular LSD sessions, individual and group. Then, with LSD out of legal reach, came the other drugs and the doctors who gave them. But it was the drug experience that was the heart of her therapy. And reaching that experience was very much conditional. Here is how Marty Goldstein describes working up to his first "super session": "I think what she really did was she gave us the belief that if we conducted ourselves in a certain way leading up to the session, for which we had to be worthy or we wouldn't even be given the opportunity—it only came a certain amount of times during one's life. This was it. You can see the ritual coming through.

"And now you're all ready. You've got the whole cast. People are going to come in, going to bless you, being with you, you're going to be welcomed into the bosom of Abraham. Home.

"You come to group the Thursday before and you've gotten into a little bit of trouble and now you have to do penance. And Betty has you cleaning up the tiles on the bathroom floor the night before the session to do a few things, including tire you out, you know? And you're not sure that she's going to go ahead and let you have the session because she's going to review that floor, and there better not be a speck on it. At least that's what you think. And you have her inside of you. And boy you really better hold yourself to the standard this time."

The words could be those of a religious acolyte at a Zen monastery, describing the experience leading up to a meeting with the *roshi*. They describe an initiation rite, a celebration of the transition from one stage of life to another. The words are Marty Goldstein's, and show that Dr. Eisner's drug therapy wasn't passive, Freudian. It was revolutionary, psychedelic, beyond Jung or anyone else.

For some patients, those of the mechanical engineering mindset, it was frequently necessary to go through a period seen as "going crazy" before the mystical experience could be attained. The therapeutic community provided an opportunity for controlled, structured, committed, ritualized expression of taboo thoughts, feelings, and actions—all in the service of the higher good, under the leadership of a wise teacher.

There were all forms of structure. Basic structure consisted of three things:

1. Seat belts had to be worn at all times in moving vehicles;[64]
2. Unprotected sex was forbidden unless conception was planned;
3. Patients were not to take drugs unless they received authorization in advance from Dr. Eisner.

Violation of these three basic rules guaranteed a strong response from both therapist and group, former patients say. (It was for violating the third rule that Bill Sturgeon was expelled.)

Discipline in Group was intense. One patient left California to obtain an advanced degree, but said he remained in weekly contact with Dr. Eisner, reporting faithfully on all details of his life. Slapping and yelling were routine parts of Dr. Eisner's therapy, much like the bamboo disciplinary rod used by Zen teachers. Some former patients report reaching a condition of continual psychological imbalance.

Another response was akin to the "doubling" described by psychiatrist Robert J. Lifton. Group members developed external and internal personas. Some Group activities couldn't be shared with most outsiders, with parents, coworkers, old friends; they wouldn't understand. So a Group persona arose, along with a social persona. Some of the former patients describe a process that also might be called "tripling," keeping some small, secret part of their identity in reserve.

"Doubling" is the production of a new personality to allow the individual to function in a high-stress situation. The new personality may even predominate, a specially reinforced, reflexive response by the individual to a system of powerful rewards and punishments.

Dr. Eisner saw doubling as culturally pervasive. This was the pattern of interlocking neuroses and psychoses. From the psychologist's perspective, drugs offered her brilliant, overrationalizing patients the opportunity to pass through the sense of "madness" that comes with the loss of an old, inadequate identity and the adoption of a new one, shaped and liberated with her unique perspective and practice. The title of her unpublished book on group therapy reflects her basic concept: *I Can't, You Can't. But We Can!*

*   *   *

Nowhere is the strong mystical element of Eisner's therapy more apparent than in the patterns of group relationships. Recreating the childhood milieu meant reconstructing "naughty," taboo, forbidden thoughts and memories, then re-experiencing them either through overt acting-out or by therapeutic, drug-enhanced abreaction, and releasing the psychic energy that had been blocked by the now-resolved trauma.

To break down the usual constraints on self-disclosure, she used drugs; communal living, group language, private, group, and written confessions, and a powerful sense of sacred mission to give her patients two identities: the regressed child under (her) authority inside Group, and the bright, self-confident professional/student/honest-laborer/parent to the rest of the world. This was the natural result of the initiation process.

*   *   *

Marty Goldstein's therapy with Dr. Eisner revolved around many issues, but one constant theme was his diabetes. "Someplace in, I think about two years, we started thinking that I had come so far that maybe I started seeing a difference in my blood sugar, in my need for insulin.

"You have to understand that when I was 18 or 19 that's when I got diabetes and I first went to a doctor who basically didn't like taking the fun out of teenagers, so he allowed higher blood sugars. Well, one of the things that happened was I didn't have anything bad happen. Gave me a lot of confidence that my blood sugar could be up there.

"We didn't see it in the lowering of my blood sugar. All I saw was Betty saying, 'Don't worry about blood sugar. Blood sugar is—all that is is a measure of blood sugar.' "

Though Marty Goldstein was expelled from Group and Dr. Eisner's practice before Noel Kramer's death, Dr. Eisner's relationship to his treatment of his diabetes was to form one of the major allegations against the psychologist when the state went after her license.

SINGING THE BODY ELECTRIC

Hank Walker had tried traditional therapy, and it failed. He wanted to be released from what seemed to be a permanent, underlying foundation of depression. His story: "I had seen two different therapists in Indiana at different times in my life, and I had had problems in school. My father died, which had been a terribly painful experience for me. I hadn't really found direction in life, and the idea of you know [taking] something to intervene and see reality from a different point of view"—the vision held out in Caldwell's book—held a strong appeal.

"I had decided that therapy was for the birds, that there really wasn't anything to it, that it was just a game. That you went to see a therapist until you realized that there wasn't anything to it, and then you were sort of on your own, you know. Kind of grown up. Some kind of a weird bastard Zen or something, that once you realized that you're on your own—just a sort of metaphysical rite of initiation that without really any substance to it. Almost like a kind of a joke or something, a bad joke."

Walker had lost his father in 1965, when he was nineteen. By 1969, his anguish still unresolved, he was ready for acid. "Psychedelics were a big thing in the '60s, and if you were an aware young person, there was lots of information about it coming from lots of sources in all the media," he said. "The first time I took mescaline it was definitely psychedelic, but there was nothing really haunting, no aspects of the bad trip. I got very much in touch with my body. I think my first insight, my first psyche-delic insight, was that people are afraid to see all the beauty that there is in life. And that's what I really felt. I felt just overwhelmed by the sensation of beauty in nature, in music. I had never really appreciated classical music probably until my second or third trip on psychedelics. I'd always said, 'Yeah, that's nice.' I'd liked it, but I just sort of became struck with the intense beauty of—I remember listening to Vivaldi. . . .

"My first two or three psychedelic trips were with a friend of mine that I'd met at [Buckminster] Fuller's World Game"—he laughs—"in New York. We got to be good friends, and he obtained some LSD in New York, and I'd invited him to visit me back in Evansville. Somewhere along the line we came up with some organic mescaline. We took that, had this incredible trip. I think we'd read things about music, listening—about things to do when you're on psychedelics to enhance the experience."

Fuller's role in Walker's life must be considered, too. It was, after all, the Atomic Age of Anxiety, and Fuller offered a strikingly different view of reality. War, dirty politics, institutionalized racism had tarnished the American ideal, and pollution, the dark side of the once-glorious Industrial Revolution, was threatening the future. This was the generation of *On the Beach* and *Dr. Strangelove*, of the Cuban Missile Crisis, of assassinations, a generation that had practiced regular nuclear-attack drills in schools.

Fuller's contention was that humanity was sheltered by once-valid institutions that now threatened our very survival, a perception hard to dispute. Humanity must cease to think of itself solely in terms of nation-states, religious blocs, racial groups, and political parties. People must recognize each other and themselves for what they really were, *world citizens*, fellow passengers on *Spaceship Earth* (a term he coined).

No lesser perspective could be permitted, because history had now proved that all actions carry unintended consequences. What was required was an analysis of available resources, coupled with an in-depth analysis of human needs—what Fuller called "bare maximums." He created the World Game, which is an ongoing effort to create a comprehensive inventory of planetary resources, material, social, and individual, to be fed into a computer programmed to provide models of the most efficient ways of distributing "bare maximum" amounts to all humans in the shortest times. He and his followers had developed impressive scenarios in which all humanity could be raised to a standard of living unimaginable to even the most powerful nineteenth-century absolute monarch. Fuller defined his vision of human potential in the title of one of his books, *Utopia or Oblivion*. He was to inspire one of the seminal documents of the era, the *Whole Earth Catalog*.

But it was another book that was to transform Walker's life. He found W. V. Caldwell's *LSD Psychotherapy* on the shelves of a shop in La Jolla, an affluent beach community, "just a few weeks before I found Betty," he recalled. He had come to California, leaving his native Indiana because he wanted to work on an advanced degree, and he had read an article in *Newsweek* painting an attractive picture of the University of California system. He enrolled at the University of California at San Diego, at a time when the universities were in a state of ferment.

Fuller, his father's death, social ferment, his chronic depression, inability to focus on university class work, tantalizing drug experiences, and the Southern California scene were powerful forces on a child of the Sixties with a bachelor's in philosophy who had come to question virtually every aspect of his experience.

There were other influences. One was his fascination with what practitioners and users call "bodywork." This term embraces a wide range of practices of varying degrees of scientifically established proof of effectiveness. "Bodywork" is an attempt to systematize physical contact in a therapeutically relaxing manner, although the process itself may be painful.

To gain approval of its explorations of body, the founders of modern medicine had to agree to leave the domain of "soul" to the Church. Traditional psychiatry, an enormously costly, lengthy secular process, remains inaccessible to most; and medicine offered nothing like the simple power of physical contact with another human (something Dr. Eisner clearly understood). "Various psychedelics, including LSD, really opened me up," Walker says. "I had been depressed before. I had seen a couple psychiatrists in Evansville Indiana where I grew up—at different times in my life. I didn't feel that I'd gotten any benefit from it. And I still had pain and problems that I didn't feel like I had a handle on."

The psychedelics, LSD and psilocybin (from so-called "magic mushrooms) in particular, "have specific effects on the serotonin system" of the brain, which regulates the level of a key piece of brain chemistry. Serotonin is a neurotransmitter, a chemical passed from one brain cell to another which will produce specific chemical effects on each cell. Serotonin plays a powerful role in shaping mood and behavior. The safest, most effective antidepressant medication now on the market has effects on serotonin in the basal ganglia similar to those produced by LSD, but without the hallucinations.[65]

"LSD . . . got me in touch with the Universe, and got me in touch with myself in a lot of ways, got me in touch with life in a lot of ways. But it also got me in touch with my body, and I started feeling tensions and pain in my body I hadn't been aware of before. It got me out of being in my head so much, where my energy was just trapped in my head. So it sort of opened me up. But it was a kind of a trade-off. I started feeling new kinds of pain (laughs), but I felt I was more alive. I had broken down some internal barriers but I still needed some help. I started having weird dreams and so forth, and I thought, 'I think maybe I should consider therapy again.' "

Physical pain and tension first fully recognized under the drug created an interest in a rapidly evolving field where most of the important events were happening in California. Sam Keene, theologian-turned-psychologist/journalist, summed up the spirit of the movement in the title of an article he wrote for *Psychology Today*, "Sing the Body Electric."[66] His highly influential piece, describes his physiological and psychological discoveries made during a ten-session course of Rolfing, an intense, defined mix of massage, deep tissue manipulation, and metaphysics. It is also known as Structural Integration.[67]

Rolf training was available in Los Angeles. So was Arthur Janov's Primal Institute. Janov is a Beverly Hills therapist who devised a therapeutic technique which is described in his book *The Primal Scream*. Janov declared that he had discovered a time-slashing practice which would allow patients to live through their most traumatic experiences, including physical birth. The "primal scream" sounds like anguished blasting. Celebrities had endorsed the technique and the media had ballyhooed the therapy, not always in a friendly fashion. To Walker, in those early, heady days before the media euphoria faded, the technique seemed promising.

Walker, disillusioned with school and living in Del Mar, just up the coast from the university, traveled north to Los Angeles one day in June 1971 to seek either admission into the primal scream process or, that failing, to meet the woman he had admired both through Caldwell and another book.[68] "I thought, just because my experiences in therapy haven't been fruitful, maybe [primal scream therapy] can be fruitful. I thought, 'I feel like I need some help anyhow, so let's hope that there is.' So I thought, 'Maybe I'll try to find one of these therapists I've heard about who's worked with LSD.' I was living in La Jolla at the time, or Del Mar, just outside of San Diego.

"So one day I went to LA—this is in early June of '71—and decided I'd make a couple stops. My first stop was the Primal Institute, and they said, 'Well, come back in August—we have an eight-month waiting list. We aren't accepting new people onto the waiting list until August.' I was discouraged, because I was in pain and felt like I needed some help right then. So my second choice was Betty. So I went over to see her. I mean, if they had said, 'Come in, we'll take care of you,' I might not have ever gone to see Betty."

Walker had also adopted another discipline rare in a culture where the most significant eye contact with individuals outside the immediate family can be with the television newscaster or game/talk show host. Many people avoid prolonged eye contact. "It's not polite to stare." But eye contact could be fascinating. When a short experiment revealed to Walker that everyone whose gaze he didn't turn from turned from his, he began a six-month experiment that encompassed his last months in Bloomington, Indiana, and first months in Southern California. One of those who held his gaze was a waitress at a health food restaurant—after a long stare-off, she invited Walker to join her and go find a UFO to board and levitate together off the planet. The other gaze-holder was a close colleague of Buckminster Fuller, now an influential New Age researcher.

Caldwell's book singles out "eyeballing" as "one technique for un-covering problems" where "therapist and patient stare fixedly at each other, to arouse in the patient an awareness of a variety of problems of inter-relation which might not otherwise come to conscious attention."[69]

After his disappointment at the Primal Institute, Walker knocked on the door of the Westwood Boulevard office unannounced. "My six months of doing eye contact hadn't ended. So I remember meeting Betty. I knocked on the door, she came to the door. That's probably one of the reasons I wanted to meet her. I wanted to make eye contact. And these eyes like big headlights came out at me. I mean, there's a certain amount of intensity.

"One of the things I noticed in my six-month inquiry into eye contact: there were some people who made fairly long eye contact, and they had really kind of soft, warm eyes. I was impressed. When I had long eye contact with them—I always maintained eye contact longer—but they weren't doing it to make eye contact for a long time; they were doing it just because they were warm open people who enjoyed making contact. With Betty it was more of an intensity. And that was intriguing to me. 'This woman is heavy duty. She's not just out passing the time of day. There's something going on.' So I was intrigued by that, too. So I ended up noticing, 'Boy she made real good eye contact with me.' "

He smiles, laughs. "Well, you can see I was almost foreordained to find this woman as my therapist. I thought, 'Wow, this is really interesting. I'm really into eye contact now and here's this woman who has this intense involvement with her patients' eyeballing.' "

So impressed was he that, unlike Sturgeon, he remembers little about the psychologist's office. It was the eyes which impressed. The conversion was completed at his first Ritalin session in the therapist's home, on an exclusive street in one of California's most exclusive neighborhoods, a street of houses that today cost in the seven-figure range. Her living room ceiling sweeps upward, the high wall containing a fireplace. The room is comfortable, visually elevating, yet quite human in scale, and the tile-roofed, thick-walled Spanish architecture harmonizes pleasantly with the Southern California environment, cool in summer, warm in winter.[70]

"I came to see her on a Monday," recalls Walker, "knocked on her door. The following Monday I saw her in her office, which may have been the only time I ever had an appointment in her office. And the following Friday I had my first drug session at her home, [which] was Ritalin. I went to see the M.D. and had a physical during that week. He okayed me for drug therapy, and that Friday I had some Ritalin, came back to Betty's house and was hooked up to a [biofeedback] machine—I know at some point she put her and Bill's faces right next to me and I looked at them and I started crying. I remember talking to [a friend from his Fuller days] about it, and he was impressed because 'this was the archetypes, the male and female archetypes that Betty was using.' He was translating it into Jungian terminology. I thought 'Yeah, yeah, she was using archetypes! Wow!' I was impressed too." He laughs. "At any rate, that was the first drug session.

"I've got my first and second session reports right here. I'll read it out loud. 'My first session with Betty Eisner and her group was Friday morning June 11. Repeating the commitment was my first task. . . .' "

*   *   *

Dr. Eisner often used other faces—her own, her husband's, her children's, other patients'—during the drug sessions. "Psychedelics and people as adjuncts of psychotherapy" was the title of a paper she presented at the First International Congress of Social Psychiatry in London in August 1974.[71] The drugs Dr. Eisner gave her patients profoundly altered their awareness. That's why she used them. Different drugs had different effects, and sessions were structured according to the effects of the drug and the effects of the milieu. One element of the milieu was other individuals who could serve as stand-ins, surrogates, for significant others in the patient's past, with whom conflicted feelings were being experienced. Those feelings could then be resolved through interacting with the surrogate.

Group blasting ritual often involved mutual surrogacy on the part of two patients, and was encouraged, former patients say, by rooting from the other group members. Surrogacy was by definition an aspect of a therapy which sought to create the early childhood environment to resolve psychological disturbances with roots in unresolved childhood conflicts incorporated in the core personality.

Several patients report undergoing a deep bonding with the therapist at the first drug session. Walker took Ritalin, which is a stimulant, a drug that arouses. Arousal is a critical concept, because it appears to be a state in which emotional attachment can be switched from one object to another. An example often cited by psychologists is the way teenage boys and girls might go to horror shows to get aroused by fear, then channel the arousal into behavior that once earned drive-ins the name "passion pits." Arousal enhances bonding, conversion, and initiation.[72]

Now here was his therapist and her spouse, literally thrusting their faces in his. The impact was profound: Hank Walker cried, expressed grief, feelings associated in part with the loss of a parent, in part with loneliness. Similar openness in the communal homes and group sessions created similar bondings, which was precisely the purpose of Group—to use drugs, sex, discipline, relationship, and structured compliance to recreate and free the primitive emotions and liberate enormous latent creative energy.

It was into this environment that Hank Walker plunged. He was to become a Group bodyworker, providing massages to other members during and after drug sessions. It was he who assisted the psychologist the day of Noel Kramer's death, and who was to become one of the most powerful witnesses against his former therapist.

"DEATH . . . AT THE HANDS OF ANOTHER OTHER THAN BY ACCIDENT"

First to pass judgment on the case of the death of Noel Ronald Kramer was a coroner's jury.

In addition to the cause of death, the coroner is charged in California with determining the "mode" of death, the "how" as well as the "why." The law recognizes four modes of death: "natural," "suicide," "accidental," and "at the hands of another other than by accident."

All findings of non-accidental death at the hands of another must, under Section 27504 of the *California Government Code*, be referred to the district attorney's office for possible criminal prosecution.

When there is doubt about the "mode" of death, the county corner in California is allowed to present the case before a jury selected from the same county pool used to try criminal and civil cases. Based on the evidence, the jury then chooses from among the four modes of death. The hearing is not a trial. The jurors can listen to hearsay testimony, inadmissible in a criminal case. The hearing officer is not bound by the rules of evidence; and the only grounds for excluding evidence are privileged communication (attorney-client, doctor-lawyer), self-incrimination, and irrelevance (which is decided by the hearing officer).

In the death of Noel Kramer, the case was presented to a jury on 11 January 1977, less than two months after the fatal afternoon. The hearing began at 9:55 A.M. in Room M, on the second floor of the New Criminal Courts Building. In 1977, the coroner's office for Los Angeles County held hearings on an average of three to four cases a week; in all other deaths in the sprawling county, the mode was considered self-evident.

Conducting the hearing was Frederick E. Lacey, chief of the Inquest

Division of the Los Angeles County Coroner's Office. Seven witnesses were questioned by Lacey and by Robert L. Schibel, attorney for Dr. Eisner.

First to the stand was Dr. Eugene Carpenter, a pathologist. He performed an autopsy on Kramer's body.

"The cause of death was a severe heart irregularity brought on by severe oxygen deprivation, essentially a near-drowning," said Dr. Carpenter. But "near-drowning" didn't mean that the dead man had been submerged for a long time; rather, he'd been sufficiently deprived of life-sustaining oxygen to produce the same physiological effects as drowning.

What Carpenter found on the autopsy table was a body whose internal organs were filled with small hemorrhages, where the capillaries, the smallest of the blood vessels, had oozed blood into the surrounding muscle, nerve, and organ tissue, causing massive congestion. There was a particularly widespread hemorrhage within the inner lining of the heart, which had produced the fatal irregularity. Smaller diapedeses (leakages) were found throughout the brain, lungs, liver, kidneys, spleen, and adrenal glands. These hemorrhages are produced when the oxygen level of the body drops in suffocation and drowning. There was nothing else about the body to indicate a cause of death, no significant pre-existing heart condition, he said.

Lacey asked whether the physician discovered anything in the police reports to indicate what might have brought on the condition. "The individual was apparently undergoing some kind of psychotherapy which includes hydrotherapy work in a tub; at the same time, the idea was to scream at the top of one's lungs to vent one's hostility as a character type of maneuver, psychologically speaking. Under these circumstances the noise would be partially muffled by an attendant so that the neighbors weren't alarmed. When you do that, when somebody is yelling and fixing their diaphragm and expelling air from their lungs and it is being obstructed at the mouth to some extent . . . what will happen in the chest is [that] the blood flows back to the heart and will be impeded to some degree.

"Also, part of this would be a situation of hyperventilation, which means overbreathing. The problem with overbreathing is that the impulse to breathe comes from the amount of carbon dioxide in the lungs . . . and carbon dioxide alone is a stimulus to take the next breath. So when one breathes rapidly, one breathes off carbon dioxide, and as far as the respiratory center is concerned, there is no impulse to breathe."

Hyperventilation, he explained, is a technique practiced by competitive underwater swimmers, allowing them to stay submerged without a breath for as long as a minute-and-a-half. The problem is, while one doesn't feel the need to breathe, the body still starves for oxygen, and if the state continues, the kind of tissue damage found in Noel Kramer's organs is produced, the pathologist testified.

Kramer apparently had two baths, according to the police reports, and in the second put his head underwater "and remained there. I don't know the time intervals. And it was finally when the attendants had to pull him from the pool . . . he got out of the pool again, sat down, and apparently shortly thereafter collapsed and he was dead."

A blood test also revealed the presence of methylphenidate, Ritalin, which Carpenter defined as a "very mild stimulant" that he felt played no role in Kramer's death.

Robert Schibel, Dr. Eisner's attorney, now had his chance to ask questions. Did Dr. Carpenter, in light of the police report statement that Kramer's head was submerged, find water in his lungs? "There is always water in the lungs," he responded. "This is sort of a popular superstition. When somebody drowns you might find water in the stomach. We find water in the lungs, but we wouldn't know if that water came from the outside or water that backed up into the lungs [from other bodily tissue] because the heart was failing. The significant finding in drowning—and there are not too many at autopsy—is the presence of foam in the airway." The foam is produced by the unconscious victim's lungs pumping against a closed mouth while the body is thrashing underneath the water. "This individual," Kramer, "did not drown," he said. "But you can compare it to a situation where somebody has been drowning and somebody rescues him"; if too much damage has been done, the victim dies after resuscitation.

Lacey had one last question for the pathologist: Could the death have resulted from "a natural cause or heart attack that may happen at any time?" Dr. Carpenter's response: "No, any individual put under this type of oxygen stress—it could have happened to anybody."

Next to the stand was Sgt. William Brucker of the Santa Monica Police Department, who had investigated the death. He had interviewed three witnesses: Dr. Eisner (whose name was spelled "Isner" in reports), her spouse, Bill Micks, and the man who had assisted Dr. Eisner with Kramer's bath, Hank Walker.

The story Brucker received from Dr. Eisner was that Noel Kramer had received a Ritalin prescription from a physician she worked closely with, and he had taken some of the medication at his home before coming to her house at 4:30 that afternoon for a hot mineral bath session. This was his report of what the psychologist told him: "During the first hot bath, Mr. Kramer did yelling and screaming, expending most of his anger, and was extremely tired from most of the exertion, which is normal. After he regained his energy, he asked to go back into the bath again . . . and he did begin to yell and scream again. However this time he stiffened up and was described as acting like he was bound at the hands and feet with his hands behind his back, and said nothing, and suddenly flipped over into the bath, at which time an assistant, Hank Walker, helped right Mr. Kramer. And he was then . . . wrapped up in towels and placed in bed to rest, because he was again tired from this procedure.

"It was a short time after that that it was noticed that he was having difficulty in breathing and he was placed on a masseuse table face down and there was noted a . . . considerable drain of mucus and blood from his mouth. He stopped breathing at this time and the paramedics were called to revive him."

Brucker had then questioned William Micks, who "related pretty much the same thing. He was present there for the bath but not for the resuscitation."

Then Brucker had questioned Hank Walker, "who is a licensed masseuse in the City of Santa Monica. He stated that he usually assists Dr. Eisner in these therapy sessions and his main function is to hold down the subject when he becomes violent or extremely active in the tub to cut down injuries. Also he does massages to calm down the people after therapy. He basically stated the same thing, except he did think that Mr. Kramer had mumbled something about drowning before he turned himself over in the tub. But Mr. Walker felt that Mr. Kramer had not taken any of the water into his lungs because he wasn't coughing or exhibiting any kind of actions like that."

Schibel had no questions for the officer, and Lacey then summoned William Michael Curtis, the paramedic who had been first through the door into the psychologist's home that night. "We were called to the residence and we found a person who was unconscious, not breathing, no heart rate, and we performed our medical duties and tried to resuscitate this person," he said.

"We entered through the front door and saw a patient or person on a medical examination or operating table face down with an Indian-type blanket and a towel over his body. There was a sheet under his body. As we walked in the house, there was an entryway. It was crowded with clothes, sweaters, overnight bags, shoes. And about fifteen to twenty people were circled around this table holding hands and interlocking arms. Two men were doing what we call a back lift arm method of resuscitation. His head was hanging over the end of the table.

"When we arrived there, we turned him over face up, and he had some blood and mucus in and about his mouth. He was hot, particularly in the chest area, which we exposed right away to detect if there was a heartbeat or anything."

The eyes were dilated and not responsive to light. The paramedics began emergency breathing with an Ambubag and started closed chest heart massage, "the whole technique." When Curtis asked what had happened to the man, an older woman came forward and told him "he had been down approximately fifteen minutes and not breathing." Had he taken any drugs, Curtis asked. Yes, she said, Ritalin.

The paramedics were able to establish a heart rhythm, and after they had administered the intravenous medications, "We had a few spontaneous respirations and then the patient went downhill after that." He was never conscious.

Schibel asked if "somebody was having a problem with fluid in their lungs or spitting up mucus, would I use the mouth-to-mouth resuscitation method?"

"Yes," Curtis answered, "if you wanted to revive them you would."

Next to the stand was Dr. J. Reynolds O'Donnell, the physician who had prescribed the Ritalin Noel Kramer took the day of his death. The drug, he said, was a mild central nervous system stimulant which produces "a very low level of increased awareness." The drug, he said, was used as an antidepressant and "to some extent—although I think its use has been abandoned—in the treatment of hyperactivity" in children.[73] The drug was safe at the dosages Kramer had used, up to 200 milligrams (or more than three times the currently recommended maximum adult dosage).[74] O'Donnell had given Kramer yearly physicals, including an electrocardiogram, since 1971. "He was a well male and he had no disease," the doctor said.

William Micks, consulting engineer and Dr. Eisner's spouse, came next to the stand. The Thursday afternoon when Kramer started his mineral bath, Micks was attending a class. When he arrived at his home between 5 and 5:30 P.M., he walked in the front door to be greeted by the sounds of "someone shouting as though getting out hostility, and I knew that there was a session going on." He went about his own business until "a little bit later." When Kramer was getting out of the tub, Micks helped the patient into the nearby bedroom to rest.

Micks said he stood at the foot of the bed and looked at Kramer, who, now covered with a blanket, was "making various body motions." Also present, he said, were Dr. Eisner and Hank Walker. Sometime between 6:15 and 6:30, Dr. Eisner sent her spouse to one of the communal homes, where she was to have met with "Young Group" for a brief session before the adult Group gathered. He was to bring the older Group over to the psychologist's house if she didn't call, "and this is what happened: "The young group had their meeting and then as the adult group arrived, I informed them that we were going over to La Mesa. And I also said something to them about the fact that Noel was having a session and I felt it would be good to have them there to give Noel support. And then everyone went over to La Mesa."

Micks came back into La Mesa through the back door about seventy minutes after he had left. "I glanced into the room where Noel was resting," and saw Kramer, "leaning over. And I saw a bucket and it looked as though he was getting something out of his mouth or—well, maybe vomiting. I don't know, because I just walked past." He walked into the living room, where Group was assembling, and turned on more lights.

"And then about this time someone . . . helped Noel into the living room," he said. "Noel was put on the table . . . face down, and I think there was perhaps some more drainage." The bucket was again at hand. "After . . . he had gotten rid of water he had in his mouth, I felt that I could get his attention. And I suggested that he sit up and let me talk to him. So people on that end helped him to sit up. I was at the foot of the table at this point, and I said (something) like, 'Noel, Noel. It's okay. We are all here. We're all here to support you. You've . . . done what you needed to do. It's okay.' "

Kramer's eyes were closed when he was first sat upright, Micks said. But Micks said that as he talked to Kramer, "he opened his eyes and he looked right at me and I said, 'Noel, it's okay.' But his eyes were focused and looking directly in my eyes and I thought, you know, 'Fine, he's right here.' Then it was as though his eyes—well, I guess he shut his eyes. I don't remember, but it was like he looked at me for a minute and then wanted to lie down or shut his eyes. I don't remember. But at the time he was—well, there were people back supporting him, so whether he did it or whether they did, I don't know. But he lied back down. And it was just shortly after this that Dr. Eisner said to me to call the paramedics, so I did."

Lacey seemed puzzled by Micks's use of the word "session." What did he mean by it? the hearing officer asked. "Well, it was—it's a therapeutic technique that Dr. Eisner uses that helps people. This kind is basically getting out hostility, working on problems in some way. But this one involved the salt bath, and that is what I mean by session."

Under Lacey's questioning, Micks said that he frequently volunteered to help at sessions. In the case of mineral baths, it could be "anything from taking wet towels to the dryer or whatever. And sometimes it helps if someone is there to give—to give support in some way."

He acknowledged that when he returned from the communal home and saw Kramer sitting up in the TV room, "Dr. Eisner was supporting him."

Kramer was moved the twenty feet from the TV room to the massage table because it would help "drain anything out if he had something in his chest . . . and also to have the group around to give support . . . just moral support." At some point Micks said he looked into the bucket and saw "some very small flecks of blood in the phlegm." He insisted Kramer was conscious when he made eye contact on the massage table.

Micks couldn't remember whether or not he had helped bring Kramer out and on to the table, but he didn't think he did, nor did he recall who else might have. At no time did Kramer speak, Micks said.

At what point, Lacey asked, was Group asked to stand around the table to give support? The reason Noel Kramer was placed on the massage table was to give him support, Micks said. "Everyone walked up and placed their hand on Noel at some place, you know, just to, you know, reassure him and let him feel that everybody was there with him. So people were standing around the table" from the time he was placed there.

> LACEY: "Now of course for someone to be assured in some manner, they would have to be conscious of the act being performed. Again, I would ask you at the time these individuals were requested to perform this particular act, was the decedent conscious or was he unconscious, in your opinion as a lay person?"
>
> MICKS: "Well, in my opinion he might have been able to hear these things, but he didn't respond in any way I could see to that part, to the people placing their hands on him. I didn't see a response to that. But he may have been hearing it. I don't know."

Schibel had only a few questions: How soon after Kramer had looked at Micks did the artificial respiration start? "It had to be less than a minute." Prior to when artificial respiration was started, had Kramer experienced any breathing difficulties? "He was breathing, but there was a noise, that sort of rasp or wheeze." And how soon after artificial respiration began were paramedics called? "It was within a minute or two, something like that."

Lacey had a few more questions: When Micks returned from Young Group, did he notice if Kramer appeared wet, or if his hair seemed wet? No, he did not notice. Neither had he noticed any blood around the mouth or any bruises on the body.

*   *   *

Then Dr. Eisner was called. She had heard the testimony, he said. What was her account of the events of that afternoon and evening?

"Can I go back a little?" she asked.

"Yes, ma'am," Lacey answered.

She held up a blue and white box, labelled *Murietta Mineral Salts*. "I brought this so you could see. . . .

"In the spring of 1976 the group of us went down to Murietta Hot Spring and we thought we'd try the bath out. And they were extraordinary. They were much like sessions for the work that I did.

"People had all kinds of unusual and strange experiences, which they said, you know, were their long sessions that they did."

Noel Kramer and one other Group member had two baths on each of the two separate weekends—March 6th and April 24th—the group visited the spa, she said. "We do a lot of things together, the group. It's not just therapeutic," she said. "It's really gone beyond that. We are sort of trying to fulfill our potential."

A return trip had been planned for September, "and then we had word that we had some trouble on the woman's side." The spa was going to make the women's baths cooler, and Group members who said they'd had the cooler baths reported "they didn't do as much," so the September trip was canceled. Meanwhile, someone had discovered the commercially packaged mineral salts, "so we decided to try doing our own."

She ran the first session on 1 October 1976, with Elaine Patterson.[75] "It was extraordinary for getting out hostility, just something about that bath." Recalling the earlier trips to Murietta, she said, "people got very angry and then they went through different kinds of experiences and things, what we call 'sessions.' "

After the first session, she said, she "went back East for a few weeks." Hank Walker administered several baths to fellow patients "with very good effects," but without Ritalin. Walker "is very talented with bodywork," she said. He had had the first half of the Rolf training, "which is a body technique I use a lot in my work." She often sat through her patient's Rolfing sessions, she said. "Really, in psychotherapy, you will find many of the problems are set into the body and that just talking doesn't always help the people the way it should."

Although she normally administered the mineral bath sessions on Friday, Noel Kramer had been particularly eager for a bath, and Wednesday of that week—when Group gathered to rehearse a play they were going to present at the local civic auditorium—he asked the psychologist if she could give him a session on Thursday instead. She agreed, and the two discussed the dosage of Ritalin he should take prior to the session. They agreed on "sixty or seventy" milligrams, she said; the prescription allowed for up to one hundred.

The afternoon of the session, Dr. Eisner and Hank Walker arrived fifteen minutes late for the four o'clock appointment. The patient was already in the house, ready for the session. The bath was run, and Noel Kramer first entered the water around four-thirty, she said. She had already dissolved a packet of salts in the tub.

Walker was there only by chance. Dr. Eisner said he had asked her the previous night if he should come, and she had answered, "I don't see any reason why." When Walker said he wanted to come, she gave her assent, she said.

At this point she asked to correct "incorrect reports on two things."

"You may," Lacey said.

"When we spoke to the sergeant, I thought we had made it very clear that to the best of my knowledge—and I was there and watching the whole time—Noel's head never went under water. There was a big

fight. I mean, there was a tremendous fight and Hank, by his strength—
he's a very strong young man—kept his head out of water. That was
one of the things that was incorrect. Anyway, so—and then I have to
explain blasting to you.

"When I work with patients who are called character disorders—and
one of the problems with character disorders, they have a great deal of
difficulty handling their hostility. It is buried very deeply and it is very
hard to get to. And Noel's was particularly hard to get to, and that's why
he welcomed any technique such as the baths or Rolfs or drugs to help
him get to his anger. And with blasting we have people go like that [demon-
strating] to each other for the blasting. And usually they put a towel in
their mouth, sometimes a towel or a washcloth in their mouth so that
the sound doesn't sound too upsetting, because we start group meetings
by all blasting and it sounds—we would be in a uproar if everybody yelled."

Dr. Eisner said she initially set the "dinger" (timer) for the first bath.
"My normal thing would be fifteen minutes, and if it didn't work then
to set it a little longer." After the timer went off, "nothing had happened.
He hadn't even felt any anger, and he didn't blast. And we said, 'Why
don't you blast?' And I reset the 'dinger' for twenty minutes." Then Kramer
took the towel and began to blast, "but it didn't seem to be very effective."

It was during the second, twenty-minute phase of the first bath that
Dr. Eisner "noticed something strange. Noel kept his legs together, his
knees and ankles just touching each other and his hands were behind
him, sitting on his hands." She only noticed the peculiar posture toward
the end of the session. "I thought, 'That's strange,' but people do a lot
of strange things in these sessions that we give."

Sometime during the session, she said, she noticed the water had
gotten cold. She filled a tea kettle and a pot and put them on the stove.

When the timer went off at the end of the twenty minutes, the
psychologist said she asked Kramer if he wanted to leave the tub, and
he said, 'Yes, I would like to.' "

Earlier in the session she learned that her patient had taken eighty
milligrams of Ritalin, rather than the sixty or seventy they had discussed,
"but the Ritalin evidently had no effect," she said.

He was dried, then taken to the TV room where the single bed had
been covered with beach towels over a layer of plastic. Kramer was covered
with a towel and a blanket. He blasted "a couple of times lying on the
bed, and he said, 'I just can't get it up. . . . I just got to get through this."

While lying in the TV room, Kramer told Dr. Eisner, "I really want
to get through this," and begged to be allowed back in the tub. She added
water from the stove and another packet of mineral salts, helped Kramer
to the tub, and set the time for twenty minutes. The whole second bath
Kramer spent with ankles together and hands behind his back, making odd

movements in the tub. "I didn't ask him what was going on, because I have seen many strange things going on, and it interrupts the process of what goes on. But I did say to Hank, 'Be careful he doesn't hit his head.' "

The undulating movements lasted about ten minutes, she said, and sent water all over the bathroom.

"Then suddenly it was—Noel made a sudden movement and it was as though he freed his arms and feet. . . . then he said, as far as I could hear, it sounded like 'drowning', and then he turned—he turned and tried to submerge himself." Kramer and Hank Walker struggled, she said, with Walker getting soaked. "But I could swear he didn't get his head under water."

About the same time, the 'dinger' sounded, and Dr. Eisner said she told Walker, "I think we ought to get him out." They helped him up and Walker "half-carried him" into the TV room and lay him back down on the bed.

"Then, when we laid him down, I got the first good look at him and covered him up and he was very gray. It bothered me for the color. Now I watch color very carefully in the tubs," because a patient can get too red, too hot. "But Noel never got very red." Now, lying on the bed, his face was ashen. "I patted him on the cheek, 'Come on Noel, you got through it. It's fine. You're all right now. You're resting now.' And very slowly the color came back in his cheeks."

Her patient went through more unusual motions with his arms and legs, his eyes closed at first, then opened but unfocused. "Now the lack of focus of his eyes I have seen a number of times in sessions where people are into their own reality, whatever they are doing, either going back to some kind of difficulties of the past."

Next came a period of relative quiet followed by more unusual motions: Kramer braced his legs on the table and raised his pelvis. "It's a strange thing," Dr. Eisner said, "but the closest way I can describe that was like a woman giving birth. Now that sounds strange, but that is the closest way I can describe the motion."

Kramer became calm once again and laid back on the bed, "quietly, and his face changed. . . . It was about the same color, maybe a little grayer, but he suddenly looked older." He "appeared to be in something else." His face looked "older . . . maybe drawn and thin," and he failed to respond to her. At this point she directed someone—Hank Walker or her husband—to call Naomi Feldman, the woman Kramer lived with, the mother of their daughter. About the same time, Bill Micks left for the other commune where Young Group was meeting.

When Feldman arrived, Kramer was entering what Dr. Eisner described as "this third phase." Prior to this point, she said, he had had no difficulty in breathing, but now "there began to be some kind of a wheeze and it sounded as though he had some mucus."

"We felt we ought to drain that out. And I keep buckets, because people do spit up a lot and they vomit and they do cough stuff up," she said, so "we sat Noel up and there was a lot of green stuff that came out of his nose."

But sitting, propped up by Hank Walker, seemed to tire the patient, so they laid him back down. Walker had to leave, and asked the therapist, "You are sure you will be all right?" Dr. Eisner said yes, explaining to Lacey, "we had seen many strange different things at sessions."

After Walker left, Kramer remained non-responsive and began the raspy breathing again. Dr. Eisner and Feldman rolled the man over on his side and held the bucket under his head. "A whole lot more of green stuff came out of his nose, and this time some mucus came out. This was the mucus. And I felt better getting the mucus out, because I felt this was making the breathing hard."

It was now 7:20 P.M., three hours since Kramer first entered the hot tub, and well over an hour since he had spoken his last word. Naomi Feldman had to leave for her home to relieve the baby sitter, a fellow patient. Alone in the house with her patient, Dr. Eisner rolled him onto his side several times to drain the mucus that kept coming; the "green stuff" from the nose had finally stopped.

She was concerned now about the mucus, anxious for Group to arrive.

When the group finally began to assemble, she told one of her stronger male patients, " 'I want to take him in, put him on the table. I want to get this mucus out of his chest.' So I went in ahead to make sure the table was set up and there was a towel on it." Two patients brought Kramer into the living room and placed him on the massage table.

"Now I was very relieved to see, when once we got him on the table, that the mucus had some—just a little streak of blood in it, because we have learned in sessions when people go through a traumatic event, no matter—they can just be sitting there, they would not have blasted or anything, they will cough up—oh, and I tried to get Noel to cough during this time, but I was only able to get him to cough once—that they quite often cough up and just—it seems totally unrelated, we know of no reason, for mucus with just a little streak of blood. And I say a streak because it doesn't look [like] a fleck, like a little line of blood. And I was very relieved when we had him upside down to find this coming out. Because I felt that this would clear his chest and that that was a signal that we were after for the session. Whatever the traumatic thing, we're getting down to it. Hostility was over and had been completed."

At some point, she didn't recall when in the course of the session, Kramer bit her finger as she was keeping his mouth open to keep the drainage flowing from his lungs. "And then Bill, my husband, said that he felt if we sat him up and talked—talked to him, we would get his attention, and this would help. In the meantime, when we got everybody in there—there was some people in the living room—and they all formed a circle, which we often do with people in sessions, and they put their hands on him."

Meanwhile, said Dr. Eisner, Rachel Goldstein was at the foot of the table, taking Kramer's pulse "the whole time before the paramedics came," and that the pulse rate was sixty beats per minute when Kramer had just been placed on the table; eighty just before the paramedics arrived. Also present were Elaine Patterson and another member of Group, world-renowned musician Les McCann.

Though Dr. Eisner said she didn't see Kramer's eyes open and focus on Bill Micks, her husband, McCann, Patterson, and Rachel Goldstein all told her they had seen it. It was just after that that "Noel threw his head backwards—that is what it looked like to me—and his eyes went up and his lips turned blue."

It was at that moment, she said, that she asked if anyone knew artificial respiration, and one of the young male patients began the arm-lift technique. The paramedics, Dr. Eisner said, were called immediately and arrived in about twelve minutes. Group gathered around the table to give Noel support, "and I think the paramedics thought it was strange because we were all holding hands in there."

The paramedics worked for fifteen to twenty minutes. At one point one of them reported a "strong pulse in the groin," she said. The IV was started, there were problems with the radio link to the hospital, and finally an ambulance was summoned and Kramer was taken away.

With that, the morning testimony ended. The hearing reconvened after lunch.

When Lacey resumed his questions, he asked Dr. Eisner if she had received "any type of medical training at all."

She answered, "Well, I don't know whether you call it medical training—during the war [World War II] I worked as a volunteer nurse's aide and they trained us down at County [the Los Angeles County-University of Southern California Medical Center] and we were on the ward and took care of people and they had us do visiting nursing and had us work at different hospitals. I don't know if you consider that training. And I cared for my mother, who had a lot of difficulties before she died, and my first husband who died, where he had cancer that metastasized to the brain. I nursed him."

But she had received no training in CPR or mouth-to-mouth resuscitation.

The questions turned to her original discovery of the use of hot mineral baths in psychotherapy. She had years ago gone to another spa and taken a "tule bath." "I remembered how interesting it was and how it seemed to bring up a lot of psychological stuff," she said. At that resort, bathers went through two baths, and were then wrapped tightly in a sheet. "I felt like kind of a containment, and it was a lot of psychological stuff," she said.

Earlier, Dr. Eisner had referred to "trouble" at Murietta which had led Group to give up the resort. Lacey wanted to know what had happened.

"Well, one—I can only assume something happened, but specifically with respect to the group, one of our group—either a man passed out or something happened after his—I don't think he passed out—but the attendant said—and I didn't know this until just very recently when I started asking about these things—said you shouldn't come back and have any more Murietta—I mean any more tule baths—because that's what they're called, tule baths—because you're not the right body type."

*   *   *

At least two other factors resulted in the group's abandonment of Murietta: "After we go there for the first two times, one of our members went down there on her own and she said that they took her blood pressure and were very reluctant to have her bath very hot."

Then they learned that bath sessions had now been limited to twenty minutes, and that hot baths were no longer being given. "It would be warm, but not hot," Dr. Eisner said they were told.

She testified that the psychiatrist who worked with her at sessions involving the use of other drugs had observed one of the bath sessions, apparently at her home. "We don't know what makes them work, sir," she told Lacey. "This is what is very puzzling."

What did she feel was the psychological benefit of the sessions?

"Well," she answered, "I think there is great value and I think all of the people who have had them could testify to this. And I had one myself of the Murietta Salt, not with the Ritalin—because I always take them before I give patients things. I feel that it makes available deeply buried anger. And our society, you know has—people in our society have so much trouble with anger that it's either pushed out so much and then when it comes out, it comes out with such a rush. I have found therapeutically for people to have access to their anger so they can feel it and express it harmlessly, such as blasting as we call it or beating on a punching bag, and that then they are able to deal with the problems of their lives more easily."

How long had Noel Kramer been a patient of Dr. Eisner? Five-and-a-half years, it turned out. "I looked up my first appointment with him, it was May 3, 1971."

There was more discussion of the experience at Murietta Hot Springs.

"I felt everybody who had one benefited from it. I benefited myself. I had quite an extraordinary one down at Murietta myself." Noel Kramer had reported the March and April spa sessions "helped him enormously."

More questions followed about the baths of Noel Kramer's last session, and the three "phases" of the session following the baths. "The third phase was where he rested [after the peculiar thrusts] and when his face changed. He looked like somebody different. But this is common. People do look like different things in going through different phases of sessions. He was sort of gone and my feeling was he looked like an old man. It didn't look like Noel, I mean—but this is, as I said—I just had somebody on the Friday before who would look like that, looked like he belonged to another time or place or something like that."

No, she had not become alarmed when his features turned ashen. "I didn't think it was physical because I have seen that many times in sessions," she explained, so had the psychiatrist she worked with, he "has given many sessions along with me to our group, different kinds of sessions And he is right there and he has seen that and we have discussed that kind of thing. And we have seen them go through these experiences and then sit and come out and they feel better afterward."

When had she first noticed Kramer's unusual breathing sounds? About five to ten minutes after her husband left to attend the Young Group meeting, she answered. The symptom returned several times, and would end after they had turned the man over to drain more mucus from his mouth, she said.

Then came this exchange between Dr. Eisner and the coroner's official:

LACEY: "Was the decedent conscious from the time that you first heard this wheezy sound until the time you called the paramedics?"

DR. EISNER: "I can't say conscious. You see, there is a conscious, [an] unconscious, and another state of consciousness. I would determine that he was in another state of consciousness. In working with drugs and the sessions we do, we see a lot of other states of consciousness."

LACEY: "Have you ever seen Ritalin cause this problem?"

DR. EISNER: "Well, I don't consider it a problem, other states of consciousness. Many people—you see, the mystic experience is considered another state of consciousness in some people. It can either be something that is a problem—if somebody is going through a problem—or it can be something that is very good and beneficial. And working with drugs, [as] we have for so many years, we have seen many of these in many different forms."

LACEY: "Are you saying that you did not consider it a problem at that time or you do not consider it a problem at this time, knowing what you know?"

DR. EISNER: "I do not consider other states of consciousness a problem."

LACEY: "I mean, the condition the decedent was in—I don't know how to describe it—psychologically."

DR. EISNER: "I still did not feel that there—I do not feel that that was the problem. I think the problem occurred when—after he sat up in the living room."

The wheezing, she said, was a problem she felt "was taken care of by the draining.

"And as soon as it was not taken care of by the draining—either because the condition worsened or I physically could not do it by myself, could not drain it as well—that I considered it a problem and I was very concerned about it. And I was very eager for them [Group] to get there so we could get him in onto the table, upside down on the massage table, so that whatever was in there could drain."

There were more questions about the bloody mucus; did she have any idea why her patients coughed it up?

"Well, it is a puzzlement to me, but it usually occurs when people cough up stuff after sessions, after they have gone through some kind of traumatic experience, either internally without anything showing, or they may sit up and blast somebody."

At some sessions held in her living room, she said, patients don't need to use a rag to muffle their blasts because the sound doesn't carry to the ears of neighbors. "It's after that . . . they start getting stuff and we pound them on the back and they cough up something, and that usually signalled the end of a problem. And I have seen it a number of times and with different kinds of sessions."

That night, however, "it was very different," she said. "It was the same thing with Noel, but it was a lot more of it. He didn't cough up the phlegm with the blood streaks and then go to the clear mucus. He coughed up quite a bit more than I had ever seen of the phlegm with the blood. It's a little tiny thin line. It just never is flecks. I would never describe it as flecks."

There were questions about the minutes before the paramedics arrived, when Group was circling Noel Kramer. "We have found that hands have a great deal of healing force in them, and that touching . . . somebody with love and affection aids them."

Was Noel Kramer conscious at that point? "No," she answered. "Again, I would say he was in another state of consciousness. Probably to somebody coming into it who was not aware of these other states, he would be called unconscious."

There were a few more questions, and the psychologist was turned over to her attorney, Robert Schibel. She had never seen the green discharge from the nose before, she said. The paramedic who said Noel Kramer hadn't been breathing for fifteen minutes was wrong.

As for the Ritalin, it was prescribed for people in Group for two reasons: "One was that for the sessions when they were given, and the other was for some of the students who had trouble staying awake. And they would—they had found that they could use the Ritalin to stay awake."

*   *   *

Dr. Eisner was the last witness called by the coroner's office. Robert Schibel called only one witness, Elaine Patterson, who testified that she had taken one of the Ritalin-and-bath sessions at Dr. Eisner's home about six or seven weeks before Kramer's death.

"When I got into the bath," Patterson said, "the bath was just hot enough so I could, you know, be comfortable in it. And it took, I would say, five or six minutes before I began to feel physically uncomfortable; and by that I mean I began to get very angry. And I felt a lot of what I call resistance to come up to remaining in the bath and I really wanted to get out of the bath. But I didn't do that because I was in the bath for my—for a reason. And that was to help me express some of the anger that I was feeling. So I stayed in the bath. . . . I found relief."

Lacey asked a few questions. He learned Patterson had had the baths at Murietta, without Ritalin, and the one session at the psychologist's home, and that she experienced no "ill physical effects" during or after the La Mesa bath session. Then she stepped down.

*   *   *

The evidence had been presented. Now Lacey told the jurors what they must do. They must chose among the four death "modes," and they could choose only one.

"The evidence before you in this matter has made it quite obvious that you are not to be concerned with any question of natural causes or suicide, but rather whether the manner of death herein was by accident or at the hands of another person other than by accident.

"Death by accident can refer to a variety of events. Some of these involve natural phenomena, such as death by fire, flood, or earthquake in which no human agency is involved. Another species of accident is the kind which results from human acts or conduct. It is this second species that inquests are usually concerned with.

"Death by accident, where a human agency is involved, is best defined as the unintended or unexpected results of human conduct. The term 'accident,' as it applies to these proceedings, is an unforeseen event, misfortune, loss, act or omission. Where the decedent's death was caused by the conduct of another human agency, the same not being intentional in nature, before said conduct may be classed as accidental, you must first find it to have been free from any gross negligence.

"The phrase 'at the hands of another person other than by accident' is not a definable legal concept, but can only be defined to mean that which it in itself expresses; namely, 'death at the hands of another person other than by accident.' It is either an intentional act which directly causes the death of another, or an act or omission to act [an action or a failure to take action] constituting, in the eyes of the law, gross negligence which causes the death of another.

"Therefore, in the absence of an intentional act on the part of the actor, before you may find the death herein to have been at the hands of another person other than by accident, you must first find an act or omission to act on the part of the actor amounting to gross negligence.

"The term 'gross negligence,' as is used in these instructions, means *the failure to exercise any care or the exercise of so little care that you are justified in believing that the person whose conduct is involved was wholly indifferent to the consequences of his conduct, as to the welfare of others* (emphasis added).

"In your deliberations, if you find from all of the evidence of this inquest that the decedent's death was the unintended or unexpected results of human conduct, then you will find the decedent's death to have been by accident. In the event you find conduct by a human agency other than the decedent's was the cause of the decedent's death, then you must further find such conduct free of intent or gross negligence before you may find the death herein to have been accidental.

"In your deliberations, if you find from all of the evidence of this inquest that the decedent's death was not by accident, then you will find the decedent's death to have been at the hands of another person other than by accident."

The jurors were not required to reach a unanimous verdict. Their verdict on mode of death was to be determined by a "preponderance of the evidence," meaning "such evidence as, when weighed with that opposed to it, has more convincing force and the greater probability of truth."

The jurors were to retire, elect a foreperson, then immediately commence deliberations. The jury retired at 2:30 P.M.

*　　*　　*

The verdict was unanimous, signed by all seven. Death was determined to be "cardiac dysrhythmia, due to or as a consequence of hypoxia, near drowning; and from the testimony introduced at this time, we find this death to have been at the hands of another person other than by accident."

THE MEDICAL BOARD MOVES

The body regulating the conduct of psychological practice in California has an impressive name: The Psychology Examining Committee of the Division of Allied Health Professions of the Board of Medical Quality Assurance of the Department of Consumer Affairs of the State of California. Mercifully, the body is usually referred to as the PEC.

Dr. Eisner had come to the agency's attention even before Noel Kramer's death. The first complaint had come from Mara Huston. Dr. Eisner, she said, practiced something called "restraints" therapy, in which patients were tied to a bed, clad only in their underwear, for days on end, forced to lie in their own urine if their bladders wouldn't hold out till the appointed bathroom time.

Mara Huston had entered therapy as half a lesbian couple and eventually joined a "Group house," one of the patient communes. She told a bizarre tale: After a suicide attempt she had voluntarily permitted herself to be tied down in a bed, under Dr. Eisner's supervision, for the purpose of forcing her to give up her own will, and thus achieve a psychological breakthrough.

As one of the conditions for release, she said, she had agreed to make a "three-dimensional commitment to life" and give up her cigarets—which were already taboo in Group. After Dr. Eisner had left for a trip to Northern California, Huston had been caught sneaking a cigaret and forced back into restraints by other Group members, headed by Dr. Eisner's husband.

She said she was forced to lie in her own bodily waste, was subjected to extremes of heat and cold, and given a dose of Ritalin so powerful it caused hallucinations.

There was more to her story. She said she had been repeatedly directed into sexual encounters with different fellow patients, for which she was paid on at least one occasion. She also told Marty Goldstein's story. Dr. Eisner was directing Goldstein to stop taking insulin, and he had gotten sick, Huston said.

The investigative staff of the California Board of Medical Quality Assurance (BMQA) was assigned to look into her complaint, under the direction of the state Attorney General's office, which represented the agency in disciplinary actions.

Kramer's death gave new impetus to the investigation.

Meanwhile, Santa Monica police and the coroner's office had referred the death of Noel Kramer to the medico-legal section of the Los Angeles County district attorney's office. The complaint was rejected for prosecution on 31 March, despite a request from Santa Monica police detectives that Dr. Eisner be charged with involuntary manslaughter.[76] The language of the negligence finding reached by the coroner's jury was virtually identical to that in the state's involuntary manslaughter statute as then in force: a death resulting from "the commission of a lawful act which might produce death, in an unlawful manner, or without due caution and circumspection."[77]

*　　*　　*

When Noel Kramer died, Group split. Five of the patients confronted Dr. Eisner and left Group and her care. They raised other charges, and substantiated those of Marty Goldstein and most of those raised by Mara Huston.

The decision to prosecute is always political, especially for a small agency with a limited legal budget. But for the PEC, the case of Betty Eisner offered the opportunity to establish not one but several standards of the limits of practice of a profession notoriously loose around the fringes. The agency resolved to take action. Former patients were interviewed; police were consulted; experts gave advice.

On 12 May 1977, Leda Deyonge, acting executive secretary of the PEC, signed Accusation D-2010, a nine-page document charging that Dr. Eisner had "exhibited gross negligence in her practice of psychology in that the therapy techniques and modalities which she uses in the treatment of her patients, which are particularly described herein as follows, all constitute an extreme departure from the standards of the community in the practice of psychology."[78] The document alleged she practiced seven grossly negligent techniques:

> *Mineral Bath Therapy:* the Ritalin and mineral salts bath technique.
>
> *K-Therapy Technique:* in which patients were given doses of a mind-altering anesthetic by a psychiatrist under Dr. Eisner's supervision, then received a deep massage.
>
> *Meduna Technique:* in which a physician administered doses of a mixture of gases patients inhaled under Dr. Eisner's supervision after first receiving Ritalin.

Restraint Therapy: the treatment alleged by Mara Huston.

Sex Surrogates: the second of Huston's allegations.

Physical Illness Approach: Marty Goldstein's treatment, in which it was alleged the psychologist considered "that physical illness is merely an outward manifestation of a psychological problem and a characterization of hostility which the patient is evidencing" against Dr. Eisner and or Group, with banishment from therapy as punishment for noncompliance.

Mandatory sessions: Here the Friday night social gatherings were considered. "At these sessions respondent Eisner would dress in a black leotard and read chapters of a book which she is writing to her patients." Patients were charged for the sessions, the accusation declares, and were required to attend other for-fee sessions if a Friday night was skipped.

The PEC was seeking action on several grounds, most of them derived from the *California Business and Professional Code*, which regulates the practice of state-licensed professionals, including physicians, psychologists, nurses, attorneys, and engineers. Also cited were several sections of the *California Administrative Code*, including section 1397.4 of Title 16, which provides "that a psychologist shall not knowingly undertake any activity in which temporary or more enduring problems in the psychologist's personality integration may result in inferior professional services or harm to patient and client."

After laying out the charges, Deyonge "prays that the Psychology Examining Committee hold a hearing on the matters alleged herein and following that hearing issue a decision revoking the psychologist certificate licensure No. PL-0591 heretofore issued to Betty Eisner."

While the accusation would ultimately decide the fate of her license, Dr. Eisner could continue to practice. So the state acted on a second front, seeking an order through the state civil courts either to stop her from practicing altogether or to set defined limits on her therapies.

*   *   *

Los Angeles County Superior Court Civil Case 201820 was filed 2 June 1977. It was titled "Complaint for Injunctive and Other Equitable Relief."

The California Attorney General's office, on behalf of its client, California State Health Director Jerome Lackner and his agency's regulatory body for psychology, the PEC, wanted the injunction, citing the practices cited in the accusation. (An injunction is a court action halting the defendant from performing acts specified in a formal order.)

Judge Charles H. Phillips refused to bar Dr. Eisner from all forms of practice, and issued the temporary order that day only against the specific practices alleged by the PEC, with the whole issue to be reopened in a review in the presence of both sides twelve days later.

In preparation for that hearing, Dr. Eisner and her attorneys assembled an impressive collection of sworn statements of support from twenty-three present patients, five former patients, and eleven licensed professionals.

One of the current patients was Leo Breiman. He said: "Dr. Eisner has always been extremely responsible and highly professional in her therapeutic work with me. In fact, she is a staunch supporter of extremely old fashioned values. For me, she has been a master teacher in the areas of honesty, personal responsibility and communication.

"My years in therapy with Dr. Eisner and as a member of her group have been years filled with personal growth, creativity, and warm relationships. She is a remarkable responsible, caring and perceptive human who has done everything she could to assist me in my growth."[79]

Another came from Les McCann, the jazz musician, a patient for fifteen years and one of the two men who performed artificial respiration on Noel Kramer before the paramedics arrived: "In the complex, crazy world of show business and with the responsibilities of being a boss employing many people on many levels, Dr. Eisner's advice and guidance has always been the main factor in helping me solve the many problems that have come up over the years. On request, I have received sound advice as to the changes I needed to make in my personal life in order to deal with the responsibilities that come with being a band leader.

"Travelling on the road has been a joy but the problems that come up have been of such nature that, without Dr. Eisner's help, I don't know how I would have made it through. I know that no matter what the problem, if a phone call didn't handle it, she would be on the next plane to be by my side and I've never known *anyone* to be such a complete friend.

"I can think of one word that speaks my feelings most as a result of working with Dr. Eisner. Thanks. Thanks for helping me find myself, for helping me know that I'm somebody. Before Dr. Eisner, I felt as hopeless, and I, a black from the South with little confidence, blamed 'Whitey' for all my problems, and to make matters even more difficult, I fell in love with a woman who just happened to be white. I know I had lots of problems, yet there was part of me that wanted to make my life meaningful and to do something constructive in this world. Through Dr. Eisner's help, I have seen my life change and many of my dreams become realities. I've seen the barriers that got in the way of [the] learning process stripped away with each new change. With hard work, I've even come to know the meaning of responsibility in many areas, but mainly in my relationship with my wife and, for that, I shall forever be thankful to Dr. Eisner."[80]

*   *   *

Dr. Eisner appears on the back cover of McCann's 1975 album "Hustle to Survive." McCann is there, wearing a crash helmet and the Group shirt, the huiple, leaning against the fender of his car. Behind the wheel, also wearing a huiple, sits the coauthor of five tracks on the album, "Rev. B."—Dr. Betty Grover Eisner, who is also author of the album liner notes. The photograph was taken by her spouse, Bill Micks.

"Rev. B" appears as coauthor of all the tracks on McCann's 1976 "River High, River Low" album, and as author of the lyrics of all but one of the tracks on his 1977 disc, "Change, Change, Change." Group members receive album credits for engineering, Rolfing, and general support. On "Change, Change, Change," the final note of thanks is to "my dear friend Rev. B for the Lifeline."

Because of his heavy road schedule, McCann was an infrequent visitor at Group. His spouse, however, was a part of Dr. Eisner's close circle, according to all the former patients interviewed.

*   *   *

A declaration also came from Oscar Janiger, who had then known the psychologist for two decades: "Throughout our long acquaintance, I have regarded Dr. Eisner as a responsible, professionally competent and skilled practitioner of psychotherapy.

"She has a good deal of interest and concern for her patients and has made many innovative contributions to her field.

"It is my opinion that Dr. Eisner is a sincere and experienced therapist who has been of great help to many troubled people."

Another testimonal came from a highly respected full professor of psychology and psychiatry at the University of Southern California who had sought out Dr. Eisner five years earlier after he had discovered her research papers and "been impressed with her special expertise in forms of intensive psychotherapy.

"Since that time I have met with her on numerous occasions to discuss professional issues and have sat in as an observer at therapy group meetings she led. I have been very impressed with her innovative approach to therapy, her clinical skills and her high level of professional conduct. I saw no evidence of unprofessional or unethical behavior, and have since recommended her to other colleagues and students as a resource for information on her orientation to intensive, community-based therapy."[81]

One professional whose credentials were especially impressive was Philip Oderberg.

"I received my Ph.D. from UCLA in psychology in 1955," he wrote. "I have been president of the Los Angeles County Psychological Association and Chairman of the Psychology Examining Committee."

Oderberg had headed the very body that was now moving to pass judgment on his colleague's career. Who better to state whether or not Dr. Eisner had been practicing within state-authorized limitations? He wrote: "I have always known her to be a creative, intelligent, perceptive clinician of considerable skill and competence. I have never had any reason to mistrust her or doubt her honesty, sincerity and intentions to be of help to others. Quite the contrary, I have known her to be one of the most dedicated professionals I have known, both with her work with patients and as seen in the extraordinary efforts she has made to improve the lot of young rural children in Mexico."

Another endorsement came from Albert V. Freeman, Ph.D., past president of the Los Angeles Society of Clinical Psychologists, a member of the board of directors of the Los Angeles County Psychological Association, past chair of the California State Psychological Association's Task Force on Sexual Mores, a full professor in the California State University system and codirector of a "growth center" in Santa Monica. He declared: "As an innovator myself, I admired and still admire Dr. Betty Eisner's courage in working with new techniques in the psychopharmacological area. While daring and inventive, she has always had the good sense and caution to work with physicians knowledgeable in her field of special interest. She is a very caring person and I have, on occasion, referred families to her when teenagers were considered 'behavior problems'. Even there, her thinking is original and very cogent.

"As further evidence of the fact that any charge of negligence is unfounded, and psychologically most out of character, is the fact that Dr. Betty Eisner, every year for the last five or six years, has been instrumental in organizing a team of people who volunteer their time in a school they organized and developed for impoverished orphans in Mexico."

Indeed, the School for Learning, Inc., was cited throughout the favorable declarations. All those who participated in this Group project commented favorably on its impact on the young rural Mexicans. To succeed financially in that part of Mexico required skill in dealing with English-speaking tourists. Group gave the students that skill. Leo Breiman and Marty Goldstein speak with evident pleasure of the successes they have seen through the years.

An endorsement of two of three therapies covered by the court order came from a physician who had practiced ophthalmology and psychiatry. Dr. Lee S. Sannella had administered over a thousand Ritalin-and-carbogen sessions between 1960 and 1970 "with excellent therapeutic results in neurotic, psychosomatic, and psychotic disorders."

He adopted Ketalar as a psychological tool "from 1970 through 1975. I worked with Ketalar with excellent results in inducing mild hypnotic states in which suggestive therapies and ventilation were facilitated with

.02 milligrams per pound" of body weight given by hypodermic into muscle tissue. "More profoundly altered states for use in basic alterations in character disordered persons were induced with .07 milligrams. Results obtained with this agent were in every way as good as those reported by other investigators using 100 to 500 microgram doses of LSD."[82]

A detailed endorsement of the legitimacy of each of the seven alleged practices came from a fellow Westwood psychologist and researcher who had worked extensively with Ritalin and who had known Dr. Eisner for years. Dr. Virginia Johnson said her colleague "is highly qualified to work with the behavioral effects of hallucinogens and psychotropic drugs since for about fifteen years this has been her area of specialization." She continued: "Recently, I have not been present as an observer during Dr. Eisner's sessions with clients. However, in the past, when I was closely in touch with her work and in first-hand contact with persons who had been under her supervision, I know of no instance in which Dr. Eisner was either irresponsible or unethical. She was under medical supervision in her programs, made recordings of most of her interviews conducted under the influence of drugs, and kept careful notes. Interested professionals were welcome to observe her methods or participate if they wished to do so."[83]

Dr. Eisner's strongest defense on the drug therapies was the presence of a psychiatrist at most of them, including all the Ritalin-and-gas sessions and the Ketalar injections. He was not present for the events of the day Noel Kramer died.

Ernest B. Katz was a Phi Beta Kappa graduate of UCLA who went on to earn his medical degree from the University of California, San Francisco, Medical School in 1956. His internship was at Los Angeles County General Hospital, followed by a psychiatric residency at the University of Maryland Hospital Psychiatric Institute from 1957 to 1960. Following military service, he joined the staff of a Los Angeles area clinic, entering individual private practice in 1965. That same year, he joined the UCLA clinical faculty. He was one of the pioneers in the experimental use of lithium carbonate to treat manic-depressive disorder.

He learned the Ritalin and carbogen technique he used in Group from Dr. Lee Sannella in 1964, and over a period of twelve years he administered more than five hundred gas sessions with and without the use of Ritalin. "The 'letting go' which characterizes the breaking of a psychological block is usually a letting go of controls and not a lapsing into unconsciousness," Dr. Katz wrote. Only one session in four produced even momentary unconsciousness, and then without any noticeable spasms or convulsive movements.

Dr. Katz and Dr. Eisner varied their techniques.

"For abreactive methods," he wrote, "the procedure of intravenous Ritalin and carbon dioxide will on occasion necessitate adding two or three people or a person onto the individual to increase the level of intensity."

In addition to "piling on," the number of breaths taken would be varied, with the intent of discharge of unresolved past psychological traumas, recall of repressed experiences, anxiety reduction, or an increased level of tension to aid in talk therapy. "This method reduces symptoms such as stuttering" and "aids in dealing with resistances," Dr. Katz said. The only situations in which the treatment was likely to have negative consequences were those involving patients undergoing paranoia, other psychotic episodes, and, possibly, obsessive-compulsive patients exhibiting symptoms of the disorder. Katz described the technique he practiced with Eisner: "The patients are given the gas supported from behind by Dr. Eisner, who holds the mask over their face and we count the number of breaths out loud.

"The patient's hands are held by two people, one on each side, and a third individual, on occasion, lies on the patient in order to restrict the abreactive movements or the abreactive experience. The presence of the weight, warmth and closeness of another human being may act as a security and reassurance device.

"The inhalation of gas under the circumstances described appears to be a specific for the abreaction of traumatic experiences. It is as though the individual goes directly to an area of discomfort and abreacts it—to a large extent with his body. Occasionally the patient will remember some sequence of images and exactly what happened, as with the ex-Marine who 'worked through' traumatic battle experiences; and often the patient will speak loudly enough to be heard through the mask, such as the one maintaining stoutly, 'I won't shit! I won't shit!' Many times a patient's body movements will give a clue as to what is occurring; however, one may conjecture that in many instances the events which are being excised or abreacted took place so early in life that there is no memory or verbalization available to communicate their meaning, and there may be no body movements—only unintelligible sounds.

"The inhalation of carbogen has been found to be a most effective psychiatric technique to abreact traumatic events from the past, to lower barriers to enable unconscious materials to emerge, to eliminate barriers to feelings not only of rage but also of love, and to tutor the patient in the creative aspects of 'letting go' against which they have so rigidly defended.

"However, it may be a very unpleasant experience, and patients approach the gas with anxiety on occasion. Many patients experience what they term a 'death' experience, which appears to have a therapeutic effect. There is also the positive reinforcement of having added courage and fortitude to one's self concept after having gone through the experience."

Ketalar, the brand name for a chemical also known as ketamine hydrochloride, cyclohexane and phencyclidine CI-851, had been commercially available in the United States since February 1970, Dr. Katz said.[84] The psychiatrist first learned of the drug's potential as a psychotherapeutic aid through articles published in the medical journal *Psycho-Somatics* in late 1973. The psychiatrist first tried the drug on Dr. Eisner and himself, and the two began conducting sessions with it on 3 June 1974. "The procedure that Dr. Eisner and I use is for me to inject intravenously from 10 to 55 mg. of ketamine, depending on the body weight of the patient, with the patient lying supine on a thick foam rubber pad covered with a sheet while the patient is covered with a blanket. Several patients can be injected in succession, and the reactions are continuously monitored by Dr. Eisner and myself and several other people attending and helping out at the sessions."

Ketalar sessions were scheduled at the psychologist's home from noon to three o'clock on Friday afternoons. Typically, each patient's session consisted of two phases: the first, a period of "internalness," lasting from five to twenty minutes, during which unconscious material may rise to awareness; the second, which Dr. Katz described as one of "insightfulness or creative rumination," lasting from thirty minutes to three hours, "during which . . . patients prefer to be left alone to go through their own inner feelings.

"It is during this period of rumination that Rolf-type or deep massage is reported effective by patients in removing blocks if patients request it, and it is reported by patients to be helpful in 'draining' material which manifests itself as bodily pain."

On some occasions, when patients were particularly anxious, the ketamine injection might be preceded by four to eight breaths of carbogen, he said. Dr. Katz declared that he never left the sessions sooner than forty-five minutes after the last patient had been injected, though he would leave the room occasionally to smoke.

Very small doses, ten to fifteen milligrams, "were given to couples experiencing difficulties in relationship. These low doses enabled barriers to be lowered, communication to take place and feelings to flow. At least one marriage and several living situations were saved by occasional sessions of this type at critical points of conflict.

"I have found ketamine to be a very effective dissociative agent, making possible access to unconscious material which is otherwise not available, allowing abreactions of deeply buried traumatic events, giving access to deeply hidden feelings and allowing integration of insights and feelings during the ruminative period following the active part of the session.

"I have found it a very safe and effective psychiatric agent which aided patients in dealing with their problems. The method which we have developed to treat patients seems a careful and effective one, and we have had no traumatic occurrences of a physical or psychological nature."[85]

THE PSYCHOLOGIST'S STORY
"MISUNDERSTANDING AND CONFUSION"

The longest of the declarations, forty double-spaced pages, plus seven single-spaced pages of bibliography, came from Dr. Eisner herself. She opened with a recitation of her academic credentials, listed her writings (seventeen items, including seven journal articles, two books [one published], three original anthology contributions, and five unpublished papers). She told of her inclusion in *Leaders in American Science 1964-65, Who's Who of American Women 1966-67, Contemporary Authors 1972*, and *Who's Who in the West 1967-68*. She had given oral examinations for the Psychology Examining Committee license applicants for five years. This is from her declaration:

There appears to be a good deal of confusion and misunderstanding with respect to my practice, probably because of the auxiliary drug work and also because of perceptual distortions due to bias from negative transference.

Basically, my practice consists of four parts: evaluations of patients at an in-take interview of an hour and one-half with subsequent referral and/or suggestions for life changes; patients accepted for short-term psychotherapy following the one and one-half hour in-take interview who are given life-change suggestions and referred for the Rolf series and usually not seen again until after that is completed and then seen in individual therapy; patients who are found to be likely candidates for drug therapy and are referred to J. Reynolds O'Donnell, M.D., for a complete physical examination; and the 'group,' a group of about 40 to 50 of us, including children, who are dedicated to the removal of barriers which stand in the way of the fulfillment of our potential. The group also serves as a matrix for individuals coming in for drug therapy for the removal of specific symptoms (one needs a matrix for rapid change). The group members, whoever is free and can, help at the initial drug sessions which is a commitment to non-violence, and at any other sessions which are necessary for the individual while he or she is in the group matrix. Since the removal from the market of injectable Ritalin, there have not been many patients who have been accepted for short-term drug therapy, so most of the sessions and certainly the ketamine sessions have been experienced by and of benefit to group people.

In other sections, I have expanded on the categorical denial that there is any such thing as physical illness therapy or restraint therapy. . . . Further, there is no sadistic "treatment" on my part or on the part of any group member. Painful or harmful behavior is aborted immediately on detection, by a slap if necessary. In the early days of drug work at group drug sessions (at which a physician was always present) and before the establishment of the commitment session, I have had to slap patients to keep them from physically attacking others. I have also slapped hysterical patients to bring them into reality and I have, on rare occasions, slapped a person who was dissociating in a harmful way. For Keith Lowenstein to say that I would slap anyone at length or humiliate them in front of group is not only untrue but ridiculous and for him to say that I jumped on him (physically, I take it) after his Ritalin and mineral bath and 'proceeded to choke me to the point of unconsciousness' is insane. I quote from his report of that session, starting about one and one-half hours after the bath:

> *When Betty and Hank started to work on me, Hank on my neck and Betty on my chest, I felt a really sharp burning pain in my leg, and I started to scream. I felt like I was dying and at one point had a very strange flash of someplace I'd never been before.*
>
> *Following that, there were three or four more past lives that Hank helped me to get out by working on my neck. I felt as though I was choking to death. People in the room said that as I went from past life to past life, I looked very strange, at times like some concentration camp victim in Germany.*
>
> *This sessions has really made a difference in my life. The main thing I can say is that it not only got a lot of stuff out, and specifically got several past lives out, but it also gave me a chance to see some of my inadequacy mechanisms in detail. I have found that I've been able to take concrete action to reverse my habit patterns of picking up and reinforcing feelings of inadequacy.*

Reports of any drug session are required of patients and have been since the beginning of my practice. Dr. Katz receives a copy of all ketamine reports. Patients may put whatever they like in the reports but are encouraged to make the reports as full as possible as a record of their therapeutic process. I have all reports of all patients (except those which were stolen from my files when my home was broken into last month), and these reports and letters from the patients to me clearly refute the specific charges. . . .

It is unintelligible to me that neither Beatrice nor Keith Lowenstein spoke of her dissatisfaction with his session at their therapeutic meeting with me the following Tuesday. When I expressed concern because Keith had looked so marvelous after his Friday session and he looked ill to me on Tuesday, he was very evasive, saying he thought he had a load from his sister. Beatrice said nothing at all. I was shocked to learn from another member of the group later how Beatrice felt about Keith's session since Beatrice hadn't lied to me for a long, long time.

With respect to families and my attitude toward them, that appointment with the Lowensteins was to enlist my help in planning for his parents' imminent arrival, and we worked out details of activities that would be pleasant for the senior Lowensteins but would not entail an excess of time that Keith needed to spend with them since he got very neurotic when he was around his parents for too long a time.

Parents and relatives are the stock from which we spring; they are part of us and we of them, and if we deny them, we deny a part of ourselves. It has always been my position that comfort with one's parents is directly correlated with level of maturity, and I worked constantly and consistently to maintain and improve relationships of group members with their families.

The group as it is today probably dates its beginnings to 1970 when the young students got together and rented a house on Euclid in Santa Monica. That was the first experience in community living and was such a success that one of the young group then bought a house which became the first group commune. There are presently four communes, all of which have six or fewer occupants in conformity to the laws of Santa Monica. The first year of the house on Euclid was a hard one, and there were innumerable occasions when I would have to referee disputes among members or help work out guidelines for successful living in close harmony. However, they worked out a set of rules, which they recorded in the house book, and that set of rules (which I have never read) is the basis on which all the communes operate, with changes according to the specific house. It has been at least a year since I have been asked to sort out difficulties in a group house. They all manage their own affairs.

Membership in group houses stays relatively stable with occasional shifts when people leave for or return from college or jobs in other places. Younger group children live with their mothers (in two cases, there are no fathers), and teenagers sometimes live with parents and sometimes with other teenagers with special surrogate parents.

Speaking of authority, the allegation that 'being under authority' means being under my authority is nonsense. The correct phrase is 'being under the authority of reality' which means being subject to cause and effect and not to neurotic mechanisms. Obviously, as the therapeutic authority, my words carry more weight in certain areas than those of other individuals. However, most of the individuals in group have areas of specialty and they are the expert in that area because of background and experience, as I am in mine. Group members help each other in whatever way they can and areas of expertise is an important one. Decisions which concern the whole group are made by the group on the basis of input from all of the members and in such cases I am one of the group members just as is everyone else.

I have never used sexual surrogates in any part of my practice. Nor have I 'ordered' any individual to go to bed with any other individual. I did, on one occasion, express strong disapproval (to the point approaching prohibition) of a man in group having sex with a woman who was in a very precarious position. However it didn't do any good because he later claimed that he didn't hear me and he went ahead and seduced her with some very unfortunate consequences. I do discuss patients' sex lives with them as I discuss all aspects of their lives in some detail. I try to come to an understanding of what is best for the patient in the overall situation and then help the patient arrive at a decision as to what to do. I considered that there has been a bilateral agreement (especially when another person is concerned and present) when a patient comes to a decision, and I feel rather strongly there should not be a change in the decision without prior mutual review.

As I have said, patients consult me on all sorts of matters—from the largest decision as to what might be the best career direction, to the smallest one of what the best menu might be for an important dinner party. In all cases, I try to elicit from the patient what he or she really wants to do, and then we examine the alternatives as to whether this would be possible and best for the individual. Many times patients have neurotic over- or under-evaluation of themselves and must be helped to see accurately what is possible for them. Once that can be ascertained then it becomes a matter of finding out which action is the appropriate one in the situation. When there is no immediately apparent solution, I usually suggest we leave it to life, and before long an indication of the action to be taken will occur.

There is no denying that a therapist has a great deal of power and authority over individuals who are looking for help with their problems. However, the power and authority lie much more in the projection from the patient than in the actual situation. It is impossible to control another human being if he or she does not want to be controlled, and it is foolish to try. I see no creative purpose that control would satisfy. True 'control' lies in the reality of the situation and what the necessities dictate. It behooves doctor and patient alike to attempt with their best *efforts to ascertain the reality of any situation and to discover the best alternative which will satisfy the situation best, in general and in the specifics, and both long- and short-range.*

With respect to mandatory sessions, there has never been a mandatory session to the best of my recollection. I have, on many occasions, told patients who asked that I didn't feel that they needed a session. Some patients love sessions not only for the good it does them but also for the excitement and attention. Since patients are usually the ones to request sessions, care must be taken to balance the need for a session with the benefit which will come from it.

There is one further aspect to a group setting. There is no doubt that when the group and the therapist leading the group concur in a decision or opinion that there is unstated pressure from the situation. Often the patient is in resistance toward doing something or seeing something that may be painful but is necessary to help with the problem. It is easy to see how such a patient might feel that psychological coercion is being used against them. However, in my knowledge and to the best of my recollection, I have been extremely careful not to allow such a situation to occur. It appears to me that the great control the witnesses claim I exercised was merely a projection of their own perception of the early childhood situation with their mother.

There is not now, nor has there ever been, any so-called 'physical illness therapy.'

I have never advised a patient not to see a physician. On the contrary, I have always suggested that any patient see a physician for any physical condition and, at times, I have insisted on this, as I did with Marty Goldstein the latter part of December, 1975, when I insisted that he return from Mexico early in order to consult his physician. . . about his physical condition which had deteriorated because of a case of the 'touristas' Mr. Goldstein had contracted, coupled with Mr. Goldstein's refusal to eat.

All patients who come to me for intensive psychotherapy are referred to J. Reynolds O'Donnell, M.D . . . for a complete physical examination and are further required by Dr. O'Donnell to have a continuing annual checkup. This condition for annual physicals is enforced by Dr. O'Donnell by not prescribing medication for a patient until the requirement is met. . . .

There appears to be a great deal of confusion and misunderstanding with respect to the use of the word 'blasting'. Blasting means nothing more or less than the discharge of anger vocally—the getting of anger out of one's system. One can blast someone on the phone for having done what they said they would do; one can blast someone in person for having crumpled your fender; one can blast another individual at any time (after securing their permission) to relieve feelings of anger and even rage. Anger, to the point of rage and violence, is so much a part of our culture that methods must be developed to keep the level of anger down or drained off so that no physical destructiveness occurs.

In the group setting, blasting occurs under two conditions: at the beginning of both young group and big group after the commitment to non-violence has been made in unison; and at sessions when the person having the session feels anger coming up and asks to blast—usually blasting me but quite often it being Dr. Katz or another group member (such as a husband and wife). Also, group members, when they are angry either at another group member or at someone else they can't blast (such as a boss), or someone out of their childhood, will often request permission to blast either the individual they are angry at or someone who is a stand-in for that person. Permission is supposed to be requested and granted before an individual blasts someone, thus preventing the person being blasted from being taken off guard and perhaps not being able to deal with being blasted or the strength of the feeling emerging.

Everyone in group blasts (at an appropriate time and place) to get rid of the anger which rises in them every day. Group members also punch bags, run and use other techniques to get rid of the anger which is an inevitable concomitant to our high-pressure, fast-moving (and violence-prone) society.

Blasting occurs most of the time without a wash cloth. Wash cloths or small towels are used when there is likely to be too much noise; for instance, as with eight to twenty people blasting in unison after the commitment to non-violence with which we start our group meetings. The group meeting blasting takes place in two phases: there is the initial group blasting of everyone in unison; and then there is the subsequent blasting when group members go around blasting each other. They all make sure to blast me and some one of the older men in the group to be sure and get out anger at male and female authority figures. People in a relationship blast each other, as do members of the same living unit in order to make sure the air is clear. We have found that a much more insightful and serene group meeting occurs after blasting.

There is a great deal of misunderstanding about the wash cloth or small towel. It is in no way a gag and it is dry, not wet. It is held between the teeth of the person blasting (because biting helps to get out the anger and also holds the wash cloth in place), sometimes held in place by the individual blasting, and sometimes held in place by the person being blasted. This has only to do with keeping the wash cloth from slipping out of the mouth. When I am being blasted, I have the individual blasting me put both hands on my shoulders and squeeze tight (it seems to help), and I hold the wash cloth in place so that it will not fall out of the person's mouth and onto the floor, with one hand and with the other hand I hold a plastic-lined bucket with Kleenex in case the person coughs something up as a result of the hostility discharge. Sometimes I or another group member whack the individual blasting on the back between the shoulder blades when they start coughing to help the process.

I should like to repeat: the wash cloth never is and never has been used as a gag, and the only reason that it is held by the individual or someone else is so that it will not fall out of the mouth with the yelling.

Noel Kramer was in no way gagged or his breathing restricted when he was blasting while in the bathtub. Noel blasted perhaps twice, or at the most three times, the first time in the bathtub. My recollection is that it was twice and that he held the wash cloth himself the first time and Hank Walker held it the second time to keep it from slipping into the water, as Noel was at that point sitting on his hands. With the mineral baths we noticed that when the wash cloth became wet it ceased to function properly—it had to be rung out, was unpleasant for the person blasting and was hard to manage. With Noel, the wash cloth never got wet at all, as Hank was holding it for him in front of his mouth. Also, it was not more than four or five times at the most that Noel blasted into the wash cloth the second time in the bath and the interval of blasting lasts about five to ten seconds.

The safe release of anger is very important for an individual trying to live a creative life in our society today. We have found that in group our commitment to non-violence plus our methods of getting out anger daily, such as with blasting, the punching bag, running, etc., is a valuable catharsis for all of us which helps keep us centered, with our goals more clearly in mind, and it enables us to move more freely and creatively toward these goals.

In my opinion, the use of Ritalin, carbogen, mineral baths and Ketalar have been useful psychotherapeutic modalities and have resulted in successful treatment of many patients. This opinion is based upon my education, observation and experience as well as on the published material in these areas as partially indicated by the bibliographies attached . . . to this declaration.

MINERAL BATHS

Bathing in hot mineral water for therapeutic purposes has been known from Greek and Roman times. In Europe, the use of hot mineral baths both for neurological and psychiatric difficulties has been widespread for at least the last 150 years. Specific articles fill the Index Medicus on Balneopsychiatry, the use of hot baths for psychiatric disorders. However, the practice of using hot baths for psychiatric disorders did not spread to the United States except in modified degree and in isolated places.

Some 15 or 20 years ago, when I was married to my first husband (who died twelve years ago), we spent a weekend at what was then Gilman Hot Springs. While my husband played golf, I took what was called a mud or tule bath (very hot mineral water with roots from tule plants) for a specified amount of time, spent another period in hot mineral water bath, and was then wrapped tightly in a sheet, covered with a blanket and left by myself for a period of time. Following that, I was given a massage. During the period by myself, I went through the equivalent of a drug session with a strong psychedelic with much benefit. The particular benefits I remember experiencing were the letting go of controls (probably because of the tight wrap of the sheet), the imagery and the insights that followed.

In the spring of 1976, I was looking for some method to reduce the resistance of body armoring of a few of my patients in long-term character analysis, patients whose bodies were so defended that our Rolfer could not easily get through the hard outer muscle layers to the structures which needed work. I remembered the earlier experience at Gilman Hot Springs, found out that it no longer existed but that the Murietta Hot Springs was less than 100 miles away and it had been in existence at least for 30 years. We decided to make a group weekend of it and all of the group (including the group children and the Mexican children we have up for the school year) went to Murietta the weekend of March 5th and 6th, taking the man who does our Rolfing and his wife. All of us who had the baths and then Rolf work and our Rolfer were enormously excited about the potentials of the hot mineral baths to lower the resistance of body armoring. Noel Kramer and [John Cunningham][86] were so enthusiastic that they had tule baths (followed by a hot mineral bath) both days while the rest of us had only one on the weekend. It was reported to me later that Noel Kramer may have taken Ritalin on the occasion of one of the baths, although when he asked me about it I said I didn't think that it was a good idea at that point.

The outing was so successful and the therapeutic (both psychological and physical) effects of the baths were so beneficial that the group went down again on April 24th and 25th accompanied by Dr. Katz who had been to Murietta Hot Springs many times as a child. Again, both Noel Kramer and [John Cunningham] (and possibly Hank Walker) had two baths while the rest of us had one. At Murietta at the time there were no trained assistants; on the women's side the attendant was a girl who wanted to be a singer and in March was working toward her massage license; on the men's side was a man who had been at Murietta around 20 years. There was no registered nurse, no physician, no one who had studied balneotherapy—nor did there seem to be need for such in the group's experience with the baths.

Again all of the group experienced such therapeutic benefits from the hot *tule and mineral baths that several members (those with body armoring) subsequently drove down from time to time just to have mineral baths.*

Throughout the summer, it is very hot at Murietta and a number of us were teaching at our school on the small ejido in rural Mexico. When we returned from Mexico, someone told us that Murietta Mineral Salts were sold at several of the local drugstores, and I purchased a box. They were in the house on October 1, 1976, when Elaine Patterson had taken 60 mg. of Ritalin prior to having a massage with Hank Walker. She said that she felt a mineral bath would help her relax before the massage and I didn't see any contraindication. The bath was outstandingly successful and she was able to reach a depth of anger not reached before. Further, Mr. Walker was able to get much more out of her body with the massage afterwards, and she reported that she felt better than she ever had and the session was the best one ever.

I should like, at this point, to correct a number of misstatements and misconceptions about the mineral baths. There was never either an intramuscular nor intravenous injection of Ritalin given prior to immersion in the bath. There is no protracted *immersion in hot mineral baths and the patient is free* to leave the bath at any time. *There is no "obstruction of the airway" when the patient blasts. The wash cloth is bitten on by the person getting the anger out and is held in place to keep from falling out in case the mouth opens either by the person blasting or by the person being blasted. Periods of blasting are from five to ten seconds, and take place three to five times during the fifteen-to-twenty minute immersion in the tub. With Noel Kramer, there were, at the most, three times during the first immersion of Noel Kramer, and, at the most, five times during his second period in the bath. I should like to repeat, the patient was free to leave the tub at any time. Patients left the tub when they felt they had had enough. It was very clearly stated by Eugene Carpenter, M.D., the Deputy Medical Examiner who performed the autopsy on Noel Kramer and who stated at the inquest that neither the hot bath nor the Ritalin (a "low therapeutic dose" as he characterized it) nor a combination of the two could have caused Noel Kramer's death. J. Reynolds O'Donnell, M.D., who was Noel Kramer's personal physician also testified that Ritalin is a very safe and "harmless" drug, and that the dose that Noel Kramer had was a low therapeutic dose. There is a misstatement I would like to correct, which is that Noel Kramer's head went under water. Dr. Carpenter reported in the autopsy that he didn't know how long Noel's head had been in the water and that "he had to be pulled from the pool." At no time did Noel's head go under water; Hank Walker did a marvelous job of keeping him from submerging his head which was very difficult as Noel was fighting very hard.[87] I was there watching all the time.[88] The procedure with the mineral baths is as follows: Water is run into the tub at a temperature comfortable to the patient stepping in. At that time, one packet of Murietta Mineral Bath Salts are put into the tub. The patient sits down and water is run into the tub as warm as the patient can stand. A timer is set from the time that the patient gets into the tub and it has never been set for more than 20 minutes. At any time, the patient may get out of the tub, although the patient is urged to stay in until beneficial results occur. In the case of Noel Kramer, the first time he went into the tub the timer was set for 15 minutes, and then for an additional period of 20 minutes when it was found that the hot water had run out because my husband had turned down the thermostat without my knowledge. Noel had also requested that he stay longer than the original time since he had very little appreciable effect from the bath.*

When the timer went off the second time, Noel stepped out of the tub with both feet and was made to step back in the tub. For the safety of patients, when patients got out of the tub, they were requested (1) to hold on to the overhead shower rail and (2) to step out of the tub one foot at a time for safety's sake. The bath mat was on the floor to step on and the patient first put one foot out which was dried, and then the other foot and that was dried. Two considerations were uppermost: that the patient not slip and fall coming out of the bath and that he not get cold after having been in such a warm bath.

After being dried off completely, the patient was wrapped in another large towel and taken a few feet across the hall and placed on a bed which was covered with a large towel over a plastic sheet. A large dry towel was placed over the patient and that was covered by a blanket. The period after the bath was from 20 minutes to half an hour.

Alternate arrangements were made when, after the bath the patient was dried off and taken into another room where he was placed on a massage table, covered by a towel, and a masseur worked to drain material out of his body which had been loosened by the hot bath.

In Noel Kramer's case, his first mineral bath was followed by a period of about 20 minutes on the bed during which time he asked to be put back in the bath again since he hadn't had much effect the first time.

There were four occasions subsequent to the date that Elaine Patterson had her session that Ritalin and mineral baths were given, the fourth one being November 18th when Noel Kramer died.

RITALIN

My work with Ritalin, methylphenidate hydrochloride, began in collaboration with Marion Dakin, M.D. on August 25, 1959 when a young 18-year old patient of psychopathic character structure with paranoid elements who had become mute out of rebellion was injected with 10 mg. of Ritalin intramuscularly by Dr. Dakin. The girl's parents and I were present, and the three of us walked the young girl back to my office, a distance of half a block. We had been in the office no more than ten minutes when it was as though a dam had burst— the young girl burst into tears and began to pour out all her troubles with great rushes of feeling. We sat spellbound as insights and information we had not been able to obtain in six months came pouring out. Ritalin was indeed being shown a drug helpful in emotional catharsis as Dr. Alvarado Pearson, Director of the Los Angeles Country Clinic on Alcoholism, had reported in the spring of 1959—a beneficial emotional catharsis even without therapeutic interventions.

After having an injection of 10 mg. of Ritalin from Dr. Dakin myself, Dr. Dakin and I began using injections of Ritalin on patients of mine and of two other psychologists with whom Dr. Dakin collaborated. Complete physicals were given to all patients before they received Ritalin, and EKG's were given in conjunction with any dose over 50 mg. Dr. Dakin, and especially her husband at the time who has since become a physician himself, became very interested in the work with Ritalin and especially high and split doses. From August, 1959 to July, 1968 when we prepared a paper, my work with Dr. Dakin covered 138 patients, aged 15 to 72 with a total of 1,246 administrations of Ritalin alone and in conjunction with other drugs. Ritalin was administered orally (10 to 70 mg.): intramuscularly (10 to 50 mg.) 583 times along with 74 times with massage; and intravenously 25 times alone and 11 times in conjunction with sodium amytal or pentothal and 402 times in conjunction with carbogen (under the supervision of Ernest Katz, M.D.). Split doses ranged from 20 + 20 mg. IM. to 200 + 200 mg. IM, while dosages used by Virginia Johnson, Ph.D. in collaboration with Dr. Dakin and other physicians ranged from 400 to 800 mg. IM.

Chemically, Ritalin is a central nervous system stimulant somewhere in potency between the amphetamines and caffeine. According to Koutsky it has very little effect on the central nervous system below the brain stem. While its physiological mode of action is clear, this does not account for its psychiatric action in lowering barriers, enhancing rapport and facilitating verbalization; nor does this account for the cases in which Ritalin has acted as a psychedelic.[89]

In 1964, Dr. Virginia Johnson gave a symposium on Ritalin to which I was an invited member, and in 1965, I attended an international conference where I reported on aspects of the Ritalin work. In 1966-1967, Dr. Katz and I prepared a paper which I was to present in Prague in 1968, but after I was in Europe, the Russians entered Czechoslovakia and the conference was called off.

The work on which Dr. Katz and I collaborated for the last twelve years *(during which time J. Reynolds O'Donnell, M.D. has been the physician who has given my patients initial physical exams and annual check-ups) utilized the combination of intravenous Ritalin and carbogen. The latter work, also referred to in the declaration of Dr. Katz, has recently consisted of carbogen alone in the traditional method which has been in use for the past thirty-five years. This consists of a progressive number of breaths from four to eight and twelve up to where the patients experiences [sic] the "letting go of controls." Dr. Katz and I have also used the carbogen much less frequently since the advent of ketamine since ketamine performs most of the same functions as carbogen in a much simpler, more efficient way. The patients tend to dislike the carbogen, but they will have the sessions when needed and recommended because of its therapeutic benefits, but it is subjectively extremely unpleasant, especially when there is no Ritalin to lighten the effect afterwards. Since January 1, 1975, there have been only six occasions on which carbogen was given and twelve patients to whom it was administered.*

KETAMINE THERAPY

Ketamine hydrochloride, also known as Ketalar, cyclohexane and phencyclidine CI-581, is also a dissociative anesthetic and analgesic agent which is also used for psychiatric purposes at reduced dosage levels. When used in amount one-third of anesthetic dosage, patients have access to unconscious material which is otherwise unavailable, making possible the abreaction of early traumatic events and also putting the individual in touch with suppressed feelings and memories. The active period of the drug varies from five-to-twenty minutes, and it is during this time that strong abreactions occur. This active period, during which an individual may slip over into unconsciousness but very rarely does, is followed by a period of creative rumination during which insights, intuitions, images and feelings occur. This insightful, creative rumination period may last from half an hour to three hours and is characterized by the patient lying quietly with eyes closed, occasionally asking a question or responding to some stimulus in the environment. Music (a Mozart Concerto) is playing throughout the sessions because music has been found to be useful in helping the patient to "let go."[90] *The progressive safe letting go of control is one of the most important aspects of all drug work.*

It is during this ruminative period that Rolf-type deep massage is used if the patient requests it. It is very helpful in releasing blocks to the expression of feelings and is helpful in "draining" material which manifests to the patient as bodily pain. We have found in the many years that we have worked at a deep level of therapy with character disorders that many of the problems are set into the body and that psychological change follows body work. The Rolf technique is particularly helpful to patients with psychological problems, and it is very common for me to refer a new patient to a Rolfer for the series—at the end of which the presenting problem has quite likely disappeared.

Dr. Katz has described how he injects ketamine. If there is an abreactive experience, it usually helps the patient to have people supportively holding their hands or sometimes lying on them. We have found with work at a deep unconscious level that there is a feeling of security and reassurance and support to proceed through the difficult work when there is body contact. Furthermore, the weight of an individual lying on top of the patient helps prevent schizoid dissociation.

I first heard about ketamine when I was in Mexico Christmas, 1973. (We have for the past six years conducted school on an agrarian commune in rural Mexico during the summer and sometimes at Christmas.) Dr. Salvador Roquet was doing extensive work with ketamine and datura at his Instituto de Psicosintesis in Mexico City. We knew several people who had been there, and I heard Dr. Roquet speak and saw his films at the house of a colleague in Hollywood.[91]

I told Dr. Katz about ketamine and we began a review of the literature, focusing especially on those articles which dealt with its psychiatric use. When we were satisfied that ketamine appeared to be a valuable psychiatric tool, Dr. Katz injected me intramuscularly with a small dose (as I remember it was 40 mg. IM), and I went through a period of very strong imagery, problem solving and insights for about 45 minutes to an hour. I felt that here indeed was a most valuable tool for access to the unconscious.

On June 3, 1974, Dr. Katz and I started with low dose intramuscular injections with stable patients of mine who were in long term character analysis. We soon switched to intravenous injections because ketamine is more effective at lesser doses and for a shorter duration of time when given intravenously. From June of 1975 through May of 1977, there have been over 500 administrations of ketamine with universally beneficial therapeutic results and without ill effects. The allegation that [George Martinsin's][92] rib was broken under ketamine is totally false since [Dr. Martinsin] left treatment with me in June of 1971, and we didn't start using ketamine until 1974. With respect to Marty Goldstein's breaking his cousin, Naomi Feldman's rib, my recollection is that it occurred while she was on Mr. Goldstein's massage table, which would have meant that it was not an occasion when ketamine was used. I was very angry that the rib was broken since we are committed to not hurt ourselves or others, and we spent a good many therapeutic hours unravelling the reasons for the injury.

Under Dr. Katz's direction, ketamine was injected on a few occasions following four-to-eight inhalations of carbogen (70% oxygen, 30% carbon dioxide [sic]) in the fall of 1974. There was always an interval between the inhalation of the gas and the injection, and there has been no use of carbogen and ketamine since 1974.

A careful search of session records showed that five patients took oral Ritalin (one took it twice), four doses of 60 mg. and two of 100 mg. approximate[ly] 45 minutes before being injected with 25 or 40 mg. of ketamine. The patients were apparently having difficulty letting go to the ketamine (they are among my most defended patients) and felt that the psychological "relation" of the oral Ritalin helped. I cannot recollect that it made any difference. The fact that neither Dr. Katz nor I could remember oral Ritalin being taken prior to ketamine (and it took a painstaking search of the session records to find the instances) is a comment on how little difference the Ritalin apparently made.

PHYSICAL RESTRAINT THERAPY

There is no "physical restraint therapy".

On three occasions patients have been, at their request, strapped to a bed with hospital restraints under the supervision of doctors.

The first occurrence was about 1967 with [Carole Wilson][93] after she had made three separate suicide attempts and Dr. Oderberg had dismissed her from therapy with him. This restraint of [Mrs. Wilson] was under the supervision of Dr. [Arthur MacTaggart].[94] [Mrs. Wilson] has not been suicidal since.

The second occasion was in February of 1969 with [Gael Burton],[95] a patient of mine who was taking lithium under Dr. Ernest Katz because of severe manic-depressive episodes. [Miss Burton's] mania became so intense that she was unable to take care of her daughter or function in her job teaching school. She refused to be hospitalized because of fear of losing her teaching job in a school she loved and requested that the restraints be tried. After several days of confinement under the supervision of Dr. Katz, [Miss Burton] was able to travel with her daughter back east to visit her mother, where she remained.

The third occasion was on January 25 and 26, 1972 with [Leopold Casimir][96] who had heard of the method and requested that he be allowed to experience it since he was fearful of his rage. I agreed, provided that the members of the student commune where he lived would take responsibility for his physical care under the supervision of [Dr. George Gelson].[97]

[Mr. Casimir] wrote a report of this session, the first paragraph of which follows:

> *My restraints session on January 25th and 26th was one of the best things that has happened to me. The session has done many things for me. It has*

provided an opportunity for me to get up and release my rage, and then as a result, I have had a great number of insights into myself and how I have behaved in relationship to people.

With respect to the allegations that I restrained Mara Huston from May 29 to June 4, 1972 (or any period thereof), they are utterly false.

[Yvonne Demerest][98] and I left Los Angeles in the early morning of May 26 for Big Sur where I planned to work on the manuscript of my new book. On May 30, we drove up to Palo Alto. I quote from [Mrs. Demerest's] diary:

Left at 3:00 and Be. read manuscript on the way to Palo Alto. We stopped and ate—way of nourishment. At group house (an enclave of college student Group members temporarily in that San Francisco Peninsula community—writer)—good to see [Jen].[99] Beatrice and Keith (Lowenstein). Dinner. Called home.

To the best of my recollection, this is the first that we heard about Mara Huston (who had earlier made a suicide attempt after not being able to deal with having seduced her stepfather) being in restraints.

The "Mara Log" kept by her commune is a diary of instructions of how to take care of Mara and of all contacts with her. The "Log" begins: "The patient went into restraints voluntarily on the evening of Sunday, May 29, 1972."

On Sunday, June 4, 1972, there is this entry: "Then we told Mara that she is restricted to her room as before but will not be in restraints and is to study straight thru to tomorrow morning when [George Gelson] will work on her again."

From [Mrs. Demerest's] diary of May 30, 1972: "When we arrived in Palo Alto, Be. and I exhausted—to bed early," since the next day we left very early to visit two patients of mine, [Mark Washington] at Folsom State Prison, Folsom, and [Bud Vermont][100] at the Medical Facility at Vacaville. Following this, [Mrs. Demerest] had a late appointment with a man near Vacaville about the math book she had just completed.

The next day, June 1, [Mrs. Demerest] and I returned to Big Sur until Friday afternoon June 9 when we drove back up to Palo Alto for the activities surrounding . . . [Jen's] graduation from Stanford, June 10 and 11. [Mrs. Demerest's] diary indicates the she and her husband drove back south on Monday, June 12 and has the notation, "At La Mesa by 6:30. Had drink with B and B" (my husband and me), so we must have returned to Santa Monica either Sunday after graduation or Monday, June 12.

GROUP PEOPLE LEAVING

It seems a little anomalous that on the one hand I am pictured as a sadist, i.e., over-controlling and insane, and on the other hand, the affidavits [of the state's witnesses] speak of the worst punishment as being kicked out of group. The testimony of the witnesses seems to be at great variance with itself.

As I have said, from the beginning, patients have come to me for the special work that I do, have been accepted into the group matrix in order to speed the therapy, and then at the successful completion of their therapy, have left treatment. For instance, a patient (Y.E.) came to me in May of 1967 to be treated for such a severe case of stuttering, that he could not recite in his classes. After five treatments of carbogen and Ritalin (May 19, 26, June 2, 1967 and December 6 and 13, 1968), he was symptom free and left treatment January 6, 1969. The patient remains completely free of stuttering eight years later and has even taught college classes. He subsequently married and consulted me several times on marital problems, but he has had no contact with group. There are scores of patients in this category, but this patient seems a good example since stuttering is a very difficult problem to overcome, and he has been totally symptom free for eight years and has had no contact with group during that time.

Besides the patients who come for specific symptom removal and who join group only in order to have a matrix during their treatment and period of fast change, there are people who join group for a period of time in order to benefit from the exposure to the group matrix and the learning experience with relationship which that exposure makes possible. [Dr. Mel Langer][101] who first came to see me in September 16, 1966 and left March 14, 1973, is an example of the latter. [Dr. Langer], whose affidavit is separately filed, came from his previous therapist who had used Ritalin in his treatment but who was retiring. She referred [Dr. Langer] to me, and he was given Ritalin therapy and carbogen and Ritalin and was in group five years learning how to relate to people. When both he and I felt two years ago that he was no longer benefitting from the group experience, he left group. He has since consulted me several times when he has felt the need, and he has had two ketamine sessions with Dr. Katz and me, one in 1974 and one in 1975 with good effects.

Just as with [Dr. Langer], there are any number of patients who came for the drug therapy that Dr. Katz and I do, joined the matrix of group for a period of time (sometimes for a number of years), and then left group because their interests diverged from those of group. Many students have come, been with group until they straightened out their academic problem, and left when they graduated from college or were well established in graduate school.

There is a third category of patient, the patient whom I dismiss from therapy because they do not follow conditions which have been agreed upon between us. The only recourse a therapist has with a patient who will not follow rules of health and safety (to which there has been mutual agreement) is to dismiss the patient from therapy. Dismissal from therapy usually means dismissal from group, although not always, since group has a great deal to say about its own membership. Dismissal from group very rarely means dismissal from therapy, as more than half the patients who have left group still consult me from time to time about their problems.

With respect to Marty Goldstein, it was necessary for me to terminate therapy with him (giving him two suggestions of alternate therapists whom he knew and regarded highly) because he would not follow the dietary rules set down by his diabetic physicians, and I could not take responsibility for a diabetic who was not on some form of insulin and would not follow the orders of the physician who had given him those orders.

Mr. Goldstein came to Mexico with a number of us for Christmas vacation 1975. The condition under which he was allowed to come was the same as the one which had been set up by his diabetic physician: that he must eat often, as much as he could, and a diet high in fish and poultry. Unfortunately, Mr. Goldstein developed dysentery in Mexico and had trouble eating. He ceased trying to eat and was going out of our home one morning into the hot sun for a rather long walk to get his ticket home without eating anything at all. (It was I who insisted that he go home a day early because he was not feeling well, and I was concerned that there were not enough diabetes experts in the vacation town in Mexico where we were.) Mr. Goldstein was helped to pack, taken to the airport, group members were called to meet him, and the request was made that the neurotic side of his behavior not be reinforced. He was given instructions to see his diabetic physician immediately on arrival. I was subsequently told that Mr. Goldstein went into Santa Monica Hospital, but that he did not experience a diabetic coma— although that was what he alleged to have been wanting according to the testimony of the woman he was in relationship with and his wife at that time.

In conclusion, I should like to emphasize the fact that I am working with the most difficult type of patient, the character disorders. And even more remarkable, these individuals with character disorders really want to undergo deep and basic change. I have treated many suicidal patients (and none have committed suicide). I have treated heroin addicts who are no longer addicts. I have treated alcoholics who are dry and stutter[ers] who no longer stutter. I have treated many violent patients, I have treated criminals (who have not returned to jail), and I have treated one woman who had had 25 years of psychoanalysis and began treatment after she had thrown herself under a subway train in New York. The patients who I have treated are the most difficult type of patient, and they are not normally amenable to the more intellectual types of therapy such as insight therapy or even behavioral modification. These patients have not been able to change while undergoing the usual form of "talking" therapy; they need methods whereby their resistance is lowered and it is possible for unconscious material to emerge which is not available under other circumstances. I have found that it is only drug therapy which has made the type of therapy I do possible.

The drug therapy that I do is extremely important to my patients, especially the ketamine sessions which are given in collaboration with Dr. Katz. There are patients whose progress will be retarded, there are patients who at this point are in very much pain and anguish because we are unable to get beyond the level of their defensive operations. We do have our body work (and Rolfs) and they are helpful, but they do not reach the area of unconscious creativity and insight that the drug sessions allow. We very much need this technique and would like to request very respectfully that we no longer be prohibited from the use of the drug therapy as one of our most important therapeutic tools.

JUDGMENT

A series of hearings followed, first before Judge William Caldecott, and then before Judge George M. Dell. The end result was a compromise reached by lawyers for both sides and approved by the court 12 July 1977, which covered only three of the seven practices: the mineral bath, Ketalar, and the Ritalin and gas sessions. Under the order, those therapies could be practiced only in a nonresidential setting under the supervision of a physician providing the doctor had at hand "such equipment as [he] deems necessary and proper" to insure the health of patients. The order would remain in force until after the PEC had conducted its hearing on the accusation.

Before the state hearing, another body, the California State Psychological Association (CSPA), of which Dr. Eisner was a member, passed judgment on her. While membership in a professional association isn't a requirement for a psychologist, to be a member of the CSPA and its national counterpart, the American Psychological Association, is to be a recognized member of the professional psychological community.[102]

Dr. Eisner was accused of violating the code of ethical principles adopted by the American Psychological Association in December 1972. A hearing was conducted by the committee, with Dr. Eisner represented by attorneys. Witnesses were called, testified under oath, and a record was made of the proceedings.

The CSPA hearing gave Dr. Eisner and her attorneys a chance to see the witnesses under direct and cross examination, and the questions raised and decisions made by the body would give an idea of how expert witnesses would perform at the later, more critical, state hearing.

The hearing was held behind closed doors, and the psychologist herself testified along with current patients to rebut the evidence introduced by the witnesses who were also the key sources for the state's action. After listening to the evidence and arguments, the committee took its vote and turned the results over to the organization's board of directors. In October 1977 a notice, printed on bright red paper, was mailed to the members of the California State Psychological Association headed:

CONFIDENTIAL MATERIAL————————FOR MEMBERS ONLY On 9/18/77 THE CSPA BOARD VOTED TO EXPEL DR. BETTY GROVER EISNER FROM MEMBERSHIP FOR VIOLATION OF ETHICS PRINCIPLES 1, 2(a), 2(b), 7(h), 7(i), 16(i), 16(l) (APA ETHICS STANDARDS, DEC, 1972).[103]

Her fellow professionals had decided Dr. Eisner had violated the general standards of her profession; failed to protect the welfare of clients; failed to exercise proper care in administering treatment; administered treatments in an inappropriate setting; failed to exercise proper supervision of drugs by her cooperating physician; failed to protect research subjects from possible long-term effects of experimental procedures; failed to take adequate precautions in research involving powerful, mind-altering drugs, and demonstrated an inability to provide professional, dependable service.

The CSPA board, after confirming the ethics committee's decision, expelled the psychologist and sent word of its action both the to parent American Psychological Association and the Psychology Examining Committee.[104] Dr. Eisner was subsequently dropped from the rolls of the American Psychological Association, losing the malpractice insurance coverage provided automatically to members.

The scene then shifted back to the administrative law forum, and the state challenge to the psychologists's license. The hearing is basically a public trial conducted by an administrative law judge who is charged with conducting hearings under the *California Administrative Code*. The defendant is present, usually with a lawyer, and the state agency involved is represented by the California Attorney General's office. There is a court reporter keeping notes that can be turned into a transcript. Witnesses testify under oath, and perjury is a crime as it is in any other judicial proceeding. Witnesses can be subpoenaed, as can documents, records, and other evidence, and the admissibility of both testimony and other evidence can be challenged under the *California Evidence Code*, the same law governing other legal proceedings.

Administrative Law Judge Ronald M. Gruen conducted what was the longest, costliest hearing ever held by the PEC to that time. The hearing opened 9 January 1978 and was conducted over sixty-one days, involved the testimony of dozens of witnesses[105] and the admission of fifty-five exhibits. The accusation was modified after the hearing began to include two more allegations not specifically included in the original papers: improper conduct after the Noel Kramer and Keith Lowenstein mineral bath treatments.

Dr. Eisner was represented by two attorneys, Robert L. Schibel and Lynard Hinojosa, and the state by Mark Levin and Deborah Monheit.

"My initial reaction was, 'This is going to be a headache,' " Levin recalls, "and I didn't want to get involved." But "the case bothered me. So I took it over. And the more I got into it—it's like any case. When you're a stranger to it, it's a pain in the butt. And then you start getting involved in it, and it becomes a part of you or you become a part of it; it's hard to tell the difference. And you start getting a feel for it. . . . and to me it looked like a cult, like these people were prisoners.

"And then you start to get to know the witnesses. In this case there were witnesses you couldn't help liking and feeling sorry for . . . it was amazing to me how all these people, particularly with such high intelligence, such fantastic education, could be so thoroughly controlled and dominated by this one personality. Basically, they couldn't make simple, everyday decisions without [her]. All these people were needy people. All these people needed approval. They needed support. They needed validation. And she could provide it not only individually but she would tell the others when to provide it to the individual who was seeking it—and when not to. Which emotionally made people want to please her and do what she expected them to do."

Today, Levin is an attorney in private practice, specializing in defending clients, like Dr. Eisner, facing the loss of professional standing.

Levin believes that one of Dr. Eisner's biggest problems at the hearing was self-created. Every day, without fail, she appeared in court wearing the Group uniform, a dark blue Mexican shirt with a huiple "plaque." "No question about it," Levin said, had she worn a business suit or more formal dress, she would have appeared the professional. Bob [Schibel] and Lynn [Hinojosa] were top-notch lawyers. I think there was a certain lack of client control—which wasn't their fault. I mean, we all encounter people like that, and it's tough."

*   *   *

On 17 November 1978, Judge Gruen issued a nine-page, single-spaced decision, covering each of the alleged treatments, starting with the mineral bath technique itself. The judge found that Dr. Eisner had administered the hot bath and stimulant treatments to "about 11 of her patients" in October and November 1976. After an oral dose of Ritalin, patients got into a *hot* mineral bath [emphasis added] and a "cloth would be placed over the patient's mouth to muffle the screams. Sometimes a body massage would also be performed after the mineral bath." He continued: "On or about November 18, 1976, Noel Kramer, a patient of respondent, underwent said mineral bath therapy and as a result thereof died. Medical testimony established that the therapy produced cardiac dysrhythmia due to hypoxia, deprivation of oxygen to the brain and other vital organs, and over-exertion of the heart, thereby causing Kramer's death."

As used by Dr. Eisner, the technique was "a new and innovative procedure," and the psychologist "was not aware of any literature regarding the use of a hot mineral bath in conjunction with Ritalin and blasting." Before Dr. Eisner started using the therapy on patients, the judge held, she had not discussed the technique with a physician or fellow psychologist, nor with the physician who had prescribed the Ritalin. The therapy was practiced "without the supervision or presence of a physician to monitor patients for potential hazards attendant to said therapy. . . .

"In using said mineral bath therapy without any medical consultation or supervision, respondent failed to recognize the limits of her training and background as a psychologist, and was thus unable to evaluate the medical risks involved. She assumed there were none."

Her conduct was grossly negligent, Judge Gruen held, detrimental to her patients.

He then turned his attention to "K-Therapy." Here, he found, "The drug and medical aspects of the therapy were controlled by and were under the supervision of a duly licensed physician-psychiatrist," Ernest Katz, who, Gruen found, had no previous clinical experience with the drug, and "minimal" training and knowledge in its use in psychotherapy. "Literature on its use as a psychotherapeutic drug was practically non-existent."

The psychiatrist had erred: "Sound medical practice required the presence of patient monitoring apparatus, and rescue devices including medication to counter the potential adverse effects of the drug. No such provisions were made."

"The psychological aspects of the therapy were supervised and controlled by" Dr. Eisner, who had "accepted and relied" on the psychiatrist's assurances the drug was safe for her patients, Gruen wrote. "She also knew that the psychiatrist lacked clinical knowledge with Ketalar and should have known that he lacked knowledge of the pharmacology, posology [the basis for determining correct doses] and predictability of effects" in psychotherapeutic use. She "failed to consult with other physicians for an independent evaluation."

Because she relied on a physician/psychiatrist's advice, Gruen ruled, she was not grossly negligent. However, her failure to conduct a broader investigation of the drug and reliance on "the opinion of said sole psychiatrist" was "not within the standard of sound practice of psychology." In other words, she made an error, but not a professionally lethal one.

While evidence showed that one patient suffered a broken rib in a post-drug massage, that did not establish that the psychologist had administered treatments which were detrimental to patients within the meaning of section 2960(k). "The potential for detriment did exist but the evidence did not establish that detriment in fact occurred."

As for the Meduna sessions, where carbogen was administered, initially with previous injections of Ritalin, here too, Gruen held, the key factor was the presence of the physician-psychiatrist. Here, the evidence showed, Dr. Katz was knowledgeable, trained, and experienced in the use and benefits of the technique. Unlike Ketalar, carbogen had a long history of therapeutic use "and is considered to be safe when rendered under proper medical supervision."

While expert witnesses had disagreed on medical standards and techniques for ensuring patient safety, Dr. Eisner "had no duty to 'second guess' a psychiatrist she reasonably believed to be competent in the administration and medical management of the therapy." The evidence didn't establish any detriment to patients or improper conduct on the psychologist's part. There was no negligence, gross or otherwise.

In the case of Mara Huston, Gruen ruled that the evidence established that "in May and June 1972," Dr. Eisner "approved the use of a therapy technique whereby she knowingly permitted patients under her care and treatment" to place Mara Huston in restraints. "Huston was strapped on a bed in a supine position, so as to be unable to move. The bed had a plastic or rubber sheet to allow Huston to relieve herself. She was fed or released to go to the bathroom only at designated times. Huston was in restraints initially for a period of two or three days and then for a second period of approximately six days. While in restraints, she was subjected to abusive treatment and indignities.

"The restraints were instituted shortly after and as a result of a suicide attempt by Huston. [Dr. Eisner]'s contentions that she lacked the authority to prevent the restraints are rejected as being without merit. Respondent owed a duty not to abandon patient Huston and had the authority to prevent the restraints. Huston's consent was obtained under circumstances of duress and fear. Respondent knew of these circumstances and abdicated her professional responsibility for Huston's care and treatment to untrained, unlicensed laymen with psychological disorders of their own. Respondent failed in her duty to supervise the restraints, and in fact was absent from the locale for the entire period of the restraints.

"Respondent considered said restraints to be therapeutically useful for Huston in dealing with feelings of omnipotence and rage. However, there was no evidence showing that Huston was violent, dangerous to others or in further danger of harming herself."

Dr. Eisner, ruled the administrative law judge, was grossly negligent "for failing to exercise minimal care and judgment in using restraints as a therapy, by improper delegation of duty, and by abandonment of patient Huston." The treatment of Mara Huston was detrimental within the meaning of section 2960(k).

Gruen ruled "untrue" the second allegation involving Mara Huston, that Dr. Eisner practiced a sex surrogate therapy where homosexual patients were requested or required to have sex with heterosexual patients.

The next issue was the "physical illness approach." Here, Gruen ruled against the psychologist, using the strongest language in the decision: "In or about 1970 through 1976, respondent Eisner utilized a therapy technique involving an approach to physical illness whereby her patients who were experiencing physical ailments were discouraged from consulting physicians or following their medical advice. Respondent's theory was the physical illness was merely an outward manifestation of a psychological problem.

"In two instances, failure by the patient to heed respondent's wishes not to consult a physician for medical treatment met with condemnation of the patient by the respondent.

"In the first instance, from 1970 through 1975 Marty Goldstein was a patient of respondent's. He was an insulin dependent diabetic which respondent knew. Respondent repeatedly counselled and instructed Goldstein that he could overcome his diabetes without insulin, by solving his neurotic problems. Respondent told Goldstein he was being 'taken in' by medical advice in that his diabetes was not a medically treatable disorder. Respondent told Goldstein that his diabetes was symptomatic of a neurosis, curable by respondent in conjunction with proper diet and exercise. In March 1974, brainwashed by respondent's conduct, Goldstein discontinued taking insulin which he needed. As a result, in December, 1975, he was admitted to a hospital in a diabetic coma.

"In the second instance, Keith Lowenstein, a patient of respondent experienced chest pain resulting from K-therapy massage. He desired to see a medical doctor. Respondent stated that Lowenstein was neurotic and any physical damage would heal by itself. Lowenstein thereafter did not consult a physician."

Dr. Eisner, Gruen held, "failed to stay within the limits of her competence and training as a psychologist in diagnosing and treating physical injury and disorder as psychological problems. She knowingly went beyond her limitations in her conduct in diagnosing and treating in medical areas beyond her expertise, with consequences that were almost fatal in the case of Marty Goldstein." Her treatment of Goldstein and Lowenstein was grossly negligent and detrimental to their well-being.

Two additional allegations had been added by the state after the hearing opened. Because of the wording of the original accusation, Dr. Eisner wasn't originally charged with negligence for her conduct after Noel Kramer's and Keith Lowenstein's mineral baths. Over the objections of Dr. Eisner's attorneys, Judge Gruen accepted the amended accusation. In both cases, the jurist ruled after the hearing, Dr. Eisner's conduct had been grossly negligent. Gruen wrote: "During the mineral bath session administered to Noel Kramer . . . and for a period of approximately three hours following the bath session, Noel Kramer was in a state of unconsciousness and in obvious need of medical attention. Respondent was present and knew of Kramer's condition and failed to summon medical assistance during the above period of time." Failure to summon help, Judge Gruen held, "constitutes gross negligence" on Dr. Eisner's part. The judge was making the same finding reached by the coroner's jury. Noel Kramer died as a result of the therapy, and Dr. Eisner's failure to recognize that her patient was in medical danger was beyond the bounds of what the law could or should allow on the part of a licensed healer.

He then turned his attention to the last mineral bath administered Keith Lowenstein, at which both Dr. Eisner and Hank Walker had been present. Lowenstein had received two mineral bath treatments that November. "Pursuant to respondent's instructions, Lowenstein ingested 80 mgs. of oral Ritalin. While Lowenstein was recovering from the effects of the second mineral bath, respondent began choking him around the neck and instructed another patient to choke Lowenstein at least three more times. Lowenstein lost consciousness each time he was choked.

"Respondent had told patient Lowenstein that the choking technique was designed to work Lowenstein's past lives out of his system." Dr. Eisner's negligence was two-fold: "for extreme use of aggression as a therapy technique, and the improper delegation of therapy duties to a layman (in the event choking can be considered to be therapeutic)."

*   *   *

The five counts of gross negligence were "serious offenses that must be dealt with in a harsh manner, that is, revocation of the respondent's license." On 18 December 1978, a month and a day after Gruen had reached his decision and exactly one month more than two years after Noel Kramer's death, the Psychology Examining Committee of the Board of Medical Quality Assurance of the California Department of Consumer Affairs ordered the immediate revocation of Dr. Eisner's license.

APPEAL AND *TRIAL DE NOVO*
"SIGNIFICANT RISK . . . TO THE PUBLIC"

The law provides for appeals from administrative law decisions. The subject of an agency action can, within thirty days of the decision, petition for a *writ of mandate* from the Superior Court, seeking a *trial de novo*. There is no new testimony, but both sides can raise legal arguments and challenge both the procedures and the findings before a civil court judge, who reviews a transcript of the hearing along with written papers filed by attorneys for both sides, who also present oral arguments, with the judge asking questions and raising issues. A decision may follow immediately, or later, in writing.

With only hours to spare, on Wednesday, 17 January 1979, Robert Schibel and Lynard Hinojosa filed a petition, signed by Dr. Eisner herself, with the clerk of the Los Angeles County Superior Court. The psychologist said none of the findings was substantiated by evidence, and that the judge and the PEC failed to consider her "previously clean records, practice, position in the community and otherwise meritorious service" in her 22-year-long career. She asked the court to halt the state's enforcement of the PEC decision pending the outcome of her appeal. After hearings 25 January and 5 February 1979, Judge Vernon G. Foster denied Dr. Eisner's request to be allowed to practice until her appeal was decided.

The psychologist now had a serious decision to make. She could press her appeal, but at huge cost. To have an appeal meant to have a transcript, and to have a transcript meant to pay the court stenotypists to translate their coded notes back into the original words. Transcripts can be prohibitively expensive, and in the case of a two-month hearing as much as double the more than $100,000 in estimated legal costs she had already incurred.[106]

Dr. Eisner had lost in three forums so far: the inquest, the state psychological association hearing, and the licensing action. What were the chances she would prevail in a fourth? And at what cost?[107] Quietly, a month later, her attorneys filed a small paper with the court, withdrawing her appeal. The PEC's action would stand—although the law provided that she could appeal to the state agency every year after the anniversary date of the original decision.

In an appeal, the burden of proof shifts from the state to the individual. License appeals are governed by Title 16 of the *California Administrative Code*, which holds that as a precondition for relicensing the petitioner must prove his/her own rehabilitation "by a preponderance of the evidence." The committee must consider the length of time between the negligent actions and the filing of the appeal petition, as well as the nature and severity of those actions.

On 8 November 1980, the PEC met in San Diego to consider the therapist's first appeal to be relicensed. Dr. Eisner wasn't represented by legal counsel; the Psychology Examining Committee was—by Deputy Attorney General Deborah Monheit, who, with Mark Levin, had represented the agency before Judge Gruen. Dr. Eisner testified, along with three witnesses she brought: psychologists Philip Oderberg and Margaret Hartman[108] (a former patient and long-time friend), and a young doctor-intern who had attended medical school with a relative of the psychologist. All three testified that Dr. Eisner was an innovator, ahead of her field, and a person of great personal integrity. The most insightful testimony came from the young physician: "I think that, to me, that the most outstanding characteristics of Dr. Eisner are that she is as a person one of great honesty and integrity. I think that since I've known her that's been really an outstanding quality in her. She is scrupulous in her dealings with friends and people. She is a person who follows through on what she says, and I think that's a very important thing for you all to know. That's clearly an outstanding characteristic that she has.

"And I think that the other thing that comes through in her dealings with other people is that she has a real deep commitment to help other people to the point of being selfless with her time and her energies.

"As a person, she's always enthusiastic. As a friend, she's the kind of friend you want when you're moving or when you're in trouble or when you need somebody to just be a friend. That's the kind of person she is. And I think there are numerous instances of that and I think she may be too modest to go into some details.

"I think that there was a friend of hers that literally was having her house washed away a year or so ago, and she was able to organize some friends of hers and peripheral friends to literally save a house, working and sanding and so forth. And it was her effort in a crisis situation which meant an awful lot to a lot of people. And I think that when people have had to move or have had to do something in terms of a physical nature or in terms of their lives—make a change—that she's the kind of person that is there always to just be there and be supportive.

"She's the kind of person you'd want as a good friend.

"I think that, to me, a very interesting thing that again she's I think been a little modest about, is that there are—working with the Mexican children—I came into this very late, and as an outsider, observed some of the children that she'd had over. I'm not a group member. I have attended some Wednesday night meetings and I have met several of the Mexican people that they've helped, and this is a really incredible thing."

The young doctor, who met the psychologist after the revocation action, saw Dr. Eisner as insightful, generous, and gifted, deserving of the right to treat others. "I think it's been hard on her," he said, "because she's been terribly restrained. She's had lots of ideas in terms of her own thoughts about where holistic medicine's going, where the potential of body/mind interaction is going. She's been very frustrated in her attempts to do anything about it as you might suspect she would be because she's a very active sort of person, a can-do sort of person. She doesn't sit. She runs.

"And so, I think she really should have a license. I think she'd be a fine therapist."

Dr. Eisner testified that the years since the revocation had been a time of reflection, writing (a novel and several short stories), editing the writings of others, gardening, and exercise. "I have also done a great deal of thinking [about] where at least I could make a continuing contribution to society. Volunteer work is one possibility open to me, and I have offered a class in CPR for a group of people and another class in the defensive use of tear gas, mainly for friends who live alone.

"In the past I have spent thousands of hours in the Red Cross as a volunteer, Kate's House Hospital, visiting nurse, blood bank. But I believe this work should be for younger women."

"In examining how best I may make a contribution during the rest of my life, the conviction came more and more deeply that I should make use of the profession for which I have trained and in which I practiced twenty-two years, providing as much as possible with the reinstatement of my license."

Her professional experience, starting with the LSD research conducted with Dr. Sidney Cohen and leading on through the later drug therapies, plus her special training and experience as a therapist made her a skilled diagnostician—a psychologist who could evaluate patients referred to her by others. "This evaluation process is very significant and I think helpful," she said, "particularly so today when there is so much meaninglessness and alienation in the lives of so many people. And I think the fact that

I have been so well trained and worked so deeply with different methods [and] diagnostic tools [has] enabled me to interpret layers of personality and see a possible path to the individual of his or her fulfillment of potential, because I believe very deeply that just as we need proper food and rest and exercise for the physical body, we need meaningful relationships and the movement toward fulfillment of our own unique potential for the psychic body.

"My deep and truest desire is to help set people on the path toward their own realization, and after much soul-searching and thought, I think that this is where I can make the most valuable contribution in this world of increasing tension and conflict."

She wanted her license back so she could practice "individual therapy, mainly evaluational, and perhaps some group work of an educational nature, such as teaching healthful ways of life, new friction [?] exercise, relaxation techniques, and all of those methods which were coming forward to help individuals lead a more balanced and creative life."

The psychologist then sought to challenge some of the evidence on which Judge Gruen had based his findings and recommendation. But Administrative Law Judge William Mevis, who presided at the appeal, told her "we are not going to retry the case" and barred her from presenting anything to challenge what had happened before the revocation. That issue had been decided the moment she dropped her appeal in superior court. All the PEC wanted to know was about her life since the revocation. Had she taken any ongoing professional training classes, as are required for all professionals in California? Yes. She had taken one course on human sexuality, two others entitled "The Healing Brain," and a symposium on "wellness."

Had she maintained any contact with former Group members? "Well, I have had continuing for the last ten years since we brought Mexican children up to learn English from the school we had down there. I have on Wednesdays had a group of people to dinner. My husband and I, that has continued this social event on Wednesdays. Although the last Mexican boys went home in July when they finished high school. Every Wednesday we have dinner together, a group of people who helped with the schools."

While many who attended the Wednesday night meetings were ex-Group members, not all were, Dr. Eisner said. Among those who came from Group were Naomi Feldman, the mother of Noel Kramer's child, and Yvonne Demerest, "my best friend," and six others. They weren't therapy sessions, just a "social gathering," she said, usually lasting about two hours. There would be dinner—refried beans, salad, tacos and tortillas were the staples—and sometimes an interesting guest.

Did Dr. Eisner retain "fairly good social contacts with peoples who used to be members of your therapy group?"

Eisner answered: "That's hard to answer because these are friends through the years of the Mexican school. These are my friends and I see them socially. I do not see them as 'past group members.' I see them as people I am fond of."

Since her revocation, she had talked to colleagues—Philip Oderberg and another psychologist who had testified for her at the PEC hearing—"but I did not feel that what had happened to me necessitated me to go into psychotherapy. . . . There's a great deal of disagreement about my actions and the findings and the actions which took place, and there were a lot of absolute inaccuracies which I can support documentarily.

"Remember, my license was taken away at the time of Jonestown, and it just seemed people said that probably had some effect."

How did Jonestown affect the PEC's decision, asked Dr. Maria Nemeth, a psychologist and the committee's secretary?

"Just with hysteria of the time of anything that looked like a group of people doing a cult-sort of thing which the attorney general's office made it look as though therapy involved with a cult," Dr. Eisner said.

"All right," Dr. Nemeth continued, "so, you don't believe that your actions were in any way reprehensible or unethical?"

"I do not believe that my actions were reprehensible," she replied. "I am obviously terribly disturbed that someone died at the end point. I do not think that it was the paramedics. That again is another thing with who came in between.

"As to it being unethical, I don't feel unethical. Perhaps people can call me unethical, but I don't feel unethical."

Dr. Eisner admitted she had made mistakes, but "of judgment, not of action." She did not consider herself to have been grossly negligent. As for Noel Kramer, after the mineral bath, she said, he "was not unconscious. He was in an altered state of consciousness and this was difficult for Judge Gruen to understand because he was not there. He didn't understand psychological terms. He didn't even understand self-destructiveness and holistic medicine. He thought I was crazy because I believed in holistic medicine. "But when Noel was in the altered state of consciousness, after his—the mother of his child came and [he] cried and responded physically to her. When he didn't come out of his altered state, I should have called Dr. O'Donnell."

But had she violated the standards of practice? another committee member asked.

"I was a very unusual psychologist," Dr Eisner said. "So perhaps I was outside the bounds. I don't know. At the time, I didn't think I was. I thought I was doing—I was helping my patients. Their great, deep character disorders were changing. . . . I think people see psychologists differently from the way I do. I do not think I was unethical and I do not think I did reprehensible acts."

On 8 December 1980, the PEC issued its decision. Dr. Eisner's license would not be restored. The committee cited five separate grounds for its actions:

- Dr. Eisner had failed to grasp the potential dangers of three therapies: mineral baths, Ketalar, and restraints. She also "failed to demonstrate sufficient use of safeguards" when using therapeutic techniques "which expose the patient to risks which could involve emotional, psychological or physical harm."
- Moreover, there was "insufficient evidence of efforts at systematic self-evaluation through psychotherapy," consultations with other professionals on the ethics of therapy, and attendance at seminars and workshops on ethical issues in therapy.
- There was also "insufficient evidence of an ability to distinguish between casual relationships and psychotherapeutic relationships," and the lack of a "clear theoretical basis for her philosophy of treating patients as friends."
- Finally, she hadn't demonstrated a knowledge of current drug therapies employed in psychological treatments, "which she says she would practice or refer her patients to."

*   *   *

On 22 July 1983, Dr. Eisner submitted her second appeal, accompanied by thirty-five supporting affidavits and letters, some from colleagues, some from former patients, some from friends, and one from the attorney who represented the psychologist in the wrongful death suit filed by Noel Kramer's family on behalf of the dead man's daughter.

One of the letters was from Ann Hiller, volunteer coordinator for California legislator Tom Hayden, state assemblyman from Santa Monica, former SDS radical and Chicago Seven defendant and then-husband of actress Jane Fonda. Hiller wrote: "Dr. Betty Eisner has been a volunteer in our office three days per week for the last eight months. She has performed a variety of tasks, including typing and editing our heavy correspondence, compiling a report on Mr. Hayden's coauthored legislation, and occasional phone answering. In every way Dr. Eisner has been an asset in our office: she is dependable, efficient, intelligent and perceptive. We have deeply appreciated her dedication and assistance."[109]

This time she also submitted a list of courses she had taken, and a letter from a psychologist who had given her counselling after her failure to win her first appeal. That psychologist, Dr. Charles Ansell, was also the current chairman of the PEC Ethics Committee.

The Psychology Examining Committee met in Los Angeles on 28 January 1984 to consider the appeal. Dr. Eisner was represented by Robert Schibel, who conducted an aggressive defense of his client. The state was represented by Arthur M. Taggart, a deputy attorney general. Administrative Law Judge Paul M. Hogan presided, and six members of the PEC were in attendance.

Schibel called six witnesses, including Dr. Eisner. Three of the others had testified at the 1980 appeal—Philip Oderberg, Margaret Hartman, and the young physician, now a cardiologist and assistant professor.

Dr. Eisner acknowledged that she may have been negligent in her practice, and she reluctantly acknowledged that "in terms of the findings it was gross negligence." But she had trouble seeing it that way, she said. "You see, gross negligence to me means a total disregard of the welfare of the patient, and I don't feel that I had a total disregard of the welfare of the patient."

As a result of her therapy with Dr. Ansell, she came to see that "I was doing something which is—was—outside of the usual and the known, that I saw had a different viewpoint about it from other people, and that I viewed things differently. I came to understand things differently. I came to a different point of view. I understand more the circumstances and the point of view of myself from other people." Were her license reinstated, she would confine her practice to "the realm of the known and the usual," without the drug and other therapies which had ended with the loss of her license—which, she said in answer to a committee member's question, had been both unknown and unethical.

Dr Eisner had asked Philip Oderberg to recommend a therapist for her to consult, and he came up with the name of Dr. Ansell, the ethics committee chair, who had treated her from April through October of 1981. In addition to his service with the PEC, Dr. Ansell was then serving as editor of the California State Psychological Association newsletter. His writings had appeared in various professional journals, and in an anthology of writings by religious psychologists.

Dr. Ansell testified that "on one occasion I was asked to observe her group" with her in a meeting at someone's home. "This was a group, apparently, that remained close to Dr. Eisner, and it was essentially a social group." Dr. Ansell talked to the group about the summer he had just spent in England at Oxford.

In his capacity as a member of the PEC Ethics Committee, he said he was convinced that the psychologist "had undergone a thoroughgoing and adequate educative experience" in ethics as required by the state Administrative Code. Dr. Eisner was fit to practice, he said.

In his letter to the committee,[110] Dr. Ansell outlined three conditions he would recommend: probationary practice under the supervision of a licensed psychologist for a period of time to be set by the PEC; that she enroll immediately in a course in ethics and the law (which she had by the time of the hearing); and that "if she wishes to return to her research into psychopharmacological drugs," she do so only with the consent of her probationary supervisor, and only then under a physician competent in the field.

In his letter, Dr. Ansell had written that he was "also mindful of the widespread response of the psychological community that called Dr. Eisner to task which ultimately led to the revocation of her license. But one is also mindful of an individual's capacity for growth and for change. Dr. Eisner has spent several years chastened by the experience of earning her colleagues' disapproval, years in which she was compelled to turn away from the profession for which she trained and for which she engaged in original research."

The PEC heard the testimony, and a month later, 7 March 1984, issued a four-page decision, which began with a history of Dr. Eisner's license and the earlier action: "At the hearing on respondent's petition for restoration of 1980, she evidenced no understanding of the danger her unusual therapies posed to her clients. At that time she set forth a stonewall defense of her practices found indefensible by the Committee which revoked her license." At the 1984 hearing, the committee held, she "has shown little change from her position of 1980. "She states she will 'abide by the rules,' but it is evident she has little regard for conventional and acceptable modes of psychotherapy. In sum, respondent believes she is on the cutting edge of psychological research. . . . Respondent will treat these clients without regard to significantly dangerous physiological and psychological risks."

At the 1984 hearing, the committee held, she "was less than candid with respect to her answers" about the pre-1978 therapies. "The committee can only infer from her answers that she still believes she did no wrong, despite the manifest harm resulting, and that her statement of intent to follow the Committee's 'rules' (sic [in original]) amounts to no more than an artificial act of contrition.

"Respondent, if licensed, would pose a substantial danger to the public. She is intelligent, articulate, and charismatic. It would take very little effort on her part to persuade her clients to involve themselves in unproven, high-risk therapy. Given her lack of insight, coupled with her experimental use of high-risk, unproven modes of therapy, restoration of her license would present a significant risk of harm to the public at large."[111]

The revocation would stand. Dr. Eisner was ordered to "cease and desist all actions, whether directly or indirectly, overtly or covertly, constituting the practice of psychology," and to mail copies of the decision to all former clients seen between 1 January 1974 and 18 December 1978.

*   *   *

On 1 June 1984, Dr. Eisner filed for a writ of mandate from Los Angeles County Superior Court. Just as in the case of the original hearing, the PEC's dismissal of her appeal could be challenged through the civil courts. This time, the transcript would be short and cheap. There were only eighty-two pages of testimony from the 1984 hearing.

The psychologist won a pyrrhic victory. Los Angeles County Superior Court Judge Irving Shimer ruled that the PEC's decision in the 1984 appeal hearing went beyond the evidence introduced at the hearing. As a result, three of the committee's findings were struck down, namely, that Dr. Eisner was more interested in research than in the treatment and relief her patients' distress; that she "conducted group therapy sessions under the guise of social events" (the Wednesday night dinners); and that "her patients or clients are, in fact, laboratory subjects."

The PEC prepared a revised decision, based on the court's findings, which the committee adopted 4 January 1985, and which Judge Shimer approved on 28 May 1985. However, the PEC's decision to continue the revocation of Dr. Eisner's license stood. At the time of this writing, the psychologist had made no further appeals.

On 12 January 1979, the Board of Medical Quality Assurance filed Accusation D-2277 against Ernest B. Katz, M.D., seeking to revoke or suspend his license on the grounds of incompetence for his participation in the K-therapy.

The psychiatrist's attorney, Maurice Levy, Jr., worked out a compromise agreement, a stipulation, which was approved by Mark Levin of the Attorney General's Office on 7 June and adopted by the Division of Medical Quality on 24 July 1979. Dr. Katz agreed to stop using "ketamine or its derivatives," to take an examination on the use of psychoactive drugs in abreactive therapy, to submit quarterly statements of compliance, and to meet yearly with a BMQA consultant. In return, he would be allowed to continue his practice, and probation would be lifted after five years.

There were no further actions against him as of the time of writing.

*   *   *

In an interview for this book, conducted in May 1989, Oscar Janiger described his former colleague this way: "I think my experience with Betty now—and I see her on occasion—is that she's a woman who has looked back and assessed the past. And I don't think she carries any bitterness with her. My impression is, she's integrated a lot of things that have happened, and she's at this time a woman who's not unreasonable, doesn't do therapy anymore, isn't involved in these issues, has made a settled life for herself, and is, I think, generally speaking, a pretty reasonable woman at this stage in time and place. I think she'd be the first to acknowledge some of the excesses that she and many others have committed during that rather heady period, and that altogether it could have had a much more serious ending than it does now for her. . . .

"I'm sure that all of us will contribute in this respect that we might set up a system of reasonable safeguards, and above all, a much more profound appreciation of the power, the extraordinary virtuosity of these medicines."

*   *   *

In 1988, fifty years after the first synthesis of LSD, the Albert Hofmann Foundation was inaugurated in California.[112] Created with the blessings of its namesake, the nonprofit educational corporation is based in Santa Monica. Its president is Robert D. Zanger, a psychologist; Oscar Janiger, M.D., is vice-president.

The foundation's purpose is "to establish a library and world information center dedicated to the scientific study of human consciousness. Our future library, art gallery and conference center will house an extensive collection of books, journals, tape recordings, news clippings, research reports and art, and will be open to researchers and the public."[113]

In the summer of 1989, the Albert Hofmann Foundation issued the premier edition of its *Newsletter*. The column by president Robert D. Zanger included an announcement that "Betty Grover Eisner, Ph.D., research associate of the late Sidney Cohen at UCLA," had been appointed to the foundation's Board of Advisors. The next issue (Fall 1989), welcomed Dr. Eisner as a new "Charter Member" of the foundation and thanked her for a $1,000 donation.

The same issue of the newsletter described the work of a Swiss psychiatrist, Dr. Peter Bauman, who conducts a government-approved group LSD therapy practice in Zurich.[114]

NOTES

1. *American Medical Association Encyclopedia of Medicine* (New York: Random House, 1989), pp. 1046–47.

2. Los Angeles County Coroner's Autopsy Report 76–13951, p. 2.

3. Robert L. Schibel, Esq., letter of 26 July 1989 to writer.

4. Letter to writer.

5. Declaration of 22 June 1977.

6. Martin A. Lee and Bruce Schlain, *Acid Dreams* (New York: Grove Press, 1985), p. xiv.

7. Lee and Schlain, op. cit., p. 71.

8. Ibid.

9. W. V. Caldwell, *LSD Psychotherapy* (New York: Grove Press, 1968), p. 46.

10. Anais Nin, *The Diary of Anais Nin, Volume Five, 1947–1955,* ed. by Gunther Stuhlman (New York: Harcourt Brace Jovanovich, Inc., 1974), pp. 255–262. Others who tripped with Janiger included Jack Nicholson and Stanley Kubrick.

11. Anais Nin, *The Diary of Anais Nin, Volume Six, 1955–1966,* ed. by Gunther Stuhlman (New York: Harcourt Brace Jovanovich, Inc., 1974), pp. 130–131.

12. Ibid.

13. Ibid., p. 260.

14. Betty Grover Eisner, *The Unused Potential of Marriage and Sex* (Boston: Little Brown Co., 1970), p. 196.

15. Nin, op. cit., p. 170.

16. Janiger was Watts's personal physician (as well as a cousin to another guru of the acid age, poet Allen Ginsberg.)

17. According to Hank Walker, whose father was also an attorney.

18. Betty Grover Eisner, testimony before the California Psychology Examining Committee, 8 November 1980, p. 10.

19. According to Hank Walker.

20. From Bill Sturgeon, Hank Walker, and Marty Goldstein.

21. Testimony, 8 November 1980, Psychology Examining Committee, p. 61.

22. University of California Library, Education and Psychology thesis section, LD 791.9 P9 E362.

23. Betty Grover Eisner, op. cit., p. 1.; *curriculum vitae.*

24. "Subjective Reports of Lysergic Acid Experiences in a Context of Psychological Test Performance," *The American Journal of Psychiatry,* Vol. 115, No. 1, July 1958.

25. In *The Journal of Nervous and Mental Disease,* Vol. 127, No. 8., pp. 528–539.

26. The source is Janiger, reminiscing to Hubbard in a 1978 videotaped meeting of psychedelic researchers held at Janiger's home.

27. Leary and colleague Walter Pahnke's Good Friday experiment showed the drug could produce a euphoric, awe-full experience when given in a religious context (a music-filled chapel during Good Friday services.)

28. Betty Grover Eisner, *curriculum vitae.*

29. See, for example, John Ranelagh, *THE AGENCY: The Rise and Decline of the CIA* (New York: Touchstone Books, Simon & Schuster, 1987), p. 211.

30. Jay Stevens, op. cit., pp. 84–87.

31. Letter to writer, 13 December 1977.

32. Laudably reviewed in *Urology,* March 1988, XXXI:3, 223–24, by Stanwood S. Schmidt, M.D., of the University of California School of Medicine, San Francisco. "The Sturgeon Vas Cautery, and inexpensive, reusable battery-powered modular unit, had been used in 600 consecutive vasectomies with a minimum of complications and without equipment breakdown," reads the abstract.

33. One of Dr. Eisner's contemporaries was a patient of one of the Westwood acid

therapists. An actress whose experience with the drug led her to earn a UCLA psychology doctorate. She describes her experiences in a remarkable volume called *My Self and I* (New York: Coward McCann, 1962), written under the pseudonym "Constance A. Newland." The sessions she describes are very similar to those staged by Dr. Eisner: pleasant, professional environment, therapist at hand, eye masks, music, interpretation of drug-induced visions, session reports.

34. Eisner, op. cit., p. 196.

35. Caldwell, op. cit., p. 74.

36. Psychology Examining Committee testimony, pp. 62–63.

37. Eisner, op. cit., pp. 4, 160.

38. Ibid., pp. 231–32. According to Mary Baker Eddy, the very concept of "lack" is erroneous. "The divine spirit supplies all needs," she writes in *No and Yes* (Boston: Christian Science Publishing Society, 1908), p. 42.

39. Ibid., p. 215.

40. Other techniques to express rage were kicking and pounding mattresses, punching-bags, and cardboard boxes. Group members would also stage mock combats with foam-filled therapy bats.

41. A pseudonym.

42. A Group euphemism for an acid trip.

43. A pseudonym.

44. Op. cit., p. 114.

45. In a presentation to the American Medical Association Clinical Convention in Las Vegas, Cohen "called for LSD research centers, where applicants, after extensive screening, could take the 'psychedelic drug' in a scientifically controlled environment." From a story by the writer in the *Las Vegas Review-Journal*, 1 December 1966, p. B-1.

46. Lee and Schlain, op. cit., pp. 90–91; Jay Stevens, op. cit., pp. 182–83.

47. For an excellent, sobering account of this project and its ramifications, see Gordon Thomas's *Journey Into Madness: The True Story of Secret CIA Mind Control and Medical Abuse* (New York: Bantam Books, 1989).

48. It was to be one of Huxley's last trips. He died of cancer the day of Kennedy's murder, flying on acid into oblivion, according to his wife, Laura Archera Huxley.

49. Cf. Keith S. Ditman, et al., "Dimensions of the LSD, Methylphenidate and Chlordiazepoxide Experiences," in *Psychopharmacologia* (Berlin) 14, 1–11(1969); and Ian Martin M.D., " 'Ritalin' and 'Sodium Amytal': An Alternative to L.S.D. 25 as an Adjunct to Therapy," *Medical Journal of Australia*, 31 December 1966, pp. 1264–67.

50. A pseudonym.

51. Within anthropology there is a discipline called "proximics," which studies cultural patterns of personal use of social space. Thanks to George Rich for this.

52. Caldwell, op. cit., p. 123.

53. Declaration of 22 June 1977, Los Angeles Superior Court file C201820.

54. *The Unused Potential of Marriage and Sex*, p. 4.

55. Op. cit., p. 140.

56. Op. cit., p. 216.

57. Op. cit., p. 122, 129.

58. Op. cit., p. 216.

59. Ibid.

60. Jay Stevens, op. cit., p. 85.

61. Declaration of Betty Grover Eisner, Ph.D. in opposition to motion for preliminary injunction, 22 June 1977, p. 2.

62. 1959, pages 438–441.

63. Another controversial therapeutic group had evolved in Santa Monica at the same time as Dr. Eisner's Group. This was Synanon, which, like Group, was founded on the charismatic personality of an authoritarian personality—Chuck Dederich, who split off from AA, rejecting its demand for anonymity.

64. Ironically, Dr. Eisner and her husband were passengers in the back seat of a car which was rear-ended by another car on 10 July 1987. They sued the driver of the car that hit them. In a response to their suit, the driver alleged the psychologist had failed

"to utilize available safety equipment"—that is, seatbelts. (Los Angeles County Superior Court case WEC 126385).

65. One of the most extreme and baffling human afflictions is obsessive-compulsive disorder, in which individuals are forced to act out endless rituals which destroy their social lives and create endless guilt and self-recrimination. Drugs that increase serotonin in the basal ganglia of the brain seem to slow or stop the disturbed behavior. The basal ganglia, among other things, relay movement commands to the skeletal muscles, which are the vehicles for acting out obsessive-compulsive behaviors, such as hoarding, showering a dozen or more times a day, and hair-pulling. For an excellent description of this disorder and its implications, see *The Boy Who Couldn't Stop Washing*, by Judith L. Rapoport, M.D., chief of the child psychiatry branch of the National Institute of Mental Health (New York: Dutton, 1989).

66. *Psychology Today*, October 1970, pp. 56ff. In a sidebar describing his own Rolfing, Keen concludes: "Thus the grounding of awareness in the body is both a joyful homecoming and a heavy trip into the humus, the ground and end of human existence, the first and last truth." Keen's eloquence induced me to "get Rolfed."

67. The writer underwent the ten Rolf sessions twenty years ago, during the course of which he lost a spouse and forty pounds. If nothing else, the technique forces the patient to confront habitual tensions, a process that sometimes leads to the recollection of an event perceived as having caused the distress. Whether that memory is accurate or not may be irrelevant. The simple fact of its release produces tangible relief and reduction of stress. Certainly, it is a field deserving of serious scientific scrutiny.

68. A collection of writings on psychedelics whose name he no longer recalls, in which she had made statements striking Walker as truly wise and insightful, refreshing in their lack of academic language and footnotes. Today, he said, he's more prone to look for the footnotes.

69. Caldwell, op. cit., p. 75.

70. Description based on documents, interviews, and a brief visit inside the home courtesy of Dr. Eisner's attorneys.

71. Betty Grover Eisner, Ph.D., declaration, 22 June 1977.

72. "Arousal" is also the tool advertisers exploit in turning a car or a stick of chewing gum into a sexual symbol.

73. Dr. O'Donnell was incorrect; the two primary medical indications for use of the drug are hyperactivity in children and narcolepsy, a disorder charcterized by daytime attacks of sleep, which may last from seconds to hours. See: *Physician's Desk Reference* (Oradell, N.J.: Medical Economics Co., 1988), pp. 890–891; H. Winter Griffith, M.D., *Complete Guide to Prescription and Non-Prescription Drugs* (Los Angeles: The Body Press, 1989), pp. 642–643; and *The American Medical Association Encyclopedia of Medicine*, pp. 715, 942.

74. *Physician's Desk Reference*, loc. cit.

75. A pseudonym.

76. "Judge Orders SM Psychologist to Halt Practice," Santa Monica, CA, *Evening Outlook*, 3 June 1977, p. 1.

77. *California Penal Code*, section 192.2.

78. PEC Accusation D-2010 paragraph 5.

79. Eisner declarations, preliminary injunction motion, p. 114. Breiman reversed his position a year later, after he left group, on account of Dr. Eisner's treatment of Marty Goldstein.

80. Ibid., pp. 117–118.

81. Ibid., p. 73.

82. Ibid., pp. 69–70.

83. Ibid., p. 62.

84. It is also chemically close to the street drug PCP, or "angel dust."

85. Ibid., pp. 41–55.

86. A pseudonym for another patient.

87. Hank Walker testified then and now that Noel Kramer's head *did* go underwater, for a brief instant, and that, in the process, the blasting rag became wet.

88. Patient testimony on this point was conflicting, as were statements made in contemporaneous declarations and subsequent testimony by the same witnesses.

89. Mara Huston was to testify that one dose of Ritalin she was given by a fellow patient, allegedly at Dr. Eisner's direction, produced a psychedelic effect while she was being held strapped into a bed in her underwear in a room where the temperature was made to fluctuate between extremes.

90. Hank Walker grew tired of the scratchy record; Bill Sturgeon retains fond memories of the same disc.

91. Dr. Roquet was the subject of a stunning article by Craig Waters in the 19 August 1977 issue of the leate *New Times*. Titled "The Cruel Age Acid Quest," Waters's article describes sessions in remote mountain Indian village where Dr. Roquet administered mixtures of LSD and ketamine. Waters notes the following: "Dr. Salvador Roquet Perez, 56, a former public health officer, is now a psychiatrist with a private practice. He has experimented with psychedelics for nearly 10 years, and conducts some 2,000 illegal psychedelic sessions. In 1974, he was arrested by Mexican police and imprisoned for five months; Salvador became more discreet. During the past year, he has conducted several psychedelic sessions in New England." Op. cit., p. 31.

92. A pseudonym.

93. A pseudonym.

94. A pseudonym.

95. A pseudonym.

96. A pseudonym.

97. A pseudonym. She does not refer to "George Gelson, M.D." as she refers to other physicians because "Dr. Gelson" is not an M.D. She doesn't mention that he is a chiropractor.

98. Pseudonym for an older Group member close to the psychologist, according to former patients.

99. A pseudonym.

100. Both pseudonyms.

101. A pseudonym.

102. The same is true for the American Medical Association and state and local medical societies. A physician who isn't a member is free to practice.

103. From an original furnished to the writer.

104. From a story by the writer, "Psychology Group Expels Dr. Eisner," Santa Monica, Calif.: *The Evening Outlook*, 26 October 1977, pp. 1, 13.

105. Including the writer, who testified that about the contents of a note he had seen passed between the psychologist and one of her attorneys. At his own request, the writer was taken off the story afterwards, but was later directed to resume coverage by the editors of the *Evening Outlook*.

106. From a story by the writer, "Panel revokes SM therapist's license," in the 19 December 1978 (Santa Monica) *Evening Outlook*, pp. A-1, A-10.

107. In yet another legal action, the wrongful death suit filed against Dr. Eisner by Noel Kramer's parents, "an award was made to the daughter of the patient who died." Eisner, Betty Grover, *Petition for Restoration of Revoked or Suspended License*, 22 July 1983, p. 3.

108. A pseudonym.

109. Dated 26 September 1983.

110. Dated 8 July 1983.

111. Action L-31274, pages 2, 3.

112. The organization was formally incorporated in October, 1987.

113. From *The Albert Hofmann Foundation Newsletter*, Vol. 1, No. l, Summer 1989, p. 1, Santa Monica, Calif.

114. After group drug sessions lasting until as late as 10 P.M., his patients usually go home with him and spend the night at his house. Op. cit., p. 9.

SO WHY CALIFORNIA?

Nearly two decades ago, before I was a Christian Scientist, I was a member of a communal household under a charismatic leader who dispensed mind-altering drugs to his followers for use in carefully controlled circumstances.[1] I earned my keep as scribe and editor for the leader, a Hindu from India, who also performed the rites for my marriage to the mother of my son. With my blessings as the household astrologer—an art I learned from the guru—some of the group members went to India. I stayed behind. Those who went sickened, living in the guru's attic, tended by astrologers and folk healers.

One woman died: I had specifically and sincerely urged her to go, based on my reading of her horoscope. When they finally took her to the hospital, it was too late. They brought her ashes home to her parents; the second of their children they had had to bury.

There was a time in my life when I believed in psychic surgery. Well-known psychologists told me it was real, showed me films.[2] I would have tried it—fortunately, the need never arose.

*   *   *

In *Influence: How and Why People Agree to Things*, Robert D. Cialdini, professor of psychology at Arizona State University, gives a wonderful plain-language report on what he calls "compliance strategies." These are the calculated persuasion techniques used by parents, Hari Krishnas, Nazis, Chrysler dealers, doctors, teachers, television comedy producers, and advertisers to get other folks to change their minds, to do what they want them to do. They go for the reflexes, using thousands of tricks and techniques. Yet behind a majority of the tactical adaptations Cialdini finds six basic strategic principles that can make us act unquestioningly:

Consistency. Once people commit to a decision, they change their thought and behavior to conform with their commitment. Advertisers call it brand loyalty; religions call it fidelity.

Reciprocation. "You scratch my back; I'll scratch yours." As social beings, humans expect favors to be returned, and to return those others do them. We do unto others who have done unto us.

Social proof. People look to others to see what actions are appropriate in the context of the moment. "When in Rome, do as the Romans do." Uncertainty produces imitation.

Authority. "Follow the leader." "Leave it to the experts." "Listen to mother." "I am the teacher here." Social existence mandates authority.

Liking. Human beings are more inclined to listen to and be influenced by people they find likeable. Hence, the con game victim's "How could he do that? He was so *nice.*"

Scarcity. The harder something is to get, the more value it gains. Humanity survived by learning to value and conserve scarce resources, and that habit has carried over into everything we do.[3]

Drawn from a wide range of published research, Cialdini's categories are useful guidelines for analyzing the success and failure of charismatic groups, and for understanding behavior. They allow us to find relationships between events that might at first seem dissimilar. They offer a scientific tool for seeking an understanding of seemingly irrational acts.

There's a valid social reason, written in genes, culture, language, for each persuasion mechanism. They enabled humans to form cohesive societies capable of sharing sophisticated observations and accumulating progressive understanding of techniques for controlling the environment. Belief systems have given humans the ability to endure tragedy. Survival isn't always unblemished, but it *is* survival. Belief systems give people a way of identifying with something enduring, transcending death itself.

Belief systems differ in externals. Hari Krishnas wear funny robes and do strange things to their hair. Scientologists have intense stares. Jehovah's Witnesses are always standing around with their magazines. Mormons are well-groomed young people who come to the door in pairs. Jesus people shop at the sign of the fish. But cultists share one perception: They have a corner on The Truth, the scarcest of all commodities. Each is equally sincere, honest, and out to serve.

Group members are likable to each other because they are alike in having subordinated their personal sense of responsibility to a designated "Authority Figure." To a great degree they have successfully "put personalities aside."

*   *   *

Another set of filters has been proposed by Robert Jay Lifton, to whom we are obligated for the concept of "loaded language." He describes eight basic characteristics of "ideological totalism," employed initially in his study of Korean War victims of Chinese "thought reform"

> *Milieu control.* What the LSD researchers called "set and setting," which are internalized as cultic rules governing conduct in given situations.
>
> *Mystical manipulation.* Disciplines and practices adopted in a seemingly spontaneous manner, but which in fact result from directed cues of authority figures.
>
> *Demand for purity.* The system/savior cannot fail; only the believer fails. Purification is an unrelenting demand.
>
> *Cult of confession.* Confession, often in front of others, is a mandate, often a hypocritical ritual designed to mask some unrelinquished fragment of individuality.
>
> *Sacred science.* Believers have a scientific franchise on truth; since the nineteenth century humans have deferred to scientific authority.
>
> *Loading the language.* Words convey hidden doctrines and set behavioral constraints.
>
> *Doctrine over person.* If feelings and doctrine conflict, doctrine rules over what Mary Baker Eddy called "personal sense."
>
> *Dispensing of existence.* If the scientific doctrine demands the supreme sacrifice, either of believer or infidel, so be it.[4]

Each of these elements is incorporated in unconventional healing. Milieu is all-important. Environment is controlled. There is some form of mystical manipulation (prayer, testimonial, hymns, chants, meditation, bells, directed study, reservations). There is a demand for purity, for some form of austerity, of thought, of diet, of other conduct. Transgression—violation of the rule of "doctrine over person"—is conditionally associated with guilt and sin, and must be confessed, atoned for, and absolved. Healer and patient share some mystical bond based on coherent, revealed/discovered scientific principles that take precedence over mere "material models." All share their mutual belief through loaded conversations, punctuated by puns, knowing laughter, and nodding heads. Even an individual's existence is expendable.

*   *   *

There is another set of perceptual screens to consider.

Garrett Hardin is Professor Emeritus of Human Ecology at the University of California, Santa Barbara, and a provocative, original thinker and writer. In *Filters Against Folly*, published in 1985,[5] he makes a powerful case that no thought can be truly critical unless it successfully passes through a series of three filters:

Literacy. For an idea to be accessible it must be effectively communicated. Before you can load the language you must know the language.
Numeracy. For one claim to be tested against another, each must be tested within defined limits. The numbers tell the story.[6]
Ecolacy. The recognition that all literate and numerate definitions are limited; that planned real-world actions always carry unplanned consequences. The "wow"/"oops" phenomenon.

* * *

Traditional psychiatry and psychotherapy have focused on the individual. But human beings are not normally isolated individuals. They exist as members of social groups, and social groups play a vital role in shaping the sense of individual identity.

We all belong to groups. We might call them our families, our "circle of friends," our "colleagues" at work, our fellow parishoners in church. For most of us, members of our groups are fairly scattered, isolated from each other and united only by our participation in each—unless we have fallen into a totalistic environment, one that promises to meet all our needs in return for submission to revealed authority.

In *The Healing Web, Social Networks and Human Survival*, Mark Pilisuk, a community studies professor, and Susan Hillier Parks, a behavioral science researcher,[7] examine the role of social support systems in physical and psychological health. They have discovered that one index of human psychological functioning is the size of the individual's social group.[8]

Psychotics, they found out, typically have no friends and a circle of associations restricted to four or five family members. "People with less serious mental disorders also have certain distinguishing social network characteristics," they write. "Here the network seems to be somewhat larger, say ten to twelve persons. Frequently there is a significant tie to someone who has moved far away or perhaps to someone no longer living. The active ties tend to be negative and with people not connected with one another."[9]

Among an average population of human beings, "a typical person's social network, we find, consists of fewer than ten people who are intimately known, and most of whom are well known to each other. Beyond this, the individual is likely to see an additional thirty or so individuals on a regular basis. The typical size of one's active social network appears to be in the vicinity of forty people."[10] For a typical individual, this social circle is grouped into a half-dozen or so clusters of subgroups, the members of one unknown to others.

What this begins to resemble is a clan, a tribe, or a herd. With animals and in pretechnological tribes, the groupings can easily be seen because they remain fairly cohesive. But with modern humans in a technological society, frequent job changes and moves, the patterns are harder to discern. But they are there: Healthy humans have groups of three or four dozen; disturbed people have smaller groups, often with one or more members who are dead or distant; severely disturbed people are limited to a few family members.

For Lise Glaser, conversion to Christian Science followed marriage and a move, two major life changes. Her new spouse took a job. He was a Christian Scientist, and his work brought her to the heart of the deepest possible ongoing immersion in Christian Science, Principia College. From there, they moved to L.A., and joined the most active, vital church in the Movement. She buried herself in church activities demanding constant self-discipline.

For Helene Mellas, desperation and discontent had brought her to an impasse. Her health seemed gone, her heart nearly destroyed. Then came the mystical experience she had been seeking. She hovered between life and death, and Jesus charged her with a holy mission. Her life was transformed as she was drawn into the orbit of the New Age, for which she had been prepared by her father. She got a divorce. She sought out an intense group experience, Lifespring, and started her own New Age self-exploration group, where she met a couple who told her about a strange band of living miracle-workers. That took her to a strange land where, in a private, closed-off-from-the-world healing center, a man with magnetic hands reached inside her skin and did things (she believed) to her heart. She came back to her own community and created a group conversion-and-healing experience with the help of a fellow with a long history of, as Tom Lehrer puts it, "doing well by doing good."

The role of the group can be seen most clearly in Dr. Eisner's patients, where the traditional therapeutic distance between patient and therapist had dissolved. Casualness, familiarity, was the ideal—in a structured relationship, an intentional group matrix operating under the authority of reality, in harmony with the law of cause and effect. Betty Eisner's home had become the center of the universe, the scene of social gatherings with celebrities, private drug sessions, group drug sessions. Her husband and children were part of Group, interacting with the other patients, serving as surrogates for the purpose of liberating the energies and enthusiasms lost in the interlocking neuroses and psychoses of the Atomic Age of Anxiety.

In this context, consider what happened to Bill Sturgeon, Leo Breiman, Marty Goldstein, and Hank Walker when they met Dr. Eisner. Each had experienced major geographic dislocations (a change in continents in one case). Two were haunted by deaths, one by serious disease. Two had been overwhelmed by psychedelics; the third sought them. Now they were all in Los Angeles, looking for insight and drawn to Dr. Betty Grover Eisner. But it wasn't just "Betty". It was Betty and Bill and their family and Group: an entire social structure, a complete tribe, a self-sustaining interactive social matrix with a fundamental creed: *I Can't, You Can't, But We Can!*

This was in the age of youthful social activism, when people taking to the streets were creating social pressures that were getting unjust racial laws changed, when public outrage helped end an unwinnable war. Groups could effect social change. History was a testament to that.

Dr. Eisner offered a complete package, a full social group of like-minded, attractive people, sharing a complex, highly loaded language, united behind a visionary, internationally recognized leader in the exuberant era before Jonestown. These were needy people, Mark Levin observed. And what they needed more than anything else was a supportive social network, a matrix.

*　　*　　*

From time to time, someone in Dr. Eisner's Group would print up a membership list. The January 1971 list records forty-one full adult members, including Dr. Eisner's family. Another eighteen adult names are listed in parentheses, for a total of fifty-nine names. There are at least thirty-three "group children." This is a complete human social network, a tribe, a clan, an extended family.

Most of the unmarried adults have different addresses, except for five. These, along with Marty and Rachel Goldstein, are the inhabitants of "Group House." This is the Young Group commune, an important addition, the impact of which becomes clear when compared to the October 1976 *MAIN GROUP LIST*, the list for the month before Noel Kramer's death. In less than six years, the nature of Group has radically changed. The earlier list is the product of a typewriter; the new one of a computer printer. There are now thirty-three full adult members and twenty-four adult names in parentheses—including several who had been expelled—for a total of fifty-seven adult names. The precise number of group children is difficult to calculate.

The most significant change is this: While total Group size dropped only two, from fifty-nine to fifty-seven, the number of full group members dropped by eight; and of these, twenty-seven, four-fifths of the full members, resided at six addresses identified as Group Houses—two of which are owned by Dr. Eisner, and all but one of which are within a three-minute drive of her home.

The group has become younger, communal. Group had come to

resemble the Pilisuk and Parks general social model even more. Now there were distinct subgroups. While members of each household knew the others in Group, each house was a social unit of its own, wheels within wheels. At the center of it all, the only one to whom all reported, was the therapist, the acknowledged authority figure.

*   *   *

Why in California?

Sometimes the obvious is profound. Consider Lincoln's succinct division of humanity:

You can fool some of the people all of the time. These are lifetime, committed true believers. These are the folks who can conceive no sense of identity separate from the belief.

You can fool all of the people some of the time. There are moments when everyone is vulnerable to one or another influence strategy. Death, divorce, war, a major move are all times of dislocation when established relationships are shattered and new relationships sought.

But you can't fool all of the people all of the time. Which is what, if anything, will pull us through.

California stands separated by a great inland desert from the rest of the nation. To the West, California faces Asia across an open sea; to the East, before the desert, is a vast mountain range. A move to California is a literal reorientation. The state's physical and psychological climate make possible an incredible array of lifestyles.

Folks who move to California have amputated social ties. Many familiar faces will never be seen again. The move can be even more disruptive if the result of death, divorce, or loss of job. Even the normally well-socialized become vulnerable in times of loss.

So why California? Because California offers groups to meet anyone's needs, in an environment filled with people needing friends.

One final question: Will exposure of these three cases in a forum like this accompish any good? The answer, I would hope, is yes. From a standpoint of public policy, legislators and regulators need to know the issues involved in unconventional healing. State and federal authorities must grapple with the issues presented here. Christian Science lobbyists are working hard to overturn the "child neglect" statutes and win exemption from manslaughter prosecutions. Psychic-surgery promoters are working the country, selling the operations and the lucrative Philippine tours. Federal authorities are reconsidering whether or not to reopen psychedelic drug research programs, and must design guidelines to ensure maximum public safety. These are issues that won't go away, but must be decided thoughtfully in the context of a democratic society.

NOTES

1. Marijuana, hashish, datura, and yage were all provided, furnished to him as gifts from devoted followers, usually those living outside the household and still employed.

2. At a meeting of the Transpersonal Association held at Esalen Institute at Big Sur, while I was on the editorial staff of *Psychology Today* in 1973.

3. See Robert D. Cialdini, *Influence: How and Why People Agree to Things* (New York: Morrow, 1984).

4. In his *Thought Reform and the Psychology of Totalism: A Study of "Brainwashing" in China* (New York: W. W. Norton, first published in 1961).

5. Garrett Hardin, *Filters Against Folly* (New York: Viking, 1985).

6. For a stimulating, phenomenally clear plain-language understanding of the consequences of a failure to apply this standard, see *Innumeracy: Mathematical Illiteracy and Its Consequences* (New York: Hill and Wang, 1988), by John Paulos, professor of mathematics at Temple University.

7. Both at the University of California, Davis.

8. Marc Pilisuk and Susan Hillier Parks, *The Healing Web: Social Networks and Human Survival*, Hanover and London: University Press of New England, 1986, p. 35.

9. Ibid.

10. Ibid., pp. 35-36.

APPENDIX
THE COMMITTEE ON
PUBLICATION ANSWERS

Nathan A. Talbot heads the Committee on Publication for the Mother Church.
As part of his duties, he monitors court cases involving Christian Science. He
agreed to be interviewed for the book. The session was conducted in his fourth
floor room at the Pacific Shores Hotel in Santa Monica, California, the first
day of the Glasers' trial.

Talbot is calm, personable, deliberate. He has sandy brown hair touched
with gray, handsome features, and a sharp nose. When he speaks, his voice is
quietly intense, almost painfully reasonable.

He was dressed in a grey suit, soft leather loafers, and a repp tie with
a Dior logo. We sat in two chairs at a small table near a sliding glass window
overlooking a site where, I explained, Swami Mukhtananda once held court for
his celebrity followers from a beachside, luxurious tent. Just to the south, I pointed
out the building where Synanon transformed itself from a splinter group from
Alcoholics Anonymous into a cult of personality whose founder and two believers
used a de-rattled rattlesnake to attack an anti-cult lawyer.

I began by asking Talbot about the seven criminal cases involving Christian
Scientists now.

NATHAN A. TALBOT: [These] seven cases are virtually all of the losses in
our entire denomination in the United States since 1983. I think I would
know if there were a lot of other lawsuits going on. We have a fairly
tight-knit church; we work closely together, especially since all of this
has been taking place.

We have [tried] to get some sense. . . .of how we're doing with children.

Our best effort indicates that if we were about at where society generally is, during this period of time we would have had between twenty and twenty-five losses. We're talking about children up through the age fourteen. From fifteen up, many other factors come in—drugs, accidents— we probably would even do a little better. But we're looking at the area that seems most sensitive in society's eyes. We agree with society that the government has an interest in the welfare of children.

You mentioned you have some background in Christian Science. Unless you left in a rage or something, I'm sure you have some sense that Christian Scientists tend to be, on the whole, reasonable, thoughtful people?

Conscientious, and moral—sure.

TALBOT: They're not people on the fringes of reasonableness in society— except some people would say this one point is unreasonable. We feel we're talking about rational people who are making intelligent decisions about health care for their families.

We've made an honest attempt to gather the information, and as nearly as we can tell, they are doing very well. This does not mean we haven't had losses. We've had certainly seven losses. But it does mean that society should think carefully before trying to prosecute us out of practicing this method of care. You could make an argument that if society is successful in doing that, that will mean *more* losses. We'll be pushed up into the general loss rate of society.

Why?

TALBOT: If we find we're having to go to doctors for children all the time, I think over time we will begin to reflect the normal loss rate in society, because we'll be doing what everyone else is. Right now we're substantially below that loss rate.

I think some people could legitimately say, "Well, maybe you're below it because your socioeconomic group is higher, your nutritional values are higher, and so on." But when we looked at the record, we took all that into account, and any way we did it, our loss rate is less than half that of the general public. Now, you can do anything with statistics. We did this for ourselves; we wanted to know for ourselves. What would we have said had it come out the opposite? I don't know; it didn't come out the opposite.

I have talked to doctors who take the attitude, "You can prove anything you want to with numbers." So, I don't think that's necessarily going to be convincing to someone starting with the assumption that there has to be medical care as a basic standard for society. Generally I have found that when a person has that basic assumption, it really hasn't mattered how much evidence the church has offered about how well it's doing for children.

I think part of the problem is that it's very hard to do any kind of demographic studies of this church because it's forbidden to give out numbers. So when someone with a scientific mindset oriented toward numbers and percentages looks, all one can say is, "Well, all we hear is anecdote and claim. We're not seeing anything we can test, that we can verify, nothing we can independently study."

TALBOT: We have done an empirical analysis on testimonies published in the [church] periodicals in the last twenty years. We've got around 2,400 healings that were medically diagnosed. Looking at those and the large numbers that were life-threatening or supposedly terminal, I think it's more difficult for critics to sweep this under the carpet and say, "Well, those are just anecdotes, or they could have been spontaneous remission or misdiagnosis." At some point, with enough volume of medically diagnosed conditions I think some fair-minded people are going to say: "Maybe something is happening here that we should at least look at; we should look at the evidence." I'm grateful to say that there are instances where people seem to have enough integrity that they want to know, and they're exploring it further than a few years ago.

What about the study that was just in the Journal of the American Medical Association *that tended to indicate a slightly lower longevity for Christian Scientists?*

TALBOT: We were very disappointed in *JAMA*'s publication of that. We, along with others, pointed out to them very significant flaws that a credible medical magazine should not have let slip by. We went to the statisticians at the *New England Journal of Medicine* to be sure we weren't overlooking something, and their view was that it was fatally flawed and it would never have been published in their publication.

Let me give you just one example, the most obvious that everyone picked up right away: They could not find all of the former students. [According to Talbot, in calculating the probable death rates of the missing students, the study's author did not structure in a probable rate of increase of death as he went back through the decades. Logic would dictate that deaths would increase with age. Figures for Principia accounted for all but 3 percent of the student body; for Kansas, the figure was 13 percent.]

We reworked the figures, assuming there was only a slightly higher percentage—10 percent—of deaths among the missing students, and it produced the very opposite conclusion the author had announced. We wrote to *JAMA*, we told them about this. We asked to have an article that gave some balance to this. They declined. Right now they're indicating the possibility of a brief letter to the editor.

People are establishing public policy on the basis of a study that was done by someone with a very specific point of view—someone who left Christian Science and is publishing articles with a specific attitude toward Christian Science. (The author was a Principia graduate). It's unfortunate.

I've almost been surprised at how people have grabbed on to that study and haven't thought about the implications of the fact that it doesn't have the kind of checking and challenge of the kind of study that a medical magazine like *JAMA* would normally require.

But they can't do that because you won't give them—

TALBOT: The things they let go in his study and accepted as legitimate are appalling. They would never have done that if it had been a study drawing conclusions about AIDS or cancer.

Let's assume it had been just the opposite conclusion. Would they have published *that* study in *JAMA?* I don't think too many people think so. I think they would have looked much more closely at the strength of the evidence. I think they would have questioned the weaknesses in his study.

The other study that's relevant that's come out recently is on Mormon longevity.[1] The argument that can be made is that both Christian Scientists and Mormons have similar lifestyles and Mormons have a significantly greater longevity and lower rates of cancer and heart disease. Even presuming that the study from JAMA were skewed in your favor, it probably wouldn't add up to that kind of longevity that the Mormons—

TALBOT: I don't know actually. . . . We've never claimed that we're living a lot longer. Christian Scientists feel deeply that on the whole this system has worked better for them. Not that we haven't had losses and not that we haven't had challenges, but I think that they're talking about more than just the body's function.

I suppose you could have ten people saved by medical care who were on some machinery and in a vegetative state, and yet it could be said that medicine saved all of those ten people. If Christian Science saves eight people, you'd want to know, "Well what kind of life are they living? What about some of the values of life?" You'd have to look at more of the picture than just some of the raw evidence that we often read about.

I think Christian Scientists would tend to say that it's a whole way of living that is so important to them in addition to the healing. [In] prosecuting those who are choosing this whole way of life, there's probably more that should be looked at. We're talking not just about children's welfare—although we wouldn't by any means want to eliminate that. We're talking about upbringing, values that are taught. We're talking about what a healing means in terms of spiritual and moral strengthening of a child. We're talking about a lot more than what a drug does to symptoms. If a child is healed of a cold in Christian Science, to us the significance is much deeper than if a certain pill will subdue the symptoms temporarily.

In our society, which seems so taken with the body and its condition, we don't want to lose sight of the fact that there is not only our [physical] well-being, but a whole sense of what it means to live a satisfying and fulfilling life. That has to be taken into account, and it almost seems as though that's being pushed aside as though it doesn't weigh with other factors.

But the question is for public policy makers who are in a position where they have to judge the relative effectiveness of one thing versus another thing, in a situation where you do have children involved.

Now as I understand it, in Canada, medical treatment is required for children? Yet there are active and thriving Christian Science communities there.

TALBOT: I think it always has been. England is another example.

Two points: First, it *hasn't* thrived as it has in the United States; and, second, it's our general sense that both Canada and England are much less aggressive in their intervention-oriented medical view of things. In this country a child can be clipped right out of the home and put in the hospital by a social worker in nothing flat—regardless of the parents' views. In Canada and England you probably have a doctor saying to the parents: "Keep working with the child for a while; let's just see how things come along." Maybe through a phone call. Not that there aren't exceptions, but there's very different overall feel to the aggressiveness of the medical intervention.

When a Christian Scientist is placed in a situation where care is mandated— when the scientist is under duress—that's the only circumstance in which you can continue to have Christian Science treatment and medical treatment simultaneously.

TALBOT: If he truly wants Christian Science treatment, and if he's been given care against his will, I think most practitioners would probably feel they could still be helpful in the case. But if that patient becomes the battleground between a medical approach and a Christian Science approach, [continuing Christian Science treatment of the patient is] probably not going to be helpful—and in fact it could be harmful. Our primary sense is to be concerned about the patient's welfare.

In Canada and Great Britain, where medical care is mandated, there can still be Christian Science treatment along with medical care.

TALBOT: You could find instances where practitioners even here would take a case: If a family is in an automobile accident and taken to the hospital [because] the authorities who pick them up won't let them go to a Christian Science care facility. It's quite likely the family may still want to rely on Christian Science, if the care is being forced on them.

In some areas in society there has been a growing respect; certainly in the legislative area. There has been a developing willingness to provide room for a responsible approach to spiritual healing.

There are those who are working very, very actively to get those laws off the books; but there are more of them each year. It would be rare we would ever go out and try to get a law on the books. What usually happens is that some medical group asks for some medical legislation. We become aware of it. We go to the legislature and say, "This is going to cause us to have to conform to a medical approach. May we have room to continue practicing spiritual healing?" And usually the legislature will make room.

I talked to people up in Sacramento who said that Christian Science had probably the most effective political lobbying organization that they'd ever seen.

TALBOT: (Laughs) If that's true, it's because it is genuine, democratic, real people contacting our legislators. We're very different from what you normally think of as lobbyists. There is never any wining or dining. We've always operated on the basis of the merits of our arguments.

There's another factor that comes into play in all of this, and that's the constitutional freedom, the free exercise of religion. We don't ever ask for the uninhibited right to do anything. We think there is a responsible approach to spiritual healing, and that we shouldn't have our practice of religion infringed upon if this truly is a responsible practice.

And how can you tell? You have to start gathering and looking at the evidence. And that's what earlier has concerned me, how few people were interested in the evidence.

*But you get back to the question of evidence and you have to have some
kind of a basis to draw from. The police asked Mrs Glaser: "Does
the church ever publish testimonials of failed healings? You're only talking
about the successes; what about the failures?" If you're looking at just
successes, you'll hear testimonials of success when you go to any church,
any religion, of any persuasion. People don't talk about failures. You
have to do some kind of study with numbers that looks at the total population.*

TALBOT: We have never been a statistically minded church. We are being
called upon to help the public understand almost from ground zero. Instead
of assuming that there is no evidence, there needs to be a willingness
to say: "Let's work together. Let's start looking at ways to gather evidence."

A very significant portion of our population hears about the failures
of Christian Science. The church tries to give some balance to that and
to show that there are some healings. Only a tiny proportion of the people
hear about the healing, but everybody knows the failures. Since 1983, the
failures have been publicized heavily. We've got thousands of clippings about
the failures. It is extremely rare that anyone pays any attention to the healing.

I know of two examples in the last five years: An East Coast newspaper
on the East Coast ran a story about a [Christian Science practitioner]
who fell three stories and was rushed to the hospital. He told the doctor
he did not want medical care; he wanted to handle it through Christian
Science. The doctor was sure he was going to die. A wonderful healing
came out of it, and a reporter found out and did a story. There was also
a one-line mention somewhere here in Southern California four or five
years ago about a lady healed of blindness. But that's all. I would be happy
for people to have a more balanced perspective. I certainly have no doubts
about Christian Scientists constantly hearing about the failures.

I can also think of instances in the periodicals where people have talked
about failures and how they've handled the grief, how they've dealt with
it. That is not a statistical showing—but again, where do we go from
here? If people really want some idea as to where we are, I think they
should be more seriously trying to gather some evidence.

Generally the public assumption is so strong that only one kind of
healing ought to be considered that people just aren't thinking in terms
of even gathering evidence.

*But how do you do it so that you can come up with a standard of
evidence that'll be—*

TALBOT: One thing we can do is this twenty-year study we've done. . . . I
talked with a few doctors who have said that they can't just ignore this

evidence. These 2,400 cases are all coming from doctors. When you look at them—when you look at the [healings of] cancer, multiple sclerosis, meningitis, virtually every life-threatening disease you can imagine—I think a fair-minded person would say, "It's likely that there's something more here than just misdiagnosis, and just spontaneous remissions perhaps."

[Particularly] interesting as far as the argument about spontaneous remission is the section on broken bones. There were several hundred examples of broken bones that had been X-rayed and the individual decided to rely on Christian Science, and within hours new X-rays were taken and bones were healed and knit. Those are probably some of the hardest for the critics to ignore. But then anyone who is critical enough can ignore almost anything. We're just looking for a broad fair-minded attitude.

Now as for [comparing] success with failures, we've really looked hard at how we can go about doing that, and it has not been easy. We don't check into members' lives. We don't know all the failures, obviously. But we don't know all the successes either.

We do feel sure about the number of losses of children up to the age 14. Records from the Department of Health and Human Services show over 50,000 children 14 and under are lost each year under medical care. It's something like 51 per 100,000—which isn't bad. I think the public generally is satisfied with that loss rate. We think ours is approximately 23 per 100,000.

Now there aren't a hundred thousand children out there to gauge it from, but we've looked at Sunday School enrollment and compared that to the losses we've had, taking into account that some of those parents would have turned to medical care, taking into account that some of the parents are Scientists and some not. This was the most honest sort of figure we could come up with. A critic might say, "Well, we don't know for sure that those are the only losses. You could have more." We can't give a person an iron-clad guarantee. All we can do is say what we honestly believe. And given the close attention that has come to losses without medical care, specifically if they're Christian Scientists, as nearly as we can find, the authorities have not missed one. I don't see any way for even the strongest critic to honestly say that we are doing worse than the rest of society.

And frankly I think we're doing much better: That's why you'll find we're concerned about more losses if we get pushed into a medical approach. It's a pragmatic attitude to some extent. It isn't just a dogmatic, religious dogmatic sort of thing. It's what going to be best in saving children's lives.

I think that's very hard for people who don't believe in spiritual healing to accept. I think they think we've got some sort of a religious viewpoint that it would be against God's will to take medicine, and so we just withhold medicine from the child and whatever happens is God's will. There couldn't be anything further from the truth. You heard Lise said this morning that if a parent really feels a doctor's going to do a better job, I think that parent, whatever his religion, is going to go to the doctor.

But given all the evidence, Christian Scientists—and I don't think without pretty good reason—tend to feel that on the whole, this method for a hundred years has proven itself to be a pretty dependable method. Christian Scientists aren't oblivious to the fact that, like doctors, we've had losses. When they're dealing with a serious child case, they're naturally going to do what they think is going to save that child's life. If they think Christian Science is more likely to save the child's life, then it's less likely a parent's going to something they think will loose the child's life.

A few courts even have talked about martyring the child's life, that there's no right to do that. Our feeling is that if we over the last hundred years had been always forced into a medical approach, more children would have been martyred to medical technology. The only thing about it is people would not have complained, because when children are lost under medical care, it's acceptable.

I know in this case, both before and after the baby died, Mrs. Scott called the COP. What is the COP's role in all of this—generically? Why are practitioners told to call? And what does the COP do?

TALBOT: First, there are some issues that we want to be sure parents are aware of. Let me give you an example: In Massachusetts the legislative provision for spiritual healing says the practitioner has to be accredited, and we would want parents to know that. If the parents had a practitioner who was not *Journal*-listed, we wouldn't tell them they shouldn't have that; we just want them to know what the Legislature requires if they want to be brought within that protection. We don't want someone later on telling us, "Why didn't you tell us that?"

But the larger reason and the more basic reason is that the church is part of a whole support system. The medical profession has a support system: You have a nurse; you have a doctor; you have a whole bunch of folks. With us you have a Christian Science practitioner, she's part of the support system, or he is, You have a Christian Science nurse. You may have a care facility. But you have the church too. And whenever the Committee on Publication is notified, that is a way of sort of bringing the church to support the parent. That may be in terms of comforting the practitioner or parent—whichever calls. A church is all about people caring for each other, and [from] the calls I get, that really is my more underlying feeling. I just want people to know that their church cares about them.

There isn't any other necessarily specific contact. But we do want them to know there is a resource, that the church cares. That's the more basic, which is a more spiritual reason, really.

Wouldn't part of it also be to work metaphysically to defend the church against attack?

TALBOT: I would have described it a little different. I would say is that in a serious child's case, from a Christian Science perspective, you've got a whole lot of forces of thought operating, and sometimes the church or the Committee on Publication will have a broad perspective of what some of the ways [are] that he might pray about the situation. He's [the COP's] not praying so much for the child. [That's the] practitioner's job. The church has a broader perspective in many respects, and that that can be valuable. So that's why I see it as part of the support system. It has made a real difference in our movement over the decades for practitioners to be brought in for the church through the committee office. I think it's made a real difference in terms of what we see as a very good record with children. I don't have any doubt in my mind. There have been lots of cases that would've been lost without the whole support system working. Even lost under medical care.

With numbers so hard to come by, trying to take any kind of a quantitative look at the movement, what I wound up doing was looking at churches, societies, practitioners, and teachers over a thirty-year period going through the Journals. *It's real clear that several things are happening. One is that there are fewer churches and societies, fewer practitioners.*

TALBOT: Yes.

And that there seems to be a big migration toward the Sunbelt, that to a demographer would indicate aging—traditional retirement areas. What's happening with the church?

TALBOT: Well, I hadn't looked at that aspect, the migration question. It is true, I think for a person to go through the *Journal* I think that's exactly what you would find. I'd be a little cautious about all of the conclusions. It certainly tells us is that what is represented by a listing in the *Journal*, which means an ability to be full-time available in the practice, there are fewer people. But I balance that with the fact that there are a lot of people who are practicing part-time, and they don't appear in the *Journal*. How many there are, I don't know. At meetings that were held in recent years for those who are giving time to the practice, over the period of a couple of years which those meetings went on in different regions, something like 10,000 attended.[2] So I do know there are a lot of people out there, although I wouldn't underestimate the fact that there are fewer who are giving their full time.

There're fewer churches.

TALBOT: But that also indicates something about people and formalized organized activity. There is certainly evidence that there are plenty of people around who are reading, studying, and practicing healing to some extent but not formally associated with the Church. But I don't think it changes the fact that for whatever the reason there are fewer listed. I see it as some parallel with some other churches. Catholic priests and nuns. I see a lot of areas where even some Protestant churches that have had dwindling membership. Although some others have had growing.

The Mormons are.

TALBOT: Yes, the Mormons are. And some fundamentalist groups.

So, where do we stand? I find that's pretty hard. I try to be a little careful. I don't want to be alarmed on statistics that may have balancing factors, but I don't want to be naive about implications. I find myself standing in about a middle ground: Not feeling either naive or alarmed, but feeling that we've got lots of work to do.

Our movement has never been large. We have always been somewhere in the ballpark of what we are now. Our swings have not been as drastic as people say. We're a modest-sized group of people. But that has never been the determining factor for us. Mrs. Eddy put that provision in the *Manual* about not numbering the people. She did it when the church was growing very fast, and I think there's a lot of wisdom in that. I think it's much more important for us to say: What are we contributing to society? When I look back at what has happened to spiritual healing since Christian Science came on the scene, I think we have had a very significant impact on Christian healing, [especially] in the last ten years even. I have even found that these court cases have stirred a lot of people to start thinking more about spiritual healing. And they should.

Right here in Santa Monica today, if Methodists had been praying [for a child] and [death followed] a twenty-seven-hour illness, would they have been prosecuted? They might have been, even if they normally would have used medicine. What does this say about the whole idea of any Christian who finds it natural to pray for their children? If a child happens to die while you're praying, unexpectedly?

But the Methodist can still take the child to a doctor and pray, because the way they conceive prayer is different than—

TALBOT: That's right. But they might not have. There are lots of instances where a child suddenly dies. I think this case has some implications for those folks, even if they would have gone to the doctor otherwise. The prosecutors I have talked to—and I've talked to a number of them—feel strongly that no matter how much a parent might feel that prayer has a role to play: "Their thought should be medicine—that is the answer."

If you take that to the point of prosecuting parents, the idea really is to crowd praying out, at least in a very practical sense. You might give lip service to it, but if parents are afraid of going to prison if they happen to be praying, there are not too many options. I see all this having a lot to do not just with whether Christian Science treatment is acceptable in society, but what about prayer in our society? I don't think it's an irrational argument to say that prayer is being prosecuted. It's considered such a weak alternative to modern technology that there's an effort to crowd it out of the picture. That's pretty chilling for a religion whose members are basing their whole lives on a sense of praying about issues. Especially the ones they care most about, like their children.

So is it in the best interest of society to prosecute the parents if a child dies under Christian Science treatment? I don't think that question's really being examined thoroughly. I think the real interest is the interest in promoting and sanctioning one method of healing.

Dr. Robert Mendlesohn is a pediatrician in Chicago. He's written several books, and he's a guy who is willing to say things not all doctors will say. He wrote a nationally syndicated column that said what's happening with Christian Science is that the religion of modern medicine is attempting to establish hegemony over other religions.[3] When I read that, I thought, "My gosh, that's kind of a bold statement to make." He said both medicine and Christian Science are belief systems, and you've got one attempting to control the other. There's some truth to what he was saying: He was raising a question people need to think seriously about.

A little closer to home, Dr. Eugene D. Robin of Stanford Medical School, wrote that if doctors were held to the same standards these Christian Scientists are being called on to adhere to in these trials, there would not be enough jails to hold all us doctors.[4] And that's almost an exact quote.

It's interesting to see that some doctors are concerned about what's happening here.

In the Manual *Mrs. Eddy states that COPs should preferably be male, and the overwhelming majority is male. But if you look at the practitioners as a population, it's about 87 percent women, about 13 percent male.*

TALBOT: I'm really in the minority I guess.

And if you look at the teachers, it's a male majority by one.

TALBOT: So it's about equal.

But a majority male.

TALBOT: Probably that's because when they draw the class together, probably they try to balance the class with men and women would be my guess.

The same with the COPs. And the other thing—has there ever been a majority of women on the board?

TALBOT: No. There are two women and three men. There's certainly no rule that would prevent that.

I don't know just exactly what Mrs. Eddy was thinking of on that question about the committees. She was a realist in lots of ways. She was down to earth and had a very realistic view of things. It might have been that she simply felt that given our world, even with women's lib and everything else, that there might be some logic in putting men in this particular position. There are lots of challenges in dealing with some of the hostile critics, and she might have felt that in that battle, men needed to be willing to be right up front there. I really don't know just what all was in her thought.

I think the average conception of Christian Science is that it's a woman's religion. And you certainly get that idea going into the church because there tend to be a lot more women in the pews.

TALBOT: Right.

And in the practitioner's offices, too. Yet when you look at the administrative hierarchy, as soon as you hit the teacher level on up, it's always a male majority.

TALBOT: I think there may be some truth to that, although I've never counted or tended to look through lists. But I have a feeling it's changing.

When Mrs. Eddy she established the roles of First and Second Reader, she wanted one a man and one a woman, and she didn't say which should be which. She did talk about the most spiritually minded being the First Reader. But to me that's a little clue that she saw a certain kind of equality there, and I have the feeling it's less important to us as time goes on.

The church was also started at a time when women didn't have the vote. And didn't have political power. And it raises questions about how much of that might have been relative to the time frame.

One of the big differences between Christian Science and Mormonism is that Christian Science is essentially a complete and final revelation, governed by a Manual, which is unalterable. Mormonism allows revisions. Blacks couldn't be in the priesthood, and then they could be. Their president, the head of the Council of the Apostles, is conceived of as having the same revelatory powers as Joseph Smith and Brigham Young.

TALBOT: As far as the theology of Christian Science, that's established. Now as far as the *Manual* goes, I have heard people outside the church comment on the fact that this remarkably slim little document makes room in its relatively modest provisions to govern an entire denomination, making lots of room for the church to function and operate as society evolves.

Talking about men and women in the church in various positions, it might have been our church sort of reflecting society to some extent. You look at organizations and all through society you might have found men holding those positions and women more often at home. And maybe just [being] part of changing society, we'll tend to reflect that back and forth. But if anything, our church would have made room for women to hold room at the top. It certainly wouldn't have discouraged it. So that's going to change.

But that isn't part of the revelation. That's more the human application. I see lots of room for the human application within our church structure.

But also I don't see the church as playing the role that it does for many other people. I think in some ways it's more significant; in other ways, Christian Scientists—people who study it, practice it, live it—aren't necessarily going to be involved in church. I can't think of anywhere Mrs. Eddy ever said that one's salvation depended on church membership, where in many churches that would be part of their teaching.

I think Christian Scientists more often might feel it is a blessing, a special opportunity to participate. [For me] it's been a wonderful sort of working relationship with others and [a] learning process to serve the church. But I still see my basic work as being out in the field as a practitioner, and I'll go back out in the field one of these days. I see that as my highest calling is the healing ministry, and that's the theological heartbeat of our church. If we haven't got healing going on, then the church really doesn't have the framework it needs to hold it together, which is why these cases are particularly important to us.

Presuming that the worst did come to worst and the courts said, well okay, you have to have medical treatment for the children? Obviously the examples of Canada and Great Britain show the movement would adapt.

TALBOT: I know what we would do. We would go right back to the legislature, just as we've always done. We wouldn't see ourselves as fixed in that position.

Historically, the legislatures which reflect more the will of the people have tended to make room for spiritual healing. For five years now the critics have been mounting a remarkable effort to get the laws off the book, but I don't know of a single example where that has happened. In a couple of instances the wording has been watered a little bit, made a little less clear. But I know of dozens of examples where over these five years the legislatures have continued making more room. One of the most significant examples happened a few months ago in Texas. That was one state out of fifty. That was the major one out of fifty states in our whole history where we never had protection for the care of children, and this year the Texas legislature placed some very strong protection in its laws against prosecution. While I see a lot of effort being made to stop the protection, I don't see that it has been that successful. I can't say it's not going to happen. I can't say there won't be examples where a few laws are lost here and there, but certainly the whole thrust of things has clearly continued to be in the direction of at a grass roots level society saying, we will make room for this healing.

Do you know we have a bill here in the [California] legislature right now? We don't know what's going to happen, [but if we lose] we'll probably keep coming back each year. Right now the bill would effectively overturn the *Walker* decision.

The *Walker* decision is very interesting. What the court says is "This is what you Christian Scientists are saying—that's not what the legislature meant." Well, we won't disagree with the court, but we know what we talked over with the legislature. John Knox, the assemblyman who carried the [original exemption] bill, testified about what the legislature intended. They did not want Christian Scientists criminalized for practicing spiritual healing.

That's a very delicate subject nowadays, and it's being worked out day-by-day and month-by-month. We've had temporary setbacks in Florida and Santa Rosa—we think there should have been total acquittal. But in all three of the cases where there has been a trial court resolution, the manslaughter charge has been thrown out. No one has wanted to criminalize us with manslaughter. With the lesser charge of child endangerment, in all three cases that has to some extent stood. Whether it'll stand on appeal is still in question, and some of these cases could eventually get to the U.S. Supreme Court.

The Supreme Court has said "You can't martyr your child." Nobody's disagreeing with that. The critics are trying to put it in that framework. They're saying "This is really children's rights versus church's rights, or a child's right to live versus a parent's right to have dogmatic religious conviction." As long as it can be kept in that framework, I think we're going to find it very challenging. But I think the real question is, what is best for the child? What's the most effective care?

But is anybody going to really listen unless you come up with numbers?

TALBOT: No. I think we've got to come up with numbers. And we are starting to [do that]. You can always say, "But there are some limitations." My answer is, "We're just beginning in these last couple of years starting from scratch."

We aren't necessarily going to come up with what a doctor's numbers would look like with a controlled laboratory experiment. But, I'm not convinced that society necessarily thinks that is the only way to assess an issue. As people in this office have explored this whole thing, we've become very interested in how much decision-making is made in the medical field on the basis of what they are calling our "anecdotal evidence." It's quite remarkable. "Anecdotal evidence" has almost become something a doctor uses to [dismiss] anything he doesn't want to deal with—when at the same time medicine is using a lot of anecdotal evidence.

I know of one doctor who wanted to do a study on us. I don't know how far he's going to go on it. [He's] very friendly and is convinced that we have a lot less trouble in childbirth than the general public. He's interviewed Christian Science practitioners and nurses and doctors who have delivered Christian Science children, and he talked about writing an article for the *New England Journal of Medicine* that would be based on anecdotal evidence.

I raised the question with him, "Gee, I thought that was kind of anathema to doctors." I don't remember his exact words—but my impression was that there is a place for anecdotal evidence. You have to determine how much weight to give to it, but you don't want to ignore all the various kinds of evidence.

We all want to be real careful as we look at the whole realm of spiritual healing and what it means to society that we not just rule out a kind of evidence just because it happens not be medical. I don't anticipate that what courts or legislatures or others will ultimately be willing to accept will necessarily just be what a doctor says has to be his kind of evidence.

I think that pretty well covers my bases.

TALBOT: I understand that in your book you're going to deal with a number of areas. Christian Scientists—and this is more the official perspective— tend to feel sometimes sensitive to being discussed in the context of a couple of the other examples you've described. The reason is because sometimes there've been television shows where they've had a psychiatrist, where they've had a guy that practices acupuncture, they've had a holistic medical practitioner, and they've wanted a Christian Scientist. We haven't always participated in that if we think it sets us up as just one more thing people can pick from.

We don't want to mislead society and say, "Well try Christian Science, or try that." It calls for a kind of commitment and it's such a whole way of life that people need to know that it isn't just part of the cafeteria you can pick from. So as you're thinking through this, that you find a way—we would consider ourselves quite distinct in terms of a whole way of life rather than a method, just a method of healing.

I try to draw the distinctions clearly.

TALBOT: In fact, you can do a lot more in a book in trying to discuss issues than a short newspaper article. I've seen a lot of newspaper articles that I shake my head over. However, even though we've gotten some real hard press, I still feel a real gratitude for the press. I'd hate to think of our country without a free press. It can be a challenging context to work within, and I do work quite a bit with the press, and we just have to take our knocks. At least when we perceive we're not well represented, we just realize we've got to come back and keep doing a better job of explaining ourselves, and it's not easy to explain Christian Science. I mean, at least you've got one leg up in having some background, and some perception of where Christian Science is coming from. You take a jury, take the trial setting. I would say that is perhaps the most difficult and challenging context in which to try to help people understand Christian Science. Almost impossible really. And yet the attorneys are working at it.

NOTES

1. Published in the *Journal of the National Cancer Institute*, 6 December 1989.
2. I was one who attended such meetings, when I was a Christian Scientist.
3. This article appeared in a number of newspapers on or around 10 March 1988.
4. Dr. Robin's article appeared in the Riverside, California, *Press-Enterprise*, 13 June 1988.

SUGGESTED READINGS

For a further exploration of some of the issues raised in *Deadly Blessings*, the reader is referred to the following sources:

CRITICAL THOUGHT

Claims of the miraculous must be thoughtfully examined; yet the skills needed for such an examination are woefully lacking in the mass culture of the Electronic Age. Why? Perhaps because critical thought is dangerous to social structures that rely on the unquestioning acceptance of questionable claims of the sort that prevail in commerce, politics, and all spheres of social life.

Influence, How and Why People Agree to Things, by Robert B. Cialdini. New York: Morrow, 1984. One of the most important yet overlooked books of recent years, *Influence* is nothing less than a consumer's guide to the process of choice. A social psychologist and a clear writer, Cialdini has synthesized the fruits of decades of research into an account enabling anyone to understand how and why they can be motivated by others, often against their own interests. His book is as much about Jonestown as it is about buying a deodorant or a used car, and it answers some of the most perplexing social questions now facing society.

Vital Lies, Simple Truths: The Psychology of Self-Deception, Daniel Goleman. New York: Simon and Schuster, 1985. A psychologist (he taught at Harvard) and journalist (his present employer is the *New York Times*), Goleman draws on contemporary research to give a clear, concise account of our extraordinary ability to create *schemas,* cognitive structures that shape the experience of the moment, recall of the past, and anticipation of the future. Of special interest are sections recounting the extreme fallibility of memory.

Filters Against Folly: How to Survive Despite Economists, Ecologists, and the Merely Eloquent, by Garrett Hardin. New York: Viking, 1985. An ecologist, Hardin proposes that no human problem can be reasonably assessed without a three-filter approach: literacy (ability to communicate an idea in words), numeracy (the ability to test and quantify claims), and ecolacy (the recognition that intentional causes invariably produce unintentional effects). A fundamental work of critical thought.

Enhancing Human Performance: Issues, Theories, and Techniques, Daniel Druckman and John A. Swets, eds. Washington: National Academy Press, 1988. The National Research Council, a branch of the National Academy of Sciences, was commissioned by the Army to look into various techniques claimed to improve physical and mental skills of the sort needed by combat soldiers, strategists, and spies. Particularly interesting are sections dealing with paranormal powers (psychic spoon-bending and the like) and a supplemental paper on the nature of anecdotal evidence.

Innumeracy: Mathematical Illiteracy and its Consequences, by John Allen Paulos. New York: Hill and Wang, 1988. A mathematician and writer, Paulos demystifies the realm of numbers and allows a reader with little mathematical background to understand what numbers mean and have to tell us about the world.

Flanagan's Version: A Spectator's Guide to Science on the Eve of the 21st Century, Dennis Flanagan. New York: Alfred A. Knopf, 1988. A cofounder and editor of *Scientific American*, Flanagan is a superb journalist whose unique multidisciplinary, common language approach to science communication reveals the developing patterns behind the startling discoveries of modern science.

CULTS/GROUPS

Individuals cannot be understood outside the context of the groups in which they find themselves. A "cult" is a group which holds different values and beliefs from the cultural mainstream; today's cult may be tomorrow's culture.

Cults: Faith, Healing, and Coercion, by Marc Gallanter. New York, Oxford: Oxford University Press, 1989. A psychiatrist who has studied two widely known charismatic religions (the "Moonies" and the Divine Light Mission), as well as Alcoholics Anonymous, explores the personal, cultural, and biological roots of the cult phenomenon. Highly valuable.

White Night, by John Peer Nugent. New York: Rawson Wade, 1979. A gifted journalist's examination of the tragedy of the Rev. Jim Jones and the People's Temple. Jones was a charismatic leader who managed to combine the skills of a California cult leader, a psychic surgeon—he performed psychic surgery during some church services—and a savvy political strategist.

Combating Cult Mind Control, by Steve Hassan. Rochester, Vermont: Park Street Press, 1988. Hassan is an "exit counsellor," a former high-ranking Moonie who now specializes in helping others leave cults. Unlike the so-called "deprogrammers," Hassan believes coercion is an unacceptable method for pulling members out of charismatic groups. He has some very clear insights on the "group conversion" process.

Snapping: America's Epidemic of Sudden Personality Change, Flo Conway and Jim Siegelman. Philadelphia and New York: J. J. Lippincott, 1978. One of the first examinations of the cult conversion experience, which the authors describe as a kind of "information disease."

Cults in America: Programmed for Paradise, by Willa Appel. New York: Holt, Rinehart and Winston: 1983. An anthropologist's plain-language examination of the cult phenomenon, with a valuable section on the physiology of brainwashing.

Thought Reform and the Psychology of Totalism: A Study of "Brainwashing" in China, by Robert J. Lifton. New York: The Norton Library, 1969. First published in 1961, Lifton's study of the forced conversion of both Western and Chinese prisoners to Maoist orthodoxy is, in fact, a study of cults. His findings have broad application, as do his later studies of Hiroshima victims (*Death in Life: Survivors of Hiroshima*) and Nazi death camp physicians (*The Nazi Doctors: Medical Killing and the Psychology of Genocide*).

The Healing Web: Social Networks and Human Survival, by Marc Pilisuk and Susan Hillier Parks. Hanover N.H.: University Press of New England, 1986. A penetrating study of the role groups play in maintaining psychological and physical health. Especially significant are the authors' insights on the cross-cultural nature of groups.

PSYCHEDELIC DRUGS

The Acid Age awakened millions to the illusory nature of many prevailing cultural beliefs, but for many the experience ended in a flight to other, equally illusory beliefs.

Acid Dreams, The CIA, LSD and the Sixties Rebellion, by Martin A. Lee and Bruce Shlain. New York: Grove Press, 1985. A wonderful social history of the psychedelic revolution and the bizarre twists woven into the script by the savants of the Central Intelligence Agency. An essential document for placing the drug within the context of an age.

Storming Heaven: LSD and the American Dream, by Jay Stevens. New York: Perennial Library (Harper & Row), 1988. Although it covers much of the same ground as *Acid Dreams,* Stevens mentions Dr. Eisner and her place in the Westwood group.

Journey into Madness: The True Story of Secret CIA Mind Control and Medical Abuse, by Gordon Thomas. New York: Bantam, 1989. The tragic story of the patients of world-renowned psychiatrist D. Ewen Cameron, who used CIA sponsorship and a Canadian mental hospital to conduct bizarre brainwashing and conditioning experiments with LSD and other drugs in the 1950s.

LSD Psychotherapy: An Exploration of Psychedelic and Psycholytic Therapy, by W. V. Caldwell. New York: Grove Press, 1968. Caldwell's laudatory treatment of mind-altering drugs is notable as a mass market book that prominently featured the work of Dr. Eisner, and which was responsible for drawing many members to Group (including Hank Walker and Marty Goldstein). An influential work, written at the height of the psychedelic revolution.

My Self and I, Constance A. Newland (Thelma Moss). New York: Coward McCann, 1962. Psychedelic-drug therapy in the Westwood model, similar to that practiced by Dr. Eisner and Oscar Janiger. "Newland," an actress who became a psychologist as the result of her experience, was a friend of Leo Breiman (who sat on her doctoral committee at UCLA), and attended several Group social functions.

Intoxication: Life in Pursuit of Artificial Paradise, by Ronald K. Siegel. New York: Dutton, 1989. A UCLA psychologist and former colleague of Dr. Eisner, Siegel is considered the world's leading authority on mind-altering drugs. He argues that intoxication, far from being a "deviation," is a basic organic drive found not only in humans but in other members of the animal kingdom. Solid, well-written, and provocative.

The Drug Experience: First-Person Accounts of Addicts, Writers, Scientists, and Others, David Ebin, ed. New York: Evergreen Black Cat, 1965. Originally published in 1961, in the days when LSD research was very much alive, Ebin's anthology reflects the exuberance and optimism of the day. Dr. Eisner's talk at the second Josiah Macy Foundation conference on LSD is quoted. Allen Ginsberg and Aldous Huxley are also quoted.

THE "NEW AGE"

A definitive history of the New Age movement remains to be written. Until it is, the following works give good descriptions as to what the movement is, what it claims to be, and how these claims stand up to serious scientific scrutiny.

Going Within: A Guide for Inner Transformation, by Shirley MacLaine. New York: Bantam, 1989. The unintentionally tragic story of a self-absorbed celebrity who falls prey to today's most flagrant (and wealthy) practitioner of psychic surgery, the Rev. Alex Orbito. Full of inaccuracies, but revealing as a sadly sincere account of the most prominent of the New Age advocates.

The Aquarian Conspiracy: Personal and Social Transformation in the 1980's, by Marilyn Ferguson. Los Angeles: J. P. Tarcher, 1980. The volume most responsible for popularizing the New Age movement, tracing (incompletely) the origins of anything-is-possible thinking to the LSD revolution and showing its gradual penetration of the establishment.

The New Age Catalogue, by the editors of *Body, Mind and Spirit* magazine, New York: Dolphin Doubleday, 1988. An unabashedly uncritical account of the wide diversity of ancient and modern myth and pseudoscience at the core of the movement.

Not Necessarily the New Age: Critical Essays, Robert Basil, ed. Buffalo, N.Y.: Prometheus Books, 1988. The best single collection of criticism on the New Age movement, written primarily from a skeptical perspective. The most significant essay is "The Occult Establishment," by the late James Webb, surveying the old origins of the New Age. Other essayists include Martin Gardner, Carl Sagan, Ted Schultz, and J. Gordon Melton. A must for anyone who wants to understand the reality behind the claims of MacLaine, Ferguson, et al. Flawed only in its lack of an index.

Understanding the New Age, by Russell Chandler. Dallas: Word Publishing, 1988. As religion writer for the *Los Angeles Times*, Russell Chandler dwells in the heart of lotus-land, and has encountered first-hand many of the most prominent New Agers. Chandler gives a broad overview, reserving the last chapters for his evangelical Christian judgments. No index.

The Fringes of Reason: a Whole Earth Catalog, Ted Schultz, ed., New York: Harmony Books, 1989. A one-time believer in the magical claims of the New Age, Schultz became a skeptic with the insight of a former insider. *Whole Earth Catalog* was the inspiration for millions in the Acid Generation, but Schultz's anthology flows against the countercultural stream, while still presenting fairly the ideas of believers.

The Upstart Spring: Esalen and the American Awakening, Walter Truett Anderson. Reading, Mass.: Addison-Wesley, 1983. Located on a bluff atop a rugged Central California seacoast, Esalen Institute played a seminal role it the events of the '60s and '70s. The prototypical "growth center," with its nude baths and endless rap sessions, Esalen has been haven to psychologists, physicians, mystics, visionaries, acid trippers, and rock musicians. Dr. Betty Grover Eisner was an occasional visitor, as were most of the pioneer acid therapists and many of the key figures in the emerging New Age movement.

The Spiritualists: The Passion for the Occult in the Nineteenth and Twentieth Centuries, Ruth Brandon. New York: Alfred A. Knopf, 1983. Today's "channellers" are yesterday's "mediums"; the "New Age" is merely the latest incarnation of what earlier decades labeled "spiritualism." With the exception of psychic surgeons like Brother Joe and sleight-of-hand artists like Uri Geller, today's "channellers" have largely forsaken one of the spiritualist's primary claims— the ability to "materialize" spiritual forms, to give them sensible, tangible reality. Brandon's book shows why: with no exceptions, the claims of the spiritualists were fraudulent. Her delightful historical account describes the gullible, the gullers, and the inevitable debunking (despite which many believers remain).

PSYCHIC SURGERY

An "Old Age" fraud that has found new life in the New Age, psychic surgery appeals to the desperate and the confused.

Healing: A Doctor in Search of a Miracle, by William Nolen. New York: Random House, 1974. An American physician explores the world of Philippine psychic surgery. Most of the major practitioners he describes are still in business. Absorbing reportage.

The Realms of Healing, by Stanley Krippner, and Alberto Villoldo. Berkeley Calif.: Celestial Arts, 1986. Two believing academics—Krippner is one of the most respected living parapsychologists—provide a glimpse into the world of miraculous healing. Krippner is the more skeptical of the two. The book is valuable not as science but as a study in perception.

Flim-Flam!: Psychics, ESP, Unicorns, and Other Delusions, by James Randi. Buffalo N.Y.: Prometheus Books, 1982. A masterful magician and a MacArthur fellow, "The Amazing" Randi has picked up the mantle of Harry Houdini and offers a standing $10,000 reward to anyone who can demonstrate any miraculous, "paranormal" feat. His account of human self-deception includes a lengthy, well-illustrated section on the "art" of psychic surgery.

A Guide to Spiritual & Magnetic Healing & Psychic Surgery in the Philippines, by George W. Meek. Ft. Meyers, Florida, privately printed, 1973. The sixteen-page brochure Victorino P. Mapa sold prospective clients during his days with Phil-Am tours, and which was offered to Brother Joe's patients. An exposition of the rationale psychic surgeons use to sell their services to the suffering.

CHRISTIAN SCIENCE

The primary sources for the orthodox view are the "authorized editions" of Mary Baker Eddy's works, available in Christian Science reading rooms and furnished by local churches to most public libraries.

Science and Health, with Key to the Scriptures, by Mary Baker Eddy. Boston: Christian Science Publishing Society, 1906. "The Textbook," the foundation on which the church is built. Mrs. Eddy's Victorian prose, improved by a professional editor, sets forth the basic tenets of her religion. Supplemented by a 100-page section of anonymous testimonials.

Prose Works, Other than Science and Health, by Mary Baker Eddy. Boston: Christian Science Publishing Society, 1925. A collection of articles, notes, pamphlets, and shorter books, some in question-and-answer format and designed to supplement "the textbook."

Church Manual of the First Church of Christ Scientist, in Boston, Mass., by Mary Baker Eddy. Boston: Christian Science Publishing Society, 1908. The constitution of the "Mother Church," setting forth its unique political structure and relation to "branch churches." This document concentrates all authority in a self-appointing Board of Directors.

A Complete Concordance to the Writings of Mary Baker Eddy, Boston: Christian Science Publishing Society, 1916. A 1,107-page recitation of virtually every word in all the authorized works. An invaluable reference.

Spiritual Healing in a Scientific Age, by Robert Peel. New York: Harper & Row, 1987. The leading church apologist places Christian Science in the context of modern scientific discoveries, arguing that the religion is not inconsistent. Impressive, well-argued, but ultimately highly limited and selective in its use of evidence, Peel's book is the best single source for a modern statement of Mrs. Eddy's religion.

Christian Science, by Mark Twain, Buffalo, N.Y.: Prometheus Books, 1986 reprint of Twain's 1907 original. America's master humorist turns a sardonic eye on Mrs. Eddy's Church, which he thought was heading for world domination. Twain's interest was both professional and personal. As a student of social movements, Christian Science was a natural subject for him; and as a husband, he was troubled that his own ailing wife had turned to Christian Science. A contemporary, critical, and insightful work that is both satirical and grudgingly respectful.

The Quimby Manuscripts, Horatio W. Dresser, ed. Secaucus N.J.: Citadel, 1976 (reprint of 1921 edition with notes from 1961 Julian Press edition). The most telling indictment of the plagiarism with which critics have charged Mrs. Eddy since well before her death. Phineas P. Quimby was her one-time mentor, a "mesmerist" who coined many of the terms his disciple later appropriated, and who may have been the source for much of the key chapter of *Science and Health* used in class instruction.

Christian Science, by Walter Martin. Minneapolis: Bethany House, 1957. A biblical literalist, Martin was a conservative Christian who made scholarly attacks on any religion he considered cultish or heretical. This 32-page booklet is a stinging attack on Mrs. Eddy, most interesting for its detailed allegations of plagiarism.

A NOTE ON BIOGRAPHIES

Robert Peel, a dedicated church member, is the only biographer who has been allowed full access to the Mother Church archives. His trilogy, *Mary Baker Eddy*, is an impressive work of orthodox scholarship. It is impossible to judge either its thoroughness or its possible failings without access to the original source material; the church was assiduous in buying and locking up early manuscripts, letters, notes, written recollections, and other documents. The would-be biographer or historian is forced to rely on contemporary critical accounts, most notably Georgine Milmine's *The Life of Mary Baker G. Eddy and the History of Christian Science*, New York: Doubleday Page & Co., 1909. Milmine and other journalists working for *McClure's* magazine interviewed those who knew Mrs. Eddy from childhood through the peak of her career, and came up with a far different picture than the authorized version. Unfortunately, Milmine's work is almost impossible to find. Another critical biography is Edwin Franden Dakin's *Mrs. Eddy: The Biography of a Virginal Mind*, New York: Charles Scribner's, 1930, which draws heavily on Milmine as well as other sources.

MIND AND HEALTH

No medical research is more controversial or exciting than the gradual discovery of the links between physiological and psychological conditions. That there are direct correlations between health and thought cannot be denied, although the extent of the connections and the way they operate are still very much at issue, despite the writings and pronouncements of the more exuberant students of "psychoneuroimmunology," or PNI. The following is a representative listing of mass market works (which, by the nature of the market, tend to be highly positive).

The Healing Brain: Breakthrough Discoveries about How the Brain Keeps Us Healthy, by Robert Ornstein, and David Sobel. New York: Touchstone Books, 1987. A collaboration between a psychologist (who is a devotee of Sufism) and a physician whose specialty is patient education, this is a well-referenced introduction to PNI. Research is well covered, and the authors make the very telling point that most of the medical research to date has gone into looking for the causes of illness, as opposed to the causes of wellness. Illuminating.

Who Gets Sick?: How Beliefs, Moods, and Thoughts Affect Your Health, Blair Justice. Los Angeles: Jeremy P. Tarcher, 1988. A medical journalist turned psychologist, Justice provides a clear, easy-to-read overview of PNI. Though the conclusions drawn sometimes outstrip the evidence, Justice has written a thoughtful, considerate work. Well-referenced and indexed.

Mind Matters: How the Mind & Brain Interact to Create Our Conscious Lives, by Michael S. Gazzaniga. New York: Houghton Mifflin, 1988. Best known for his research on "split brain" patients, Gazzaniga is a psychologist who has devoted his career to understanding the physiological foundations of conscious thought. While the author is not primarily concerned with the healing of disease (he does discuss it, however), *Mind Matters* is a wonderfully lucid account of what science has discovered about the contents of our skulls.

The Faith Healers, by James Randi. Buffalo N.Y.: Prometheus Books, 1987. Randi is a long-time student of claims of the miraculous. In this work he turns his attention to nationally known faith healers, exposing some as outright charlatans and hucksters, others as (at best) dangerously misguided. A stunning indictment of fraud and deceit.

Patients and Healers in the Context of Culture: An Exploration of the Borderland between Anthropology, Medicine, and Psychiatry, by Arthur Kleinman. Berkeley: University of California Press, 1980. In the not-so-distant past, "medical treatment" was at best risky, and at worst life-threatening or even fatal. In the more-distant past, the roles of healer and priest were one, and the patient's *feelings* about disease were the primary object of treatment. Western physicians have concentrated on physiology, but in many traditional societies sufferers still have the option of consulting folk-healers. Kleinman, a professor of psychiatry, looks at the culture of Taiwan, where both forms of healing are practiced, and draws conclusions relevant to contemporary post-industrial society.

The Other Medicines: An Invitation to Understanding & Using Them for Health & Healing, by Richard Grossman. New York: Doubleday, 1985. A careless, misguided book that defines and advocates all manner of unconventional treatment.

The Alternative Health Guide, by Brian Inglis, and Ruth West. New York: Alfred A. Knopf, 1983. An encyclopedic account of alternative health systems written by two English writers who appear to believe in most of them. The book is well-organized, tightly written, and well-referenced. It falls short, however, in that it fails to include critical claims.

Examining Holistic Medicine, Douglas Stalker and Clark Glymour, eds., Buffalo N.Y.: Prometheus Books, 1985. An anthology of critical articles providing an excellent counterbalance to the works of Grossman and Inglis and West. Selections deal with a variety of unconventional health claims, and the text is supplemented by an excellent glossary and bibliography. No index.

INDEX